Renouncing the World Yet Leading the Church

Renouncing the World Yet Leading the Church

The Monk-Bishop in Late Antiquity

Andrea Sterk

HARVARD UNIVERSITY PRESS
Cambridge, Massachusetts
London, England
2004

To Tony, Timmy, and Peter

Library of Congress Cataloging-in-Publication Data

Sterk, Andrea.
  Renouncing the world yet leading the church : the monk-bishop in late antiquity / Andrea Sterk.
    p. cm.
  Includes bibliographical references and index.
  ISBN 0-674-01189-9 (alk. paper)
1. Leadership—Religious aspects—Christianity—
History of Doctrines—Early church, ca. 30–600.
2. Asceticism—History—Early church, ca. 30–600.
3. Basil, Saint, Bishop of Caesarea, ca. 329–379.
4. Gregory, of Nyssa, Saint, ca. 335–ca. 394.
5. Gregory, of Nazianzus, Saint.
6. John Chrysostom, Saint, d. 407.   I. Title.

BR195.L42S74 2004
262'.12'09015—dc22   2003056717

Acknowledgments

Most of the research and writing of this book took place in three different stages in Princeton, New Jersey. It began as a dissertation on Basil
of Caesarea at Princeton Theological Seminary. For critique, direction,
and advice during that period I am indebted to Karlfried Froehlich, Paul
Rorem, and especially my adviser, Kathleen McVey, who has provided
ongoing support and encouragement. Graduate seminars with Peter
Brown at Princeton University and with the late Father John Meyendorff
at Fordham University also provided inspiration for different parts of
this book.

The second major phase of research and writing took place at the
Center of Theological Inquiry in Princeton, where I was a member-in-
residence for nine months in 1997. Though I had intended to complete
the book during that period, the project expanded into a broader study
than I had originally envisioned. The wonderful facilities of the center,
the supportive environment, and the easy access to the fine collections
of the Speer and Firestone Libraries made this a very productive time.
The final phase of writing took place in Princeton once again, this time
at the Institute for Advanced Study. Though it was my husband and not I
who was a fellow there, I am indebted to the institute for providing such
a fine living and working environment and to Giles Constable for wel-
coming me into the engaging group of scholars who made up the medieval seminar. Both the Center of Theological Inquiry and the Institute
for Advanced Study do all they can to accommodate scholars with families and to meet the needs of academic couples.

In between these more focused periods of writing, I have taught at
Calvin College, the University of Notre Dame, and, most recently, the
University of Florida. I am grateful to supportive colleagues at each of
these institutions. During and after his brief tenure as director of the Medieval Institute at Notre Dame, Patrick Geary provided moral support

v

and practical advice at several crucial junctures. Special thanks are due to Dave Jenkins, the Byzantine research librarian at Notre Dame, who provided professional assistance in a number of ways. The Byzantine reading group he organized translated one of the major hagiographic texts I discuss in the epilogue. This group turned a potentially tedious project into a fruitful and truly enjoyable collaboration during an otherwise difficult year.

Parts of this book were first presented as papers at meetings of the American Society of Church History, the North American Patristic Society, the Byzantine Studies Conference, and at the Conference on Byzantine Monasticisms held in Toronto. I am grateful for audience questions and responses, for the comments of Susanna Elm on two occasions, and for the participation of other panelists who helped me to clarify and sharpen my treatment of certain issues. Claudia Rapp went beyond the call of duty in passing on bibliographic information, even sending one of her own articles before it appeared in print.

For reading and commenting on different chapters of this book I wish to thank Frederick Norris, Ute Possekel, Peter Brown, Philip Rousseau, and Nicholas Constas. I would also like to thank the two outside readers at Harvard University Press and my editor, Margaretta Fulton, for their sane comments and suggestions. Any errors that remain are of course my own.

Finally I am indebted to my husband, Howard Louthan, who was my chief critic, support, and encourager through the long and often lonely project. It spanned the births of three boys, and twelve moves—including three different countries and four different states. Though our three delightful boys certainly delayed its completion, they also provided a sense of perspective that enabled me to continue through the long haul. It is to them that I dedicate this book.

Contents

Introduction

In the last few decades of the fourth century the monastic settlements of Nitria were in their heyday. Situated on a rocky promontory above the southwestern streams of the Nile Delta some forty miles southeast of Alexandria, Nitria functioned as the gateway to the Egyptian desert and the meeting place of monks with the wider world.[1] But it was neither the distinctive geography or topography of this wilderness nor its relative accessibility to visitors that made it well known in Egypt and far beyond. Its fame was due to the reputation of the holy ascetics who inhabited the desert region—devoted Christian men and women who had renounced all worldly possessions, temporal affairs, and even ecclesiastical ambitions.

Among the ascetics of Nitria lived a monk named Ammonius who had been trained by the great Pambo. Like his spiritual father, Ammonius became renowned for his rigorous austerities and extreme renunciations.[2] Not only did he deny himself any cooked food other than bread but also, to tame his passions when desire arose, he heated an iron in the fire and applied it to his limbs. However, while Pambo had been an illiterate savant, his disciple was a man of considerable erudition, said to have learned the whole of the Bible by heart as well as a multitude of texts from the writings of Origen, Didymus, and other fathers. Given his intellectual capacities and his reputation for sanctity, it is perhaps not surprising that inhabitants of a nearby Egyptian city should approach their archbishop with the request that the learned ascetic be appointed bishop over their diocese. Aware of the monk's renown for both piety and learning, Bishop Timothy of Alexandria asked only that the citizens bring

Ammonius to him for consecration. The eager Egyptians set out with alacrity to fetch the holy man and bring him back to Alexandria in compliance with Timothy's instructions. A simple task, they must have thought, in order to gain so prominent and worthy a bishop for their see.

The monk, however, had no desire to abandon the peace of the desert for the tumult of ecclesiastical affairs. When the envoys arrived at his cell Ammonius pleaded with them to leave him be, swearing that he would not accept episcopal election. They, for their part, would not budge; none of the monk's remonstrances could sway them from their intent. Seeing their resolve and realizing he was likely on the verge of being forcibly dragged off to Alexandria for consecration, Ammonius knew he had to act quickly and decisively. Without further hesitation, he seized a pair of shears and in full sight of his pursuers suddenly cut off his entire left ear.[3] He then announced to his astonished onlookers that he was disqualified for ecclesiastical office since the law forbids ordination of a mutilated man to the priesthood.[4]

The envoys left in dismay, their plans foiled and their hopes dashed. After they had recounted the horrific deed to Bishop Timothy, however, the wise prelate informed them that while this law might well be kept by the Jews, it bore no weight with him. In fact, he explained, "If you bring me a man with his nose cut off, but worthy in other respects, I will ordain him." With renewed hope the emissaries set out a second time to retrieve the holy monk, this time begging him to submit to ordination and serve as their bishop. The forcefulness of their entreaties was matched by the intensity of Ammonius's response: "If you compel me," he threatened, "I will cut out my tongue." No doubt loathe to witness another act of mutilation, the envoys finally relented, left the learned ascetic, and returned home in defeat. As for the monk, Ammonius was henceforth surnamed "the Earless," and we know of no further attempts to submit him to the episcopal yoke.

One of the famous four Tall Brothers of the Egyptian desert, Ammonius appears in several different accounts of monastic and theological developments of this period, owing to his connection with John Chrysostom and his persecution by the ex-Origenist turned rabidly anti-Origenist patriarch, Theophilus of Alexandria.[5] The monk's dramatic refusal of episcopal office is not central to most of these narratives, but the story is relatively well known nevertheless. Though among the more extreme examples, this peculiar incident does not stand alone in the history of episcopal recruitment in late antiquity. We find many vehement reactions of eastern monks to the proposal of priestly or episcopal ordination, ranging from self-mutilation to simple flight. Well before the time of Ammonius, the monk Dracontius had been rebuked by the patriarch Athanasius for fleeing the burden of the episcopate. More famous monastic pioneers, like Pachomius and Macarius the Egyptian, were also known to have resisted enrollment in the clergy.[6] Nor were these rebuffs limited to Egypt. In Syria the holy ascetic Acepsimas had immured himself in a cell for some sixty years and agreed to accept the priesthood only when he knew that he was about to die.[7] A monk in Palestine jumped from a roof of his monastery and escaped when he learned of plans to ordain him; though eventually forced to succumb to priestly ordination, he persisted in his refusal to celebrate the liturgy.[8] In fifth-century Asia Minor some monks were explicitly warned against refusing ordination, for one of the brothers had bitten off his finger to avoid his impending fate.[9] Even a famous bishop like Gregory of Nazianzus fled both the priesthood and the episcopate. In both cases he penned an eloquent justification for his actions.[10]

Those familiar with the biblical literature and its patristic exegesis will not be surprised by the expectation of certain ascetic qualities in a religious leader. After all, the patriarch Abraham was called by God to abandon his homeland, his relatives, and his possessions, and the prophets Elijah and Elisha were both models of abstemiousness and conspicuously unwed.[11] Following in their path, John the Baptist is well known for his ascetic renunciations: withdrawing to the desert, clothing himself in coarse camel's hair, and eating only locusts and wild honey as he preached his message of repentance. The life of Jesus himself was marked by fasting and temptation in the wilderness, physical deprivations, and periods of withdrawal, and he clearly called his would-be disciples to a life of renunciation patterned after his own.[12] The exhortations to Timothy seem more moderate, exacting blamelessness and self-control but allowing the Christian leader to be the husband of one wife, the father of children, and a good manager of his household.[13] However, the apostle Paul's descriptions of his own ascetic regimen left little room for marriage or family life. He wrote of the importance of rigorous physical training, noting how he pummeled his body to keep it under control. While making concessions to the weak, in view of the shortness of the time he explicitly counseled against marital relations, possessions, and unnecessary involvement with the material goods and affairs of the world.[14] Indeed the significance of ascetic themes in both the Jewish Scriptures and the New Testament, and especially in the interpretation of those texts by Christian authors of the late Roman world, has been the subject of several major individual and collective projects in the past two decades.[15]

Certainly biblical models are not unique in such ascetic emphases, for the Greek ideal of *ascesis* was prized by philosophers and educators from Homer to Plotinus and Porphyry.[16] In his classic study of early Christianity and Greek *paideia*, Werner Jaeger explained that the Greek philosopher's whole life was a process of formation through "philosophical ascesis."[17] Not only philosophers but also outstanding civil and military leaders in antiquity were often characterized by ascetic virtues. The Tarantine Archytas (c. 380–345 B.C.E.), a successful army general, commander-in-chief of his flourishing city as well as a Pythagorean philosopher and mathematician, provides an apt example. Known for his lofty morals, self-control, and rigorous asceticism, Archytas was greatly admired by Plato and likely served as a model for his philosopher-king. Likewise in Virgil's *Aeneid*, the worthy ruler of others is the one who has learned to master himself.[18] In the late antique period, from the Stoic Marcus Aurelius to the last pagan emperor, Julian the Apostate, we find a similar emphasis on moderation, if not abstemiousness, and various forms of self-denial as an ideal for virtuous rulers.[19] Michel Foucault has alerted us to important differences between the ascetic goals of the ancient Greeks and Romans and the asceticism of their late Roman and Christian successors.[20] Nonetheless, without denying certain distinctive features, the late antique Christian valuation of asceticism in the lives of prominent members of that community was part of a broader phenomenon of spirituality that marked the age. It is but one aspect of a continuity, rather than a sharp break with classical genres and motifs, that has been demonstrated in Greek art and literature from the second century up to the Arab invasions of the seventh.[21]

Turning to the ecclesiastical context, the idea will be equally familiar to Christians of the Orthodox tradition that the church's leaders, bishops, are generally chosen from the monastic world. That bishops should be monks has been long assumed and largely unchallenged in that religious community, though recent polemic has begun to call certain aspects of this model into question.[22] Whatever its modern implications might be, among Byzantine historians it is well known that a monastic episcopate became firmly ensconced during the middle Byzantine period (641–1081) and would eventually become the norm for leadership of the Orthodox churches. But the social, political, intellectual, and theological origins of this paradigm have been largely ignored. Scholars have tended to mention or assume this development in ecclesiastical authority rather than examine the phenomenon. While certain ascetic models of leadership predated the monastic movement, what is puzzling in light of the incidents recounted above is why such a class of seemingly isolated, world-renouncing, and often recalcitrant monastics should have become an increasingly normative model for leadership and eventually an institution within the hierarchy of the post-Constantinian church in the East.

The pattern that emerged seems paradoxical on at least two levels. First and most obviously, it is odd that men decidedly removed from the world and even, apparently, from the church should be so eagerly pursued for positions of ecclesiastical authority. Certainly the value of a philosophical disposition or a certain degree of detachment in the governance of church and state would have been widely recognized by elites of the late antique period. However, in the highly politicized setting of the late Roman and Byzantine worlds one might well expect that significant administrative experience and political savvy would be considered prime attributes for oversight of the Christian communities of the East. Needless to say, these qualities were not normally nurtured by the long periods of ascetic withdrawal or isolation that typified the life of a monk. A second paradox has to do with peculiar developments within the monastic movement itself. The rapid spread of ascetic ideals and the rise of monasticism as a distinctive movement in the fourth century brought new challenges to the church and to society as a whole. In fact many contemporaries viewed the new movement of enthusiasm with concern or even disdain, and this anxiety was not limited to men of letters, civil officials, or pagan despisers of the Christian faith. From within the very ranks of the ecclesiastical hierarchy ascetics were not infrequently regarded with suspicion, especially in the first half of the fourth century. By the end of that century, however, the leadership of the church had gradually shifted from caution or suspicion to widespread acceptance of the monastic movement. We find an increasing number of clergy and bishops being recruited from monastic communities. This process accelerated in the Christian East to such an extent that from the sixth century on monasteries are said to have served as virtual "seminaries for bishops."[23] Eventually a monastic model of ecclesiastical leadership became the norm for Byzantine Christianity.

My purpose in this book is to examine the origins of the long tradition of the monk-bishop in the Christian East and the reasons for its ultimate triumph in the Byzantine world. To be sure, other patterns of episcopal leadership preceded and coexisted with that of the monk-bishop. With the rise of the monepiscopate by the early second century, bishops were raised to elite positions within the Christian community, and the privileges accorded them by Constantine, along with the exponential growth of the church in the post-Constantinian era, gave bishops increased public prominence and influence. Their social and spiritual duties were endorsed by law, and the office was sought and filled by *curiales* and even senators as late as the sixth century.[24] Yet a monastic-episcopal paradigm steadily increased and ultimately prevailed in the eastern church while such other career patterns waxed and waned. By the sixth century the church had assimilated the monastic movement, and monks had become bishops of many of the major sees. From the world-rejecting monasteries and desert hermitages of the East came some of the most powerful leaders in the church and civil society as a whole. The image of the model bishop also underwent significant development as episcopal identity was gradually reframed in accordance with monastic values. The reasons for this transformation, the key individuals, ideas, and social contexts that caused a monastic ideal of leadership to flourish and eventually dominate, are the subject of this book.

Beginning with the first half-century of monastic organization in the Christian East and concluding with the post-iconoclast period, several foundational arguments are woven into the fabric of this study. First, I hope to demonstrate that Basil of Caesarea was a pivotal figure in the emergence of the monk-bishop ideal, both through his embodiment of the paradigm and through his active advocacy of monks in church office. Certainly Athanasius of Alexandria played an important role in the asceticization of the church as a whole and the clergy in particular in fourth-century Egypt, and many other bishops and theologians helped to shape and popularize ascetic ideals in church office. But with regard to the particular monastic-episcopal model that was increasingly adopted throughout the Byzantine world, the pattern set by the Cappadocian most consistently comes to the fore. His influence did not wane after his death, for he became a dominant image for episcopal leadership in ensuing centuries. While the details may vary in later portrayals of Basil of Caesarea, the outline remains the same. Basil the monk and holy man was also represented as the bishop par excellence by succeeding generations of Christians.

I will also examine the nature of the monastic ideal of episcopal leadership, showing why it was attractive to so many and such diverse groups of people in the church and in late Roman society as a whole. It transcended geographic, chronological, and even theological boundaries. Indeed it was the very flexibility or adaptability of the model that facilitated its transfer to later ecclesiastical and cultural contexts. In describing the origins of this paradigm I will often speak more broadly of ascetic ideals in church office, but as time progressed it was cenobitic monks more often than mere advocates of ascetic or contemplative life who were increasingly appointed to episcopal sees throughout the Christian East. Despite many studies of eastern monks, bishops, and individual monk-bishops published in the past few decades, the rise and triumph of a monastic episcopate as a broader phenomenon has been overlooked. Even several fine studies that have underscored relations between ascetics and bishops in late antiquity have tended to pit the former against the latter in a rivalry for authority and status, while neglecting the equally fascinating story of their convergence.[25] What we will observe simultaneously, then, is a process of asceticization of an institution, the episcopate, and the near institutionalization of asceticism in the ascendance of the monk-bishop. Theological conceptions of the bishop's role and requisite attributes will be central to this investigation, without minimizing social, political, and economic factors that shaped ecclesiastical developments. Building on recent discussions of asceticism and power, I wish to illuminate a new or distinctive type of leadership that emerged in Christianity. The model of the monk-bishop defies Max Weber's categories of "world-rejecting" and "inner-worldly asceticism," for it fused the increasing institutional authority of church office with the spiritual power and appeal of the holy ascetic.[26]

It has often been assumed that the rise of a distinctly monastic episcopate in Byzantium dates roughly to the eighth century, or to the iconoclastic controversies and their aftermath. During this period monks, who had won the favor of the masses and proven themselves champions of orthodoxy, gained a definite monopoly over episcopal sees.[27] Though we will be considering the *longue durée* of this model of leadership, the chronological core of the study is the late antique period, for the ideal of a monastic episcopate was already well established in the East by the late sixth century. The patriarchate of Constantinople was still often governed by humanist scholars and secular clergy in the centuries following the Triumph of Orthodoxy, but there too monastic leadership was gradually gaining ground. In the Epilogue I will reflect on a few of the later episodes and review some of the underlying themes in the ultimate triumph of the monk-bishop throughout the Byzantine world—from the shores of the Black Sea to the medieval Serbian kingdom under the Nemanjić dynasty to the Byzantine capital itself.

My primary concern, then, is not the way in which a monastic party finally gained the upper hand in episcopal elections, though the growing social status and political influence of monks are factors inextricably intertwined with their increasing dominance of episcopal sees. My focus is the development of an ideal and its implications for structures and positions of authority in the Christian church. Though an ascetic ideal of leadership had both classical and biblical roots, it found particularly fertile soil in the monastic fervor of the fourth through sixth centuries and in the social and political uncertainty of the late antique era as a whole. It was during this period that the notion of the monk-bishop arose as an ecclesiastical ideal and the reality of monks in the episcopate began to spread. The particular conceptions of spiritual authority that developed at this time amid the social, legal, and theological ferment peculiar to the eastern Roman world explain the eventual triumph of a distinctly monastic episcopate in the Byzantine church.

I have chosen to limit this study of the monk-bishop to the East, despite the emergence of a similar pattern of ecclesiastical leadership in the West. While many of the same theological ideals underlay the selection of monks for bishoprics in Italy, North Africa, and especially Gaul, different circumstances and a number of different doctrinal emphases also came into play. These factors not only generated a slightly different model of episcopal leadership but also ultimately led to a celibate Roman Catholic priesthood as well as episcopate.[28] An analysis of western patterns and ideals of church leadership, while often intertwined with theses presented in this book, would require the development of separate arguments that have in part been made elsewhere. My own treatment of the monk-bishop focuses on the particular context of Christian traditions in the eastern Roman Empire and what became a distinctively Byzantine ecclesiastical model.

Among many scholarly guides on the issues of authority and asceticism I am particularly indebted to the work of Philip Rousseau, whose analysis of similar trends in the western church provided much of the initial inspiration for my own work on the East.[29] Also stimulating have been Henry Chadwick's brief presentation on the bishop in ancient society, along with its accompanying responses, and Rita Lizzi's work on episcopal power in the newly Christian Roman Empire.[30] More recently a two-volume collection of essays on bishops and pastors in the Theodosian era has made available a wealth of information and reflection on the episcopate in this period.[31] On the social function of ascetics and holy men and their status vis-à-vis bishops, the work of Peter Brown has been foundational, and recent revisions, reassessments, and applications of his seminal work have added valuable new insights and perspectives.[32] Gilbert Dagron's monumental volume on monks, bishops, and emperors has been particularly helpful for the themes and figures examined in the Epilogue.[33] Finally, Harold Drake's study of Constantine and the bishops examines issues of episcopal leadership from a different vantage point, that of imperial politics. If, as Drake has demonstrated, fourth-century bishops became "power players" in the "game of empire," then monks were not far behind them.[34] In the peculiar figure of the monk-bishop we see their rise to dominance in eastern Roman society and the church as well as a critical dimension in the dynamics of leadership in late antiquity.

I

Basil of Caesarea and the Emergence of an Ideal

1

Monks and Bishops in the Christian East from 325 to 375

"A monk should by all means flee women and bishops," wrote John Cassian, generally regarded as the interpreter of eastern monasticism to the West.[1] The admonition to avoid bishops was in no way intended to spurn the church hierarchy but was rather written as a warning to monks who eagerly sought out episcopal office. Nevertheless, these words expressed an important impulse that lay behind the monastic movement, namely, separation from the world. Monks, after all, had fled to the deserts precisely to escape the entanglements of the world and what many considered an increasingly worldly church. Many bishops, meanwhile, were skeptical of these new ascetic enthusiasts.

Egypt

Early monasticism in Egypt was marked by an ambivalent relationship between monks and the bearers of church office. Relations were influenced in part by the geography and climate of the region, which were conducive to the particular types of monastic life that emerged. Emphasizing the distinctive topography of Egypt, Peter Brown suggested that the harsh conditions of life in the desert or on its fringes inevitably shaped the monastic communities that were established there. The Egyptian had to transplant into the desert "the all-absorbing routines of the villages of the *oikoumenē*," he explained. "To live at all, the man had to remain in one place, earning his living from manual labour, from pottery and reed-weaving . . . The monastery of Pachomius was called quite simply The Village."[2] Since communities became of necessity almost

13

self-sufficient, there was apparently little need for contact with the *oikoumenē* and relatively little interaction with the hierarchical church. These early Egyptian monasteries, then, would seem to pose no threat to men in church office.

Despite a real physical distinction between desert and arable land, however, recent studies of Egyptian monasticism have helped to correct misconceptions about the movement based in part on faulty geographic or demographic assumptions. Aside from the interior of the delta in Egypt, the desert was everywhere close to villages and towns, if not cities. Populated localities were rarely situated more than twenty kilometers from the desert proper, and even large villages sometimes hugged its borders.[3] James Goehring has helped to expose other misconceptions about Egyptian monasticism, particularly the myth of Antony and Pachomius as founders of anchoritic and cenobitic monasticism, respectively. Such myths have arisen largely on the basis of later literary sources that were shaped by "the ecclesiastical desire for ideological conformity" in monastic life.[4] This concern on the part of church officials often served to suppress or erase the memory of diverse forms of ascetic life that coincided with and even predated what became the institutionally acceptable paradigms.

The reality of ascetic development in Egypt was far more complex than the simple bipolar division might lead us to believe. Prior to the spread of the anchoritic and cenobitic models represented by Antony and Pachomius, groups of men known as *apotaktikoi* or "renunciants" practiced forms of asceticism in the towns and villages of Egypt. These men followed an older pattern of virgins and widows who lived communally and combined lives of personal renunciation with active service in the church. Papyri evidence reveals that *apotaktikos* was once a rank in the church and suggests more active engagement in both the civic and the ecclesial community than was once assumed of Egyptian ascetics. In fact the earliest known technical use of the term *monachos,* occurring in a documentary papyrus in Egypt in 324, likely designated a member of this early apotactic movement.[5] It referred specifically to a certain town or village ascetic who, together with a church official, intervened to protect a fellow villager from an attempted assault. Alongside the documentary evidence for *apotaktikoi,* the circumstances surrounding this early usage of the term *monachos* helps to dispel both geographic and typological myths regarding Egyptian monasticism.

Despite the assertion of an absolute "antithesis" in the mind of Egyptians between the desert and the settled areas, even anchorites were more actively engaged with the secular world than was once assumed.[6] Nor should we imagine that self-sufficient cenobitic monasteries were completely isolated from the life of the church. The *Life of Pachomius* reveals many incidents of encounter or interaction between monks and residents of nearby towns and villages.[7] In his detailed treatment of the emergence and spread of Pachomian communities in Egypt, Philip Rousseau has shown that numerous links—social, economic, and ecclesiastical—tied these communities to the society around them.[8] The economic productivity of the monasteries was impressive and soon gained the attention of church officials. Increasing interest in monastic life among the leaders of the church, however, was coupled with a certain suspicion or anxiety. Two factors in particular produced tension. First, economic relations between the monasteries and the villages had not been worked out. Second, and more to our point, the distinction or relationship between the ascetic community and the broader Christian body was not clearly defined. This ambiguity fostered ambivalence on the part of both monastic leaders and the church hierarchy. The former questioned the benefits of clerical services and support, while the latter wondered about the contribution of ascetics to the official structure of the church.[9]

Any consideration of relations between monks and bishops in fourth-century Egypt must, of course, take some account of the pattern set by Antony the Great. This paragon of ascetic life was allegedly on good terms with the ecclesiastical hierarchy and showed special deference to officers of the church. According to his *Life* he honored all clergy above himself, bowed his head before priests and bishops, and gave priority to them in prayer.[10] It is not insignificant that the dying Antony left his mantle to two bishops, Athanasius and Serapion.[11] By his words and deeds he also sought to cultivate respect for church office among his disciples.[12] Priests and bishops, for their part, sought out the famous holy man. A close friendship between Antony and Athanasius had been long assumed until more recent studies began to question the evidence for their direct interaction. Certainly the Patriarch of Alexandria wholeheartedly embraced the monastic movement and endeavored to ally its leaders with his own goals for the church in his region.

Caution must be exercised, however, in using the relationship between Antony and Athanasius as representative of relations between monks and the church hierarchy in fourth-century Egypt, let alone elsewhere in the Roman Empire. First of all, documentary evidence has helped to reveal a very different portrait of Antony and early Egyptian monks than the one drawn by later literary sources on monasticism, particularly the *Vita Antonii*. Far from indicating the illiterate but orthodox peasant of the *Vita*, the letters attributed to Antony, now increasingly accepted as authentic, present an early fourth-century ascetic teacher shaped by Platonic philosophy and Origenist theology and more concerned with *gnōsis* and self-knowledge than with *ascesis* and the struggle against demons.[13] Moreover, in the letters we find only a few passing references to the church and no mention whatsoever of bishops, priests, or an ecclesiastical hierarchy.[14] In reading the historical recollection on Antony's life that eventually took the form of his famous *Vita* we must remember that it is Athanasius's biography of the great holy man that provides us with most of the details of Antony's life and interaction with the church that have long been accepted as paradigmatic. It is not surprising that the bishop most noted for his struggle against the Arian heresy should put into the mouth of the famous monk the words of Nicene orthodoxy.[15] Some scholars have argued very forcefully that Athanasius's primary purpose in composing the *Vita Antonii* was to combat Arian soteriology, which may have been gaining ground in certain Egyptian monastic circles.[16] It was certainly to Athanasius's advantage to emphasize good relations between the monastic movement and the church hierarchy. In his protracted battle for the Nicene faith, the patriarch stood in opposition to the imperial government and for this reason found himself almost constantly in exile. He needed the support of popular forces. Groups of Melitians as well as Arian monks threatened his ecclesiastical power, while many other monks proved able and willing allies in the cause of orthodoxy.[17] In short, the circumstances surrounding Athanasius's involvement with monks and monasticism were unique, and his relationship with Antony should not be regarded as normative for Egypt.

Nonetheless, admiring the monks' way of life and recognizing their potential usefulness to the church, Athanasius placed as many pro-Nicene monks as possible at the head of dioceses and in other ways put them into the service of the church. In one letter alone, he mentioned no fewer than seven monks ordained to the episcopate.[18] In this letter of

354 Athanasius endeavored to convince the monk Dracontius, who had fled his episcopal election, to return and accept his appointment to the see of Hermopolis Parva. It was apparently no easy task to find suitable monks who were willing to serve as bishops. Although in the *Vita Antonii* the monastic father's great respect for bishops is undeniable, we should also remember that Antony himself managed to avoid ordination. Exposing the suspicion with which some Egyptian monks viewed the hierarchy of the church, in his letter to Dracontius Athanasius acknowledged that many of them looked down on bishops. Some had apparently advised Dracontius to refuse the episcopate because it was an occasion for sin and would compromise his character. In response to such allegations Athanasius attempted to allay the monk's fears that ordination would harm his spiritual condition or hinder his progress.[19] The interaction between monks and bishops suggested by the *Life of Antony* was clearly not always as harmonious as the patriarch would have liked.

Equally revealing in this epistle are the reasons Athanasius enumerated for why the monk ought to embrace episcopal office. He emphasized the situation of the church, its need for unity and order, the threat of filling episcopal sees with unfit persons, and the example of biblical saints who had served in prophetic and pastoral roles. As for personal qualifications, Dracontius was an able teacher of the Scriptures and a proven leader of others. Like the other monk-bishops Athanasius listed, he had substantial administrative experience, for as abbot of a monastery Dracontius had already served in the capacity of an overseer.[20] His moral and spiritual qualities were also of great importance, since the Christian laity needed models for imitation. However, Athanasius pointed out, even if the man considered himself unworthy of the task, which was frequently the case with those called to such ministry, Dracontius had been chosen for the bishopric not merely by a unanimous hierarchy in Alexandria but by God himself, and he should not despise or reject this grace that had been given to him. Though far from expressing a developed theology of ordination, this letter presents appointment to church office in sacramental terms.[21]

In several ways Athanasius equated the roles of bishop and monk, for effectiveness in both depended on moral effort rather than position, and both involved care for others. The convergence between monastic and episcopal leadership is especially clear at the end of the letter, where

Athanasius again criticized Dracontius's monastic advisers. They had counseled him to refuse the episcopate while they themselves wanted presbyters among the monks who could "teach" and "preside," acting in very much the same capacity as bishops.[22] Strikingly absent from this appeal, however, is any reference to the ascetic virtues of the monk as necessary qualities for episcopal leadership. Though asceticism is not absent from the letter, it plays no role in qualifying the monk for his prospective role as bishop.[23] The letter does not express ambivalence about monastic life, nor should it be read as a mere political ploy to recruit the reluctant monk as an ally against episcopal competitors.[24] Though Athanasius highly valued the ascetic vocation and recognized the spiritual powers that issued from a life of renunciation like Antony's, when it came to the office of bishop he had other primary qualifications in mind. Though ascetic practices were not mandatory for effective leadership of the church, in his *Festal Letter* of 368 it is clear that Athanasius continued to favor the appointment of monks. After listing the bishops who had taken office that year, he added approvingly, "and all of these men are ascetics, being in the life of monasticism."[25] The list includes the monk-bishop Isidore as the replacement for Dracontius, showing that the reluctant monk eventually succumbed to Athanasius's ardent appeal.

Returning to the early Pachomian communities, we find what may be a more representative model of relations between the nascent monastic movement and the hierarchy of the church in Egypt. Here too, however, we must bear in mind that the Pachomian tradition has been shaped by later Pachomian monks after the death and glorification of the movement's founder.[26] Pachomius, like the Antony of the *Vita*, is shown to have held bishops in high regard. He instructed his monks to obey the church and to render honor to bishops and priests. He considered bishops the fathers of Christianity and the heirs of the apostles, and he cited the apostle Paul's injunction to pray for them.[27] At the same time, Pachomius himself hid among the brothers when Bishop Serapion wanted Athanasius to consecrate him priest over the monks of his diocese.[28] He staunchly resisted the ordination of monks. According to the *Vita Prima*, he "frequently told them that it was not good to ask for office and glory . . . [for] 'clerical office is the beginning of contemplation of the lust for power.'"[29] It was striving after position, the temptation to love of power, and the consequent envy and jealousy in the community

that Pachomius opposed, not ecclesiastical office in itself. Nevertheless, despite his respect for church officials, he tended to keep them at a
distance.

In contrast to more distant bishops like Athanasius, local prelates, vis-
à-vis the monastic movement, found themselves involved with a force
they did not completely understand and a source of spiritual authority
that they could not easily contest. Pachomius's own trial before a synod
of bishops at Latopolis in 345 highlights certain underlying tensions between monks and the church hierarchy that were not easily overcome.[30]
Present at the trial were villagers, soldiers, and monks, as well as local
bishops. The issue in question was Pachomius's spiritual discernment,
his alleged ability to see into people's hearts. In a speech to the bishops
the abbot defended his unusual ability several times as *to charisma tou
theou,* the gift of God. The bishops are said to have marveled at his
candor and humility. We also learn that two of the local bishops participating in this synod were former Pachomian monks, for Pachomius
himself queried, "Were you not ever together with me in the monastery
as monks before you became bishops? Do you not know that, much like
you, by the grace of God I love God and care for the brothers?"[31] Given
the setting and tone of these questions, Pachomius may have been pre-
scient regarding the problems posed by ordaining monks to church office. At the same time he implicitly acknowledged a close connection between the tasks of monks and bishops: both were to love God and care
for their brethren. Immediately following Pachomius's speech a man
with a sword arose to slay him, "but the Lord saved him through the
brothers who were present, since a great tumult arose in the church."[32]
The event of this trial demonstrates the monks' alliance with the local
rural population, their connections with powerful patrons in the city,
and their cautious collaboration with members of the church hierarchy.[33]
It was such incidences of interaction, alongside a growing incorporation of monks among the clergy itself, that marked the communities of
Pachomian inspiration.

Despite Pachomius's apprehensions and warnings, the practice of ordaining monks to church office increased. It was in Nitria and the Cells
that a monastic priesthood first emerged. It is difficult to determine the
function of *presbuteroi* in the early ascetic communities.[34] It seems that
some ministered only to physical needs, while others performed liturgical services. Eventually some exercised a teaching function among their

fellow monks. The rise of ordained clergy in the Egyptian ascetic milieu, both in Nitria and eventually in the Pachomian communities, brought the monasteries into closer relations with the church and led to attempts at episcopal control of the movement. While monks were initially ordained for ministry within the ascetic community, their services were increasingly demanded for tasks outside the monastery. Monk-priests became well accepted and perhaps even commonplace in Egypt by the fifth century. However, relations between monks and the church hierarchy did not progress in exactly the same manner throughout the Christian East.

Syria

The Syriac-speaking church had a long tradition of close relations between ascetics and church officials. Unfortunately the common conception of Syrian asceticism has been shaped by an emphasis on its severity and even its *bizarrerie*. This image has been formed largely on the basis of later sources like Theodoret of Cyrrhus's *Historia Religiosa*, Palladius's *Historia Lausiaca*, Sozomen's *Church History*, and especially the *Lives of Symeon Stylites*, for the saint atop his pillar in his "splendid isolation" has become a favorite—if somewhat distorted—icon of Syrian asceticism as a whole.[35] These are texts that reflect the monastic ideals of certain fifth-century Syro-Byzantine circles rather than third- and fourth-century Syria and Mesopotamia. We will return to portrayals of more radical ascetic life toward the end of this section, for they are neither unfounded nor irrelevant to our inquiry. For the earlier period, however, Ephrem the Syrian (c. 306–373) and Aphrahat "the Persian Sage" (fl. 336–345) are our primary witnesses. In their writings we find that the premonastic asceticism that was an important feature of Syrian Christianity in the early centuries was tightly intertwined with ecclesiastical organization.[36]

Members of the *bnay* and *bnat qyama*, generally rendered sons and daughters of the Covenant, were seen as the core of the early Syrian church. These ascetics took vows of celibacy and pledged themselves to be *ihidaye*, "single ones" or "singles," on the occasion of their baptism. The Syriac term *ihidaya*, though often identified with the Greek *monachos* in its Christian usage, had several different connotations and a deeper primary sense than might be implied by the adjective *single*. Indeed several scholars have suggested that it may actually have been the Syriac usage of *ihidaya* that prompted Greek-speaking Christians to adopt the term *monachos* to describe a celibate ascetic.[37] For the early Syrian fathers it may have chiefly signified a "putting on" or an imitation of Christ, who is himself described several times in the Peshitta New Testament as the *ihidaya,* that is, the Single One or the unique son of God the father (John 1:14, 18; 3:16, 18).[38] In these passages *ihidaya* is used to translate the Greek *monogenēs.* The Christological significance of the term was almost always prominent in both Aphrahat's and Ephrem's references to the *ihidaye* who served the church.[39] At the same time, *ihidaya* implied a singleness of mind or heart as well as the separation from wife or family that is usually associated with the term *monachos.* But unlike the "monk" of organized anchoritic and cenobitic monasticism, these "single ones" often lived at home or in small informal groups and ministered within the church community as members of the *qyama,* or Covenant. Ephrem the Syrian, long considered the major theologian of the early Syriac tradition, and Aphrahat, whose *Demonstrations* illumine the ascetic life and spirituality of the Syrian church, were closely connected with the *qyama.* Both these men pursued the ascetic vocation. At the same time, Ephrem served the church as a deacon, and Aphrahat was the spiritual leader of the *qyama,* if not a bearer of church office as well.[40]

We also have indications from Ephrem that bishops in Nisibis exercised many of their pastoral duties through the sons and daughters of the Covenant or were themselves members of the *qyama.* In a series of hymns devoted to four consecutive bishops of Nisibis, Ephrem revealed much about the functions and expectations of bishops in fourth-century Syria as well as his own ideal of a leader in the Christian community. In his exhortations to Abraham of Nisibis, Ephrem began with the proclamation, "You have no wife, as Abraham has Sarah. Behold, your flock is your wife. Bring up her children in your faithfulness."[41] He then instructed the young bishop to order his flock like the Old Testament patriarch Jacob, and he listed female and male virgins alongside priests as distinctive groups within the church that Abraham must pastor.[42] Elsewhere we are told that Abraham governed his flock with the aid of a "fold of herdsmen," and in yet another hymn Ephrem explicitly referred to the *qyama* as an order that should shine under the bishop's leadership.[43] Particularly revealing of Ephrem's expectations of a leader in the church is a passage in which he commended to the young Abraham a long list of qualities he ought to emulate as a bishop. Prominent among them are those virtues normally associated with the ascetic life: the fasting of Daniel, the chastity of Joseph, victory over avarice like that of Simon Peter, the purity of Elisha, the continence of Elijah, and especially the poverty of Abraham's own episcopal predecessor and mentor, Bishop Vologeses.[44]

Abraham himself is elsewhere compared with Vologeses, an ascetic bishop to whom Ephrem devoted another of his hymns in praise of bishops.[45] Exalting Vologeses as a model for all the people, Ephrem noted specifically that he was *ihidaya* in his body and *ihidaya* in his house.[46] Indeed among the bishop's many virtues his asceticism stands out alongside his education and his gift for preaching. In another hymn in honor of three bishops of Nisibis whom Ephrem served, he particularly praised the ascetic virtues of Jacob of Nisibis, the first metropolitan bishop of the city and the most famous of the trio. Though Ephrem's description of Jacob is far less exotic than the picture presented by Theodoret of Cyrrhus a century later, his references to Jacob's labors and fasting on behalf of the people suggests that the bishop lived as an ascetic even after his assumption of high church office.[47]

From shortly after the middle of the fourth century there is evidence suggesting that a number of Syrian bishops had been monks in the more formal sense of withdrawal from society.[48] Ephrem, who moved from Nisibis to Edessa some time after Emperor Julian's defeat and the subsequent ceding of Nisibis to the Persians in 363, was himself exposed to new anchoritic and cenobitic forms of ascetic life coming from Egypt and Palestine. He apparently looked favorably on these monastic models, for in a series of hymns he praised the hermit Julian Saba, who was among the earliest Syrian representatives of the anchoritic ideal.[49] In *Carmen* 29 Ephrem hymned the ascetic life and forbearing character of Barses, who served as the first bishop of Harran (Carrhae) before his transfer to Edessa (360/361). Barses may have even dwelt in an anchoritic settlement near the city during the early years of his episcopate while the largely pagan city of Harran was being evangelized. According to Sozomen, Barses' successor, Vitus, also belonged to a monastery outside Harran prior to his episcopal consecration.[50] The beginning of his episcopate corresponds with the beginning of the reign of Emperor Julian the Apostate, and Vitus's zealous struggle for the conversion of the pagans may have been the cause of a conflict between the ascetic bishop and the clergy of Harran.[51] Both Vitus and Barses were faithful adherents of the Nicene faith in the Arian controversy and were among the correspondents of Basil of Caesarea.[52] During the episcopate of the monk Protogenes, the next bishop of Harran, the pilgrim Egeria visited Mesopotamia. From her account of visits to Bathnae, Edessa, and Harran, it seems to have become customary in these episcopal sees to choose bishops from the nearby monastic communities.[53] Yet while Egeria and Sozomen employed the term *monk* to characterize these bishops, in Ephrem's descriptions of Barses, Vitus, and the ascetics of their churches there is no mention of organized monastic life. He employed traditional Syriac terminology to describe their ascetic lives and ministry.[54]

While these examples suggest a generally harmonious relationship between ascetics and the church hierarchy, this was not always the case, especially in western Syria in the late decades of the fourth century. Compared with the desert of Egypt, the Syrian *erēmos* was not sharply distinguished from the *oikoumenē*. Settled areas were closely interwoven with uninhabited steppes or mountains, and the mildness of the climate in most areas of Syria enabled ascetic holy men to live with their desert on the fringes of society.[55] The fluidity of the village population amplified contact and interaction between inhabitants of the *oikoumenē* and ascetics who dwelt on its margins. Harvesters, skilled craftsmen, peddlers and other travelers, soldiers, and considerable numbers of the unemployed composed a large mobile population. Such people moved to and from mountain villages at various points throughout the year and had intermittent contact with monks and hermits. In Roman Syria, then, it was in the more "ambiguous space of countryside" rather than "the polarized images of city and desert" that various modes of religious authority met.[56]

As organized forms of anchoritic and cenobitic life spread throughout the region, the relative proximity between village and desert could have had negative implications for relations between monks and bishops. Because ascetics and holy men lived on the fringes of society and were relative strangers to the village and even to the larger Christian community, they were suspect in the eyes of many villagers. A good example of scorn for monastic life in Syria is captured by the reaction of a resident of Antioch at a slightly later period (c. 380) to the prospect of a young man of the city joining a community of monks: "Incomprehensible! he is the son of respectable upper middle class parents, with a good education, and excellent prospects for a steady comfortable life, yet he has left home and gone off to join a lot of dirty vagrants."[57] Similarly notorious descriptions of Syrian monks appear in the speeches of the pagan orator Libanius. Ascetics were often held responsible for misdeeds and even serious crimes committed in the surrounding area.[58] Moreover, the rising popularity of ascetic holy men in the later fourth and the fifth century posed a challenge to the authority of local bishops as well as magistrates. Not only did they draw large crowds and exercise power as patrons and mediators in village life, but they also assumed some of the functions that had become normative for bishops—for example, settling lawsuits and other disputes. The reasons for the rise of these unlikely candidates to prominent positions in Syrian society is a story told elsewhere.[59] Suffice it to say here that their status sometimes put them at odds with those in positions of official authority in the church. Nor were individual hermits or holy men the only source of anxiety for the church hierarchy. The very structure of Syrian monastic communities may have contributed to skepticism toward the movement. They were less rigidly organized and controlled than the Pachomian monasteries in Egypt, and monks tended to show greater independence with respect to their bishops. Together these two factors could lead to rebelliousness, as attested by events of the next century.[60] As a result, the entire monastic movement in Syria came to be held in disdain by some ecclesiastical as well as civic leaders.

But the picture of Syrian monks and holy men I have drawn in the preceding paragraph clouds and may even distort the images we have seen in Aphrahat and Ephrem of an essential integration of ascetic and ecclesiastical life toward the middle of the fourth century. We must remember that the portraits of Syrian ascetics so vividly painted for us in Peter Brown's "Rise and Function of the Holy Man" and *The Body and Society* belong primarily to a later period, beginning in the latter half if not the last third of the fourth century, and they are particularly characteristic of the fifth. Sidney Griffith, among others, has been at pains to make the distinction between Syrian premonastic asceticism of the third and fourth centuries and Greek models of organized monastic life that began to enter the Syriac-speaking world at a later date, specifically toward the end of Ephrem's lifetime (c. 373). These later varieties of asceticism involved an "individual or collective physical withdrawal" from society and from the ecclesiastical community that did *not* typify the protomonasticism of northern Syria or Mesopotamia.[61]

To be sure, both the older, indigenous ascetic life of the *bnay* and *bnat qyama* and these newer monastic forms of asceticism would continue side by side in the Syriac-speaking church.[62] Although Griffith's hermeneutics of early Syrian asceticism does not focus on relations between monks and bishops, in light of the ascetic and ecclesiastical ideals he has examined so closely in the writings of Aphrahat and Ephrem, one wonders whether his analysis might be taken a step further. Griffith himself has suggested that *anachōresis,* physical withdrawal or separation from society, was the condition of the newer form of ascetic life that characterized the fourth-century monastic movement spreading through the eastern Roman Empire. Yet it was at odds with the native ascetic tradition of the Syriac-speaking church. Perhaps, then, the very introduction into the Syrian setting of *anachōresis* as an ideal was the catalyst for some of the tensions that arose in this region between monks and hermits, on the one hand, and ecclesiastical authorities, on the other. Whatever the sources of anxiety in subsequent decades, during Aphrahat's lifetime and Ephrem's Nisibene ministry we find ascetics most often working hand in hand with ecclesiastical leaders in Syria and even serving the church as deacons, priests, and bishops.

Asia Minor

Asia Minor presents another environment in which the monastic movement emerged and spread. In Egypt the *erēmos* to which many monks withdrew in the fourth century was a true desert, isolated by climate and topography, if not by distance, from the cities and the main stream of village life. Even Pachomian monasticism, which has been justifiably described in recent scholarship as a village rather than a desert phenomenon, recreated the life of the *oikoumenē* rather than functioned within it. Though we find *ihidaye* serving the church in urban settings such as Nisibis and Edessa, throughout much of Syria the village or fringes of the village would provide the fundamental space in which the monk pursued his vocation. For the early ascetics of Asia Minor, the city was the basic point of reference.[63] If in Athansius's famous description of Egyptian monasticism the desert became a city,[64] one might well affirm that for many ascetics of Asia Minor the city became their desert. Describing early monasticism in Galatia, Cappadocia, and the neighboring provinces, Sozomen commented that, unlike the holy men of Egypt and Syria, the monks of this region "for the most part dwelt in communities in cities and villages." He explained that "the severity of the winter, which is always a natural feature of that country, would probably make a hermit life impracticable."[65] The proximity of ascetic groups to the various power structures of urban or town life in Asia Minor and their active involvement in their ecclesiastical communities produced distinctive tensions, not the least of which is seen in the relationship between monks and bishops. A survey of these dynamics provides the necessary background for understanding the mediating role played by Basil of Caesarea upon his assumption of episcopal office.

In his seminal article on monasticism in Constantinople prior to Chalcedon, Gilbert Dagron argues that the emergence of monasticism as an urban phenomenon was unique to the imperial capital.[66] It was only in Constantinople, he maintains, that monks constituted an important social group, integrated into urban life although distinct from other groups. The urban character of the movement, along with links uniting early Constantinopolitan monasticism with a moderate form of Arianism, meant that the city served as a theater of perpetual conflict between monks and bishops.[67] Dagron presents a convincing case for the distinctiveness of the monastic movement in the capital. It may be misleading, however, to emphasize the uniqueness of the urban setting as the focal point of monastic life in Constantinople as over against other cities and towns in Asia Minor where monasticism flourished.

Indeed the many small cities in western Cappadocia and especially the capital of the province stood in marked contrast to the rural character of most of the eastern half of the region.[68] Located on the Via reale stretching across Asia Minor from Ephesus toward the ancient Persian capital of Susa, the city of Mazaca, later Roman Caesarea, stood at a crossroads connecting such cities as Ancyra, Iconium, Amasea, Tyana, Tarsus, Comana, and Melitene. Primarily because of its central location the Cappadocian kings chose Mazaca as their capital, and the city continued to flourish under the Romans, who changed its name to Caesarea around 10 B.C.E. Far from a cultural backwater, by the mid-fourth century C.E. Caesarea had become a populous city of great commercial, artisanal, and intellectual activity.[69] It was in this urban milieu that Basil of Caesarea established his famous hospice, later dubbed the Basileiados. Constructed at the gateway to Caesarea during the early years of Basil's episcopate, this foundation was established to minister to the needs of pilgrims, the sick, and the poor.[70] Basil's monastic *Rules* emphasized the value of work and engagement in social, educational, and charitable activities. These features of the cenobitic system he developed suggest that the Cappadocian envisaged monastic communities situated in or near cities and towns, where the monks could be at the service of the church and the general population.[71]

Although Basil's monastic synthesis ultimately succeeded in embedding itself in the life of the church, he was not the first ascetic in Asia Minor to demonstrate a commitment to the urban population. Eustathius of Sebaste, whose pioneering role in the ascetic movement has been highlighted in recent decades, was similarly involved in the cities of the region. It was in large part Eustathius's commitment to urban life that initially attracted Basil and inspired some of his own monastic ideals.[72] From early in his career, however, Eustathius ran into difficulties with ecclesiastical authorities. He was born in or slightly before 300 in Sebaste, the most important city of inland Pontus and the capital of Roman Armenia.[73] His father, Eulalius of Sebaste, was the bishop of the city, and Eustathius himself was enrolled in the clergy by 325. At some point he had assumed the garb of an ascetic and a philosopher, apparently as a sign of contempt for worldly affairs. This attire so angered his father, who considered such dress unbecoming of a priest, that the bishop expelled his son from the church.[74] It may have been this dispute with his father that prompted the young man's journey to Egypt where, according to Basil, he became a disciple of Arius. In Antioch he allegedly attempted to gain admission to the clergy but was excluded by the bishop because of his Arian views.[75] Eventually Eustathius moved on to Caesarea in Cappadocia, where he was ordained as a priest by Bishop Hermogenes after presenting the staunchly Nicene bishop with an orthodox confession of faith. After the death of Hermogenes he traveled to Constantinople and became acquainted with Eusebius of Nicomedia. Eustathius soon had a falling out with Eusebius, however, apparently because of the former's ascetic activities. As a result, he left the capital city and returned to his native Pontus.[76] During the next few years Eustathius began to attract disciples and organize groups of ascetics in Armenia, Paphlagonia, and Pontus. His rigorous ascetic discipline and certain practices and teachings associated with him provoked considerable controversy. According to the church historian Sozomen he was excommunicated by a synod in Neocaesarea around 340 and shortly thereafter by the Council of Gangra.[77] Despite a series of condemnations and depositions, however, by 357 Eustathius had become bishop of the metropolitan see of Sebaste in Armenia and managed to remain in his ecclesiastical position until his death around 377.

Connected with Eustathius of Sebaste and particularly with his followers, the decisions of the Council of Gangra are important for several reasons. First of all, they reveal the kind of teachings and abuses on the part of mid-fourth-century ascetics that church officials feared and condemned. An examination of the specific anathemas makes it clear that Eustathian ascetics resided in the cities of Anatolia and Armenia and were involved in various ways in the churches of these regions. It was their presence and activity in these population centers that made them particularly threatening to clergy and bishops as well as to certain members of the laity. The council also has a broader significance for the history of monk-hierarchy relations in Asia Minor and beyond. Along with the Councils of Ancyra, Neocaesarea, Antioch, and Laodicea, the acts of the Council of Gangra constituted the disciplinary corpus of the church of Antioch at a time when this metropolis was still in anti-Nicene hands. Eventually attached to the canons of Nicaea, this corpus formed the nucleus of early Greek canonical collections and of almost all future collections of canon law.[78]

The precise date and circumstances of the council that met in Gangra, in the province of Paphlagonia, remain somewhat obscure. A twenty-year discrepancy between the accounts of Sozomen, who put the council before 341, and Socrates, who placed it after 360, is further complicated by the fact that there is no indication of the episcopal sees of the thirteen bishops who participated in the council.[79] The presiding bishop at Gangra was a certain Eusebius, often identified as Bishop Eusebius of Nicomedia. In this case the council may well have been part of a larger dispute between Eusebius, who was favored by the emperor, and Macedonius, who was supported by the ascetic party, in the struggle for ascendance to the see of Constantinople.[80] Sozomen noted Eustathius's familiarity with Macedonius and especially with his disciple Marathonius, a wealthy social reformer whom Eustathius himself influenced to embrace the ascetic life and who would later serve as a deacon under Macedonius.[81] This may help to explain Eusebius's prejudice against the

Eustathians, who likely supported his opponent in the contest for Constantinople. Eusebius was eventually transferred from Nicomedia and appointed bishop of Constantinople by Emperor Constantius II around 338, though his death in 342, shortly after the presumed date of the Council of Gangra, led to renewed conflict for succession to the increasingly important imperial see.[82] In any case, as the official representative of the Arian imperial church, Eusebius was clearly no friend to ascetics.

The acts of the Council of Gangra consist of twenty canons along with a synodical letter from the bishops of Pontus to the bishops of Armenia.[83] The letter refers specifically to the asceticism of Eustathius and his followers as the cause of the council and enumerates the irregularities of which they were accused. The acts of this council have been analyzed from different angles, but for our purposes it is most helpful to consider the ascetic abuses condemned at Gangra in terms of two major, if occasionally overlapping, categories. One set of canons denounced the transgression of accepted social norms. Prominent among these abuses was the condemnation of or contempt for legitimate marriage and the concomitant exaltation of singleness and virginity (canons 1, 9, 10). The Eustathians apparently overturned or undermined other established familial and social relationships as well. Anathemas were pronounced against parents who abandoned their children (canon 15), children who neglected their parents (canon 16) under the pretext of piety, and ascetics who encouraged slaves to despise their masters or forsake their service under the pretext of serving God (canon 3). Innovations on accepted customs were also condemned. Offenders included those who despised the eating of meat (canon 2) and those who wore the *peribolaion,* the pallium of philosophers and monks, and who looked down on people clothed in the ordinary fashion (canon 12). The practices of ascetic women were the subject of three canons.[84] Some women had apparently forsaken their husbands to pursue the ascetic vocation (canon 14). Others were condemned for wearing male apparel (canon 13) or for cropping their hair, a sign of subjection, from pretended piety (canon 17). Though not mentioned in the canons, the accompanying synodical letter included yet another transgression of accepted social standards: the Eustathians allegedly condemned the rich, claiming that those who did not forsake everything had no hope of salvation.

Practices or teachings believed to undermine the authority of the church hierarchy make up the second category of abuses condemned by the Council of Gangra. Though they lived within the cities and towns of Asia Minor and Armenia, it seems that some Eustathian ascetics avoided or scorned the regular services of the church (canon 5) and the celebration of "agapes" (canon 11), most likely referring to feasts that rich Christians gave on behalf of the poor. They neglected the commemoration of martyrs (canon 20). They particularly objected to married priests, according to the synodical letter, and taught that one should refrain from participating in eucharistic services conducted by married clergy (canon 4). The Eustathians were condemned for holding their own private services without the presence of an approved church official (canon 6). Misappropriation of church offerings was the subject of two canons. The attached letter to the Armenian bishops clarifies the background to these anathemas: some Eustathians wrongly considered themselves the rightful recipients of ecclesiastical offerings by virtue of their exceptional sanctity. In response, the council strictly forbade the acceptance or administration of gifts and offerings without the authorization of the bishop (canons 7 and 8). Ascetics who fasted on Sundays (canon 18) or failed to observe the traditional fasts of the church (canon 19) were also condemned for their pride and presumption.

The canons of Gangra suggest that Eustathian ascetics were considered suspect not because they had fled the world but rather because they had sought to pursue their ascetic vocation *within* the world and in the church. Their presence as a kind of countercultural community within the urban milieu would naturally stand as a challenge to the status quo. Their specific teachings about marriage and the family and their condemnation of riches and other socially acceptable practices would be especially irritating to some citizens. Moreover, by residing in the cities and towns of Anatolia and Armenia they more easily attracted recruits from within the ecclesiastical community. Although they scorned a number of its practices, despised the married clergy, and condemned accommodations to the world that the imperial church was willing to tolerate, it appears that Eustathians were very much involved in the church and tried to influence the mass of Christians with their distinctive ascetic ideals. In fact the bishops assembled at Gangra were particularly concerned about the attempt of the Eustathians to impose their rigorist beliefs and practices on all. The teachings of these ascetics, such as they are presented by the council, would have clearly challenged the authority of church officials.

The bishops assembled at Gangra viewed the urban asceticism of the Eustathians as a nuisance and as an actual or potential hindrance to their own exercise of spiritual authority. They did not, however, want to leave the impression that they were opposed on principle to the ascetic vocation. Therefore, they concluded the canons with an epilogue affirming what they perceived to be a positive asceticism in contrast to what the Eustathians taught:

> We write these things not to cut off those in the church of God who wish to practice asceticism according to the Scriptures but [to cut off] those who undertake the practice of asceticism to the point of arrogance, both by exalting themselves over those who lead a simpler life and by introducing novel ideas that are not found in the Scriptures or in the writings approved by the church. For this reason we admire virginity [when practiced] with humility and we approve of self-control [when practiced] with dignity and piety; we also approve of withdrawal from worldly affairs [when it is done] with humility; and we honor the noble union of marriage; we do not disdain wealth [when used] with righteousness and [the giving of] alms; we praise plainness and frugality of dress, with simple concern only for the body; but we do not approve of going about in lascivious and effeminate dress; we honor the house of God and we approve of the meetings held in them as holy and beneficial, not limiting reverence to the houses but honoring every place built in the name of God; and we approve the communal meeting in the church of God for the benefit of the community; and we bless the brothers' abundant good works on behalf of the poor, because they are performed in accordance with the traditions [established] by the church; and to sum up, we pray that the things transmitted by the divine Scriptures and the apostolic traditions be done in the church.[85]

While clearly expressing the bishops' objections to the alleged arrogance of the Eustathians, their innovations, and their disrespect for the official church and its leaders, this addendum left room for forms of monastic life that might be harmoniously integrated into the life of the church.

In one sense the decrees of the Council of Gangra cannot be considered an accurate reflection of the monastic movement throughout Asia Minor. Scholars have questioned to what extent the teachings and practices condemned by the council represent the ideals of Eustathius himself as opposed to a malevolent caricature of his admittedly austere ascetic principles. Already in the fifth century Sozomen suspected that Eustathius's ascetic teachings had been misrepresented by the bishops at Gangra.[86] If he had truly espoused all the extreme views condemned by the council, it is improbable that the ascetic pioneer would have risen to the metropolitan see of Sebaste by 357, let alone that he would have had such a great influence on the monastic ideals of Basil's family. Moreover, according to Bishop Epiphanius of Salamis, while Eustathius himself was serving as bishop of Sebaste his former disciple, Aerius, broke away from his movement and established his own more radical ascetic group in the surrounding forests.[87] The fact that the bishop was plagued by the emergence of a more extreme splinter group within his own movement suggests that he was himself inclined toward a somewhat more moderate form of asceticism. Rather than being a radical extremist, Eustathius likely represented a pattern of ascetic life that was already common in parts of Asia Minor, an asceticism resembling the indigenous Syrian model praised and embodied by Aphrahat and Ephrem. However, either Eustathius himself or some of his disciples began to depart from or even disdain established ecclesiastical practices and norms. These ascetics ministered on a parallel plane, which some authorities considered dangerously competitive, rather than in harmony with the church and in submission to its hierarchy.

Even if the abuses described by the bishops at Gangra represent an exaggeration of Eustathius's ascetic ideals, the decrees of the council stand as an important backdrop to the development of relations between monks and the church hierarchy in Asia Minor. They reveal a nascent monastic movement in this area that, unlike the cenobitic monasticism of Egypt and somewhat closer to the protomonasticism of Syria and Mesopotamia, sought to operate within the urban or semiurban context and in close relation to the church community. The Eustathians did not succeed in this endeavor, not least of all owing to their leader's eventual fall into doctrinal heresy.[88] But their failures forewarned the next generation of monastic leaders of extremes to avoid, suspicions to allay, and potential tensions to resolve.

We have ample testimony that the issues that dominated the Council of Gangra represented ongoing tensions at least into the early years of Basil of Caesarea's episcopate (370–379). Basil himself alluded to antagonism toward the monastic life when he first resolved to pursue this vocation. Many people, he claimed, hoped to deter him from this course, apparently because of the association of ascetic circles with Eustathius of Sebaste.[89] The attempt to dissuade him from joining with these serious and austere ascetics suggests that the ghost of Gangra still lingered at the outset of Basil's monastic career. In the early years of his own episcopal tenure Basil expressed deep sorrow at the hatred of monks in Caesarea and the efforts of many to malign or discredit their way of life.[90] In Neocaesarea in Pontus it was the clergy in particular who felt animosity toward monks, and indeed toward Basil himself for his association with them. In a letter to the clergy of this city the Cappadocian endeavored to defend the monastic life and to heal the breach that had arisen between monks and the church hierarchy.[91]

Gregory of Nazianzus provides similar evidence of both a general suspicion of monks and particular tensions between monks and bishops. In one of his earliest orations (c. 360) he lamented the fact that the monastic vocation was often the object of scorn, in part because many people simply disdained the contemplative life and in part because unworthy monks had given the movement a bad reputation.[92] Elsewhere he described the monks of Nazianzus as the "overzealous part of the church" who arose against his father, then serving as bishop of Nazianzus, and himself.[93] Gregory devoted an entire oration to this conflict and its eventual peaceful resolution, referring to himself as a friend of the brothers and one who had shared their way of life, a way of life he lauded.[94] Yet he did not hesitate to criticize the monks of Nazianzus. They had been excessively zealous, even combative, according to Gregory, for they had rebelled against their bishop and destroyed the unity of the church. "For the sake of love we have practiced hate," he said, and he went on to harangue his listeners with an exhortation to maintain the fragile unity that had so recently been restored to the Christian flock.[95] However, Gregory did not always censure monks for their opposition to the church hierarchy. When a dispute arose between Bishop Eusebius of Caesarea and Basil, who was then assisting his predecessor as a priest and adviser, the monks of the city supported Basil and conspired to revolt against their bishop.[96] Rather than chastise the monks, Gregory commended the prudent course that Basil had adopted on this occasion, withdrawing from the metropolis for a time to avoid causing further division in the church. His allusions to both these affairs, in Nazianzus and Caesarea, respectively, make it clear that monks were a force to be reckoned with in the cities of Cappadocia and a potential source of conflict with leaders of the church. Uneasy, if not occasionally hostile, relations between monks and the church hierarchy were certainly not exclusive to Constantinople.

Relations between monks and bishops in the fourth century varied substantially from region to region. Complicating any attempt at generalization is the need to take account of such ascetics as the *apotaktikoi* of Egypt, the *bnay qyama* of Syria, and the Eustathians of Asia Minor and Armenia alongside the better-known cenobitic and anchoritic models of monastic life that became more deeply entrenched and more regularized as the century progressed. To emphasize either general harmony or protracted conflict with the church hierarchy would be to misrepresent the distinctive features of the early monastic movement that took root in diverse locations and differing social, political, and ecclesiastical contexts. On the one hand, many people recognized that monks, especially proven ascetic leaders, were particularly well-suited for episcopal office. This is evident in the long tradition of ascetic bishops in Syria, in the appointments of Athanasius, and in the popular support for Eustathius, who rose to the metropolitan see of Sebaste despite a history of friction with ecclesiastical leaders. On the other hand, for a variety of reasons tensions increased toward the middle of the century as monastic life rapidly spread throughout the empire. If the withdrawal of monks to the outskirts of towns and villages provoked suspicion among some ecclesiastics in Syria, the tensions that marked early monastic expansion in Asia Minor were due in large part to the spread of ascetic communities *within* cities and towns. The Council of Gangra testifies to fears and suspicions monks provoked among men in positions of authority in the church. Though early monastic leaders and orthodox bishops made little reference to the decrees of this council, perhaps because of its links to the anti-Nicene imperial church,[97] the tensions exposed at Gangra continued into subsequent decades. It was in this setting of malaise that Basil of Caesarea would take the reins of the young movement of ascetic fervor and try to harness it to his broader purposes for the church.

2

Asceticism and Leadership in the Thought of Basil of Caesarea

Basil's connection of asceticism with the Christian life in general and even more strongly with the leader of the Christian community had roots in the Cappadocian milieu of his youth. Unfortunately Basil himself maintains almost complete silence on the subject of his family and upbringing. He remarked in passing that he was preserved from error and raised in the knowledge of sacred Scripture by Christian parents. In several letters he mentioned the nurturing role of his grandmother Macrina.[1] Gregory of Nazianzus described in greater detail the hardships of Basil's paternal grandparents. A noble and pious Christian couple from Neocaesarea, they endured seven years of exile in the Pontic forests during the persecution of Maximinus II (310–313).[2] We also hear of the piety of Basil's parents. Gregory pointed specifically to their care for the needy, their austere lifestyle, and their dedication of a portion of their goods to God. The elder Basil, a teacher of rhetoric, is said to have trained his son in both learning and virtue.[3] Even from his earliest years, then, Basil's family provided a model of serious religious life—devoted to God, to Scripture, and to meeting practical needs.

Formative Influences

Basil's exposure to varieties of ascetic living dates from this early period as well. His own family seems to have practiced a form of household asceticism, a custom that was popular in Asia Minor and Syria through the middle of the fourth century.[4] He probably came into contact with ascetic groups of Eustathian inspiration living in or near the urban centers of northeast Anatolia during his youth.[5] He passed part of his child-hood years on property belonging to his father's family in the vicinity of Neocaesarea, where the elder Basil seems to have practiced his profession as a rhetor for some time. Bishop Musonius, whose life Basil would later eulogize, was the bishop of Neocaesarea during his youth and was himself probably an ascetic.[6] Soon after his father's death, while Basil was studying in Athens, his mother, Emmelia, and his sister, Macrina, moved from Neocaesarea to the more remote family estate at Annesi in Pontus. Macrina convinced her mother to adopt the ascetic life, and gradually the whole household—mother, children, and slaves—was transformed into an ascetic community.[7] Not only did Macrina have considerable influence on her mother and her younger brother Peter, but she also seems to have played a significant role in Basil's own monastic vocation. While Basil was in Athens it was probably Macrina who kept her brother informed through letters of the ascetic ideals and growing renown of Eustathius of Sebaste. Although Basil himself is silent about his sister's influence, Gregory of Nyssa suggests that it was Macrina who won him over to the "philosophic life" after his return home.[8] Basil's brother Naucratius, who preceded him in abandoning rhetorical pursuits for ascetic solitude and whose more isolated, rustic lifestyle Basil initially imitated, also stands in the background of his early ascetic experiments.[9]

Basil has more to say about another important factor in his early formation, the heritage he received from Gregory Thaumaturgus. Highly esteemed as the missionary-apostle of Cappadocia and Pontus, Gregory became bishop of Neocaesarea around 240. His words were preserved and passed down to Basil's generation through the oral tradition and liturgical practices of the church. But Basil could also claim more intimate links with Gregory, for the great bishop had converted, baptized, and instructed his grandmother, Macrina the Elder. Basil often referred to the words, the customs, or the tradition of Gregory, and he clearly regarded him as a standard of orthodox doctrine and practice.[10] He frequently appealed to Gregory's life, teaching, and connection with his family when defending the orthodoxy of his own beliefs or practices.[11] Perhaps just as significant an influence on Basil's convictions and direction in life was Gregory's career as both an ascetic and a bishop. Born to a wealthy pagan family in Neocaesarea, Gregory was groomed for a career in law. While visiting Caesarea in Palestine before commencing his legal studies, the young man came under the spell of Origen of Alexandria. Captivated by the great Christian teacher and ascetic, Gregory postponed his plans to study law in Beirut and became a student at Origen's school, where he devoted himself to study, prayer, and contemplation. After approximately five years he returned to Neocaesarea. According to Gregory of Nyssa, Gregory Thaumaturgus initially withdrew from the bustle of city life and worldly affairs to be alone with God.[12] Despite this alleged proclivity for solitude he soon became the city's first bishop and is reputed to have successfully evangelized the largely pagan city. These main features of Gregory's career were well known to the Cappadocians. Basil certainly knew of his biblical and spiritual training under the great Alexandrian. Whether or not it was actually intended for the Thaumaturge, Origen's "Letter to Gregory" is included in the *Philocalia,* an anthology of his spiritual writings that Basil and Gregory Nazianzen compiled during their retreat together in Annesi (c. 358).[13]

Not only were Gregory's theology and spiritual preparation exemplary for Basil but stories about his life and exercise of episcopal authority also must have deeply impressed the future bishop. Both he and his brother Gregory of Nyssa referred to the Thaumaturge as "Gregory the Great," and in a number of passages Basil portrayed him as an ideal leader.[14] His most complete eulogy appears in *De spiritu sancto.* Against the background of heresy and the weak and factious ecclesiastical leadership of his own day, Basil presented Gregory Thaumaturgus as a model Christian and bishop:

> As for Gregory the Great, what place shall we assign to him and his words? Why not place him among the apostles and prophets, for this was a man walking in the same spirit as they. His whole life he followed the track of the saints and during the course of his entire existence he strictly maintained the life of evangelical citizenship. As for myself, I say that we shall wound the truth by not counting among the intimates of God that soul who was like a great resplendent flame whose glow shone through the Church of God. By the help of the Spirit he had a fearful power over demons. But in order to lead the nations to the obedience of faith, he received such a grace of speaking that having found only seventeen Christians, he led the entire people, city dwellers and villagers, to the knowledge of God.[15]

Alongside the influence of family and spiritual models from the past, Basil's education played a role in the formation of his character and ideals. After brief periods of study in Caesarea and Constantinople, he went on to Athens to continue his education in rhetoric. According to Nazianzen, however, he never lost sight of the "philosophic life" that the two friends so longed to pursue.[16] In fact the Cappadocian's classical education in philosophy and rhetoric probably strengthened his aspiration toward this goal. It must also have played a role in the development of his views on Christian leadership. The Homeric ideals of virtue (aretē) and imitation of the hero, central elements of the earliest Greek education, were bequeathed to later epochs of antiquity. While we do not know the exact content of Basil's educational program, his study of philosophy would have presented an ideal of life comprising a strong moral element.[17] Indeed the philosophy that had come to dominate the Greco-Roman intellectual world by the third century may well have reinforced a student's inclination toward asceticism.[18] Paideia itself came to have religious as well as intellectual connotations, and to acquire paideia was in a sense to pursue the pagan vocation of holiness. Coupled with the philosopher's renunciation of worldly values and ambitions was the requirement of asceticism, for only by liberating the soul from its attachment to the body could one aspire to contemplation of spiritual realities. Purification of the soul was attained by such practices as celibacy, austere diet, and other forms of physical denial. The pagan philosopher Plotinus was known to be particularly severe in his pursuit of these methods of self-purification.[19]

Nor was asceticism restricted to the realm of philosophers and monks. It was an ideal for the ruler as well, and the fifth-century church historians incorporated it into their portrayal of Christian emperors. Theodosius the Younger was perhaps the best exemplar of a new "soldier-monk" image of the emperor.[20] But already in the fourth century we find that the ruler most antagonistic toward Christians, the pagan emperor Julian, had a significant ascetic bent. Among his marvelously detailed descriptions of the physiognomies and personal habits of late antique rulers, Ammianus Marcellinus provides glimpses into this aspect of Julian's life. The emperor had "no need of choice food, content with a scanty and simple diet"; his sleeping regimen included making his bed on the ground and at times denying himself of sleep altogether.[21] He also maintained strict sexual continence. When beautiful Persian maidens were taken as prisoners, Julian is said to have refused to touch or even look at them. Ammianus remarked that he was "following the example of Alexander and Africanus, who avoided such conduct, lest those who showed themselves unwearied by hardships should be unnerved by passion." Such explanations show how personal asceticism was linked with an ideal of leadership for pagan and Christian alike.[22]

Along with Basil's academic pursuit of philosophy, his study of rhetoric, continued from his earlier years in Constantinople, would also have had a moral aim. One of Basil's two notable teachers of rhetoric, Prohaeresius, was a Christian and an ascetic, though we know nothing concrete about his influence on the young student. The pagan Eunapius described Prohaeresius in praiseworthy terms and particularly lauded his asceticism.[23] In general, educators from Isocrates through the Hellenistic period insisted that the primary purpose of education was to instill in students good principles of conduct, and they condemned any system that neglected this moral goal.[24] Basil himself highly valued even pagan authors who wrote "in praise of virtue," for he would later encourage youths to emulate the words and deeds of good men that these pagans recounted.[25] His own strong emphasis on the moral and ascetic virtue of the Christian leader would reflect the ideals of his profane education as well as the influence of his Christian upbringing.

In Athens Basil also gained his first real experience of leadership, and it was closely connected with the pursuit of disciplined religious life. Gregory Nazianzen describes how a small group of like-minded Christian students gathered around his companion. They were distinguished by their austere lifestyle and were proud to be known as Christians among their colleagues in this very pagan city. Basil's exposure to the "moral disease" that is said to have permeated the city and the inhabitants of Athens may have contributed to his decision to dedicate his life to pastoral care and monastic formation.[26] In any case, Nazianzen implies that his friend left Athens with the intent to undertake a life of "philosophy," a goal that may well have expressed classical as much as Christian ambitions.[27]

Upon the completion of his education Basil was profoundly influenced by Eustathius of Sebaste and the ascetic communities he had formed or inspired. Much has been written about the relation of the great Cappadocian to this ascetic pioneer in Asia Minor who eventually fell away from Nicene orthodoxy.[28] Jean Gribomont has argued convincingly that Eustathius was the recipient of Letter 1, in which we learn of the young Basil's eager pursuit of the "philosopher" through Cappadocia, Palestine, Egypt, and Alexandria, missing him at every turn. The seriousness and radicalism of Eustathius's ascetic commitment attracted Basil. Reflecting on his initial encounter with ascetics organized by Eustathius, Basil later compared them with the monks of Egypt, Syria, and Mesopotamia, whose virtues and austerity they sought to imitate. He recalled with admiration the humble clothing, the subjugation of the flesh, the sobriety of their manner of life, which caused him to defend them and initially to deny the accusations brought against them. The example of these ascetics and their leader, which had so shaped the ascetic pursuits of his family during his absence, played a significant role in strengthening Basil's own resolve to pursue the philosophic life.[29]

Toward this end, sometime around 357 he withdrew to his secluded family estate in Annesi on the Iris River in Pontus, just across the river from the settlement of his mother and sister. There Basil studied the Scriptures more intensively. The *Moralia,* which he began to compose during this Pontus period, represents the fruit of his studies and reflection. It is saturated with the Bible, particularly the New Testament.[30] His friend Gregory Nazianzen soon joined him in his study of biblical and spiritual texts and his life of prayer and fasting. It seems that others also began to come under Basil's influence, though his initial ascetic contacts were with disciples of Eustathius. In fact Basil visited nearby communities of Eustathian inspiration, where he listened and responded to questions raised by the brothers. Eustathius himself, who had recently been elected bishop of Sebaste (c. 358), was a frequent visitor and companion during these years.[31]

From the example of Eustathius and his followers Basil learned of an asceticism that flourished in the urban milieu. It was not by chance that Eustathian ascetics resided in cities. In his own episcopal see, Eustathius established a monastic hospice designed to meet the practical needs of the poor, sick, and needy.[32] Basil would later establish a similar institution on the outskirts of Caesarea. The presence of Eustathian ascetics in the heart of the cities of Anatolia may well have provoked the opposition that led to their leader's rebuff. However, this involvement in urban life appealed to Basil. It was different from what he had encountered in monastic centers of Egypt and Palestine, where isolation or removal from society was more the norm. While Basil emphasized the need for silence and solitude, he also saw the value for ascetics of residing near towns so that they could be of service to fellow Christians.[33]

Along with his concern for cities Eustathius demonstrated a commitment to the church that could not have failed to escape the notice of the future bishop of Caesarea. The ascetic leader whom Basil had come to know and respect during his early career was also a man of the church. The son of a bishop, Eustathius had been ordained a priest at a fairly young age.[34] While the decrees of Gangra may have caused him to moderate more radical ascetic practices, Eustathius continued to recruit men and women for the ascetic life while serving as a priest. His rise to the episcopal see of Sebaste in Armenia, notwithstanding suspicions about his ascetic and ecclesiastical ideals, attests to his popularity with both the people and the bishops of the province. In fact, Epiphanius of Salamis, usually so scathing in his attacks against heretics, was surprisingly indulgent in his treatment of Eustathius. Despite Eustathius's Arian leanings, Epiphanius acknowledged that "no few [people] admire his life and conduct."[35] Perhaps Epiphanius's own position as both a bishop and an ascetic made him more sympathetic to his colleague's plight, for as bishop of Sebaste Eustathius had to struggle with the more radical wing of his own ascetic movement. His disciple Aerius allegedly reproached him for his acceptance of ecclesiastical office, considering it incompatible with serious monastic renunciation.[36] Though he had been given charge of Eustathius's hospice, Aerius eventually broke away from his bishop and mentor to form his own more extreme ascetic community, detached from the city and the church.

Eustathius himself continued both to advance the ascetic life in his region and to fulfill his episcopal commission, a pattern that Basil of Caesarea would follow.[37] Alongside Basil of Ancyra and Eleusius of Cyzicus, Eustathius led the homoiousian party in the struggle against Aëtius and the Anomoeans at the Council of Ancyra (358). The following year he participated in the Council of Seleucia (359). This council delegated him to the court of Constantinople to present the homoiousian position to Emperor Constantius (337–361). Like the other delegates there, he was compelled to sign the fourth formula of Sirmium and was exiled to Dardania by the triumphant Arians. He was soon recalled, however, and restored to his see by Emperor Julian (361–363). During this period Basil accompanied Eustathius not only on visits to ascetic communities but also in ecclesiastical negotiations. He traveled with him to see Silvanus of Tarsus to make arrangements for the Council of Lampascus (autumn 364), where the bishop of Sebaste again played a prominent role. He was one of three delegates chosen to present the homoiousian view to Emperor Valentinian and Pope Liberius. On their return, the members of this delegation reported on their western journey to the Council of Tyana (367), which approved the work of the commission. Basil was probably present at this gathering. He was certainly on good terms with Eustathius at this time and labored with him for the well-being of the church.[38]

Eustathius eventually became a source of deep pain and great embarrassment for Basil. Both the intimacy of their friendship and the injury caused by their rupture are described in Letter 223. Elsewhere Basil decried Eustathius's defection from the orthodox faith, suggesting the pernicious influence of Arius himself as the underlying cause.[39] Even in his bitterest reproaches, however, he recalled his earlier veneration for the great ascetic. He never directly opposed Eustathius's ascetic ideals. We find no mention of the decisions of Gangra in Basil's writings. Similarly, the Synod of Melitene, where it seems that Eustathius was deposed by the Arians because of his ascetic stance, is mentioned only with uneasiness.[40]

Basil did try to temper ascetic enthusiasm that might cause dissension or division in the church. For example, he forbade the celebration of the eucharist in private homes,[41] a practice explicitly condemned by the Council of Gangra. He encouraged temperance in eating and fasting and called for proper attention to physical needs. In general Basil's *Rules* aimed at moderation. They emphasized not extreme austerities or prodigious acts but positive deeds of love toward God and neighbor.[42] Yet the practices of the Eustathians are nowhere explicitly condemned. Nothing could erase the impression Eustathius had made on the young Basil as both a model of the ascetic life and an active leader in the church. Overshadowed by the theological breach that so deeply divided the two erstwhile friends, the similarities in their ideals and certain aspects of their careers have often been overlooked or downplayed.

Other factors also played some role in the development of Basil's monastic thought and his eventual acceptance of an ecclesiastical career. A number of older studies assumed that Basilian monasticism owed a great deal to the Pachomian cenobitic system. Actually, however, Basil had very little exposure to Pachomian patterns of monastic life. Though the young Cappadocian visited monastic centers in the east, it was much more likely that he set out on this journey in search of Eustathius than for the purpose of collecting data for his own monastic establishment.[43] Basil says nothing about visits to Pachomian brotherhoods in Egypt. He may have gleaned more from his sojourn in Alexandria, where ascetic life and clerical vocation tended to coincide, but his letters reveal that he never met Athanasius. His admiration for the great bishop and monastic advocate radiates through his correspondence, but he knew him only by reputation.[44] Significant firsthand experience of monastic models was more likely acquired from Syria, in closer proximity to Basil's native Cappadocia. It is in this direction that we might more profitably look for influences on his monastic thought, particularly with respect to his linkage of ascetic ideals and church leadership. In this region relations between premonastic asceticism and the church hierarchy were closely intertwined. Moreover, as we have seen, it was an area in which ascetic bishops were not an uncommon phenomenon.

Basil said very little about the direction his life took or the motives that drew him into the priesthood and eventually the episcopate. Yet the influence in his formative years of models such as Gregory Thaumaturgus and Eustathius of Sebaste must be sufficiently underscored. In the lives of these men he saw no opposition between asceticism and church office. Nor do Basil's pre-episcopal letters suggest the kind of reserve toward bishops that we observed in some texts of Egyptian monasticism. While many monks hesitated to accept ecclesiastical office, the Cappadocian demonstrated no such reluctance.[45] In fact, given the turmoil of the church in his day, Basil saw all the more need to hold monastic life and ecclesiastical authority in tandem. His own career became purposefully directed toward this end. Following his ordination to the priesthood in 364, his active service to the church was interspersed with periods of retreat.[46] While such respites necessarily became less frequent amid the pressing duties of his episcopate, on a personal level Basil yearned for those times of withdrawal. His official episcopal functions mirrored this dual focus. For Basil, leadership of the church as a whole encompassed oversight and care of monastic communities.

Context: The State of the Church and the Episcopate

Whatever influence family, education, or specific role models may have had in his formative years, Basil's ideas about the episcopate were significantly shaped by what he perceived as the crisis of the church in his day, particularly the spread of heresy and the foibles of contemporary episcopal leadership. The latter years of the reign of Constantius II (337–361) as well as that of Valens (364–378) saw the temporary triumph and spread of Arianism. Adherence to the homoian creed accepted at the Council of Rimini (359) and confirmed by the Council of Constantinople (360) became the rule of law. Faced with the alternatives of assent or exile, many Nicene bishops signed the formula. In Caesarea the elderly Bishop Dianius subscribed to the creed, though Basil later suggests that he did so in the simplicity of his heart and with no intention of rejecting the faith of Nicaea. The elder Gregory of Nazianzus also yielded under pressure, although he too was later reconciled with the orthodox.[47] The reign of Emperor Julian (361–363) began with a period of toleration during which exiled bishops were recalled. Soon after, however, the emperor spawned a pagan revival and initiated a campaign of direct and more subtle attacks on Christians. Athanasius was exiled once again. The Nicene party enjoyed a brief respite during the reign of Julian's successor, the pro-Nicene emperor Jovian (363–364), but his premature death ushered in the reign of the last Arian ruler.

Emperor Valens (364–378), who ruled the Christian East during the large part of Basil's ecclesiastical career, was described in the fifth century as tolerant of all save "the champions of the Apostolic decrees," against whom "he persisted in waging war."[48] Basil's letters support this later portrayal of the ruler's prejudice against the adherents of Nicaea. While the earlier years of his reign were largely occupied with military campaigns against the Goths, after 369 Valens intensified his persecution of those who resisted his religious policies. He staunchly upheld the formula of Rimini-Constantinople in opposition to both homoiousian and Nicene Christians. Numerous bishops from both parties were exiled for their refusal to sign the creed. Monks were also pressed to subscribe and punished for failing to comply.

In a series of letters to the West, Basil presented the perilous state of the church. Certain images recur in his descriptions of the situation. The church had succumbed to the attacks of her foes like a ship buffeted by the waves, and the threat of "shipwreck" was imminent. The Arian heresy had spread like a raging "storm" or "tempest" that was quickly overtaking the entire church.[49] As a result, morality was undermined and Christians were submerged in a sea of confusion and ignorance. Basil contrasted this picture of turmoil in the East with the united orthodoxy and peace of the churches in the West. Yet over the course of a few years his earnest pleas for help turned to reproaches of the western bishops for their failure to come to the aid of their brethren.[50] He warned the westerners to beware lest they too fall prey to the Arian onslaught. In a letter to the bishops of Italy and Gaul, one of his most desperate appeals for aid, Basil described in great detail the "deadly fruit" borne by the Arian blight: "The doctrines of piety have been brought to ruin and the laws of the church are thrown into confusion. The ambition of those who do not fear the Lord rushes into the foremost positions, and episcopal office is now publicly known as the prize of impiety. The result is that the worse a man blasphemes the more worthy people judge him to be a bishop . . . There is complete immunity in sinning, for those who have been placed in office by human schemes return the favor by continually showing indulgence to sinners."[51]

Prominent among such depictions of the beleaguered church is the plight of the Nicene bishops of the East. Basil recounted bitterly the exile and replacement of orthodox leaders: "Shepherds are banished, and in their places are introduced cruel wolves who rip apart the flock of Christ." Four years later the persecution of Nicene bishops had not subsided. Writing to Bishop Eusebius of Samosata in 376, Basil lamented that perverse men had established domination over the churches.[52] Good bishops, including his brother Gregory, had been expelled from their sees and replaced by slaves and destroyers of the faith. In another letter to the bishops of Italy and Gaul he spelled out the Arian strategy against Nicene leaders: "Shepherds are persecuted so that the flocks may be scattered . . . No malefactor is condemned without proof, but bishops have been convicted on calumny alone and are consigned to punishments without the least evidence having been brought forward in support of the accusations . . . They have been apprehended by force late at night, have been exiled to remote places, and have been given over to death through the sufferings of the desert."[53] Basil often wrote letters of comfort to bishops in exile, encouraging them in their struggle and exhorting them to persevere in their stand against heresy. He also commended monks victimized by Arian persecution for their loyalty to the faith of Nicaea.[54]

The spread of Arianism was not the bishop's only concern. Internal divisions had ripped apart the churches of the East. "Shipwreck is produced on the one hand from the sea being violently agitated from the external cause," Basil wrote to Athanasius, "on the other hand from the confusion of the navigators hindering and crowding one another."[55] Mutual distrust and suspicion kept orthodox eastern bishops from forging the unity so desperately needed to withstand their common enemy. Their strength was spent on vicious internal quarrels. "We jump on those who have fallen; we tear at wounds; we who seem to be like-minded launch the insults that are uttered by the heretics; and those who are in agreement on the most essential matters are wholly divided from one another because of some detail."[56] No situation of internal discord caused Basil greater grief than the schism of Antioch. His correspondence with Athanasius is almost wholly devoted to efforts to heal this schism.[57] In other disputes as well, Basil often found himself caught between rival parties. His leniency toward former Arians rendered him suspect in the eyes of more conservative brethren. In one letter he exclaimed that he was attacked on one side by Anomoeans and on the other by Sabellians.[58] The heresies of Apollinarius of Laodicea and Marcellus of Ancyra continued to gain adherents, according to Basil, and even orthodox bishops sometimes unwittingly received them into communion. Unstable and confused bishops were proliferating creeds and vying for support of colleagues in their ever-changing opinions, so that the church was increasingly divided against itself.[59] Finally, the divergence of Eustathius of Sebaste from the emerging orthodox consensus on the Holy Spirit unleashed all manner of suspicion. Some bishops suspected Basil of heresy because of his long association with the bishop; others reproached him for changing sides and betraying his former allegiance on account of a petty personal quarrel.[60] Eustathius and his disciples themselves indicted the bishop for heterodoxy. Worse still, Basil complained, some who pretended to be defenders of orthodoxy were using such dissensions as an opportunity for personal aggrandizement.[61]

Particularly painful for the Cappadocian was the fact that bishops themselves were so often promoters of strife rather than forces of reconciliation. The seizure of episcopal sees from the Nicene party had brought Arians and incompetents to positions of ecclesiastical authority. Basil denounced their overweening ambition and lust for power.[62] Yet not only the heretics were to blame. In the last chapter of De spiritu sancto, a graphic portrayal of the trials of the eastern church under Arian persecution, Basil took the orthodox bishops to task.[63] Moved by party spirit, he explained, they attacked one another as fiercely as they fought their Arian foes. They jealously contended for places of influence, throwing the Christian people into confusion. Proper leadership was wanting and authority was disdained. In a preface to his *Moralia* Basil was again quite explicit in faulting bishops for the miserable state of affairs. "What is worst of all," he reflected sorrowfully, "is that the leaders themselves are in such difference of thought and opinion among themselves, take such contradictory attitudes toward the commandments of our Lord Jesus Christ, so mercilessly divide the church of God and cruelly agitate his flock." All wished to command even over against the Lord, and none deigned to submit to his rule.[64]

From Basil's perspective as metropolitan bishop of Caesarea, one of the gravest problems facing the church amid such anarchy was the lack of suitable candidates for the episcopate. Throughout his ecclesiastical career Basil complained of this deficiency. "It is not easy to find worthy men," he wrote to Amphilochius in 374. He also advised caution "lest we unwittingly bring the word into discredit on account of the unsatisfactory character of those who are called to office and accustom the laity to indifference." In a letter to Eusebius of Samosata he described how an unscrupulous synod had chosen a man "of what sort I do not wish to speak." Premature and contracanonical ordinations had became the order of the day.[65] The need for sound teaching was of particular concern to Basil. "Everyone is a theologian," he remarked sarcastically, yet he decried the profound ignorance of Scripture and the traditions of the church.[66] Writing to bishops of the West, Basil lamented that in the eastern churches, "There are no longer any men shepherding the Lord's flock with knowledge . . . Strict observance of the canons is unseen."[67] He complained that many who had attained the episcopate were unstable and inconsistent in their theology. Confusion and lack of clear instruction by church leaders had promoted the spread of ignorance among the Christian masses, making them all the more vulnerable to the onslaught of Arianism.

Not only was ignorance increasing, but graft and immorality were widespread among bishops and episcopal candidates. Basil particularly exposed the lust for money in his letters to chorepiscopi, bishops of country dioceses located at considerable distances from the Caesarean metropolis. Writing toward the beginning of his episcopate, he expressed horror at a report he had heard that some of these country bishops "receive money from those who are being ordained."[68] He condemned the sale of church office as covetousness and idolatry that rendered its perpetrators unfit to celebrate holy mysteries. In another letter the bishop reproached his chorepiscopi for admitting men of reprehensible character into church office, in total disregard of the canons and customs of the church: "With complete indifference you have allowed presbyters and deacons to introduce unworthy persons into the church, whomever they wanted, without any examination of their life, by mere favoritism, on the basis of relationship or some other tie of friendship. For this reason in every village there are reckoned many ministers but no one worthy of the service of the altar, as you yourselves bear witness since you lack men in the elections."[69] Basil also pointed out that many were seeking admission to the clergy for fear of conscription into the military. He ended this letter with an exhortation to reexamine carefully the character and conduct of ministers and to purge unworthy priests. Yet notwithstanding Basil's efforts to guard the sanctity of ecclesiastical office, men he considered unproven and unfit were entering the episcopal ranks.

Criteria: The Good Christian Leader

Against such a backdrop of theological division and confusion, immorality and incompetent leadership, Basil formulated his views on the model bishop. Although he was imprecise in his vocabulary regarding positions of authority in the church, and unsystematic in his treatment of the subject, he had a great deal to say about Christian leadership. Both his ascetic and nonascetic writings reveal his convictions about the requisite qualities of a leader in the church. Basil treated this theme in his monastic rules, which were clearly addressed to an ascetic milieu, as well as in the *Moralia*, which was directed toward a wider audience. Along with the *Moralia*, Basil's letters and sermons reveal his standards for church office in particular. Comparing these qualifications with the attributes he sought in monastic overseers will help us assess the extent to which asceticism factored into his thinking about the episcopate.

A few remarks on Basil's vocabulary are in order here as a preface to our examination of his ideals of leadership. When addressing his episcopal colleagues or speaking about the office of bishop, Basil used a variety of titles and terms. Among the most frequent titles employed in direct address are "Your Piety," "Your Devotion," "Your Sanctity," and "Your

Charity."[70] Basil usually avoided the word *bishop* (*episkopos*), the most precise term for the head of a local church community. He preferred to speak in more general categories of the *sulleitourgos* (fellow-minister), the *koruphaios* (leader), *hoi prostatai* or *proistamenoi* (foremost authorities, superintendents), and especially the *proestōs* (literally, one who presides). This last term occurs most frequently and may refer to either a monastic or an ecclesiastical leader.[71] What may seem more peculiar with regard to Basil's usage is the fact that this acknowledged leader of the monastic movement purposefully avoided the word *monk* (*monachos*) in both his ascetic and nonascetic writings. In fact, throughout his works the Cappadocian presented the ascetic life as the norm for all Christians, not for an isolated elite. This is particularly evident in his *Moralia*, which is foundational both to his monastic thought and to his view of the Christian life as a whole.[72] Even when explicitly addressing a monastic community, as in Letter 22 or throughout his *Asceticon*, Basil used the words *brothers* or *Christians* rather than *monks*. Conversely, he wrote to a number of people pursuing occupations in the world who were also living the ascetic life.[73] It is not until much later in his career that we find the beginnings of an express division between a distinct class of monks and other Christians living in the world.[74] Even this distinction reflects the reality of increasing monastic organization rather than a change in principle. An ascetic lifestyle remained for Basil the rule for Christians in all sectors of society.

Leadership in the Asceticon

The so-called *Short* and *Long Rules* that comprise Basil's *Great Asceticon* were written in the form of questions and answers at least partly reconstructed from actual exchanges between Basil and the monks within his circle of influence. The title *Rules* (*horoi*) was interpolated by later copyists and does not reflect Basil's own thought. For Basil, Scripture alone represented the true rule or law for life. His *Asceticon* was intended only to give spiritual advice in keeping with the biblical text. The corpus was compiled in stages, and the various redactions represent different periods in the development of Basil's ascetic thought.[75] In these writings there is a clear distinction made between leaders and followers. This is sometimes implicit, as when Basil simply states that superiors or overseers of monastic communities are to be obeyed by the brothers under their care. At other times, however, he is quite explicit on this matter. He distinguishes between superiors and inferiors, those who give orders and those who are called to obey.[76]

Basil's preferred term for a monastic superior, as for a bishop, is *ho proestōs*. Subordinates were designated by a variety of words and phrases including the inferior, the one ruled, the subject, and the weaker one.[77] Each brother was given his "charism" and "rank" by God and was to act in a manner befitting his position. The highest place was accorded the leader or overseer who had the function of teaching in the community, for such a brother was entrusted with the crucial "ministry of the word" (*tēn diakonian tou logou*).[78] In response to a question about the need to study Scripture, Basil made one of his clearest pronouncements regarding leaders and followers and the implications of their respective roles:

> As the brethren fall into two general divisions [*duo tagmatōn*], those who are entrusted with leadership [*tēn prostasian*] and those whose duty it is to yield and to obey [*eis eupeitheian kai hupakoēn*], according to their several gifts, I conclude that the one, entrusted with the leadership and care of the larger body, ought to know and learn by heart every thing that they may teach all men what God wishes, showing each one his duty. But let each of the others, remembering the apostle's words: 'Not to think of himself more highly than he ought to think, but so to think as to think soberly, according as God has dealt to each man,' learn his own duty diligently and practice it, not being curious about anything else.[79]

While the *Asceticon* assumes the presence of women's monasteries and female superiors, Basil gave no specific instructions regarding their selection and few regarding their responsibilities. In many cases their duties and qualifications seem to have paralleled those of the men.[80]

Basil was very concerned that order and authority be respected in the monastery. This is particularly evident in the *Long Rules*, which reflect a later, more developed monastic situation.[81] The overseer was never to be corrected or criticized by the brothers, except by those of appropriate age and rank, lest the harmony of the community be disturbed.[82] Basil longed for concord among the brothers and often appealed to the early church as a model of unity.[83] We have seen that he viewed the lack of unity and solidarity among bishops as a primary cause of dogmatic and moral anarchy in the church. It was therefore all the more important that the communities under his tutelage or influence exemplify proper order, submission, and respect for authority, which would result in peace and harmony. The best of these ascetic communities represented for Basil all that the church should be and in this sense functioned as his "living ecclesiology."[84] In keeping with proper order, a monastic overseer should be chosen not by his own peers but by the leaders of other communities. The main criteria for selection were proven character and evidence of good deeds done and recognized by the brothers.[85] Those in positions of authority would be judged more severely for their sins. It is not surprising, then, that passages outlining the qualifications of a superior were complemented by warnings about the weightiness of his responsibility. He would have to give account of his ministry to God and must therefore fulfill his commission in godly fear. He who failed to reprove and rightly guide the brethren would have their blood on his head.[86]

The overseer's position encompassed a wide range of functions and roles, including that of arbitrator among fellow monks and distributor of tasks and duties in the monastery.[87] Particularly ponderous, however, was his responsibility as an instructor in the Word of God. Those entrusted with the ministry of the Word had to proclaim it publicly and instruct it privately, ever zealous to lead the brothers to perfection. Woe to those who taught false doctrine or failed to preach the whole counsel of God! Basil reminded those who studied and taught the Scriptures that to whom much had been given, still more would be required—more fear, more zeal, and greater faithfulness to God's commandments.[88] Because of the weight of leadership and the burden of many decisions, the superior should often seek the counsel of wise and experienced brethren. He should also occasionally meet with other overseers to discuss common concerns regarding the administration of affairs and the discipline and direction of individual monks.[89]

Basil stressed the leader's need for humility and selflessness in governing the brotherhood, a task that might naturally tempt him to vanity and pride.[90] He should correct his monks with mildness and patience. Echoing the words of the apostle Paul, Basil called on leaders to be gentle among their brethren, caring for them "as a nursing mother cares for her children," imparting to each one not only the Gospel of God but their own lives as well.[91] Leaders should be just, unbiased, and sensitive to natural aptitudes and weaknesses when assigning duties. At the same time they had to be grave and firm when necessary, taking seriously their commission to reprove and sometimes to punish those who strayed from the way of the Gospel.[92] Above all other responsibilities, the superior should provide an example of godliness to the flock entrusted to his care. This theme is perhaps strongest in RF 43, which is devoted exclusively to the qualities of the overseer and the manner in which he should lead. He "must make his life a clear example of every commandment of the Lord so as to leave the taught no chance of thinking that the commandment of the Lord is impossible or may be despised."[93] Overseers should call their brothers to imitate them as they themselves imitate Christ, and they should see themselves as servants even as Jesus deigned to serve the very earth he had formed. They should especially help the weak to make progress toward perfection.[94] Basil prefaced this imposing list of attributes with the reminder that actions speak more loudly than words, for "even when he is silent the example of his deeds may stand out more strongly than any word as a means of teaching." Little wonder that such men were hard to find. As Basil remarked elsewhere, one would be hard pressed to find two or three qualified men in a single monastic community. To his knowledge, a multiplicity of such gifted leaders had never arisen in one place.[95]

While Basil's notion of asceticism emphasized internal dispositions of the heart, external and more rigorous ascetic virtues were also assumed to be evident in the life of an overseer, for an inner life of renunciation must be expressed in outward deeds as well. All monks were called to pursue lives of self-denial and discipline and to embrace the virtues of poverty, chastity, and obedience. The *Asceticon* also gives instructions on solitude and silence, fasts and prayer.[96] The use of a hair cloth or hair shirt for the purpose of self-humbling was approved in one rule, and other types of mortification were encouraged as a necessary brake on the passions.[97] Basil was careful to warn against excesses, however, and he encouraged moderation in the practice of ascetic disciplines. He condemned the false bodily rigors of the Manichees and urged monks to attend to their physical needs.[98] Yet he also stressed the value of self-renunciation and an ascetic regimen as aids on the path toward perfection. On the value of continence *(enkrateia)* Basil wrote, "As firm flesh and clear skin characterize the athlete, so the Christian is betokened by emaciation of body and paleness, which is the bloom of continence, showing that he is truly an athlete of Christ's commandments. For he overcomes his enemy by the weakness of his body, and displays his strength in the contests of religion, as it is written: 'When I am weak, then I am strong.'"[99] If this description was the standard for all members of the monastic community, it was to be expected especially of the overseer, whom the brothers were called to emulate.

The Moralia

In a prefatory document known as the *Proemium ad hypotyposin* Basil introduced a corpus of ascetic texts that included both the *Moralia* and the *Long* and *Short Rules*.[100] This letter of Basil's assumes a wide audience and suggests that the accompanying texts were written not only for the faithful as a whole but especially for the benefit of leaders in the church—whether preachers, bishops, or monastic overseers. In the conclusion of the *Proemium* Basil explained that he was sending these precepts to recipients who should fulfill the word of the Apostle, "Entrust these things to faithful men who will be able to teach others also." He also described his purpose in these works: to give a summary of the distinctive marks of the Christian in accordance with Scripture and in the form of a rule. In like manner he proposed to delineate the attributes of "those who preside in teaching the Word of God, in whom will shine exactness of discipline and extreme purity of conduct."[101]

The *Moralia*, probably composed quite early in Basil's career and eventually supplemented by two prologues, echoes the goals of this *Proemium*.[102] A collection of New Testament quotations followed by Basil's commentary, the *Moralia* focuses on Christian character with an emphasis on the value of ascetic discipline. But in this text Basil also considered a wide range of gifts and callings within the church as a whole, demonstrating his conviction that the ascetic life was the standard for all Christians, those fulfilling diverse vocations in the world as well as those living in monastic communities.[103] As promised in the *Proemium*, he did not neglect to consider the attributes of the Christian leader in particular. RM 70, the longest rule in the entire corpus—containing thirty-seven subpoints, as opposed to only two and four, respectively, on baptism and the Lord's Supper—is devoted to the theme of leadership in the church.[104] In fact, RM 70 and 71 comprise the most systematic treatment of church leadership in Basil's writings.

RM 70 presents biblical references and instruction concerning those who hold church office. RM 71 explicitly addresses the subject of bishops and priests in one subpoint and deacons in the other. Like the precepts regarding overseers in the *Asceticon,* these two rules deal primarily with the irreproachable character demanded of a Christian leader. Priests and deacons are to be chosen prayerfully by those commissioned to proclaim the gospel.[105] Ordinations should proceed slowly and with much consideration, for those unproven face serious danger (RM 70.2). As in the selection of monastic leaders, a blameless and proven life is the main qualification for church office (RM 70.1, 2, 9, 10, 15, 24, 27; RM 71).[106] Obedience to the Gospel must undergird the leader's teaching, and good works ought to be manifest in his life. Basil also called church leaders to demonstrate mercy, sympathy, compassion, affection, and zeal toward those they teach. So important is the leader's character that Basil advised parishioners little versed in Scripture to look for marks of the Spirit in those who instruct them. Teachers who lack such indications should be rejected (RM 72.2).

As in the *Asceticon,* Basil spoke gravely of the heavy responsibility of those who teach the Word of God. He warned them not to teach false doctrines and called those instructed in the Scriptures "to test the words of those who teach."[107] Preachers must be sure to proclaim the Word of God in its fullness, for omission of some necessary point will render them accountable for the blood of those in peril. They must not seek to flatter or impress their hearers but must speak the truth with liberty and integrity, despite the opposition or even persecution that might ensue. Otherwise they become slaves of those they seek to please.[108] The content of the message must be complemented by the preacher's attitude and motivation. He must be humble toward those he instructs and should never preach the gospel out of rivalry or envy (RM 70.24, 25). Well aware of the many demands of church office, Basil called leaders back to their priorities: prayer and the ministry of the Word (RM 70.22, citing Acts 6:2 and 4).

Not only must an intellectual understanding of biblical truth be imparted to the Christian people but also their wills must be transformed. Therefore Christian leaders cannot depend on mere human skill or the power of intellect in instructing the faithful. Ultimately they must trust God to apply to the hearts and lives of their hearers the message that has been taught (RM 70.26, 27). Preaching should be buttressed by visits to parishioners to encourage and affirm them in their faith (RM 70.12, 18). Teachers should aim not only to instruct but also to improve those entrusted to them, to form them to perfection. They must labor tirelessly toward this end, teaching both in public and in private, not neglecting to pray for the spiritual progress of the people they instruct (RM 70.11, 14, 19, 31). RM 80.16–18 also suggests personal and intimate involvement of church leaders with their flocks. This emphasis on personal encouragement and training suggests that Basil considered some form of spiritual direction, common among monks throughout the Christian East, to be as much the task of the bishop or priest as that of the monastic superior.[109]

Above all, an ecclesiastical leader, like a monastic overseer, should present to those under his care "an example of every good thing." If he fails in this task he has no right to impose moral obligations on others (RM 70.9, 10, 37). Throughout the *Moralia* Basil outlined the virtues that ought to mark the follower of Christ. Alongside the call to faith, love, humility, good works, and especially obedience to God's commandments, he included practices more narrowly associated with the monastic vocation. For example, he encouraged self-renunciation for the purpose of purification (RM 2 and 80.11). He urged assiduousness in prayers and vigils (RM 56), particularly encouraging widows in the practices of prayer and fasting (RM 74). He also emphasized voluntary poverty. This was the subject of two rules and was taken up again in his specific exhortations to leaders, for Basil believed that those entrusted with the preaching of the Gospel ought not to possess more than what was personally necessary (RM 47, 48, 70.28).[110] In this respect, as with all the qualities and practices that distinguish the faithful Christian life, the leader should serve as "the model and rule of piety" (RM 80.14).

The Letters

An emphasis on character and ascetic discipline as crucial requirements for ecclesiastical leadership is no less marked in Basil's letters and sermons. In his correspondence Basil wrote not only of general principles but also of specific individuals or concrete situations in which the importance of moral character was demonstrated. His notion of the ideal Christian leader can be gleaned in large part from those passages of his letters in which he censured the moral abuses or general mediocrity of bishops and episcopal candidates. On the positive side, however, Basil lauded church leaders in whom he recognized praiseworthy attributes.

As might be expected, such adulation often appears in letters of consolation upon the death or removal of a bishop. Four of Basil's nineteen letters of consolation were written to Christian communities grieving such a loss.[111] In this context he praised the virtues of Bishops Musonius of Neocaesarea and Athanasius of Ancyra in Letters 28 and 29. He extolled their good works as well as their orthodoxy and exalted the life of Musonius as a model to all who lived around him. Basil enumerated the praiseworthy attributes of Bishop Dianius, whom he counted "among men who are most illustrious for virtue" despite his temporary, unwitting defection from the doctrines of Nicaea.[112] Esteem for the high moral character and orthodox teaching of Athanasius of Alexandria and Eusebius of Samosata radiate through his many letters to them. Similarly, he commended Bishop Elpidius for his great progress in virtue and his spiritual training, and Bishop Valerian for his purity and love.[113]

Basil's abundant use of standard classical *topoi* in such acclamations was not intended merely to fulfill a rhetorical requirement or to Christianize, and therefore legitimize, Hellenistic rhetorical techniques. Commenting on the Cappadocian's consolatory letter to the church of Neocaesarea at the demise of their bishop, Robert Gregg describes how the components of the *eulogia* were carefully crafted for a specific purpose. Basil's intention was to outline the profile of a worthy successor, Gregg suggests, for he "declares by his selection of *enkomiastika* for the departed bishop just what characteristics should be found in the next occupant of the episcopal chair."[114]

The exemplary moral qualities of the bishop seemed to be of special concern to Basil. Against a background of evil and oppression of the orthodox he exhorted the priests of Nicopolis: "in the present circumstances strive to give clear examples by deed of whatever you teach by word." Similarly he praised the monastic bishop Ascholius of Thessalonica for his virtue particularly because it was so rarely found in their day.[115] Immorality was so rampant and calumny so widespread in the church that Basil commended one priest who had not only maintained his "priestly integrity" but also managed to escape the attacks of the enemies of the Lord. "I do not know that any charge has been raised against him by those who are laying their hands upon everyone," Basil remarked with seeming surprise. In fact, he added, "no accusation against this man has even been imagined."[116] Such irreproachable character accords with the high standards that Basil presented in the *Moralia*.

In an environment of suspicion and slander, not only must the bishop be a model of Christian virtue but he must also speak and act with circumspection and prudence. He ought to receive the approbation and favorable testimony of those to whom he ministers.[117] Such an exaltation of virtue in the life of the Christian leader contributed to a distinctive conception of church office in Basil's writings. The preacher of the Gospel had to be a model of sanctity and goodness. The Cappadocian left little room for the possibility of God administering grace through unsanctified ministers.[118] His understanding of the bishop's function was so intertwined with the call to perfection that he could hardly conceive of the faithful preaching or efficacious acts of an unholy minister. Accordingly he warned his chorepiscopi that their unrighteousness disqualified them from celebrating the sacraments.[119]

In his descriptions of worthy church leaders, Basil praised upright living in general and ascetic virtues in particular. In a letter to Bishop Elpidius he commended the priest Meletius, whom he had sent as a messenger. He explained that he had almost determined to spare Meletius this charge, "because of the weakness that he willingly brought upon himself by bringing his body into subjection for the sake of the Gospel." However, he said, he finally resolved to honor Elpidius by sending a man of such high character that he would serve as a type of "living letter."[120] Ascetic ideals are even more prominent in Basil's description of the man he selected in response to a bishop's request for a worthy successor to his see. His choice was an elderly Caesarean priest whom he praised for continence and rigorous ascetic discipline to the point of injuring his flesh. The man was also extremely poor, barely supporting himself by the work of his hands, and he lived in community with other brothers. Such a worthy man, Basil assured his fellow bishop, was "well-suited for this task" of the episcopate.[121]

Two letters to Antiochus, the nephew of Basil's friend and highly esteemed colleague Eusebius of Samosata, give further expression to his monastic ideals. He wrote as an older adviser to this young man, who by 374 had been ordained priest and by 381 had succeeded his uncle as bishop of Samosata. Basil counseled him to discipline the lusts of his flesh and to guard the thought of God in his soul, being mindful of the tribunal of Christ in every word and deed.[122] In Letter 168, written during Antiochus's exile together with Eusebius, Basil fittingly upheld the value of withdrawal and solitude. He noted that in the past Eusebius had been preoccupied with an excess of affairs and concerns. Likewise Antiochus himself had been beset by the cares of life. Consequently he had lacked sufficient time to benefit from his uncle's spiritual experience and example. Thus, Basil represented their exile as a privilege for Antiochus and a deliverance from the multiple concerns that had besieged him in Samosata. Occasional periods of solitude were crucial for those in church office. As a bishop Basil recognized the value of such retreats in his own life.[123]

In a similar vein he exhorted the chorepiscopus Timothy, a man who had from childhood pursued an ascetic life. Basil had heard that he was straying from this path and becoming entangled in "the things of this world." "Why are we mixing incompatible things, the disturbances of civil affairs and the exercise of piety?" he asked in Letter 291 to Timothy. He did not imply that contemplation and action were incompatible, nor that church office was somehow inconsistent with ascetic life. He did not suggest that Timothy relinquish his duties as chorepiscopus. The problem was Timothy's preoccupation with worldly affairs. He had become overly concerned with the opinions of others, seeking to help his friends and avoid the ridicule of his enemies, and hence was distracted from what was most important.[124] Basil expressed the same concern in his instructions to church leaders in the *Moralia*. While active service as pastors and teachers need not be incompatible with the maintenance of ascetic discipline, bishops and priests had no business assuming responsibility for secular affairs.[125]

Even marriage may have been a hindrance to church leadership in the mind of the Cappadocian. While the celibate life was assumed in the monastic profession, there was not at this time any legislation prohibiting the ordination of married clergy. Nonetheless, in an early letter to Gregory Nazianzen Basil described the married state as a definite distraction from the contemplative life.[126] Moreover there are few, if any, married priests among his correspondents. While Basil said nothing explicit in this regard, one wonders whether his stringency in this matter lay behind the refusal of at least some priests to be ordained.[127]

Another notion Basil seems to have adopted from his monastic experience was the function of the bishop as a spiritual director, an aspect of leadership we have seen in the *Moralia*. The Cappadocian described how as a young man he had sought out holy men as spiritual guides for his own journey to God. Eustathius of Sebaste had played this kind of formative role in his life. Bishop Eusebius of Samosata was also an important mentor and a model for Basil's ecclesiastical career.[128] Basil seems to have served in a paternal capacity to monks in the communities under his care, and he urged monks to submit themselves to the training and example of more experienced brothers.[129] As bishop of Caesarea he assumed this role of spiritual director for several men. We have already noted his advice to Antiochus, who may well have been one of the earliest collectors of the cherished letters of his second "spiritual father."[130] Basil also served as a mentor to Amphilochius of Iconium, both before and after his consecration to the episcopate. In his first letter to Amphilochius he encouraged the younger man to enter into this relationship despite obligations to his aging father that were preventing him from coming to Basil personally. "Instruction in how to lead the Christian life depends less on words than on daily example," he wrote. Amphilochius should therefore impress upon his father the importance of spending time with a man, like Basil, who is both experienced in the spiritual life and able to impart what he has learned to others.[131] Basil admired this ability in other bishops as well. Writing to Eusebius of Samosata, he praised God that "your disciples everywhere show the mark of your dignity." Having received from Bishop Vetranius the relics of the recent martyr Sabas the Goth, the Cappadocian praised his venerable colleague, who had trained this "athlete" of Christ.[132]

Several of Basil's homilies evince the same emphasis on the ecclesiastical leader as a spiritual guide to his flock. While his sermons were generally directed toward a wider Christian audience, occasionally he referred to the duties of men of authority in the church. Not only should they nourish the souls of the faithful with sound doctrine, he said, but they must also care for their flock with warmth and zeal. The demonstration of such earnest concern would stimulate people to heed the message that is preached. The leader's goal should be to form the faithful to lives of virtue and piety.[133] The spiritual child of such a devoted teacher is "formed by him and brought into existence just as an infant is formed within a pregnant woman."[134]

Not only should a Christian leader guide specific individuals but Basil's ideal bishop also should exercise spiritual oversight of monastic communities. His correspondence suggests that Basil exemplified such engagement with the monks and nuns under his own jurisdiction. We have already mentioned his letters of comfort to monks in exile for their faithfulness to the Nicene faith. As bishop of Caesarea he was eager to keep abreast of affairs in the monasteries and urged the brothers to send information.[135] In Letter 258 he praised Bishop Epiphanius of Salamis for his concern about disputes among monks on the Mount of Olives and encouraged him in his efforts to resolve the conflict. In one of his canonical letters to Amphilochius he recommended that the bishop examine the lives of would-be monks and receive a clear profession from them.[136] Though it would be long before the church officially sanctioned this relationship, for Basil monastic life and endeavors were clearly the bishop's domain.

While ascetic ideals and practices were of prime concern to the bishop of Caesarea, they were not the only qualifications for church leadership. For example, a bishop ought to be willing and able to collaborate with colleagues, a capability not necessarily connected with the monastic milieu. Basil urged collegiality among bishops time and time again, and he himself frequently sought the counsel of trusted friends in the episcopate.[137] When problems arose or suspicions were roused against him, he considered a synod of bishops the means by which to resolve the issue.[138] He lamented the loss of that spirit of harmony among Christian leaders that he believed had thrived in the early church and hoped that orthodox bishops would recover this ideal. He encouraged monastic as well as ecclesiastical leaders to meet together regularly.[139] Among other nonascetic qualities he sought in prospective priests and bishops were prior experience in lower church office, and discernment and foresight. These latter qualities are vividly depicted in Letter 222, in which Basil described the clergy as the "eyes" of the body, surrounding the members of the body with vigilance.[140] Finally, knowledge of Scripture and orthodox doctrine were of prime importance for a leader in the church.

As we have seen in both the *Asceticon* and the *Moralia,* Basil emphasized the role of the leader as a teacher of the Word and accordingly stressed biblical education for those who would hold church office. He highly valued the learning of orthodox priests and bishops like Diodore of Tarsus, Amphilochius of Iconium, and his close friend Gregory Nazianzen, for he knew such men were sorely needed in the battle against heresy.[141] Yet he never insisted that priests or bishops have a classical education. Moreover, his own sermons are steeped in biblical citations but almost completely bereft of classical allusions. Basil's "Address to young men on reading Greek literature" demonstrates his own education in philosophy, literature, and rhetoric, and his appreciation for the value of such learning when properly used as a propaedeutic for the study of Scripture.[142] Accordingly, it was training in Scripture and doctrine that concerned him. We have observed his dismay over the lack of properly trained ministers in the church. He deplored the ignorance of apostolic teaching and the neglect of the canons among the clergy of his region. Knowledgeable, well-trained men seemed to be the exception. Recommending a certain episcopal candidate, Basil noted that alongside his ascetic qualities the man was "skilled in the canons, scrupulous in the faith."[143] Elsewhere he commended bishops who demonstrated zeal in the study of Scripture or the search for truth.[144]

Given such ideals, both ascetic and nonascetic, it is not surprising that many monks were considered to be well qualified for church office. Their daily ascetic regimen formed them in virtue, their communal life instilled in them the value of collaboration and unity, and they also acquired extensive knowledge of the Bible. The totality of Basil's monastic system was founded on Scripture. His *Rules* themselves were not commands in the strict sense but explanations and applications of New Testament texts. All monks were called to read and meditate on the Scriptures.[145] Daily psalmody, the reading of Scripture over meals, and regular teaching fostered familiarity with the biblical text and helped monks to commit many portions to memory.[146] Some men were singled out by overseers to devote themselves more intensively to study of the Bible. Those entrusted with this duty made up a kind of elite among monks and were commissioned to instruct the other brothers. The "gift of the Word" was a highly revered monastic gift.[147]

In addition to intensive inculcation of the Bible in monastic communities, Basil's correspondence with monks reveals that some were educated and well-informed of church affairs. For example, his discussion of contemporary heresies in a letter to ascetics under his care assumes considerable understanding of doctrinal issues on their part.[148] Basil was always eager to enlist the brothers in the cause of orthodoxy. After commending a group of persecuted monks for their faithfulness against Arianism, he encouraged them to remain steadfast. "Even if bishops have been driven from their churches," he wrote, "this should not shake you up. If traitors have arisen from among the clerics themselves, let this not undermine your confidence in God." In fact, as this same letter indicates, it was often the monks of Asia Minor whom Basil found to be champions of the Nicene faith when others had succumbed under pressure.[149] Such a combination of ascetic virtue, biblical knowledge, and perseverance in the true faith would surely render them able leaders of the ailing eastern church.

The Paradigm of Moses

Perhaps the best model for church leadership in Basil's estimation was that of Moses, a paradigm to which we will return in the writings of his Cappadocian colleagues. In his *Asceticon*, homilies, and letters Basil presented aspects of Moses' character as examples for emulation. This Old Testament patriarch served as a paragon of self-sacrificial love, contemplation, nearness to God, and the calmness of character and freedom from passion that produces meekness.[150] Moses modeled the wise leader who did not fail to heed good counsel.[151] Often his virtues were invoked in explicit demonstration of some quality of episcopal leadership. In this connection Bishop Musonius was said to be like Moses in his faithfulness to tradition, and Bishop Innocent was compared with the patriarch in his desire to see a successor. Eusebius of Samosata was urged to pray more earnestly for the churches, even as Moses had interceded continually for the people of Israel. Gregory Thaumaturgus was dubbed a "second Moses" by the very enemies of the church, Basil explained, on account of the many signs and wonders he performed.[152]

The most telling portrayal of Moses as a leader occurs at the beginning of the *Homilies on the Hexaemeron,* which were delivered toward the very end of Basil's life.[153] Introducing Moses as the author of the *Hexaemeron,* Basil described distinct phases of the patriarch's career. After his adoption by the daughter of Pharoah, Moses received a royal education under the sages of Egypt. Yet disdaining the pomp and power of royalty, he preferred to suffer ill treatment with the people of God. Thus he joyfully renounced the tumult of Egypt and went to Ethiopia, where for a period of forty years he devoted himself to contemplation, culminating in his vision of God at the age of eighty. He was thereby deemed ready to minister to the people. "This man, therefore, whom God judged worthy to behold him face to face like the angels," Basil declared, "speaks to us the things he has heard from God."[154]

This account reveals Basil's conception of both the model exegete and the ideal Christian leader. The description is one of the monk-bishop par excellence—a man who has been trained in the learning and wisdom of the world, rejected it for the contemplative life, and finally emerged from monastic solitude, albeit reluctantly, to lead and instruct the people of God. Basil delineated the first two stages of Moses' career in similar terms in his address *Ad adolescentes,* in which he presented the patriarch as an example for young men.[155] In the commentary on Isaiah attributed to the Cappadocian, the division of Moses' life into three forty-year periods was even more explicit:

> Indeed the first forty years he was instructed in the Egyptian disciplines; the next forty years, under the pretext of tending sheep, he withdrew to deserted places and gave himself to the contemplation of realities. And thus finally, having been judged worthy of the vision of God after the second forty years, unwillingly, with a view to the love of God among humans, he descended for the care of humanity. Yet not even then did he remain continually in the active life, but also returned frequently to the contemplative.[156]

Here the final stage was passed not in active life alone but combining the responsibilities of leadership with periodic retreats for the sake of contemplation.

This ideal three-stage progression was one that Basil himself embodied. Educated in profane learning, and having committed an important part of his life (his years at Annesi) to solitude and meditation, he devoted the remainder of his career to leading the Christian people entrusted to him. In fact, the three stages of the life of Moses would later be presented by Basil's brother Gregory as a prefiguration of Basil's own career.[157] Basil himself not only compared the virtues of great bishops with aspects of Moses' life and career but also seemed to look for the Mosaic pattern in prospective church leaders.

Surveying the situation of eastern Christendom in his day, Basil encountered a church beset by heresy, internecine rivalry, and inadequate and incompetent leadership. His writings vividly depict his perception of the plight of the Christian community. In the midst of such an ecclesiastical situation, the Cappadocian formulated, expressed, and modeled his views on leadership in the church. It has been suggested that for Basil the various duties of church leaders could be reduced to two major functions: defense of orthodoxy and proclamation of the Word of God.[158]

While he certainly placed great weight on these responsibilities, this assessment fails to do justice to Basil's frequent portrayal of the leader as
an example to the people, a concern that was paramount in his thinking
about episcopal leadership. His insistence on the moral character of the
bishop bears out Peter Brown's discussion of the holy man as an exemplar in late antiquity. Brown describes the tendency to see persons as
"classics," to view the character and actions of elites as models for emulation. To illustrate the intensity of the master-pupil relationship he
draws specifically from fourth-century Anatolia, where "the force of example was what mattered most."[159] In an early letter to his friend Gregory, Basil himself spelled out the importance of the lives of saints as paradigms for Christian behavior: "Just as painters, when they are painting
an image from another image, frequently look at the model and make
every effort to transfer its features to their own work, so too he who
seeks to make himself perfect in all aspects of virtue must turn his eyes
to the lives of the saints as though to moving and acting statues, and
make their virtue his own by imitation."[160] Basil viewed the bishop as
having much the same function as these biblical saints. Not only the
blessed men of Scripture and the holy ascetics but also, especially, the
bishops must serve as exemplars for the Christian community. In this
capacity the monastic bishop in particular would excel.

The combination of qualifications and concerns we find in the
Cappadocian's writings point to one primary conclusion: monastic virtues ought to reform church office, particularly the office of bishop. Basil
did not actively campaign for the ordination of monks *qua* monks. As
Klaus Koschorke has affirmed in his study of Basil's ecclesiology, it was
not that the monk should become a priest, but rather that the priest—
and, I would add, the bishop—should live as an ascetic.[161] However, in
view of the qualities Basil sought in ministers of the Gospel and the difficulty of finding men who met these high standards, it became his natural inclination to consider monks ideal for positions of leadership in the
church. This was also the conclusion that others would draw from his
life and thought.

Jean Gribomont has attributed Basil's aspiration to the episcopate to
his desire "to make the ascetic ideal triumph."[162] Certainly he displayed
a dual commitment to the fledgling Cappadocian monastic movement
and the enfeebled eastern church. But in one sense we should not make
so clear a distinction between the two. Although monastic communities

epitomized the evangelical way of life for Basil, he considered moral virtue and ascetic discipline to be the norm for all true Christians. Above all, he believed, those who lead and instruct the faithful must serve as models of such a lifestyle. Thus it was perfectly consonant with Basil's perspective on the Christian life as a whole that ascetic ideals should shape his conception of ecclesiastical leadership. Despite the struggles and failures he faced in church office, his theoretical views on the bishop would take practical shape and have lasting influence through his own exercise of episcopal authority.

3

Reframing and Reforming the Episcopate: Basil's Direct Influence

Basil's high view of episcopal office, expressed particularly in the *Moralia* and throughout his correspondence, inclined him toward a monastic model of ecclesiastical oversight. In his own career, as well, he endeavored to embody the qualities and commitments that he hoped would characterize Christian leadership as a whole. Yet his role in shaping new ideals of leadership in the church was by no means limited to his personal example or written espousal of any particular principle. As bishop of Caesarea, Basil wielded a great deal of authority in the political, social, and ecclesiastical realms, and his exercise of authority in these domains helped to shape and popularize the image of the monk-bishop in the latter half of the fourth century. He also employed various strategies within ecclesiastical circles to foster the harmonious interaction of monastic and episcopal concerns. Particularly important in this regard was his intervention in the selection of bishops who shared his ascetic ideals. Basil's direct action in these different spheres—whether in the capacity of patron, statesman, or metropolitan archbishop—both promoted the ideal of the monk-bishop and encouraged an actual increase in the number of monks in church office.

Patron, Statesman, and Overseer of the Church

Particularly significant for our investigation are the types of influence Basil possessed and the various ways he used his authority on behalf of individuals, groups, or the church as a whole. There is no doubt that Basil functioned in the capacity of a *prostates* in late antique society. Such patrons, mediators of power, whether earthly or divine, stood between the civil authorities and the people whose causes, burdens, or petitions they represented.[1] They used their acquaintances, political connections, and social prestige for the benefit of their community. While this function had long been fulfilled by municipal benefactors or wealthy, aristocratic families, changing economic and social conditions in the late Roman world were depleting traditional sources of patronage. Moreover, while a governor would hope to commend himself as the benefactor of his city, his patronage was always precarious, since he was obligated to represent the interests of the state alongside and sometimes against the concerns of individual citizens. For these reasons the church increasingly assumed the tasks of patronage, and the bishop came to be seen as the protector of the city.[2]

Though fulfilling the duties of patronage was always burdensome for him, Basil regarded his own episcopal vocation in this light. Indeed while still a priest he used whatever influence he possessed on behalf of those close to him.[3] The privilege of intercession had become customary for members of the sacerdotium, and the Cappadocian carefully cultivated friendships with men of power and influence so that he could exercise this prerogative with some measure of success.[4] He petitioned such high-ranking officials as governors, *comites,* military commanders, the *magister officiorum* Sophronius, and the praetorian prefect Modestus. The sheer number of Basil's letters of request or recommendation attests his concern to fulfill the duties of *prostasia.* We find him appealing on behalf of friends and relatives in distress, defending officials who have been slandered or otherwise mistreated, and recommending the appointment of a worthy administrator.[5] He represented such petitioners as an aged civil servant, a tax assessor, a magistrate, and an unnamed man of illustrious ancestry who had been unjustly accused of a crime.[6] He also took up the cause of Cappadocian *curiales* who had been constrained to flee as a result of the partition of their province. At times he appealed on behalf of the entire city or country.[7]

While friends, relatives, and officials in need of endorsement or reinstatement were typical recipients of patronage in antiquity, the bishop of Caesarea did not neglect the needs of the more humble classes. In one letter to an official he described his purpose as to plead the cause of the afflicted.[8] He proceeded to solicit aid for the indigent, specifically requesting that a hospice for the poor be exempted from taxation. Basil also sought tax exemption for clergy and monks, and pleaded for the alleviation of the tax burden for inhabitants of poorer, rural areas.[9] Indeed, special favor toward the poor and corresponding admonitions to the rich are even more pronounced in his sermons.[10]

Individual beneficiaries of Basil's patronage included a calumniated priest, a man wrongfully maligned, litigants in need of mediation, and slaves who had offended and enraged their master.[11] The case of the priest Dorotheus provides a good example of Basil's mediation on behalf of persons unjustly treated. In two letters of intercession he explained how certain authorities had illegally requisitioned the poor priest's corn, daring "to steal his only means of livelihood." In a first letter he implored the governor to ensure that the man's grain would be returned and the perpetrators held accountable for their crime. Though this brief, deferential request to the governor may well have sufficed to obtain the desired result, Basil also penned a letter to the chief tax collector for the region, apparently a fellow Christian, whose underlings had been responsible for the injustice.[12] Not only did he ask that the misdeed be quickly rectified, but he also expressed dismay that such an act had been committed against a presbyter of the church.

It was his intervention on behalf of the poor and oppressed, as well as his mediation in support of emerging monastic institutions, that set the Cappadocian apart from other aristocratic patrons of the period. Late antique patricians comprised an exclusive society which generally showed little concern for the struggles of the *humiliores*.[13] Neglect or contempt for the poor was certainly not in keeping with the classical Hellenic ideal of *philanthropia;* indeed the pagan emperor Julian exhorted his confreres to share their money especially "with the helpless and poor, so as to suffice for their need." He reproached pagan priests for their failure to practice such generosity and resented the fact that "impious Galileans" had coopted this philosophical virtue and thereby won many over to their "atheistic" beliefs.[14] Despite such grudging praise from the emperor, in the West even committed Christian ascetics from aristocratic circles tended to despise or at least overlook the common people.[15] In Basil's capacity as a patron he endeavored to act consistently with his understanding of both monastic vocation and episcopal responsibility. This is not to deny his self-interest at times, especially given an imperial system in which private and public interests were so often and so closely intertwined. But he attempted to apply the principles of the

Gospel in confronting the social and political realities of his day, even if constrained to use the occasionally obsequious, often self-aggrandizing, and always frustratingly complex tactics of petition and mediation.[16] Moreover, besides his personal involvement on behalf of the city as bishop of Caesarea, his conviction that the cenobitic community should engage in social and charitable activity put monks and nuns at the service of those in need.

Undoubtedly the most famous example of Basil's patronage and commitment to the unfortunates of his city was the establishment of what was later dubbed the Basileiados, or "new city," as Nazianzen called it, a complex of buildings constructed at the edge of Caesarea during the early years of Basil's episcopate.[17] Eustathius's foundation of a hospice to care for the needs of the poor and the sick in Sebaste very likely influenced Basil in his own vision for the project in Caesarea. Epiphanius described Eustathius's complex as "the hospice, which in Pontus is called the alms-house. For they make arrangements of this kind out of hospitality, and the leaders of the churches there lodge the crippled and infirm, and supply [their needs] as best they can."[18] Eustathius himself may even have been directly involved in Basil's undertaking by sending two ascetic disciples to aid his younger friend in his project of social welfare.[19] Aside from Eustathian inspiration, however, it was probably the serious famine that struck Cappadocia in the winter of 369 that provoked the actualization of this complex, which may well have been latent in Basil's mind for some time. Though often referred to as a "poorhouse" or even a "soup kitchen," most descriptions emphasized care for the sick, especially lepers, as a major focus of the project.[20] Judging from Basil's letter to the Cappadocian governor, Elias, by around 372 the foundation already included a house of prayer, a residence for the director, living quarters for "servants" who ministered in the complex, a hospice for strangers, rooms suitable for official imperial visitors, a hospital for the sick where physicians and nurses could perform their medical treatment, and "other buildings" required for the diverse services rendered.[21] Elsewhere in Basil's correspondence there are indications that similar establishments for the poor, though certainly smaller in scale, were operating in other areas of the province as well.[22]

Needless to say, the financial investment needed for the construction and ongoing administration of such an extensive undertaking would have been enormous, and Basil must have employed all his powers of persuasion to solicit the support of both public and private benefactors. Besides his letter to the governor defending the project, requests for tax exemption or other forms of financial aid in connection with houses for the poor are scattered throughout his letters. The extent and substantial success of his fundraising efforts are suggested by Gregory Nazianzen, who wrote that even the leaders of the people were moved to vie with one another in philanthropy and magnanimity toward the seriously ill and needy, and hence in support of Basil's hospice. Theodoret later noted that Emperor Valens himself had donated lands for the poor and especially the sick under his care.[23] Nor did Basil rely exclusively or even primarily on government funding for the project. Several of the sermons he preached during the spring and summer of the trying year of famine (369) presented clear challenges to the city's rich citizens to share their wealth and give magnanimously to their poorer, hungry brethren. The generosity stimulated by his message to the wealthy of Caesarea likely did not cease with their immediate response to the crisis but may have resulted in continual donations; hence the meaning of Nazianzen's description of the Basileiados, "where the superfluities of wealth, and even the necessities, are stored away due to his persuasion."[24]

The networks of patronage, the classical philosophic and civic precedents, and the distinctively Christian motives that underlay this tremendous philanthropic endeavor have been the subject of several careful studies.[25] Particularly relevant to the present inquiry, however, are two factors. First, Basil saw care of the poor and needy, whether physically or materially, as a task supremely entrusted to the bishop. His sermons as well as his many letters of request on behalf of those in need show how seriously he took this responsibility. Several letters also reveal that chorepiscopi who fell under Basil's jurisdiction were similarly charged with oversight of poorhouses.[26] Second, the project was very much related to and perhaps even a concrete expression of Basil's monastic vision. Strictly speaking it may be erroneous to refer to the Basileiados as a "monastic" institution, for it clearly served a multitude of functions. Yet at the least it had clear monastic overtones. Besides its connection with Eustathian ascetic endeavors, the project likely had roots in Basil's personal monastic experience and ideals. In his own description of the complex Basil mentioned simple lodgings for certain "servants of God's worship," and though these may well have been clerics as opposed to monks, here and in other descriptions of the communal arrangement there is a definite monastic feel.[27] Sozomen later noted that the poor-house in Caesarea was run by the elderly Prapidius, a celebrated Cappadocian monk who also served the episcopal function in several villages; and Gregory Nazianzen gave his memorable description of the "new city" in the context of Basil's monastic endeavors.[28] Two of Basil's letters to Amphilochius—one written while Amphilochius was yet an impressionable young ascetic, and the other once he had become bishop of Iconium—invited him to visit the hospice. In the earlier letter Amphilochius's friend and fellow ascetic Heracleidas, in whose name the epistle was written, was actually residing in the Caesarean poorhouse, where he claimed to have found the way of life "in accordance with Christ's polity" (*tēs kata Christon politeias*). He urged his colleague to join him there and especially to meet the bishop (namely, Basil himself), who customarily visited the complex.[29] For Basil, then, involvement in such a foundation was what committed ascetics as well as bishops ought to be doing. Such activity on the part of monks, bishops, and laity alike made the Gospel a living reality in the city.

In his discussion of Basil's practice of patronage, Barnim Treucker has suggested that the Cappadocian combined the selflessness of the monk with the aristocrat's openmindedness to the world.[30] One could also say that Basil fused the divine authority of the holy ascetic with the civic clout of a post-Constantinian bishop. Knowing his reputation as a monk and holy man, leaders as influential as the prefect and the emperor allegedly hoped to escape or to benefit from his mediation of divine power.[31] At the same time, the common people had confidence in his goodwill toward them as a spiritual leader and in his influence as a bishop to affect those in the upper echelons who determined their fate. In one instance when Basil found himself persecuted and even physically threatened by civil officials, outraged factory workers, artisans, and women of the city armed themselves with makeshift weapons and took to the streets in the bishop's defense. They were ultimately restrained only by the force of his personal influence.[32] Committed to the needs of the *humiliores* and conversant with, though removed from, the urban ruling classes, Basil the monk-bishop was the perfect mediator and *defensor civitatis*. In a society where the need for such patrons was expanding, the Cappadocian exemplified and advanced the role of the monk-bishop as a viable new spiritual and social model in the eastern provinces.

Basil's mediation extended beyond intervention in local affairs and in-

teraction with provincial officials. In 371–372 Emperor Valens decided
to divide Cappadocia into two smaller provinces.[33] Since ecclesiastical
boundaries customarily followed civil divisions, this partition would
have significantly decreased the area of Basil's metropolitan jurisdiction.
Ecclesiastical sources interpret the decision in the framework of the
power struggle between Arian emperor and Nicene bishop. In fact, however, Valens probably acted out of purely secular political motives in
keeping with the general policy of dividing excessively large provinces
for administrative purposes. Basil endeavored to take full advantage of
the sources of influence at his disposal to revoke the emperor's decision.
He wrote letters to friends and men of authority at the imperial court,
pleading the case of the disconsolate city of Caesarea.[34] Ultimately his efforts were to no avail. His appeals may have influenced the emperor to
transfer the capital from the remote village of Podandus to the larger city
of Tyana, but this move could have only intensified the protracted feud
between Basil and the bishop of the new provincial capital.

Despite the failure of his intercession in this affair, bishops of Basil's
stature held considerable sway over the people of their provinces, and
emperors and imperial magistrates ignored such local elites at their own
risk.[35] This may account for Valens's deferential treatment of Basil. The
Cappadocian was never exiled. Moreover, as noted above, the emperor
had even conceded imperial lands to the church of Caesarea as a gift for
the care of the poor. Valens also seems to have granted Basil an unusual
degree of independence in governing his churches, and he commissioned him to oversee the religious situation in the neighboring province of Armenia, which lay beyond Basil's metropolitan jurisdiction.
Such allowances may well have been offered as a partial compensation
for the division of Cappadocia.[36] In any case, these concessions had important consequences for Basil's episcopal authority. In particular the
task of ecclesiastical supervision in Armenia gave him increased power
and opportunity to influence the episcopate.

The province of Cappadocia in Basil's day was primarily a rural territory in which civil and ecclesiastical boundaries were still in flux. Nonetheless Basil's metropolitan jurisdiction encompassed a vast geographical area that included many imperial estates and several episcopal
sees.[37] In contrast with ecclesiastical organization in the West, the multiplicity of bishoprics was not uncommon in the Christian East during
this period. Moreover, following the partition of Cappadocia Basil made

every effort to increase the number of sees. He had at least twelve bishops under his jurisdiction, possibly more. Because of the rural nature of Cappadocia his diocese also included a large number of chorepiscopi. Gregory Nazianzen claims there were fifty of these country bishops directly accountable to Basil.[38] Although this number is probably exaggerated, it gives some idea of the extent of Basil's authority in the province. While chorepiscopi were appointed by their bishop and were not permitted to ordain priests or deacons without episcopal authorization, they were influential men in their own right. They took part in regional synods, and some were even among the signatories to ecumenical councils.[39]

As metropolitan bishop of Caesarea it was Basil's task to supervise the clergy and bishops of his province. Accordingly, concern for proper observance of the canons and customs of the church is prominent in many of Basil's letters.[40] Aside from his canonical epistles, which provide an abundance of instructions on applying the canons to specific cases, several letters disclose the Cappadocian's personal involvement in matters of church discipline. In one instance he gently reprimanded a bishop for his absence at a yearly martyr's commemoration and exhorted the man to attend the next one.[41] Basil also had to deal with far graver situations. We have already considered the content of Letters 53 and 54, which took certain chorepiscopi to task for canonical and moral abuses. Similarly, Basil penned a severe rebuke to a certain priest, Gregory, who was cohabiting with a woman. He reminded Gregory that a canon of Nicaea had explicitly forbidden *suneisaktos,* and he threatened the penalty of excommunication should the man persist in his scandalous behavior.[42] He also warned the priest not to reproach his chorepiscopus, who had apparently brought the affair to Basil's attention. Even more serious was the case of the deacon Glycerius who had been sent by Basil to assist a priest under Gregory Nazianzen's jurisdiction. The deacon apparently assembled a company of young virgins and established himself over them as their leader.[43] In so doing, wrote Nazianzen, he had scorned his priest, his chorepiscopus, and his bishop, and had upset the entire church. Gregory called on Basil to take the proper action against Glycerius. Still other letters reveal Basil's efforts to prevent or rescind uncanonical ordinations or to settle various ecclesiastical disputes.[44]

In addition to writing letters of instruction, counsel, and rebuke, episcopal oversight of the churches required frequent voyages. Despite his maladies and many complaints about the harsh Cappadocian winters, which restricted or prohibited travel, Basil managed to make a number of journeys during his episcopal career. Trips were sometimes undertaken to visit suffragans, sometimes to assist in affairs beyond his own diocese.[45] One such journey illumines Basil's work as a peacemaker between prelates in Armenia and his involvement in the appointment of bishops there. On another occasion he wrote that "many other journeys have taken me from home" and described the purpose of his visits to the provinces of Isauria and Pontus.[46] Unfortunately we know little about the actual proceedings of Basil's meetings with bishops and clergy during these sojourns. At the very least, however, they enabled him to establish or strengthen ties with the bishops of Cappadocia and neighboring provinces and to promote his own ideas.

Provincial synods provided Basil a great opportunity to orient the religious life of his region. As metropolitan bishop he was responsible for convoking and presiding over these councils.[47] Episcopal conferences were customarily held in Caesarea toward the beginning of September, in conjunction with the annual celebration in honor of the martyr Eupsychius. These meetings were clearly attended by bishops from outside as well as inside Cappadocia. Three letters in which Basil mentioned the yearly synod extended invitations to bishops from other provinces: Eusebius of Samosata, Amphilochius of Iconium, and the bishops of the diocese of Pontus.[48] Basil also spoke of synods to which he himself had been invited, and he proposed such assemblies for the resolution of ecclesiastical concerns.[49] On one occasion he asked that a meeting be postponed a few days because he had fallen ill and was unable to travel, a request with which his colleagues apparently complied.[50] Synods had multiple aims, including theological clarification, resolution of conflicts, and promotion of fellowship and trust between colleagues. The appointment of bishops was also a concern at some of these synods.[51] Through such episcopal gatherings Basil was able to influence a wide range of decisions affecting the life of the church, not least of which was the selection and discipline of ecclesiastical leaders.

Basil regarded the oversight of monastic life as another important aspect of his episcopal commission. In practice this entailed keeping himself apprised of news and developments, writing occasional letters of encouragement or instruction to monks, and making periodic visits to the cenobitic communities. He was probably present to receive the formal profession of monks, since he advised that youths, when they came of age, and others who had adopted the celibate life make a profession before the ecclesiastical authorities.[52] At times Basil felt constrained to relieve tensions between monks and the broader church community. Several letters show him as an apologist for the monastic life to critical or skeptical opponents. In Caesarea itself there were feelings of ill will toward ascetics. Basil lamented that "no occupation is now so suspected of vice by people here as the profession of the ascetic life."[53] In Pontus we hear of similar animosity toward the monastic vocation, some of it clearly linked with the doctrinal deviations of Eustathius of Sebaste, whose former close association with Basil made the Cappadocian himself suspect. In a trilogy of letters to the Neocaesareans, Basil affirmed both his own orthodoxy and the doctrines and practices of the monks under his jurisdiction. Writing to the clergy of Neocaesarea, who clearly harbored prejudices against certain monks, Basil extolled the convents of men and women "whose citizenship is in heaven."[54] They were committed to rigorous discipline, constant prayer, and work with their hands that helped to provide for the poor. He defended their practice of psalmody against allegations that they had introduced innovations departing from the tradition of Gregory Thaumaturgus, to whom the Neocaesareans were particularly devoted as the founder of their church. In fact, Basil ensured that the monastic office conformed with the offices already celebrated in the churches of his region.[55] This was one way of harmonizing monastic life with ecclesiastical practice.

Jean Bernardi has suggested that the Cappadocians' sermons most clearly reveal the focus of their pastoral activity.[56] If so, then Basil the pastor encouraged ascetic living for the laity as a whole and thus likely fostered a more sympathetic view of monasticism within the church. To the general Christian public as much as to monks, he preached moral reform and an ascetic way of life. His sermons called listeners to classic ascetic virtues: control of the passions and subjugation of the flesh, detachment from worldly goods, and the practices of abstinence, prayer, and fasting.[57] He stressed the need for peace, solitude, and withdrawal for the purpose of prayer. He described asceticism as a great benefit to the soul and departure from the world as a lofty pursuit. At the same time, in some of his sermons on the Psalms Basil censured virgins who had strayed from the discipline of the church, and he condemned sectarian groups and private religious gatherings. Worship, he insisted, must take place in the church alone.[58] These homilies were most likely delivered during the early years of Basil's episcopate, perhaps even late in his priesthood. Though they were preached before his breach with Eustathius and had no direct bearing on the doctrinal issues that would divide them, Basil was always careful to clarify the proper place of ascetics and asceticism within the context of the church and to eschew the controversial positions condemned at Gangra and associated with Eustathius. Such preaching, then, promoted ascetic ideals while at the same time upholding ecclesiastical discipline and authority.

An important part of Basil's solution to latent tension between monks and church leaders was to promote ascetic life among the clergy of Cappadocia, Pontus, and neighboring provinces. This intention lay behind sections of the *Moralia* that were explicitly addressed to leaders in the church. It is also evident in his words of encouragement to colleagues in the episcopate and in his counsel to future bishops like Antiochus and Amphilochius. He urged Antiochus to attend to the salvation of his soul by disciplining the lusts of his flesh, and his letters to Amphilochius were replete with advice on the practice of asceticism. Basil was eager to ensure that those who had embarked on the ascetic life remained faithful to their intention. In this vein he exhorted the chorepiscopus Timothy, who had become distracted by worldly affairs, to continue in the ascetic vocation that he had pursued from childhood.[59] While we have no clear evidence for a clerical monastery in Caesarea of the kind that Augustine would later establish in Hippo, a number of "servants" of the church apparently lived in rooms of the Basileiados.[60] This would have augmented Basil's opportunities to impress ascetic ideals upon the clergy of the city. Gregory Nazianzen also spoke of the close relationships the bishop formed with his suffragans and his ability to influence these men by his own conduct.[61]

Recruiting Bishops

Perhaps the Cappadocian's most important channel for furthering monastic life and reconciling ascetic ideals with episcopal authority was the recruitment of bishops. The state of the episcopate was of prime concern for Basil, and his status as a metropolitan bishop in the second half of the fourth century put him in an excellent position to influence the selection of candidates. While in the third century the Christian people as a whole played a major role in episcopal elections, the Council of Ancyra (314) marked the beginning of an evolution through which bishops became the main players in the electoral process. Canons 4 and 6 of Nicaea required the presence of at least three provincial bishops for an episcopal ordination, as well as confirmation by the metropolitan bishop and written approval of the other bishops of the province.[62] These canons mentioned no role for the clergy or the people, confirming the increasing weight of episcopal authority in the electoral process. Later canonical legislation prescribed that episcopal appointments be made at synods, implying the necessary physical presence of the metropolitan. The translation of bishops from one see to another was prohibited, and bishops were forbidden to meddle in ecclesiastical affairs of another province except in a case of extreme necessity.[63] Unfortunately, however, we cannot determine practice from these juridical texts alone. In reality episcopal elections were very irregular during this period, and canon law was often ignored.[64]

Basil expressed some of his thoughts about the appointment of bishops in a letter to Amphilochius of Iconium in late 374 or early 375 concerning the problem of episcopal vacancies in Isauria. He agreed with Amphilochius that it was best for the care and administration of the churches to be shared among a number of bishops. However, he was hesitant to fill the vacancies immediately, preferring to wait rather than appoint unsuitable candidates. He proposed the following strategy. If a worthy leader could not be found for the main city, superintendents should be chosen for the smaller villages. The appointment of a bishop to the principal see of Isauria would best be postponed so as to avoid the danger that an overly ambitious prelate would gain ascendancy. If such a delay should prove impossible, the new bishop's sphere of influence must be strictly limited. In the future, Basil concluded, "it will be reserved for us" to designate bishops for the other sees after carefully examining their lives.[65] He seemed to be alluding to an upcoming synod, which was probably the purpose of his trip to Pisidia in 376. He later claimed to have traveled there "to settle the affairs concerning the brethren in Isauria in company with the Pisidian bishops."[66]

In addition to rigorous personal examination of the lives of episcopal candidates mentioned in the letter to Amphilochius, Basil placed great confidence in the testimony of other trustworthy bishops. Paralleling his own extensive use of letters of recommendation, a similar practice carried over into his consideration of ecclesiastical promotions. The *Moralia* reveals Basil's concern that the reputation of church leaders be beyond reproach.[67] Accordingly, in several letters he requested the written testimonial of his episcopal colleagues as to the moral character of potential bishops. One candidate came to him with a letter from Pap, the king of Armenia, demanding that he be ordained bishop. Not swayed by this royal missive, Basil sought the testimony of Theodotus of Nicopolis and other bishops of the province. The candidate in question was eventually consecrated by Anthimus of Tyana, but Basil refused to receive him into communion without a supporting letter from the local Armenian bishop. He asked that such a letter be written only if the man was found to be of upright character.[68]

While relying heavily on such letters of reference, Basil the patron also set limits on the practice of patronage. Particularly, it ought not to be a vehicle for promoting unworthy candidates to church office. In certain country dioceses, he wrote, priests and deacons had allegedly introduced unworthy men "by mere favoritism, on the basis either of kinship or of some other relationship."[69] Basil condemned this convention, enjoining chorepiscopi to submit to the canons requiring episcopal approval of all appointments. By insisting on his own endorsement of candidates, Basil the patron was actually restricting the exercise of patronage by country bishops who, by their involvement in the choice of lower clergy, could enhance their own image and authority in their communities.[70] In another letter from the early years of his episcopate (c. 371) he was no less uncompromising in response to his friend Nectarius, who sought support for a particular nominee in an ecclesiastical election. "If I should have to please people," Basil replied, "either giving in to petitions or yielding to any fear, may I never be involved in this affair. For I would be not a steward [*oikonomos*], but a huckster [*kapēlos*], exchanging the gift of God for human friendships."[71] He acknowledged the weaknesses of human nature and the dangers of party spirit in the process of electing church leaders. Nevertheless, he said, ecclesiastical appointments should be decided through suffrage, prayerfully and without contention, entrusting the results to God. It was not his place to interfere.

Despite occasional misgivings about intervention in the choice of clergy and bishops, the Cappadocian was certainly not averse to using his influence and powers of mediation for such purposes. The potential for heresy and immorality in church office may well have been heightened during this period by the irregularity of elections and the neglect of canon law. Yet Basil used this very ambiguity to his own advantage. In addition to his efforts to multiply episcopal sees under his jurisdiction,[72] he took certain ecclesiastical measures prohibited by the canons. These included the appointment of bishops without synodal approval, the transfer of bishops from one see to another, and interference in ecclesiastical affairs beyond his borders.[73] A number of these maneuvers will be reviewed as we examine Basil's recruitment of specific individuals for church office. Who were the episcopal candidates of Basil's choice? Under what circumstances did he intervene, and what means did he employ to influence their election? Finally, to what extent did ascetic ideals figure in his recruitment of bishops?

Though one might expect to find a consistent pattern of episcopal recruitment in keeping with his high standards for church office, the Cappadocian was most often constrained to act as a pragmatist willing to receive less-than-ideal candidates. A letter suggesting that Basil permitted the ordination of a slave has been proven inauthentic, but there is little doubt that a worthy slave or colonus was in fact ordained by Gregory Nazianzen in preference to the installation of an Arian prelate.[74] In one instance Basil felt that the pressing need for capable, orthodox leadership warranted even the ordination of a neophyte, so long as the consecrating bishop, in this case Amphilochius of Iconium, could serve as spiritual guide and trainer to the recently baptized ordinand.[75] In another of his three letters to Amphilochius regarding the canons and customs of the church, Basil acknowledged that he himself had received as bishops two ex-Encratites, Izoïs and Saturninus.[76] There is no other mention of these two men in Basil's letters or in any other source. It is noteworthy, however, that the Cappadocian viewed the Encratites, a rigorist ascetic sect, with particular leniency. He approved of these two candidates for episcopal office despite their prior involvement in a separatist ascetic group.[77]

These cases, however, were the exception. There were several men in whom Basil showed great confidence and whose election he actively promoted. Least surprising among his choices was that of his friend Gregory Nazianzen. Both in his autobiographical poem and in his funeral oration on Basil, Gregory himself related the circumstances of his election to the see of Sasima.[78] It was part of Basil's response to the partition of Cappadocia in 372. Arguing that ecclesiastical borders should

follow civil ones, Bishop Anthimus of Tyana claimed metropolitan jurisdiction over the churches situated in the newly formed Cappadocia
Secunda. Though officially within the realm of this new province, the
see of Nazianzus, governed by Gregory the Elder, remained loyal to the
bishop of Caesarea.[79] Other bishops supported the episcopal pretensions
of Anthimus. Through a rapid and largely successful effort at gerryman-
dering, Basil hastened to establish new bishoprics in his province and to
place a network of allies in positions of leadership. Under these circumstances he appointed Nazianzen to the new bishopric of Sasima and his
own brother to the see of Nyssa. Basil did not elect his friend in the context of a synod, nor do we have evidence that he consulted fellow bishops; it seems to have been an independent decision. While Gregory himself complained bitterly about this affair, he never reproached Basil for
transgression of the canons. Anthimus apparently recognized the canonical illegality of Basil's action, however. Gregory reported that Anthimus
questioned him on many issues, including that of his episcopal consecration, and endeavored to convince Gregory and his father that they
should henceforth submit to him as their new metropolitan.[80]

Evidence of Nazianzen's impassioned reaction against Basil's decision
is scattered throughout his writings. In fact, we know little about this affair that does not come from the pen of Gregory himself. He objected
most strongly to his forced consecration because, he alleged, the episcopate would deny him solitude and the contemplative life for which he
yearned.[81] He was also infuriated because of Basil's apparent breach of
friendship in appointing him against his will and in full knowledge of
his contrary longing for spiritual calm and contemplation.[82] At the very
least, Gregory implied some years later in his autobiographical poem,
if he had had to accept the burden of the episcopate he should have
been granted a more suitable see than the obscure, backwater village of
Sasima.

> Midway along the high road through Cappadocia, where the road di-
> vides into three, there's a stopping place. It's without water or vegeta-
> tion, not quite civilized, a thoroughly deplorable and cramped little
> village. There's dust all around the place, the din of wagons, laments,
> groans, tax officials, implements of torture, and public stocks. The
> population consists of casuals and vagrants. Such was my church of
> Sasima. He who was surrounded by fifty chorepiscopi was so magnani-
> mous as to make me incumbent here.[83]

This passage suggests that there was more to Gregory's reservations about episcopal consecration than simply the loss of contemplative solitude. In any case, just as he had fled Nazianzus following his ordination to the priesthood, so again Gregory took flight in desperation. Only after his resentment had somewhat subsided did he yield to pressure from his father to return. Back in Nazianzus he preached a sermon exposing his internal struggle and explaining the reasons for his actions. Although he finally resigned himself to his fate, Gregory could never fully forgive Basil or his own father for constraining him to fulfill a vocation that crushed his deepest desires and disturbed his entire life.[84] Moreover, he never took possession of the see of Sasima. Instead he became his father's coadjutor in Nazianzus and eventually sole bishop of the city upon the death of Gregory the Elder in 374.[85]

From Basil's vantage point the election of Gregory to the episcopate seemed a natural choice. From the time of their student days in Athens they were the most intimate of friends. They held common ideals and ambitions to pursue the "philosophic life" and lived these out together for a time in their joint retreat on Basil's family estate in Annesi.[86] At the time of Gregory's appointment to Sasima he had already been serving for almost ten years as a priest alongside his father in Nazianzus. In addition to this experience in pastoral ministry, Basil knew Gregory to be a learned and articulate theologian, well-equipped to uphold the Nicene faith against the storms of heresy that raged about them. Given their bond of friendship, their shared ascetic ideals, and Gregory's doctrinal orthodoxy, theological capabilities, and commitment to the church, Basil must have seen him as the perfect ally both in his rivalry with Anthimus and in the struggles of the church as a whole.

In his anger about the appointment, Nazianzen accused Basil of pride and condescension in his exercise of episcopal power. On the other extreme, it has been suggested that Basil saw the remote bishopric of Sasima as a post peculiarly appropriate to Gregory's desire to pursue the contemplative life in relative solitude and outside the mainstream of ecclesiastical affairs.[87] More likely Basil hoped to strengthen his claim to ongoing metropolitan jurisdiction over this area through the promotion of like-minded, loyal suffragans. He seems to have simply assumed that his friend would back his agenda and to have given too little thought to Gregory's own ambitions and desires. Though a mere village, Sasima was situated on the border between the newly divided provinces of Cappadocia Prima and Cappadocia Secunda and therefore had strategic importance for Basil in his dispute with Anthimus. But exactly what he expected Gregory to do in Sasima, other than support his episcopal authority in the face of division among the Cappadocian bishops, remains somewhat puzzling. Certainly he misjudged his friend's response. This miscalculation of psychological factors in Gregory's temperament has been construed by Giet as nothing less than a grave mistake on the part of the great Cappadocian.[88]

Whatever combination of factors motivated his appointment of Nazianzen to Sasima, Basil sincerely believed that Gregory, despite and partly because of his ascetic and contemplative inclinations, could render a tremendous service to the church in the capacity of bishop. Writing to Eusebius of Samosata after Gregory's flight, Basil expressed regret that he could not offer Nazianzen a bishopric more commensurate with his gifts and abilities. "But since this is impossible," he concluded, "let him be a bishop not deriving honor from his see, but honoring his see by himself. For it is the mark of a really great man not only to be sufficient for great things, but also to make small things great by his own power."[89] Though Gregory never took over the see of Sasima, Basil's high hopes for his friend would not be disappointed. Not only did Nazianzen become a major voice for Nicene orthodoxy, but he continued to promote many of Basil's own monastic-episcopal ideals throughout the remainder of his life and, by means of his writings, far beyond.

Somewhat more surprising was Basil's appointment of his brother Gregory as bishop of Nyssa. Several passages in the writings of both Basil and Gregory of Nyssa indicate that Basil played a formative role in his brother's Christian education and introduction to the ascetic life. Gregory probably visited his brother often during the years of Basil's monastic retreat on the Iris and imbibed and adopted Basilian monastic ideals.[90] He often referred to his older brother as his *didascalos* and held him in the highest esteem. Basil, on the other hand, had very little to say about Gregory and provides no evidence that they enjoyed an especially close relationship.[91] However, while Nazianzen expressed concern that Nyssan had initially chosen a rhetorical over a clerical career, Basil mentioned neither his rhetorical background nor his marriage as a detriment or obstacle to church office, and in fact neither would have been unusual for bishops of this period.[92] He did, however, express concern about Gregory's lack of diplomatic and administrative skills. In the early years of Basil's episcopate Gregory seems to have posed somewhat of a hin-

drance to his brother's ministry. In his well-intentioned efforts to reconcile Basil with their uncle Gregory, one of several bishops who contested
Basil's election, he forged three letters from his uncle to his brother. The
discovery of these forgeries caused the bishop of Caesarea considerable
embarrassment. In a letter to Eusebius of Samosata as well, he mentioned the trouble caused him by Gregory's naïveté in ecclesiastical matters. Nonetheless, Nyssan's clumsy attempt at peacemaking, of which we
know only Basil's version, has been described as a "burlesque episode"
that ought not to be taken too seriously.[93]

Like Gregory of Nazianzus, Gregory of Nyssa was placed in a newly
designated bishopric in Basil's attempt to fortify his position after the
partition of Cappadocia. Although the exact date of his consecration is
unknown, evidence points to its connection with Basil's efforts to stay
the advance of Anthimus of Tyana following the division of the province.[94] When the ordination was called into question several years later,
Basil insisted in the name of all the bishops of his province that "no
canonical regulation be it small or great was neglected in the appointment of the bishop."[95] In the same letter he referred to his brother as
having been "forced to accept the ministry by sheer constraint." Unlike
Nazianzen, however, this Gregory showed no repugnance to episcopal
office. In fact he went to Nazianzus in an apparent effort to console and
encourage his friend Gregory, who was so greatly distressed by his forced
and unwelcome consecration.[96]

Despite certain negative or critical comments he made about his
brother, Basil considered him a faithful ally and an asset to the church.
Gregory intimated that his older brother had commissioned him to write
the treatise *De virginitate,* a work that Basil probably hoped would help
him win recruits to the ascetic life.[97] Soon after its completion Basil consecrated Gregory bishop of Nyssa. Even after his brother had served several years in the episcopate Basil still regarded him as "completely inexperienced in ecclesiastical matters," but he attributed this weakness to
Gregory's kind, trusting nature and his being unaccustomed to servile
flattery. In later letters he referred to him as "my God-beloved brother"
and commended him for patient endurance in exile; he also faithfully
defended him against the malicious charges of his persecutors.[98] Unbe-
known to Basil, Gregory would eventually fulfill some of his greatest expectations as a monk-bishop, for he assumed leadership of the monastic
movement after his brother's death.

Another of Basil's better known episcopal choices was that of Amphilochius of Iconium, whom we have already encountered at various junctures in Basil's writings and career. Around 372, perhaps at the same time as the partition of Cappadocia, the province of Lycaonia was newly constituted from portions of neighboring Pisidia and Isauria.[99] Consequently Iconium, the principal city of the new province, gained ecclesiastical importance as a metropolis. In 373 Bishop Faustinus of Iconium died, and the Iconians solicited Basil's aid in selecting a bishop to replace him. Seeking advice from Eusebius of Samosata, Basil was initially hesitant to respond to this request in light of canonical prohibitions against ordination across ecclesiastical borders.[100] We do not know the precise details of Amphilochius's election to the metropolitan see of Iconium, but it seems that Basil overcame any reluctance he may have felt about interfering. In a letter congratulating the new bishop upon his consecration, Basil hinted at his own involvement in the selection of Amphilochius: "Though you were fleeing, as you yourself say, not from me, but from the call you were expecting to receive through me, he has caught you in the inescapable nets of grace, and has led you into the midst of Pisidia in order to catch people for the Lord."[101] Judging from the rest of this letter, the bishop of Caesarea was delighted with the decision.

As with many other candidates, Amphilochius's resistance to episcopal consecration, evident in this same congratulatory letter, was allegedly rooted in his prior commitment to pursue the monastic life. After completing his studies under Libanius in Antioch, he had been employed as a rhetor in Constantinople for six to seven years. In his growing inclination toward the ascetic vocation, his cousin Gregory of Nazianzus seems to have been a major influence.[102] When Amphilochius fell on hard times, Gregory challenged him to abandon worldly affairs in order to serve God. At the time his employment looked precarious. His family situation necessitated that he leave Constantinople, for his mother had recently died and his father was living alone and in need of care. The monastic ideal, or rather the philosophical life, attracted Amphilochius. The combination of these factors motivated him to return home both to fulfill his filial responsibilities and to prepare for a monastic life, to be undertaken on his father's death.

Probably before leaving Constantinople, Amphilochius had agreed to pursue the anchoritic ideal along with a friend, Heracleidas.[103] During two to three years of relative withdrawal on his father's estate, he prepared for his eventual transition to this way of life. According to Basil's

Letter 150, he had several questions about which he wanted the advice or direction of someone experienced in the monastic vocation. In this connection he sent his friend to Basil, and Hearacleidas, or Basil writing in the name of Heracleidas, responded to Amphilochius's inquiries. Perhaps no letter expresses more clearly Basil's ideal for a Christian disciple, if not also his expectations for a prospective leader in the church. The great bishop and monastic leader had convinced Heracleidas, and hence hoped to persuade Amphilochius, that the cenobitic life was the higher calling. Specifically, he presented his vision of ascetic life in community, centered around a common commitment to the social and charitable ideals of the Gospel, particularly voluntary poverty and care for the poor. He was describing, of course, the work of the Basileiados, for it was with such an endeavor that a serious ascetic like Amphilochius ought to be involved. But the letter also stressed the importance of teaching or instruction for a would-be disciple. What they needed, Heracleidas acknowledged to his friend, was someone "to lead us by the hand" (*tou cheiragōgēgontos hēmas*), a "great and experienced teacher" (*megalou kai empeirou didaskalou*); for, he concluded, "instruction in how one ought to lead the Christian life depends less on words than on daily example."[104] For this reason he urged Amphilochius to come to Caesarea to meet Basil personally. The characteristics outlined in this letter—renunciation of worldly ambitions, formation in asceticism, commitment to the social and economic demands of the Gospel, and humble acceptance of the teaching and guidance of an experienced spiritual leader—were traits Basil sought in a Christian disciple. But they were especially necessary qualities of a leader in the church, for it was his own teaching and example as bishop that Basil was recommending to the young man. Whatever reservations Amphilochius may have had initially, before long he was persuaded by this challenge and came under the Cappadocian's sway.[105]

From this time onward Basil served in the capacity of a mentor, adviser, and spiritual father to Amphilochius, who was very soon to be consecrated bishop of Iconium. It is clear that he considered Amphilochius a spiritual son.[106] Little wonder that he should choose, or at least encourage the choice of, his protégé to fill the vacant see of the neighboring metropolis. Following his consecration, Amphilochius continued to seek the Cappadocian's counsel and instruction. Conversely, Basil always showed the highest esteem for his disciple's virtue and ea-

gerness to learn, sharing with him fundamental ecclesiastical principles as well as deeply rooted theological ideas.[107] It was in response
to Amphilochius's request for clarification on the doctrine of the Holy
Spirit that Basil wrote his great theological treatise *De spiritu sancto,* and
to Amphilochius that he dedicated the work.[108] As for ascetic ideals,
Amphilochius followed in Basil's footsteps in his efforts to reform the
moral life of the Lycaonian church by encouraging stricter monastic discipline. After Basil's death he struggled to forge tighter links between ecclesiastical authority and the monastic movement, but he was apparently less successful than his mentor in maintaining a happy balance
between the two.[109]

Basil was directly involved in the appointment of two other bishops
in connection with his commission to resolve religious affairs in Armenia. This order from Emperor Valens, following his recent political and
military campaigns to prevent further Persian aggression in Armenia,
"thrust Basil onto 'the world stage' with a vengeance."[110] It also involved
him in complex and extremely sensitive ecclesiastical negotiations between the bishops of the province, particularly in light of the tensions
between the staunchly Nicene Theodotus of Nicopolos and the increasingly suspect former mentor of Basil, Eustathius of Sebaste. On a visit to
the Roman frontier town of Satala in the summer of 372 or 373, during
which Basil succeeded to some degree in pacifying the discordant Armenian bishops, the Christians of Satala requested that he select a bishop
for them. Basil's choice for the vacant see was Poemenius, a member of
his own clergy and a distant relative.[111] Canons 4 and 6 of Nicaea required that a bishop be chosen by all the bishops of his province. Even
in the case of necessity, at least three provincial bishops had to be present and the ordination then had to be confirmed by the metropolitan
and the other bishops. The bishop of Caesarea apparently filled the va-
cancy in Satala without recourse to this legislation. His appointment of
Poemenius would have come as an affront to Eustathius of Sebaste, the
incumbent metropolitan bishop in this part of Armenia, who still maintained jurisdictional rights over the region in which Satala fell, despite
his deposition by two councils.[112] Shortly after Poemenius's consecration, Anthimus of Tyana, Basil's rival metropolitan bishop in Cappadocia, consecrated a candidate of his own choice as *catholicos* of Armenia.
Somewhat ironic was Basil's complaint to Poemenius that Anthimus had
acted "on his own authority and by his own hand, not waiting for the

vote of any of you, and mocking my scrupulousness concerning such matters," having thereby "confounded ancient discipline."[113] Even this situation was not irremediable, however, provided that "the man's life is good."

There were certainly pragmatic political reasons for Basil's choice of Peomenius as bishop for Satala, for he would clearly benefit from the presence of a friend and ally of unquestionable orthodoxy in a see of the theologically and ecclesiastically contentious neighboring province. However, the selection of Poemenius was also based on the moral qualities he possessed and his experience as a pastor. Basil assured the citizens of Satala that in sending this man he was sparing not even "the apple of his eye," an intimate friend from his boyhood whose absence would severely disappoint the people deprived of his rule.[114] This man was "a shepherd worthy of the name," one who would please "those who love orthodox teaching and who have accepted the life conformed to the commandments of the Lord." In another letter Basil described Poemenius as holy, selfless, and spiritually minded.[115] Though he did not mention specific monastic qualities other than a life conformed to the Gospel, it is likely that a man from his own circle whom he held in such high esteem was also committed to the ascetic life that Basil so heartily promoted among the clergy and chorepiscopi of his province. From Basil's perspective the virtues of such a man, coupled with the pressing need for orthodox leadership in the church of Satala, warranted the pretermission of the canons.[116]

The second episcopal appointment in Armenia in which Basil played a significant role followed the death of Bishop Theodotus of Nicopolis toward the end of 375. Basil implied that several bishops were involved in arrangements to transfer Bishop Euphronius of Colonia, a smaller outlying bishopric in the province, to the more important see of Nicopolis. Bishop Poemenius of Satala originally proposed the candidate, and Basil staunchly supported his recommendation.[117] In Letters 227–230 he defended this decision both to the clergy and magistrates of Colonia, embittered by the removal of their beloved leader, and to the clergy and magistrates of Nicopolis, who apparently disdained the Colonians for the insignificance of their see. Episcopal translations were strictly forbidden by canon law, and the people of Colonia threatened to bring the matter before the courts. The Cappadocian, however, insisted on the rightness of the appointment and the propriety of the bishops' administrative procedures. Although their bishop would henceforth reside in Nicopolis, Basil attempted to console the Colonians by presenting the arrangement as a type of incumbency in both sees rather than a transfer from one to the other.[118]

About Euphronius himself we know very little. Basil knew of him before the proposed transfer, although it seems he had never met him personally. He was dearly loved by his flock, whom he served as a "spiritual father." He was deemed a "good vessel" and a man as "worthy of esteem as his predecessor."[119] Alongside spiritual and moral qualities, it seems that the orthodoxy of Euphronius was a major factor in Basil's mind. The discovery of Eustathius's heterodoxy had been a cruel blow to the Cappadocian, and the province of Armenia was under constant pressure from Arians who were infiltrating the churches. In this context Basil extolled the church of Nicopolis. Though surrounded by heretical adversaries, she was "the nursing mother of piety" and a "metropolis of orthodoxy" precisely because of the faithful leaders who had governed the church from of old. He considered Euphronius a worthy successor to them.[120] Ultimately, however, the arrangement of Basil and his collaborators failed. The Eustathian party, supported by Basil's frequent nemesis, the *vicarius* Demosthenes, succeeded in supplanting Euphronius. In his place they consecrated and installed their own candidate, Fronto, on the episcopal throne and cast the orthodox priests of Nicopolis outside the walls of the city.[121]

The final prospective bishop for whom we have clear evidence of Basil's favor is the proposed replacement for a certain Bishop "Innocent," though the name most likely represents a later scribal insertion. This elderly bishop, whom several recent scholars have identified as Faustinus, bishop of Iconium, wrote to the bishop of Caesarea asking that he choose a successor to guide his flock after his own passing.[122] Basil referred to his colleague's diocese as a vast and famous place located a great distance from his own see. This description strongly suggests that the territory was beyond Basil's metropolitan jurisdiction. In this case his appointment of a bishop, especially without synodal approval, would supersede canonical injunctions prohibiting bishops from interfering in affairs outside their province. Moreover, while the location of this diocese is uncertain, the bishop's request itself was proscribed by the canons. Canon 23 of Antioch explicitly forbade a bishop to choose or attempt to install his successor before his death. Basil expressed no concern about the canons. He only claimed apprehension about his inability and unworthiness to make such a selection.

In response to the bishop's appeal, however, Basil proposed one of his own Caesarean priests, whom he described at some length and in the most praiseworthy terms. This man may well have been the ascetic priest Meletius, Basil's "dear brother and fellow-worker" who occasionally served as his messenger and whose rigorous asceticism Basil described in another letter.[123] In Letter 81 the presbyter in question was the spiritual son of Hermogenes, whom Basil upheld both here and elsewhere as a pillar of Nicene orthodoxy.[124] He was an experienced priest, well grounded in the canons, of scrupulous faith, and able gently to instruct his adversaries. Basil also commended the man's severe ascetic practices. He "has lived until now in continence and asceticism, although the rigor of this harsh discipline has finally consumed his flesh. He is poor and has no resource in this world, to the point that he has no means for bread, but must earn a living by working with his hands among the brothers who are with him."[125] He stood in marked contrast to a younger person who could merely attend to temporal needs, and he was even superior to the honorable candidate whom the bishop himself had apparently suggested to his colleague. If Jean Pouchet is right in his painstaking examination of this and related letters, the younger man whom Bishop Faustinus had proposed to replace him was none other than Amphilochius of Iconium. That Basil should have preferred for this post his elderly priest to his younger spiritual protégé need not lessen his estimation of the qualities of his disciple, but it certainly suggests the importance he attached to a sufficient period of ascetic testing and pastoral experience before the assumption of high church office. In any case, following Pouchet's surmises, Bishop Faustinus must have died soon after Basil's letter, and when the Iconians themselves wrote to Basil proposing Amphilochius, the bishop willingly consented. While we do not know for certain what became of Basil's recommendation, or even the identity of the proposed priest, the vivid description of his candidate of choice illustrates once again the Cappadocian's imposing standards for episcopal office.

A review of Basil's direct involvement in the appointment of bishops demonstrates that he often ignored the relevant canons. Meanwhile we find him condemning the decisions of others who transgressed these same laws. Faced with the spread of heresy, the pressure of internal divisions, and the lack of what he considered suitable leadership, Basil used his ecclesiastical authority and personal influence to their fullest potential, despite obvious inconsistency in his policies. He actively labored to infiltrate the ecclesiastical hierarchy, both within and beyond Cappadocia, with theological allies and men he deemed worthy of episcopal office. His actual choices were diverse and involved a wide variety of considerations. They do not fit neatly into a single, all-embracing category. Among them we find friends, relatives, disciples, and one man known by reputation only. At least a few were well educated, most were experienced in ministry, and all were respected for the orthodoxy of their faith. Alongside right belief, moral virtues were a crucial factor in all of the men Basil endorsed. At least four of the six were either monks or firmly committed to the ascetic vocation, and several of these came to have considerable influence within the monastic movement. Basil also approved of two men who had formerly been Encratites. Judging from these few examples about which we have concrete information, a complex network of factors entered into Basil's decision-making process when it came to the selection of a bishop, a procedure that he could not single-handedly control anyway. Even those who seemed to meet his high standards for episcopal leadership were sometimes chosen owing to the exigencies of a particular situation and for a mixture of spiritual, practical, and political motives. But amid an array of concerns regarding leaders of the church, formation in and commitment to asceticism were high on his list of qualifications. In his recruitment of bishops, as in his function as patron and overseer of the church, Basil's emphasis on monastic ideals in church office did not remain only on a theoretical plane.

Before leaving the subject of Basil's influence, we must briefly consider the direct impact of his writings on his own and succeeding generations of leaders. In Chapter 2 we examined Basil's letters for information about his own ideas on church leadership. But these epistles were written to particular people for specific reasons and must also be considered from the standpoint of their recipients. Basil's correspondents encompassed a vast and diverse assortment of individuals and groups: friends, civil officials, military personnel, clients in distress, laymen, women, clergy, bishops, cenobitic monks, and other ascetics. Well over a third of Basil's extant letters were addressed to members of the church hierarchy, and the large majority of these were bishops. Recipients included his suffragans, colleagues in other eastern dioceses, and even the leading bishops of Alexandria, Italy, and Gaul. His efforts to negotiate with the bishops of the West produced few results. Nevertheless, Basil commanded respect even in places far removed from Cappadocia. Though he was not without critics and opponents closer to home, his words carried great weight. The large number of extant letters to bishops throughout the Roman Empire suggests that he consistently attempted to influence ideas and decisions both within and beyond his diocesan frontiers.

Basil wrote no treatise on church government or on the nature of the model Christian bishop, but a large number of his letters treated issues of leadership in the church. Many dealt with the ascetic life. Some of these letters were written to clergy, encouraging them to embrace ascetic ideals. Basil corresponded with several monks and priests who would eventually ascend to the episcopate. His encouragement of such men by his personal example and his letters could well have influenced their orientation toward a career embracing both monastic ideals and episcopal office. But Basil's letters were often intended for a wider audience as well. Their stylistic qualities prompted Gregory Nazianzen to send a collection of his friend's correspondence to an inquirer as a model of letter writing. Several other friends and disciples, as well as family members, were involved in collecting or donating Basil's letters to collections in which they would be preserved for posterity.[126] In the ninth century the Byzantine scholar and bishop Photius still found in these letters a model of epistolary style and viewed all of Basil's writings as a wonderful expression of his pious life and spirit.[127] In the intervening centuries many other people had read his correspondence. The content as much as the style of these letters could not have failed to leave some imprint.

More direct in its tuition and expressly intended for a wider audience, the *Moralia* underscored Basil's vision of monastic ideals in church office. The message committed to leaders was that they ought to be paragons of virtue and ascetic discipline. Conversely, the *Asceticon,* intended primarily for monks in the setting of a cenobium, required of monastic overseers such qualities that would also make them ideal members of the ecclesiastical hierarchy. Basil composed such guidelines particularly for those in positions of teaching and authority in the church. Since the *Rules* and the program outlined therein became omnipresent in eastern monasticism, Basil's principles of leadership were also widely propagated.

Finally, in several passages of his correspondence Basil himself commented on the power of the written word. In a letter to two of his spiritual sons he explained that while bodily presence is preferable, for those who are eager to learn,

> even physical separation is not a hindrance. Our Creator, in his surpassing wisdom and love for humanity did not confine thought in the body nor the faculty of speech in the tongue . . . [so that we] can transmit teaching not only to those separated by a great distance but also to those who will be born a long time after. And experience confirms my words, inasmuch as those who have lived many years ago instruct young people by the teaching preserved in their writings. And despite the distance that separates us . . . teaching knows no hindrance, neither by land nor by sea, provided you are concerned about your own souls.[128]

Basil's own written works instructed and influenced not only his contemporaries but also succeeding generations of readers, both lay people and men of rank in the church. By means of his writings as well as his deeds and decisions as bishop of Caesarea, Basil actively promoted consonance between his ideals of monastic life and his vision of episcopal authority. One major result of his efforts was a growing number of bishops in Asia Minor who were themselves ascetics or monks and advocates of the monastic movement. This pattern was further advanced by Basil's friends and disciples, for whom the Cappadocian himself served as the monk-bishop par excellence.

II

The Development of an Ideal

4

Gregory of Nyssa: On Basil, Moses, and Episcopal Office

The ideal of the monk-bishop did not die with Basil of Caesarea. Basil's ideas and efforts gave a crucial impulse to this ecclesiastical development, but they were part of a larger process. Others who had been influenced by the monastic movement perpetuated the vision of ascetic ideals in church office. In particular Gregory of Nyssa and Gregory of Nazianzus echoed Basil's concerns about the state of the episcopate, and in their efforts to promote higher standards of leadership they often turned to the example of Basil himself. Their writings both promoted his principles and incorporated Basil's image into their particular paradigm of episcopal authority. Though better known for their theological influence, both Nyssan and Nazianzen contributed to an ecclesiastical ideal that continued to gain dominance in the Christian East. The writings and example of John Chrysostom also advanced a monastic model of leadership, despite an expressed hesitancy about the appropriateness of monks for church office. In Part II, then, we will examine the ideal of the bishop in the writings of the two Gregorys and John Chrysostom.

First, however, it will be helpful to recall certain contextual factors that lie behind these bishops' ideas about church leadership. Aside from the various phases of the Arian controversy, internal quarrels and divisions, graphically depicted in the letters of Basil of Caesarea, continued to plague the church in the eastern Roman Empire and prevented even Nicene bishops from forging the unity needed to withstand their common enemies. Contemporary pagan reflections on this state of affairs are especially apt. "Christian bishops," Ammianus Marcellinus recounted frankly, "were far from being of one mind." Commenting on Emperor

Julian's strategy toward bishops, he added: "Experience had taught him that no wild beasts are such dangerous enemies to man as Christians are to one another."[1] Though the two Gregorys and Chrysostom composed many of their writings after the Theodosian triumph, disputes and rivalry among bishops did not cease, and this spirit of dissension was always fresh in their minds.

Equally important to remember is the dramatic transformation in the status of the bishop that had occurred under Constantine, and its ramifications for episcopal office. In 257 Emperor Valerian had decreed the death penalty for all clerics, naming bishops first among them. Less than seventy years later the priesthood and episcopate had become positions of privilege, and with time the social prestige of bishops only increased.[2] Local aristocrats, often neophytes or men with little knowledge or experience of the faith, were increasingly entering the episcopal ranks. They were often supported by the masses, who preferred to have the rich and powerful in positions of influence. To be sure, ecclesiastical legislation over the next hundred years would attempt to counteract the most blatant abuses. But it is in this context that we must view the scrambling for high position depicted by Basil and the travesty of church office that Nazianzen continually denounced. For all three Cappadocians, as for their later Antiochene counterpart, the state of the episcopate represented a crisis of leadership. What was needed, they believed, was not only strict adherence to the doctrines of Nicaea but also a fresh breath of ascetic fervor among Christian leaders.

Perhaps no one held Basil of Caesarea in higher esteem or more consistently upheld him as a paragon of episcopal leadership and doctrinal orthodoxy than his brother Gregory of Nyssa. It has often been shown that Gregory continued his brother's legacy in his theological treatises and his leadership of the monastic movement in Asia Minor.[3] Indeed Nyssan came into his own as a theologian and leader in the church only after Basil's death. Because his ecclesiastical influence is generally deemed much less important than his work as a theologian, relatively little attention has been paid to his notions of leadership or his own career as a bishop.[4] Gregory would invoke the image of Basil in his efforts to shore up the ailing episcopate, but his expression of episcopal ideals went beyond his portrayal of his brother. The transformation of Moses into the image of the supreme Christian leader may have been even more important in propagating the monk-bishop ideal. We have considered the importance of Moses as a leader in Basil's writings, and we will see that the Old Testament patriarch played a role in Nazianzen's vision of episcopacy as well. But Gregory of Nyssa developed the portrait most fully. Through his portrayal of Basil, Moses, and other leaders in the Bible and more recent Christian history, Gregory may be the one who, more than anyone else, gave theological underpinnings to a monastic model of church leadership that would ultimately win the day in the Christian East.

Before considering how Basil fit into Gregory's vision of episcopal office, it is worth noting that Basil himself viewed his life and his career somewhat differently than did his admirers. While he occasionally complained about the burden of episcopal responsibility, particularly his obligation to fulfill the duties of patronage, he said relatively little about his perception of himself as a bishop. He was clearly aware of the authority inherent in his office.[5] However, in most letters in which he reflected on his ministry it was rather to decry his failures in securing peace and unity in the church. He attributed these failures both to the corporate sins of the church and to his personal transgressions. Sin, Basil suggested, was the cause of the western bishops' reluctance to come to the aid of their eastern brethren and the reason for the widespread influence of heresy in the East.[6] Similarly, he ascribed his failure to establish unity with Bishop Theodotus of Nicopolis to his own personal sins.[7] He often asked colleagues to intercede on his behalf. For example, he requested prayer that he would be turned from his dangerous ways and made worthy of the name of Christ, and for watchfulness and faithfulness in his life and ministry.[8] He recalled how he had wept for his sins in his conversion and lamented his struggles with self in his early pursuit of the monastic life, and he continued to present himself as a penitent throughout his ecclesiastical career. "I know myself," wrote the bishop of Caesarea, "and I do not cease shedding tears for my sins, if only I may be able somehow to appease my God and to escape the threatened punishment."[9] The notion of life as a perpetual act of penitence was in fact typical of monastic culture. Basil sustained this mentality in the episcopate, yet another way in which the bishop helped to transfer monastic ideals to the broader ecclesial community.[10]

In contrast to Basil's occasional revelation of himself as a failure and a penitent, Gregory of Nyssa consistently portrayed his brother as the episcopal ideal, the champion of orthodoxy, a paragon of virtue, and a model of the perfect life. It is true that a certain distance marked their relationship, and various explanations have been offered for an apparent coolness between the brothers. Their "strained relationship" has been attributed to Nyssan's chicanery in attempting to reconcile Basil with their uncle, or to disappointment over Gregory's initial choice of a rhetorical rather than monastic vocation.[11] Others have spoken of a family "axis," with Basil on one side and Macrina, Peter, and Gregory on the other, and of natural fraternal tension.[12] Whatever tension existed was certainly stronger on the side of the older brother. Gregory, for his part, always spoke of Basil with the utmost respect. We have already noted Basil's early influence on his younger brother and Gregory's consequent attribution to Basil of the title *didascalos*. Other frequent epithets include *megas, polus,* and *pater.* His esteem for his brother is also attested by his correspondence, which abounds with allusions to Basil's writings.[13]

In short descriptions scattered throughout his works Gregory praised Basil for his skill as a biblical exegete and for his accuracy in teaching the doctrines of the true faith. Speaking of his brother's *Hexaemeron,* which he proposed to complete, Gregory claimed that Basil's teaching was admired no less than that of Moses himself, for Basil had interpreted Moses' words with such exegetical skill and precision.[14] He revered Basil's great wisdom and his understanding of God, the world, and humanity, which enabled him to lead the people to true knowledge and contemplation. He described the bishop as the "mouth of the church" and the "golden nightingale of doctrine."[15] Although Gregory's theological and exegetical works generally emphasized his brother's doctrinal orthodoxy, they also described his personal and moral qualities. In his treatise against Eunomius, for example, Nyssan extolled Basil's piety and labors for the Christian people as well as his efforts to restore errant men to the church.[16] Elsewhere he celebrated his brother's virtuous character: "Just as no one would deny that the sun gives light and warmth, so no one will disclaim that Basil has been adorned with every beauty of virtue. For indeed he is praised as the sublime of the sublime, he is revered as the saint of saints."[17]

While the Encomium is Gregory's most thorough eulogy of his brother, two other works add important details to the portrait. The earliest of his writings, *De virginitate,* was composed c. 371, just prior to Nyssan's episcopal consecration. In this treatise Gregory referred to Basil's ecclesiastical rank and his own consequent responsibility to respect the authority of the great bishop.[18] Allusions to Basil, however, focus not on episcopal authority but on his supreme example of the type of life that Gregory called young men to emulate. Though he hoped to inspire his readers with accounts of those who distinguished themselves by virtuous lives, Gregory acknowledged that the memory of bygone saints alone was insufficient: "And since the examples in these accounts are not as sufficient for the proper practice of virtue as the living voice and good examples in action, necessarily toward the end of the treatise we have called to mind our pious bishop and father as the only one able to teach such things . . . In this way those who later use the treatise will not consider the advice unprofitable under the pretext that it commands young people to associate with someone already dead."[19] While virginity was presented as a cardinal virtue throughout the treatise, and Gregory regretted that he could not himself enjoy the benefits of this state, the life that *De virginitate* exalts is not one of sexual continence alone. Rather *parthenia* encompasses the life of virtue as a whole.[20] It is such a life that Basil modeled and in which he served as the perfect spiritual guide.

We have seen the importance of spiritual direction in Basil's thinking and the role he played as a mentor to several individuals, including his own brother. Nyssan emphasized the same theme, to which he devoted the final and by far the longest chapter of *De virginitate*. While he pointed to the value of written instructions for those who wish to pursue this "philosophy," Gregory was convinced that exemplary actions were more efficacious than the teaching of treatises.[21] A spiritual guide was therefore of the utmost importance and had to be carefully chosen by the serious disciple. The ideal director stands between death and life, dead to the life of the flesh, yet living and active in deeds of virtue. Should such a master be found, one should emulate his rule of conduct, for God has appointed him as a model.[22] As Gregory had forewarned readers in his prologue, the master whose attributes he presented in this chapter was none other than Basil himself.[23]

Gregory's *Vita Sanctae Macrinae* (c. 380) mentions Basil directly in only two passages.[24] Nevertheless, these texts add texture to Nyssan's portrayal of his brother. While *De virginitate* presents Basil as the model of the virtuous life in general, *Vita Macrinae* points to specific monastic virtues and links Basil's contemplative life with his ecclesiastical career. In this treatise Gregory introduced his brother as a young rhetor recently

returned from studies in Athens and a little conceited by his own eloquence and worldly achievement. Under Macrina's influence, however,
he was soon won over to the philosophical ideal and renounced fame
and secular ambitions. In their stead he embraced a life of manual labor,
poverty, and virtue in which he soon surpassed all others.[25] The renunciation of profane education mentioned in this passage echoes a stage that
Basil himself described in the life of the ideal bishop and which Gregory
would develop in other writings. Poverty and manual labor, the two features singled out by Gregory in this brief depiction, were characteristic
of the monastic life and were often highlighted in the two Gregorys' portrayals of Basil and his ideals.[26]

In the second passage of the *Vita* that refers to Basil we learn that
he ordained his brother Peter to the priesthood.[27] Earlier in the treatise Gregory suggested that Peter, who would eventually be consecrated
bishop of Sebaste, had received a monastic education and had since
childhood pursued the monastic life on the family estate in Annesi. Like
Basil, Peter disdained profane studies. Indeed he made such progress in
virtue that he was no less esteemed in this regard than the great Basil
himself.[28] Basil's consecration of Peter for the priesthood, then, provides
further evidence of the Cappadocian's approval of monks in church office. But even more revealing in this passage is Gregory's description of
the effect of ordination on both Basil and his younger brother Peter:
"And in this their life progressed toward greater piety and holiness, the
priesthood advancing their growth in philosophy."[29] Thus, not only did
ecclesiastical office pose no hindrance to the contemplative life, but it
strengthened or enhanced it in some way.

Although we find passing references to Basil and the theme of church
office throughout his writings, Gregory's ideal of episcopal leadership
appears most prominently in four works representing at least two different periods of his own episcopal career. The first two, *In basilium fratrem*
and *De vita Gregorii Thamaturgi*, date from the early 380s, the years just
following Basil's death and the period of Nyssan's most prodigious literary activity. The second two pieces, *De vita Moysis* and Letter 17, were
written around a decade later, toward the end of Gregory's life. Very
different in genre and style from each other and from the two earlier
orations, these later works nonetheless express a similar vision of the
making of a Christian bishop. Though many of Gregory's principles of
leadership as well as his own ministry as a bishop are apparent in the
sermons he preached both in Nyssa and elsewhere in Asia Minor, these

four works will be my main focus because of their direct bearing on the intersection of his ascetic and episcopal ideals.

In the encomium of his brother, Nyssan developed his portrait of Basil to its fullest extent. Though the precise date of the speech is uncertain, it may well have been delivered in Caesarea on an anniversary of Basil's death.[30] The text suggests that there was already a cult of Basil at a relatively early date and that Gregory wished to honor his brother with a new feast day in the liturgical calendar: "If Basil the Great is shown to be thus by report, so that on being compared with the great saints he is not far from them in the manner of his life, well does our sequence of feasts now bring round the anniversary which we have established to him."[31] The encomium was written during a period when Nyssan himself was no doubt feeling acutely the burden of leadership in the church. Though the death of his famous older brother had liberated him in some ways, it had also deprived the Christian community of a leading bishop and theologian as well as the organizing force behind the Cappadocian monastic movement, and Gregory himself would have to stand in the gap. He had served as a bishop for almost a decade by the time he composed the encomium, but it seems that he had little aptitude for ecclesiastical politics, a judgment rendered by no less than Basil himself.[32] His oration reveals nothing about his brother's social background and provides no historical details about his upbringing. In this and other respects *In basilium fratrem* departs from the form and content of classical encomia, which were highly schematized in the late antique period by Menander (c. 300).[33] While an encomium would normally include a discussion of the subject's homeland, ancestry, and education immediately following the *proemion,* Gregory chose instead to idealize these aspects of Basil's life in a later part of the oration. His silence regarding Basil's origins may be due to his desire to portray the bishop as the model Christian, an archetype for the emulation of all the faithful.[34] Yet alongside his presentation of virtues toward which all Christians ought to strive, Gregory described his brother as the ideal bishop, a leader marked not by nobility of birth or attainment of worldly honors but by a life of detachment and love for God.

A lengthy series of *synkriseis* comprise almost the entire oration. These comparisons between Basil and various Old and New Testament figures are intended to demonstrate that the bishop's subsequence in time to these biblical saints in no way diminishes his greatness.[35] Gregory explained that God had raised up Abraham to expose the error of godless Chaldean philosophy; Moses to destroy the deceit of the Egyptian sorcerers; Samuel to secure the obedience and purity of the Israelites; Elijah to tear down the idols of his age; John the Baptist to expose sin and preach repentance; and Paul to lead others to the light of truth. In the same way God raised up Basil, "the man of God in our own generation, the great vessel of truth," to combat the heresies of the present time.[36] Moreover, just as the biblical saints were commended for their asceticism and spiritual labors, so also Basil "was dying day by day and was ever being spent willingly by mortification."[37] He was their equal not only in his struggle for the true faith but also in his longing for God and his progress in the spiritual life.[38]

After demonstrating Basil's worthiness in faith and intellect to be celebrated alongside these Old and New Testament heroes, Gregory developed a second set of *synkriseis* (GNO X.118.20–130.6) in greater detail, in order more precisely to delineate Basil's praiseworthy spiritual and moral attributes. In this section monastic ideals and virtues are especially marked. The first of five comparisons examines the likeness between Basil and the apostle Paul. Their outstanding common characteristic is love for God evidenced by complete detachment from material possessions and worldly ambitions. All other virtues are said to be "offshoots of the root of love" for God, a love that Basil fully possessed.[39] Toward the end of the comparison Gregory affirmed that both men were crucified to the world, one mortifying his flesh and the other perfecting his strength in weakness.

In the next comparison Basil's disdain for the body and specific ascetic practices are most clearly set forth. Gregory first insisted on the foolishness of comparing anyone with so great a man as John the Baptist. However, he continued, just as John "preferred the desert to the world and yet lived much with the world," so "our teacher" was in no way inferior to John in this respect.[40] Particularly striking are the monastic ideals attributed to the bishop:

> Who does not know that he considered an effeminate and luxurious mode of life inimical, in everything seeking fortitude and manliness instead of pleasure, enduring heat from the sun, exposing himself to the cold, with fasts and acts of self-control disciplining the body, tarrying in cities as in deserts (with his virtue harmed in no way by social contact), making the deserts into cities? For neither did his intercourse with the multitude in any way change his exact and steadfast way of life; nor if he withdrew into the solitude into himself could he be freed

of those who assembled for aid; so that in his case also, after the manner of the Baptist, the desert became a city crowded by those who rushed there . . . From the beginning poverty had been a pleasure to him; his decision became an immovable rock. He desired through purity to approach God.[41]

Not only was Basil's ascetic discipline and contemplative bent revealed, but he was also shown to have succeeded in pursuing the "mixed life," a term often used to describe a balance between the contemplative life of the philosopher or monk and the active vocation of civic or ecclesiastical service. The monastic solitude and isolation that characterized the life of the desert hermit were internalized in Gregory's description of Basil. By this means the bishop was able to combine the virtues of monastic life with active pastoral care.

The Elijah comparison continues Nyssan's treatment of Basil's monastic virtues. Gregory listed general characteristics that marked the two men, such as zeal, love for God, and austere living, and drew analogies between specific incidents in their lives. Elijah's forty-day fast is matched by Basil's lifelong abstemiousness. Elijah's famine relief for a single widow is likened to Basil's care for his entire region under similar circumstances, for he sold his possessions and exchanged the money for food.[42] Even the extraordinary event of Elijah's heavenly ascension in a chariot of fire has a parallel. Through "sublime living" Basil, too, was "removed from earth to heaven, having made his virtues a chariot through the Spirit."[43]

After a brief comparison of Basil with Samuel, Gregory presented the final and longest *synkrisis* in the encomium. This comparison of Basil with Moses is especially significant for its portrayal of the Cappadocian as a model bishop. Gregory claimed that Basil intentionally imitated Moses, and a major part of the *synkrisis* evinces the nature of this imitation. He outlined three stages of the life of Moses for the purpose of comparison. First, both men received the finest pagan education yet finally rejected the glory of profane learning for the humble life of fellowship with God. Second, just as Moses retreated from Egypt to a life of retirement, so Basil "left the tumults of the city and this worldly circumstance, and would philosophize with God in great solitude."[44] He is even said to have had a vision of God akin to that of the burning bush. This contemplative experience prepared him for his ecclesiastical career, the third phase of his life in which he imitated the patriarch. As Moses delivered his people from tyranny, so the Cappadocian by his priesthood restored the people of God in his own era. At this point Gregory began to speak of Moses' acts as the prefiguration of Basil's functions as bishop.[45] He emphasized great or miraculous deeds that confirmed the bishop's authority, Basil's care for the people entrusted to him, his monastic endeavors, and the effects of his powerful preaching. Not only did Basil adorn and serve the church through his priesthood, but he also "equipped others by his own example."[46]

Marguerite Harl has commented that in this oration, in contrast to his later *Life of Moses,* Nyssan did not portray the patriarch as the type of the contemplative but rather as the guide of the multitudes and a charismatic leader.[47] These were episcopal functions that Gregory certainly felt were needed in his own day and which he hoped to impress on his audience. This assessment is misleading, however, for in the very context of the comparison with Moses, Gregory suggested that after having donned the sacerdotal robes Basil did not neglect the contemplative life: "Many times we perceived that he also was in the dark cloud wherein was God. For what was invisible to others, to him the initiation into the mysteries of the Spirit made visible, so that he seemed to be within the compass of the dark cloud in which knowledge about God was concealed."[48] This passage is followed by several examples of Basil's victories over the enemies of truth, which Gregory attributed not to superior learning or charismatic leadership but to the teacher's prayer and faith.[49] In the Moses *synkrisis,* as in the comparison with John the Baptist, the "mixed life" represents the ideal. Simultaneously engaged in pastoring his flock and pursuing spiritual perfection and knowledge of God, the monk-bishop is the model for leadership in the church. This *typos* of episcopal authority, Gregory implied, was foreshadowed by Moses and fulfilled by the bishop of Caesarea.

Gregory concluded his *synkriseis* with the same affirmation with which he had begun, that Basil the Great was not far from the other great saints in his manner of life and was therefore well deserving of the festival established in his honor.[50] At this point in the oration Nyssan moved into the eulogy of Basil. Belittling the elaborate praises typical of encomia, Gregory returned to the subject of Basil's spirituality and affirmed that the bishop was hostile to the flesh, even torturing his body in order to subdue it. "Therefore," Gregory explained, "to exalt one who was thus disposed towards the flesh on account of the noble birth of the body would be most unreasonable."[51] Besides, he continued, noble birth is fortuitous. What was truly important in the life of Basil was virtuous character, and the best encomium of the teacher is to imitate him in virtue. Focusing on Basil's poverty, detachment from worldly possessions, and complete devotion to God, Gregory ended his speech with the exhortation to honor the teacher by showing forth his instruction in one's own life.[52]

By accentuating his brother's moral and ascetic virtues, Nyssan used Basil as a model of qualities that all Christians could assimilate. But the encomium also had a more specific didactic purpose. Like Basil himself, Gregory was deeply concerned about the state of ecclesiastical leadership in his day. Basil's own successor in Caesarea, Bishop Helladius, was by background no ascetic but an influential member of the local aristocracy whom Gregory would describe in his correspondence as a pompous and presumptuous hierarch.[53] By contrast, comparisons of Basil with biblical heroes in the encomium highlight those qualities Gregory felt ought to typify the life of a bishop. While *synkriseis* were commonly employed to exalt particular virtues, here they express a comprehensive view of episcopal leadership. Since Basil's role and functions as a bishop are described throughout the oration, Gregory's purpose to portray him as a model of episcopal authority is fundamental to the entire encomium. For Gregory, ecclesiastical leadership was not primarily a question of rank or status but rather of spirituality.[54] In fact, many of the ideals he presents in the life of his brother echo the same standards we examined in the writings of Basil himself.

During the same prolific period of his career, Nyssan composed two other orations in praise of specific bishops. The first, *In Meletium,* was written and delivered on the occasion of the sudden death of Meletius of Antioch who had been presiding over the Council of Constantinople (381).[55] Following the address of another orator who had reviewed the career of the deceased bishop, Gregory delivered a short speech in his honor to fellow bishops and clergy assembled at the council. This consolatory oration emphasized the role of Meletius as a beacon of truth in the struggle against heresy. Gregory described many of the bishop's virtues and compared him with a number of biblical figures, including Moses.[56] The speech is quite brief, however, and it does not develop in any depth the themes and comparisons we have examined in Nyssan's encomium of Basil.

Much more significant is an oration Gregory delivered on the occasion of the feast day of St. Gregory Thaumaturgus. While the exact date is uncertain, the panegyric is generally thought to have been composed between 379 and 388, and probably closer to 380. At a later date Gregory revised and expanded the oration, turning it into a biography aimed at a wider audience.[57] The speech provides little help in determining actual dates or events in the life of the renowned third-century bishop of Neocaesarea. Gregory of Nyssa intended it as a panegyric of his great predecessor, and the content of the *Vita* is more hagiographic than historical.[58] However, Nyssan's relative ignorance of the details of Gregory's life has little significance for his portrayal of episcopal ideals in this speech. Indeed his particular choice and use of events in Gregory's career, whether based in fact or pure fabrication, reveal all the more clearly the attributes he valued in the life of a leader in the church.

Nyssan started the *Vita* with forms typical of a panegyric. He introduced his subject's country, city, and family. After affirming that his true fatherland was virtue and his city the very kingdom of God, he gave a few concrete details about the background of the one known as the Wonder-worker. He mentioned his praiseworthy origins—the region of Pontus, the city of Neocaesarea, and the wealth and nobility of Gregory's family. Though bereft of his parents at an early age, during his boyhood Gregory already demonstrated a keen intellect that foreshadowed future accomplishments. Abandoning the typical diversions of youth, he desired instead to seek wisdom and acquire virtues, both of which are inevitably linked in Nyssan's mind with the practice of self-control (*enkrateia*). Finally, his humble and moderate temperament was matched by a contempt for riches.[59]

While the entire oration exalts Gregory's virtuous life and presents him as a model for all Christians, two long sections of the *Vita* are particularly suggestive of Gregory of Nyssa's episcopal ideals. The description of Gregory Thaumaturgus's preparation for episcopal office is especially revealing. After briefly introducing his moral and intellectual gifts, Nyssan compared Gregory with various biblical figures, among whom Moses stands out most prominently. Just as Moses was instructed in all the wisdom of the Egyptians, so the great Gregory examined all the learning of the Greeks, discovered its weaknesses, and became a disciple of the Gospel.[60] To complete his education the Thaumaturge allegedly went to Alexandria, a city flooded with students who had come to pursue the disciplines of philosophy and medicine. There he maintained his purity and integrity despite the schemes of envious colleagues and the false accusations of a prostitute. In fact, however, there is no evidence that Gregory Thaumaturgus traveled to Egypt at any time. It seems that his namesake simply invented this episode to help fulfill the hagiographic purposes of his *Vita*.[61] It provided him the opportunity to expose the potential evils of pagan education and, more important, to identify his hero with the lives of several biblical saints.

Following this interlude in Egypt, the *Vita* describes how the young Gregory forsook the pursuit of "external philosophy" and went to study with the great master Origen, the "prince of the philosophy of the Christians."[62] Gregory progressed famously in these studies, according to his panegyrist, but he desired to return to his native land to share the riches of wisdom and learning he had acquired. His stay in Pontus was short-lived at this point, despite the admiration of his countrymen. Recognizing and fleeing the dangers of pride, he abandoned urban life for solitude in order to perfect his soul in virtue. So, the young and successful scholar bid farewell to the world, showing himself to be "the Moses of our times." Continuing the comparison, Nyssan explained: "Both Moses and Gregory left the turbulence and bustle of life, each in his own time living alone until out of the vision of God [*ek theophaneias*] the benefit of a pure life was made manifest to both. But it is said that Moses had a wife along with philosophy, while Gregory had virtue alone as a partner. Therefore they both had the same end in view, for the goal of both men in withdrawing from the crowds was to contemplate the divine mysteries with the pure eye of the soul."[63] Just as Gregory had imitated Moses in his acquisition of great learning, so now his rejection of worldly honors and his retreat to solitude are made to parallel the life of the patriarch.

Responding to the call of God, Gregory Thaumaturgus was eventually ordained bishop of Neocaesarea at the hands of the nearby bishop of Amasea. In confirmation of his call to ministry he received a vision of the Virgin and heard the voice of John the Evangelist delivering to him "the mystery of piety," namely the words of the creed that the young man was thenceforth to preach.[64] Just as Moses had penetrated the divine mysteries and emerged from the mountain to lead and instruct the people in the knowledge of God, he wrote, "so also we observe the same pattern in this great man. For him the mountain should not be understood as a visible hill but as the summit of his desire for the true teachings; the darkness is rather the sight of that which others could not comprehend; the tables are the soul; the letters on the tablets are the voice of the one who appeared to him; through all of which a manifestation of the mysteries came to him and to those who were initiated by him."[65] As a result of his training, culminating in a theophany that paralleled that of Moses before the burning bush, the great Gregory became an "athlete."[66] He had gained the experience and power needed for the many conflicts that would characterize the remainder of his ecclesiastical career. Reversing the direction of his earlier journey, Gregory Thaumaturgus emerged from his solitude on the fringes of civilization and set out for the city (*apo tēs eschatias . . . pros tēn polin*) in order to serve the church.[67]

Thus, with his ordination and initiation into ministry, a threefold comparison with Moses has been completed. After abandoning the pursuit of pagan education and following a period of contemplative solitude culminating in the vision of God, both men returned to active ministry strengthened and equipped to lead the people of God. The identification of the Wonder-worker with Moses was not Nyssan's own invention. Several years earlier his brother Basil had spoken of the great Gregory as a "second Moses," an appellation that may have been passed down in the tradition of this region.[68] But Nyssan used this comparison not only to exalt Gregory's great deeds but also to proffer a particular image of the bishop, an image that linked monastic withdrawal with the exercise of episcopal authority. Finally, as the divine choice of Moses as God's spokesman was demonstrated by the performance of miracles, so the ministry of Gregory Thaumaturgus was confirmed by a series of prodigious acts. Much of the rest of the *Vita* recounts these miraculous deeds for which the bishop of Neocaesarea would eventually gain the epithet "the Thaumaturge."[69]

If this portrayal of Gregory's training for ministry is indicative of Nyssan's preferred pattern for bishops of his day, another episode in the *Vita* helps to fill out his vision of episcopal leadership. It is the relatively lengthy account of the choice of a humble charcoal burner as bishop of Comana.[70] Among Gregory's many duties as bishop of Neocaesarea was the selection and ordination of bishops in neighboring cities. At the request of an embassy from Comana, Gregory Thaumaturgus went to that nearby city to designate a bishop for their church. The leaders of the city anxiously wondered and debated about who would stand out "by eloquence, birth or some other distinction."[71] The Thaumaturge, however, had other criteria in mind. He proceeded to consult the leading Christians of Comana, who suggested a variety of candidates, all members of the local aristocracy. Unimpressed by their qualities, Gregory asked whether there might be anyone marked rather by diligence and virtue in his way of life. Those presiding over the election were affronted by the bishop's dismissal of their candidates, and in mockery of his judgment they proposed to him for ordination a poor, lowly charcoal burner named Alexander. On meeting and questioning this man—described as dirty, ragged, ugly, and an object of reproach to most of his fellow citizens—Gregory discovered that he was not a collier by birth but had rather chosen his humble vocation as a form of asceticism. Recognizing that Alexander was in truth a "philosopher" aspiring to a life of virtue, Gregory Thaumaturgus immediately ordained him bishop of Comana. Alexander's first sermon revealed that the man was no ignoramus, for the speech was delivered in good Greek despite its lack of rhetorical embellishment, and the message was "full of understanding."[72]

This rather charming account of the choice of a bishop is important for several reasons. First, Alexander himself is a model of the qualities Gregory of Nyssa admired in leaders of the church. They were clearly monastic virtues—voluntary poverty, humility, continence, disdain for the body, and the pursuit of virtue above all worldly happiness. When it came to the selection of a bishop, the question of social status seemed of no account for either the Thaumaturge or his panegyrist. Despite appearances, however, the charcoal burner was in reality neither from the lower social classes nor completely uneducated. We are told that he did not choose his way of life by the constraint of poverty, a clear indication that the collier was born into a family of higher social rank.[73] Moreover, only a man of some learning could deliver an oration deemed both linguistically correct and so perceptive that it confirmed the Thaumaturge's sound judgment.[74] Though both the *Vita* and the encomium on Basil expose the imperfections and even dangers of pagan learning, Nyssan seemed unable to dismiss the value of education for leaders in the church, even if best abandoned in pursuit of a higher goal.

No less significant in this episode is the way it portrays Gregory Thaumaturgus himself. He is a model of discernment and courage, undaunted by the opposition of the city's leading citizens. While the people of Comana could see in Alexander only the physical poverty and ugliness of the charcoal burner, the bishop of Neocaesarea was able to perceive the spiritual riches and beauty of the inner man. Nyssan described Gregory's guiding principles in the selection of a worthy bishop: "Assigning the highest place to virtue alone, and judging that only an evil life is to be cast aside, he considered as nothing all those things that the world deemed worthy of esteem or contempt."[75] In choosing Alexander, Gregory's right judgment was matched by boldness in challenging the leaders of Comana. The struggle between bishops and local gentry in episcopal elections was a feature of Nyssan's own epoch. The Cappadocian populace in the second half of the fourth century tended to favor the selection of bishops from the curial class, and though the electoral process was shifting toward increasing episcopal control, the voice of influential city leaders could present a formidable force.[76] Nyssan's own Letter 17 to the priests of Nicomedia contesting an objectionable candidate who was apparently favored by a powerful municipal aristocracy reveals precisely such tensions. In light of these concerns, his description in the *Life of Gregory Thaumaturgus* of the bishop's courageous choice in the face of local opposition seems more than a fortuitous addition to the text. In fact the appointment of bishops and the concomitant need for wisdom and discernment preoccupied Nyssan on a practical level around the time he delivered and revised his oration on the Thaumaturge. In 381 Emperor Theodosius designated Gregory one of eleven bishops who were to serve as the measure of orthodoxy for the various dioceses of the eastern church.[77] In Gregory's case this position included the prickly task of mediation in churches outside his region.[78] His own ecclesiastical responsibilities and struggles during this period surely lay in the background of his portrayal of the wise bishop of Neocaesarea.

De vita Moysis, likely written some ten years after the encomium of Basil and the panegyric on Gregory Thaumaturgus, lays even greater stress on both the practice of virtue and the contemplative calling of a leader in the church.[79] The contemplative emphasis may reflect Gregory's own increasing inclination toward the monastic life during the last decade of his career, though there is evidence that he was still active as a bishop and ecclesiastical leader in the latter years of his life.[80] Moreover, in this work Gregory never separates the life of virtue from the practice of contemplation. Indeed the subtitle of the treatise is "Concerning Perfection in Virtue."

The purpose of the *Life of Moses* is to advise petitioners about the pursuit of the perfect life, and it is not much concerned with concrete historical circumstances. Nonetheless it contains several clear indications of Gregory's dissatisfaction with contemporary church leaders. He censured some men who, with selfish ambition and arrogance, "thrust themselves into the honor of the priesthood and contentiously thrust out those who had obtained this ministry from God."[81] The true priesthood, he explained, is of divine and not human origin. It is marked by self-control rather than self-indulgence and has nothing in common with the lives of many priests "who fatten themselves at rich tables and who drink pure wine and anoint themselves with the best myrrh and who make use of whatever seems pleasant to those who have a taste for a life of luxury." Gregory seemed to be drawing his portrait of the false priesthood from his personal experience of the pride and presumption of certain bishops.[82]

The career of Moses provides the perfect contrast to such abuse of ecclesiastical office. Since the *Life* aims to portray Moses as the model of *epektasis,* perpetual progress toward God, the various episodes of the patriarch's life are linked together to show his development. The presentation of his life is not narrowly focused on three forty-year segments as it is in some other Cappadocian writings of this period, but the same three stages we have seen before are evident. Gregory spoke of Moses' upbringing in Egypt as a period of profane education during which he clung to the nourishment provided by the teachings of the church.[83] In an already traditional Christian interpretation, he equated the command to "spoil the Egyptians" with acquiring knowledge of such subjects as philosophy, geometry, astronomy, and dialectic, which could be of use to the Christian community. Here he referred explicitly to Basil of Caesarea as an example of the proper use of pagan learning: "Such a man was the great Basil, who acquired the Egyptian wealth in every respect during his youth and dedicated this wealth to God for the adornment of the Church, the true tabernacle."[84]

Nevertheless, spiritual training was most important for Moses' career as a lawgiver and leader of the people of God. This entailed his sojourn in Midian and the consequent divine illumination of the burning bush.[85] Only a solitary life culminating in the vision of God equips a man to instruct the multitudes, Gregory insisted. He warned against presumption in advising others unless the teacher had been perfected by a "long and exacting training" such as that of Moses.[86] Nyssan described this kind of preparation in the life of his brother as well. It has even been suggested that Basil served as a model for the treatise.[87] But ultimately, Moses' long preparation and illumination represented only the beginnings of the virtuous life. It was perfected in ongoing service to God. Thus, the large part of Gregory's *Life of Moses* recounts and interprets the patriarch's deeds in conducting the Israelites out of bondage. A comment toward the beginning of the long account of Moses' ministry may provide the best summation of Gregory's message for leaders in the church: "Moses (and he who exalts himself by virtue in keeping with this example), when his soul had been empowered through long application and high and lofty life, and through the illumination which came from above, considered it a loss not to lead his countrymen to freedom."[88]

While he referred neither to his brother nor to Moses in Letter 17, Gregory's treatment of the role of the bishop in this epistle represents his mature thought about the qualifications for church leadership and shows his practical attempt to influence the choice of a bishop. It also parallels or reflects much of Basil's thinking about episcopal office. For these reasons it provides an excellent conclusion to our consideration of Nyssan's episcopal ideals. Letter 17 is addressed to the priests of Nicomedia, the metropolis of Bithynia, following the death of their bishop Patricius.[89] Gregory considered it his duty to offer counsel concerning the selection of a suitable replacement for such an important see. This sense of obligation seems to stem partly from a strong conviction about episcopal collegiality and partly from the task of supervision in Pontus with which Gregory had been entrusted at the Council of Constantinople.[90] The persistence of heresy in this region was clearly of great concern to the bishop of Nyssa, although he did not specify the source of the dissidence to which the letter refers. Division and confusion in the church of Nicomedia made it all the more imperative that a wise and strong leader be placed at her head.[91]

The portrait of the ideal bishop in this letter devotes considerable attention to characteristics Gregory deemed unnecessary or neutral in the life of an episcopal candidate. Birth, riches, and worldly acclaim, declared Gregory, ought not to be sought in a bishop.[92] Should these qualities be present, they need not disqualify the candidate so long as other necessary attributes are manifest. Nonetheless, the Bible abounds with examples of humble men of no social status or worldly esteem who were chosen to lead the people of God. Peter, for example, was extremely poor, yet richer than all because "he possessed God wholly."[93] In each church those considered great according to God are preferred to those highly regarded in the eyes of the world. We hear echoes in this passage of the lowly ascetic charcoal burner who was ordained to the see of Comana by the discerning bishop of a neighboring province.

Gregory seemed to be polemicizing against a proposed candidate who possessed external but no internal qualifications. There is evidence to suggest that this man was a certain Gerontius, a former deacon under Ambrose of Milan. According to Sozomen's later account of the affair, Bishop Ambrose had imposed penitence on this deacon for relating strange and unbecoming visions.[94] The same Gerontius scorned his bishop and left Milan for Constantinople, where he quickly made friends with influential men at the imperial court. Shortly thereafter he is said to have been ordained bishop of Nicomedia by Gregory's own metropolitan, Helladius of Caesarea, whose son Gerontius had recently helped to secure a high appointment in the army.[95] Such political maneuvering was not unusual for the attainment of positions in both the civil and ecclesiastical hierarchies of the fourth century. In fact Gregory's perspective in Letter 17 cut against the grain of the normal selection process for bishops. In a society in which social status and worldly influence were much sought after in ecclesiastical leaders, Nyssan belittled the significance of such factors. Far worse than a superfluous quest for external qualities in the life of a bishop, however, would be the selection of a man whose character definitively disqualified him for church office. Gregory compared a worldly man in a position of spiritual authority with a dysfunctional well. Such a leader might present a magnificent outward appearance, but he provides no water for the thirsty. Therefore, Gregory insisted, if someone takes undue pride in his friends, honors, wealth, or lineage, he should be abandoned like a "useless cistern."[96]

What characteristics ought to be sought in the selection of a bishop? At least four distinct qualities can be discerned in Gregory's portrayal of the episcopal ideal. The first attribute of a leader chosen by the Spirit is single-minded devotion to God. He should have his eyes focused only on God, not on the things of this life. Such were the Levites, Gregory suggested, whose portion was God alone and who were not enticed by material possessions.[97] Second, in keeping with a mind set on spiritual things, the potential bishop must not be prone to party spirit but should have in view the common good of the church.[98] The third crucial characteristic is competence borne of experience in leadership. Gregory pointed to the consequences of incompetent pilots at the helm: "How many shipwrecks of churches have already taken place because of the inexperience of their leaders!" In contrast, he compared the experienced leader with a blacksmith. Such a man knows how to soften lives in the heat of the Spirit and shape them into choice and useful instruments.[99] Gregory linked this capability with a final quality. The ideal bishop is a person of irreproachable character. Since subordinates and disciples strive to imitate their superiors and teachers, the virtues of a leader would inevitably become those of his followers. The example of a worldly man could not possibly produce a spiritual disciple.[100] A *pneumatikos,* a truly spiritual leader, must therefore be selected.

Although Gregory used only biblical examples in this letter to the Nicomedians and did not refer to his brother as a paragon of episcopal authority, there are many parallels with his portrayal of Basil. Also striking is the similarity between this description and Basil's own criteria for ecclesiastical leadership. In both prescriptions the virtues of the bishop are described in monastic terms. As in Origen's critique of contemporary bishops, worldly status and even ordination play no role in defining the true bishop.[101] Rather, an episcopal candidate must demonstrate doctrinal orthodoxy and suitability to lead by spiritual experience. He should be detached from terrestrial affairs and consumed by the things of God. Like the monastic overseer or the *pneumatikos pater* in Basil's writings, Gregory's ideal bishop must be an experienced spiritual director, able to guide souls safely into the "harbor of God."[102] As for Basil, so also for Gregory: he, too, believed monastic ideals should reform the ailing episcopate. And, as we have seen elsewhere in Gregory's writings, it was often Basil himself who embodied the desired reformation.

In his own ministry Gregory attempted to put into practice the convictions and commitments he found in exemplary leaders. But while his treatises reveal his high standards for episcopal office, his efforts to implement those ideals were often fraught with problems and met with failure as much as success. Several of his extant letters, all of which date from the period of his episcopate, open windows onto Gregory's activities and relationships as bishop of Nyssa. Letter 1 illumines a dispute to which we have already alluded. Bishop Helladius, Basil's successor in the see of Caesarea and hence Gregory's metropolitan bishop, was by background an influential member of the local aristocracy. The precise subject of their disagreement is never clearly stated in the letter, but there were certainly underlying political factors involved.[103] In 381 Emperor Theodosius issued a decree that placed Gregory on an equal level with Helladius as a guarantor of the orthodox faith for the region of Pontus and apparently commissioned them jointly with a special task of overseeing and ordering the churches. Helladius apparently took umbrage at this elevation of his gifted suffragan, a measure that also contradicted the hierarchy of episcopal leadership recently stipulated by canon 2 of the Council of Constantinople.[104] Despite the political and ecclesiastical issues in the background, Gregory, in his letter of complaint to Flavian, focused on the character of his metropolitan. He accused Helladius of pride and arrogance, precisely those vices that a monk ought to shun and despise.[105] As we have seen in Letter 17, tensions with Helladius also underlay Gregory's intervention in Nicomedia. Though his outline of a model Christian bishop for the city reveals lofty moral and monastic ideals, his practical efforts to prevent the consecration of an unworthy candidate ultimately failed.[106]

Elsewhere we learn that Gregory mediated in other churches as well. Considerably more successful was his earlier intervention in the city of Ibora, close to his family residence in Annesi and the monastic communities established by Macrina and Basil. Summoned to the city on the death of its bishop, Gregory helped to appoint a man who would eventually represent the province of Helenopontus at the Council of Constantinople.[107] Of all the appointments during his episcopate he may have been most pleased with the election of his own brother Peter as bishop of Sebaste. Peter had been directing the monastic community at Annesi, and Gregory admired his upright character and spiritual oversight.[108] Gregory was also involved in churches far beyond his borders, with varying degrees of success. The mission to Arabia was entrusted to him by the Council of Constantinople and authorized by the emperor, but the role of episcopal mediator was well known to him from the example of his brother.[109] Like Basil, the Bishop of Nyssa also served as a patron of the faithful under his charge. Moreover, throughout his episcopal tenure he maintained close contact with monks and ascetic communities in his region. His advice and authority in monastic matters were highly regarded, both in Nyssa and beyond.[110] Such preoccupations would no doubt increase in the later years of his life as his role in guiding the monastic movement deepened.

Though Gregory of Nyssa wrote no single treatise on leadership in the church, the writings considered here reveal common themes and ideals in his thinking about the episcopate. While he did not condemn what he considered external attributes for the office of bishop—education, wealth, social status—Gregory repeatedly emphasized the life of virtue as the paramount qualification. He did not give a single, consistent definition of virtue, but his examples show that it entailed the practice of ascetic disciplines and the pursuit of God through prayer and contemplation. Virtue was ultimately rewarded with an experience of theophany, a manifestation of the divine. But both training in virtue and its fruition in the vision of God ultimately prepared a person to serve the people of God. Perhaps the account of Gregory Thaumaturgus's ordination to the priesthood expresses this concern most poignantly. While the Thaumaturge feared that the burden of priestly care would impede the philosophic life, Bishop Phaedimus of Amaseia wished to place Gregory in charge of the church "lest such great good should conclude in an idle and unprofitable life." Again ordination is depicted as an enhancement of the contemplative life.[111] In the end Bishop Phaedimus won out, and Gregory was willingly consecrated bishop of Neocaeasarea.

In short, the life of virtue must not end with inaction. It is preparation for further service to God and to the church. It has been noted that in Gregory's later writings his notion of the virtuous life departs from the Platonic tradition and its Christian expression in the thought of Origen.[112] Plato, Aristotle, Origen, and Plotinus tended to view the moral life as subordinate to knowledge, and they expressed the goal of virtue in terms of vision or union with the divine. For Gregory, in contrast, virtue was not a mere step on the pathway to perfection, a stage that had to be surpassed and superseded by the mystical or unitive experience. While virtue is a precondition for contemplation, it is also the result of contemplation. Virtuous action must flow from the knowledge of God, for it is part of a continuous process of perfection. If this transformation of the Platonic tradition is generally apparent in Gregory's later theology, it is certainly characteristic of his treatment of ecclesiastical leaders. Even De vita Moysis, one of the most mystical of his treatises, concludes with a picture of the patriarch, the friend of God, successfully interceding on behalf of the people. Such things, Gregory explained, "are a clear testimony and demonstration of the fact that the life of Moses did ascend the highest mount of perfection."[113]

Indeed it is the image of Moses that perhaps best embodies Gregory's vision of episcopal leadership. The exaltation of Moses as a model of the virtuous life was not unique to Gregory. Basil appealed to the patriarch's life, and it was a fairly common *typos* among Christian and Jewish authors of the period. Nyssan himself drew heavily from Philo's *Life of Moses* in his own treatment of the patriarch.[114] But the Cappadocians found in Moses' life and career an ideal for Christian leaders in particular. Gregory of Nyssa developed most fully and consistently the three-stage pattern of his life as a model for contemporary bishops. Ideally the candidate should be educated in profane learning, abandon academic and all other ambitions for the contemplative life, and finally sacrifice even the enjoyment of monastic solitude in order actively to serve the people of God. Nyssan praised this pattern in Basil's career, implying that only an ascetic who had attained to intimacy with God through rigorous bodily discipline and the steady practice of contemplation is properly equipped for the crucial but burdensome task of episcopal oversight.

Gregory's portrayals of virtuous leaders are not merely descriptive but are carefully crafted to express, as it were, a theology of the episcopate. I use the term *theology* guardedly since it goes against the grain of its usage in the eastern tradition, where it is generally reserved for the very being of God. Moreover, in Gregory's writings on church leadership we find relatively little discussion of liturgy or sacraments and even less about the actual role of the priest or bishop in administering these mysteries.[115] Nevertheless, undergirding his descriptions and prescriptions for the good bishop are major features of Gregory's spiritual theology, a theology ideally suited to the monk-bishop model of leadership in the church.

Like Basil, Gregory longed for the reform of church office in his day. His direct efforts to effect change in this sphere were not particularly successful and may well confirm his brother's earlier judgment that Gregory was naive and had no aptitude for ecclesiastical politics. Nevertheless, at least two texts hint at the lasting impact of some of his writings on leadership discussed in this chapter. A letter of Severus of Antioch (c. 465–538) reveals that Nyssan's panegyric of Gregory Thaumaturgus continued to be read in many churches, notably in the capital. A half century later his *Life of Moses* served as a prominent model for the *Life of Eutychius,* the late sixth-century patriarch of Constantinople who was himself a monk-bishop.[116] At a time when heresy was rife and factionalism continued to plague the Nicene party, Gregory of Nyssa echoed Basil's concern about a deficit of spiritual authority in the church. Orthodox faith was clearly of prime importance in the selection of bishops, but right doctrine alone was insufficient. Gregory's panegyrics and descriptions of praiseworthy models best express his ideals of leadership in the church, ideals that would help to shape the episcopate for generations to come.

5

Gregory of Nazianzus: Ascetic Life and Episcopal Office in Tension

In keeping with his more volatile and sensitive temperament, Gregory of Nazianzus was more explicit in his descriptions of bishops and ideals of leadership than were his two close Cappadocian colleagues. This is particularly evident in his treatment of ecclesiastical abuses. In fact, no one up to this point in the fourth century was as outspoken as the Theologian in condemning contemporary bishops he judged unworthy of episcopal office. His forthrightness and specificity were not confined to negative examples, for he provided vivid descriptions of the positive preparation and character he expected of a Christian bishop. Though Gregory had difficulty reconciling ascetic and episcopal ideals in his own life, many of his positive expectations were met in the person and career of Basil—if not always in the real Basil, then at least in the bishop of Caesarea he constructed in his later writings. In fact, much of what Gregory said about ecclesiastical office, his concerns as well as his high standards, had been expressed or intimated in a different tone and in a less programmatic fashion by Basil himself. Yet the number and forcefulness of Nazianzen's writings on church leadership, a subject that preoccupied him through the greater part of his life, played a particularly important role in spreading his own perspectives as well as shared Cappadocian ideals.

In considering Gregory's career we must remember that most of what we know of his biography was carefully scripted by Gregory himself. Through his autobiographical poems and his astutely crafted orations, both purposefully directed toward specific audiences, Gregory took a very active role in projecting a particular self-image to his own and future generations.[1] While such intentionality on Nazianzen's part may distort some of the details of his past or cause readers to misinterpret them, it also illumines what he considered most important to communicate about his life and ideals. From his own reflections, then, we learn that as a young man Gregory was already strongly disposed toward the monastic vocation. Employing a standard hagiographical trope, he recounts how at his birth his mother dedicated him to God; in accordance with her prayers for him, Gregory explains, Christ "breathed into me the love of holy wisdom, and of monastic life, which is the first fruit of the life to be."[2] Any natural inclination toward a life of asceticism and contemplation became all the more pronounced through his intimate association with Basil. Gregory's admiration for Basil dates back to the years of their blossoming friendship as students in Athens. "Above all it was God, of course, and a mutual desire for higher things, that drew us to each other," he later recalled.[3] Together they pledged to devote themselves to "philosophy," "the more perfect life," upon the completion of their studies.[4]

While Basil embarked on a monastic course soon after his return to Cappadocia, Gregory himself was held back for some time. He explains on several occasions that it was reverence toward his aging parents that prevented him from joining Basil immediately. In retrospect he wonders whether his separation from Basil was not the cause of many difficulties in his life, particularly his unsatisfactory progress in the pursuit of philosophy.[5] Gregory did finally succeed in joining his friend in Annesi for some time.[6] He was not equally enthralled with the humble existence there that Basil had described to him in such idyllic terms. Finding the setting harsh and barren and the lifestyle rigorous and austere, Gregory describes the retreat in a mocking tone in two letters to his friend.[7] Nonetheless, another letter from these early years reveals that his ascetic ideals and ambitions had not diminished. After discounting his two previous letters as mere teasing, he looks back longingly to the psalmodies and vigils, the zeal for the Scriptures, the earnest pursuit of virtue, "those journeys to God in prayer and that life in some sense immaterial and incorporeal" that he had shared with Basil and other brothers in their company.[8] His yearning for such a life and his esteem for Basil remained strong.

Gregory returned to his family in Nazianzus little knowing the plans his father had for him. Though he did not disdain the active life, he claims that his proclivity toward monastic withdrawal and contemplation caused him to react vehemently against the course of life the elder Gregory had foreordained for him. In reflections on this period of his life he lays bare his internal struggles. A passage from his autobiographical poem *De vita sua* is especially telling in this regard:

> As I surveyed the actual paths to holiness it was not easy to discern the better path or the serene one . . . I decided upon a middle way between the life without ties and the life of mixing, one which would combine the serenity of the former with the practical use of the latter . . . I took the view that people living the active life, too, deserve our love. They receive their measure of honor from God because they lead people by means of the divine mysteries. Still, however much I seemed involved with people, I was possessed by a greater longing for monastic life, which I regarded as a matter of interior dispositions, not of physical situation. For the sanctuary I had reverence, but from a good distance, the effect being that of sunlight upon weak eyes. In all the ups and downs of life I had hoped for any other dignity than this.[9]

Gregory's worst fears were soon realized. He describes the "tyranny" of his forced ordination at the hands of his father. In great distress he fled back to Pontus, hoping that Basil would serve as "medicine" for his wounds. Although his panegyric would portray Basil as having perfectly combined the virtues of active and contemplative life, in his reaction to the demands of the priesthood Gregory perceived his friend in stark contrast to mundane and burdensome ecclesiastical affairs: "For there, hidden in that cloud, like one of the sages of old, practising union with God, was Basil."[10]

Precisely what he did during the ensuing period of retirement with Basil is nowhere clearly stated, but it likely involved considerable reflection on the role of the Christian leader, whether priest or bishop, and the proper ascetic, biblical, and theological preparation for such a weighty position, themes that Gregory would soon take up in his early orations. The retreat served to clarify his perspective on church office and to reconcile him personally to the tasks that he was about to assume in Nazianzus. Indeed his withdrawal was short-lived, for fear of irreverence toward his father and disobedience to God soon persuaded Gregory to return and accept his charge.[11] Soon after his return he delivered Oration 2, an apology for his flight from sacerdotal responsibility. The speech is not merely a sermon defending his actions to the congregation of his hometown but a major treatise on the priesthood that would exercise great influence on John Chrysostom's ideas in the next generation.[12] Gregory's preoccupation with ecclesiastical leadership would continue throughout his life, and many of the convictions he expressed in this oration would deepen and apply to his treatment of the episcopate some twenty years later.

To appreciate the acuity of the problems addressed in Oration 2 it is worth recalling the historical and literary context of the speech, particularly its connection with broader realities of leadership in the church of this period. During the reign of Constantius in January 360, bishops at the Council of Rimini-Constantinople had formulated a *homoian* creed affirming the likeness, rather than equality, of the Son with the Father. In the months that followed, proponents of the creed succeeded in rallying support for this position among a majority of eastern bishops, a clear victory for Constantius's religious policy and a bitter disappointment for the Nicene party.[13] Both Dianius, Basil's bishop in Caesarea, and Gregory the Elder in Nazianzus signed the creed between 360 and 361, much to the chagrin of both Basil and Gregory. A group of dissenting ascetics in Nazianzus even split off from the church as a result of this apparent defection, refusing to have their leaders ordained by their own bishop.[14] In fact, Gregory the Elder's subscription to an unorthodox formula of faith may well have been one reason for Gregory's own prompt withdrawal from Nazianzus at the prospect of ordination at his father's hands.[15] In any case, after three months of retreat in the company of Basil he had returned to Nazianzus some time before Easter 362 and delivered his first three orations as an ordained priest.

Only a few months before these events, in November 361, Emperor Julian had come to power. The first pagan emperor since the conversion of Constantine, Julian's ascension to the imperial throne threw the Christian world into confusion. Shortly after Julian's death in 363 Nazianzen would compose his famous *Invectives against Julian*. Alongside their polemic against the emperor's anti-Christian policies, these orations attempted to explain to the faithful why God would have allowed such misfortune to befall them. God was teaching Christians a lesson, Gregory suggests, for the corruption, pride, and rivalry that had arisen among them because of their success.[16] Not far in the background were the lust for power and the personal ambitions of bishops, whom

Gregory would often blame on subsequent occasions for the impiety of Christians as well as for doctrinal quarrels. If this is only an underlying critique in his *Invectives,* it is a major theme of Oration 2, pronounced in Nazianzus in the midst of the Apostate's reign. Compared with the conflicts that rage among Christian leaders, says Gregory, even this great external threat inspires no fear.[17]

Certainly the apology presents a sad picture of the clergy of his day. Like the other two Cappadocians, Gregory was all too aware of the abuses of priestly office. Yet while Basil and Gregory of Nyssa reserved their critiques of the priesthood for personal correspondence or less direct discussion, Nazianzen often brought his complaints and accusations before a wider public. In Oration 2 he expresses concern about proper order in ascending to the priestly throne, no doubt alluding to the process by which neophytes rose hastily through the ecclesiastical ranks.[18] He criticizes priests for lack of preparation, wrong motives, and reprehensible character—for presuming to lead others in the pious life while they themselves have not been sanctified.[19] Finding and recruiting worthy candidates for church office was a problem to which Gregory would repeatedly return in his discussions of the episcopate. Already in this oration composed in 362 he sees disreputable men in the priesthood as the principal fault of the church in his age. Decrying the numerous "wretched" and "pitiful" ministers who hold power, Gregory laments that "nothing in any circumstance is or has been as widespread as are such infamies and sins among Christians today. Stopping this tendency is beyond our control, but to detest it and blush at it is not the least element of piety."[20]

Shaped by classical style and themes, as might be expected of a young man who had recently completed a rhetorical education in Athens, the same oration also shows the early influence of monastic ideals on Gregory's concept of church leadership. In keeping with the prescriptions for overseers in the monastic rules that Basil had begun to compose in Pontus, Gregory stresses the exemplary character that ought to mark the Christian leader. "One must first be purified before purifying others, be instructed before instructing, become light in order to enlighten, draw near to God before approaching others, be sanctified in order to sanctify."[21] He devotes considerable attention to the role of the priest as a spiritual guide to his flock. Like the monastic overseer who applies appropriate treatment for each state of the soul, the priest must be able to apply different remedies to the wide range of maladies that plague the Christian people.[22] The medicine prescribed for each malady is some appropriate portion of Scripture rightly applied by the priest, for after presenting an overview of salvation history through the Old and New Testaments, Gregory declares, "Of this treatment we are servants and coworkers."[23] The specific image of the physician of souls to which he appeals repeatedly in this oration is more than an apt metaphor for Nazianzen. Physicians were the only "professionals" of his day who went through a lengthy and exacting professional training to equip them with the requisite skills for their vocation, and Gregory seems to be recommending this kind of preparation for leaders in the church.

In fact the final and longest section of Oration 2 considers the kind of training required for leaders in the church in contrast to the unpreparedness and consequent moral, spiritual, and theological deficiencies of most clergy in his own day. Central to such preparation is a long and deep immersion in Scripture, and not just the memorization of a few pious phrases or a brief acquaintance with the Psalms, which was apparently the boast of some contemporary clergy.[24] Thorough biblical and spiritual training would require years of preparation and could not be rushed. Little wonder, then, that Gregory's ideal minister might well be a man of gray hair and advanced age. Until a prospective priest has, through long philosophical training, mastered his passions, purified his understanding, and sufficiently surpassed others in nearness to God, it would be dangerous to entrust him with the direction of souls or to place him as a mediator between God and humanity.[25]

Here as elsewhere in his orations Gregory refers to Moses as an example of one who was suitably prepared to approach God and consequently to lead God's people.[26] He reminds us that even Aaron and his two sons who were priests were instructed to worship at a distance, "for it does not belong to all to approach God," but only to those who, like Moses, are able to confront God's glory.[27] Likewise only Moses, who alone had climbed the mountain and penetrated to the interior of the cloud, was prepared to receive God's law and instruct the multitudes. Far from being opposed to the active life of pastoral care, the life of contemplation is presented as a requirement for effective priestly service. To accept a position of authority without this spiritual experience would be folly and peril.[28] Gregory implies that it is largely because he recognized the grandeur of the priesthood that he himself hesitated to submit to this exalted calling. The refusal of public office, followed by acceptance of it at some later time, was in fact a classical political motif that would have been familiar to someone of Gregory's background and education; we need not insist on purely Christian ideals or monastic virtues behind his reservations. And he places himself in good company, for once again Moses, whom he so often invokes as a model of Christian leadership, was initially reluctant to respond to God's call.[29]

In light of this high view of priestly office and its requisite qualifications, it is not surprising that Gregory writes a letter of encouragement to Basil on the event of his ordination to the priesthood.[30] He sympathizes and identifies with Basil's love for the philosophical life, and he admits that he does not understand the purpose of the Spirit in the matter of their ordinations. Yet especially in light of the threat of heresies facing the church in their day, he urges his friend to bear the task entrusted to him. Several years later Basil had returned from Caesarea to the monastic solitude of Pontus when Bishop Eusebius's negative feelings toward him threatened to divide the Caesarean church into rival parties. The conflict seems to have been sparked by a group of ascetics in Caesarea whom Gregory refers to as "our Nazarites," the wiser elite of the church who had separated themselves from the world and consecrated their lives to God. This influential ascetic party opposed Eusebius's episcopal election, considering Basil the more suitable leader. Recognizing the danger of a split in the church, Basil felt it prudent to withdraw from the city. Gregory writes to him during this period, encouraging him to resume his sacerdotal duties in Caesarea both because his bishop needs his aid and because of Basil's better theological preparation to withstand the attack of heretics.[31] At the same time, he pens three letters to Bishop Eusebius urging him to be reconciled to Basil. He praises his friend's life and words, describing him as a priest of such high character that "in life, in doctrine, and in conduct we hold him to be the best of all we know."

Gregory considered Basil not only the best of priests but also the worthiest of bishops, despite his initial reservations about Basil's motives in accepting the episcopal dignity.[32] Writing to the people of Caesarea during the summer of 370, Gregory speaks of a bishop as "the lamp of the church," one whose character either compromises or saves the church. In the same letter he commends Basil above all other candidates, for he is a priest "purified in life and word."[33] At the start of the controversy surrounding the division of Cappadocia two years later, before Gregory himself is forcibly ordained bishop, he writes a letter of support to his friend. He expresses confidence that Basil's "philosophy" will be untainted by his present afflictions and that his long experience in the contemplative life will enable him to remain unshaken by events that are agitating others.[34]

Gregory seems to have come to view the "mixed life" that Basil represented as the ideal. He believed the active life of love and service ought to complement the pursuit of contemplation.[35] An appreciation for a kind of mixed life was not unique to Christians of this period. For many pagan philosophers of late antiquity, involvement in public affairs at a certain level went hand in hand with the life of renunciation and contemplative withdrawal. Philosophers might serve as ambassadors, diplomats, mediators, and financial benefactors of their city and its traditions.[36] What set apart the pagan ideal of "contemplative worldliness" from the mixed life of the Christian ascetic was the nature of the pagan philosopher's involvement in public life. The philosopher rendered service almost exclusively on behalf of the governing class, an upper-class urban elite. The Christian ascetic, in contrast, identified with the humble and oppressed classes.[37] The ancient virtue of *euergesia,* which wealthy and powerful patrons practiced largely in the form of gifts to their city, was transformed by Christians into the virtue of *ptōchotrophia,* support of the poor and care for the sick. As Brian Daley has argued, it was particularly this concrete Christian version of the philosophical life, a central aspect of the classical ideal of *philanthropia* that pagan Hellenism had failed to realize, that the Cappadocians saw as the goal of the Christian community as a whole and a major focus of monasticism. This is an emphasis we have already noted in Basil's career and one that Gregory would laud on various occasions.[38]

Whatever his ideological convictions about the nature of *philanthropia* or the value of the mixed life, however, Gregory continued to wrestle with a natural inclination toward monastic seclusion and a disinclination to govern the churches or engage in ecclesiastical affairs. This tension, he suggests, underlies his hostile reaction to being consecrated to the newly created see of Sasima in 372. In a biting letter to Basil he writes, "For me the greatest action is inaction . . . So proud am I of my inactivity [*apragmosunē*] that I think I might even be a standard for all of magnanimity in this regard."[39] Despite his claims here, Gregory's objections to this ordination probably involved more than a mere disinclination for ecclesiastical affairs. His comments in *De vita sua* suggest that he was particularly incensed at being condemned to such a remote village. Gregory never actually took possession of his see in Sasima but remained in Nazianzus as his father's coadjutor. Though his anger and bitterness persisted toward both his friend and his father for forcing him into the episcopate, Gregory still held Basil in high regard. While a certain distance thenceforth marked their relationship, he did not cease to praise Basil for his piety and example of virtue.[40]

Four short orations from the period of Gregory's episcopal consecration illustrate the tensions that continued to dominate his ecclesiastical career. The editor of these discourses has singled out three "thèmes privilégiés" of Orations 9 through 12: friendship, the role of the bishop, and philosophy.[41] Gregory's treatment of each of these themes juxtaposes his inner struggles and his consistently lofty ideals. In particular these speeches expose his sense of loss at having to relinquish the tranquil life of philosophy. In Oration 10 Gregory confesses, "I dreamed of Elijah's Carmel and John's desert, of that life above the world led by the philosophers. I considered the present as a tempest, and I sought a rock, a precipice, or a wall to shelter myself. I said, let others have the honors and the toil; for others the battles and the victories. For myself, let it suffice for me to flee the battles, to be attentive to myself."[42] While admitting his sadness and unable to hide the pain caused by an apparent breach of friendship on Basil's part, Gregory claims that he has now been won over by the Spirit and reconciled to his new position as well as to those who placed him in it.[43] He describes his episcopal charge in terms that reflect monastic ideals, and he appeals to Basil to teach him his pastorly art. He compares both Basil and his father in their function as bishops with the ministry of Moses.[44] Indeed despite feeling victimized by what he considered a heavy-handed use of authority, he later commended the bishop of Caesarea as the paragon of Christian leadership.

Before considering his famous panegyric of Basil, however, we must review the events in Nazianzen's life that directly preceded his delivery of this speech. Soon after his father's death in 375 Gregory fled to the monastery of St. Thecla in Seleucia, 600 to 700 kilometers from Caesarea, hoping to withdraw from ecclesiastical affairs for the sake of contemplation.[45] He remained there in relative seclusion for several years until, according to his own account, he was again wrenched away from his solitude by the pressing needs of the church.[46] With the death of Valens in 378 the orthodox community in Constantinople, which had long suffered under Arian dominance, saw its fortunes changing. The Nicene emperor Theodosius was about to establish his rule in the imperial city. Yet Christians were still deeply divided, and warring factions threatened to further rend the beleaguered church. Able leadership was sorely wanting. The small flock of orthodox Christians appealed to Nazianzen as God's man for the task.[47] He accepted the call and assumed leadership of the Nicene community in Constantinople.

The preceding scenario is based primarily on Gregory's personal reflections on the course of events. The actual religious situation in Constantinople was more complex and Nazianzen's role more ambiguous than he might lead us to believe.[48] There is no doubt, however, that once he arrived in the capital Gregory immediately found himself in the midst of controversy. While defending the Nicene faith against manifold heresies that persisted in the imperial city, he was also forced to defend himself personally against enemies who sought to denigrate his character or contest his authority to govern the church.[49] His embroilment in controversy with bishops following his arrival in Constantinople strengthened his convictions about ecclesiastical authority and puts the panegyric of Basil into proper perspective. The importance of the Constantinopolitan episode in Nazianzen's life is suggested by the amount of space he allots to it in his poem *De vita sua*. Almost two-thirds of the verses in this autobiographical poem focus on this two-year period.[50] Also striking is the amount of attention he devotes to the episcopate in his writings from 379 to 382. His orations and poems from these years show him to be a forceful and untiring advocate of ecclesiastical reform, particularly upholding an ascetic ideal of leadership in the church.

Several orations delivered during Gregory's tenure in Constantinople reflect the ecclesiastical malaise of the city. They also expose his view of contemporary bishops and his deepening convictions about episcopal authority. Both Orations 20 and 21 take up the theme of bad bishops.[51] Men in the highest ecclesiastical office are uninstructed, unpurified, and wholly unprepared for spiritual leadership.[52] Only one who has tamed the flesh and received divine enlightenment through the prolonged practice of "philosophy" is equipped to take charge of souls, Gregory insists at the beginning of Oration 20. He repeats this concern at the close of the discourse. As in Oration 2, from which much of the content of this speech is drawn, Gregory points to the life of Moses as an illustration of proper preparation for leadership. Moses alone ascended the mount, encountered God in the cloud, and finally received the law.[53] We have seen that the three stages of Moses' life served as an important episcopal paradigm for the Cappadocians, but his tripartite career was only one aspect of his appeal as a leader. His encounter with God on Mount Sinai was indispensable preparation for the task of instructing the multitudes. Gregory takes up this theme again in one of his five theological orations delivered in Constantinople during the same period. In Oration 28 he gives a detailed account of Moses' ascent and divine encounter. The vision of God epitomized by the Sinai theophany was for Nazianzen as for Nyssan the ultimate goal of monastic withdrawal and the mark of the true theologian. "In this way, then, you will do theology," Gregory declares toward the end of the narrative.[54] To teach or lead the Christian people without this revelation was for Gregory the height of presumption.

In Oration 21 Athanasius poses the contrast to unworthy prelates of the day. While the latter usurp and abuse their power, the great bishop of Alexandria is said to have exercised paternal authority, a gentleness and severity stemming from his "philosophy."[55] After classing Athanasius with a long list of biblical saints, Gregory suggests that his hero equaled or surpassed them all. Both in theory and in practice he excelled, and he far exceeded those renowned in only one or the other domain.[56] Though Athanasius was never a monk in the strict sense, Nazianzen turns him into the model monk-bishop; and it was especially this depiction of the Alexandrian that shaped later Byzantine portrayals of the patriarch. Gregory explains how Athanasius reconciled the eremitic and coenobitic life,

> showing that there is a priesthood which is a philosophy and a philosophy which needs the sacerdotal ministry. In this way he harmonized the two types of life and brought them together, both activity compatible with retreat and retreat compatible with the active life, that he might persuade everyone that the monastic profession is characterized by steadfastness in a way of life rather than by physical withdrawal, according to the principle of David, the great man of action who was at the same time a perfect solitary.[57]

As in Nyssan's portrayal of Basil, Nazianzen internalizes monastic ideals so that active ministry in the church need not be opposed to the values and practices of the monk. Such a life, he concludes, is the rule for the episcopate.[58]

Gregory's personal struggles with fellow bishops worsened with time.

Although Theodosius I himself had formally installed him as bishop of Constantinople in November 380, the legitimacy of his position continued to be questioned. Ostensibly the objections of adversaries were based on the prohibition of episcopal translations in canon 15 of the Council of Nicaea. This legislation was undergirded by a number of patristic writers who developed the notion that a bishop contracts a mystical, indissoluble marriage with his church. Gregory himself referred to this concept when arguing that he was not bound to a church that he had never occupied.[59] But worst of all the opposition, according to Gregory, were the pretensions of the rival bishop Maximus, at once a "villainous kennelkeeper" and a "poor shorn dog."[60] This one-time Cynic philosopher had been smuggled into Gregory's own church and fraudulently consecrated by Egyptian prelates, and had ultimately gained the support of the western bishops as well. The whole episode of Gregory's rise and rapid fall in Constantinople was in fact part of a larger pattern of ecclesiastical conflicts in the capital in which the bishop of Alexandria, allied with a faction of monks, opposed and eventually jettisoned the bishop of Constantinople.[61]

Debate over Nazianzen's status continued into the Council of Constantinople, over which Gregory himself presided following the death of Bishop Meletius. The rejection of his recommendation for the resolution of the Meletian schism of Antioch, coupled with ongoing polemic about his own appointment, was, by Gregory's account, too much for his sensitive temperament to bear. Though he does not mention it, the late arrival at the council of the Egyptian bishops, who had earlier backed Maximus as their candidate for the imperial see, must have sealed his doom. Pleading illness, he resigned his episcopate, took leave of the council, and returned to the family estate in Arianzus.[62] Before his departure, however, he delivered a farewell address before a group of prelates assembled at the ecumenical council. Oration 42 was probably composed in stages, and the bishops likely never heard the harshest invectives Gregory hurled at them in the final form of this speech; or it may be that Gregory's immediate audience was composed of friends and supporters rather than the hostile bishops themselves.[63] Nonetheless, it represents the epilogue to Nazianzen's tenure in Constantinople. Taken together with his autobiographical poems *De se ipso et de episcopis* and *De vita sua,* written during the same period of retirement, it contains some of his most severe criticism of the episcopate. It also provides an excellent foil for his portrayal of the ideal bishop, soon to be eulogized in his panegyric of Basil.[64]

Like Oration 2, delivered almost twenty years earlier, Oration 42 is Gregory's *apologia* for his flight from ecclesiastical responsibility. After describing his call to Constantinople, the struggling church he had come to serve, and the results of his ministry, Gregory reserves a large portion of the speech for an indictment of unworthy leaders. He censures pastors who keep the truth hidden, caring only for their own well-being and not for the health of the people entrusted to them. He paints a bleak picture of episcopal intrigues, describing contentiousness among bishops as a "holy war."[65] Moreover, many Christians seek pastors who will rival men of power, wealth, and worldly status: "For they seek not for priests, but for orators, not for stewards of souls, but for treasurers of money, not for pure offerers of the sacrifice, but for powerful patrons."[66] Gregory blames fellow bishops for the low level of the Christian laity, for leaders have all too easily accommodated themselves to the whims of the people they are supposed to lead. He begs only that his own successor would be a worthy shepherd, "one who is the object of envy, not the object of pity."[67] There is a note of irony in this plea, for his replacement, Nectarius, was almost the antithesis of Gregory's ideal bishop: a neophyte rather than an experienced priest, an administrator rather than a theologian, and a senator rather than a "philosopher."

Oration 42 has very little to say in a positive vein about bishops. However, within months of his departure from Constantinople Nazianzen found an ideal opportunity to publicize his own standards for episcopal office. It has been suggested that Oration 43, Gregory's funeral oration on Basil, forms a "diptych" with his farewell address.[68] Composed by the bishop of Constantinople, recently "emeritus" and living in retirement, it was pronounced before the public of Caesarea and later revised and enlarged for broader consumption. In this speech Basil's career serves as a contrast to the negative characteristics of contemporary bishops that Gregory had just condemned and as an example for imitation. Unlike Nyssan's highly idealized portrait of his brother in the encomium, Nazianzen's speech recounts many specific incidents from Basil's life. Despite obvious omissions in the narrative, there is also significant historical detail and a number of events parallel those related in Basil's correspondence.[69]

Following traditional headings of a *logos epitaphios,* Gregory starts his oration with a eulogy of the Cappadocian's homeland, ancestry, and parents.[70] He hopes to demonstrate that the great distinction of Basil's family was piety, which the young man both inherited and cultivated in his own life. Basil's education, especially his studies together with Gregory in Athens, is recounted in considerable detail. Nazianzen clearly valued the bishop's pagan education (*paideusin . . . tēn exōthen*), which most Christians, he remarks, wrongly reject as dangerous or insidious to faith.[71] While he stresses Basil's superiority in all academic pursuits, he is just as concerned to show that his friend's main occupation was "philosophy." Describing the common object of their zeal during this period, Gregory writes, "The sole business of both of us was virtue, and living for the hopes to come, having retired from this world, before our actual departure hence. With a view to this, were directed all our life and actions."[72]

Approximately half the oration deals with Basil's ecclesiastical career. In the background lies an implicit and occasional explicit critique of contemporary prelates. Introducing the topic of Basil's priesthood, Gregory reiterates familiar complaints. Church office is becoming the object of ridicule because men uninstructed, inexperienced, and spiritually unprepared for leadership are being promoted to the sacred thrones.[73] Villainy and power rather than virtue and worthiness are often the standards for advancement. Basil, however, was exalted to the priestly throne by God. "And in what manner? Not by precipitate advancement, nor by at once cleansing and making him wise, as is the wont of many present candidates for preferment: but bestowing upon him the honor in the due order of spiritual advancement." Similarly, Gregory recounts Basil's rise through the ecclesiastical ranks: he was first a reader, then a priest, and finally a bishop, "attaining the office neither by stealth nor by violence, instead of seeking for the honor, being sought for by it, and receiving it not as a human favor, but as from God."[74] Basil's temporary retirement in Pontus during his priesthood is described as "philosophical and wonderful," yet his return to Caesarea in her time of distress was "even more admirable." Though he served thenceforth as his bishop's assistant, he actually governed the church from his position of lower rank, being better prepared for such leadership than his predecessor.[75] Among the activities of his priesthood Gregory highlights his personal care for the victims of famine, comparing Basil's provision of food for the hungry with his nourishment of souls with the Word of God.[76]

Gregory's representation of Basil's episcopate continues his polemic against bad bishops. Though envious Cappadocian prelates attempted to prevent Basil's ascent to the episcopal throne, God's intentions were not thwarted. Nor did Basil's promotion compromise his calling or character in any way. He continued to live consistently with his own philosophy, making constant progress in virtue.[77] In his efforts to bring peace and unity to the church he is said to have influenced "principally by his conduct rather than by argument."[78] In Basil's interaction with the emperor and the prefect Modestus, Gregory ascribes to the bishop miraculous powers of healing. Yet in confrontations with enemies and persecutors of the church Basil's moral character and asceticism are paramount. He is described as a man "free from passion, whom the angels revere, at whom women do not venture even to look"; as a "martyr without bloodshed"; as a prelate whose reputation far outshone that of his colleagues.[79] Concerning the partition of Cappadocia, Gregory affirms that Basil turned this evil situation to good by multiplying the number of bishops to care for the churches. In this context he refers to his own forced consecration, and even his praise of the bishop cannot hide his disappointment at a friend's callousness and disloyalty. Nevertheless, he ends up excusing Basil because he had greater concern for his duty to God than for any claims of friendship.[80]

Following his chronological account of Basil's career, the orator breaks into a eulogy of Basil's virtues. While he does not neglect the Cappadocian's intellectual and theological exploits,[81] it becomes especially clear in this section of the oration that the bishop was a monk who joined to his exercise of episcopal authority a wholehearted commitment to ascetic ideals. Gregory extols Basil's life of poverty and concomitant avoidance of publicity, saying that he was "poor and unkempt, yet without ostentation." He praises his temperance with regard to all physical needs and desires, pointing to "his single coat and well worn cloak, and his bed on the bare ground, his vigils, his unwashedness . . . and his most sweet food and relish, bread and salt."[82] In contrast to those leaders concerned only for their own earthly comforts, the Cappadocian consistently exemplified a life of charity in practical care for the weak, the poor, and the sick.[83]

We learn also of Basil's love of virginity and his efforts to influence others to embrace the monastic life. He reconciled the contemplative and active vocations reflecting Gregory's personal quest for a *via media* between the two. Specifically, the bishop managed to unify two streams of the monastic movement that were occasionally at odds. Both solitary and communal life *(tou erēmikou biou kai tou migados)* have benefits and pitfalls, Gregory explains, but Basil "brought them together and united them, in order that the contemplative spirit might not be cut off from society, nor the active life be uninfluenced by the contemplative."[84] Here as elsewhere in the oration Basil's life and ideals embody the perfect mixture of *philosophia praktikē* and *philosophia theōrētikē*. These Aristotelian terms are used by both Nyssan and Nazianzen to denote different types of monastic life,[85] but in the person of Basil they are perfectly combined. Having rejected the values and practices of the world, the monk-turned-bishop nonetheless served the world in active deeds of love and care.

Using almost the same words he employed to condemn unworthy bishops in Oration 42, Gregory insists that Basil was innocent of the many vices of his colleagues. Rather, he says, the pursuit of virtue dominated his career. In a long series of *synkriseis* toward the end of the oration Gregory compares Basil with a host of biblical heroes whom he equaled or even surpassed. Alongside his theological prowess, which receives more attention here than in Nyssan's treatment of Basil, monastic ideals and virtues are prominent. Comparing him with Jacob, for example, Gregory describes Basil's ladder, "which he ascended by successive steps toward virtue." Similarly he rivaled John the Baptist in ascetic discipline.[86] Nazianzen caps off this list of comparisons with a note about the bishop's admirers. So great was Basil's virtue that some, hoping to gain notoriety, sought to imitate even his physical defects. Finally, in his last moments of life, the bishop is said to have ordained to the priesthood some of his "most excellent servants" so that the church might not be deprived of his disciples.[87] The concluding account of the Cappadocian's death and funeral emphasizes once again his roles as mediator and model for monks, clergy, and laity alike.

In light of the foregoing analysis, Gregory's purpose in the funeral oration must have encompassed more than a desire simply to honor Basil, to preach orthodox doctrine, to defend his relations with his friend, or to create a harmonious synthesis of classical and Christian cultural traditions.[88] All these motives entered into his composition of the speech, but they do not in themselves do justice to the themes and emphases examined above. We must not lose sight of the broader context of the oration. Gregory had recently left Constantinople embittered by his personal battles with prelates, disgusted by the low state of episcopal leadership, and particularly incensed by the choice of his own successor. This scenario certainly lies in the background of his portrayal of Basil's life and ecclesiastical career as a model for the episcopate.

Gregory Nazianzen's notion of spirituality, particularly his portrayal of the progress of Basil's life, has much in common with the traditional Platonic and Origenistic pattern of ascent. Nyssan's notion of perfection ends in ceaseless striving and, as we have seen, virtue is as much the purpose as the precondition of contemplation. Nazianzen expresses the goal of the spiritual life in terms of illumination or the vision of God.[89] A Platonic bent in his thought may help to explain the constant vacillation in his own life. Gregory viewed the episcopate as a position of prime importance, which only the best and most philosophical of men were equipped to fill. The true philosopher or monk had progressed through a pathway of ascetic practices and moral purification to intellectual enlightenment and contemplative union with God—necessary preparation for a Christian leader, yet difficult to reconcile with the active duties of a bishop. Gregory tried to bridge a seeming impasse by advocating the mixed life as the highest ideal. It is such a life that he found embodied in men like Basil and Athanasius. But in the back of his mind lay the deeply ingrained Platonic ideal of the philosopher, largely removed from the affairs of the world. Combined with a natural inclination to a life of contemplative withdrawal, this image provided a constant source of angst whenever he personally faced the burden of ecclesiastical duties.

Whether or not Nazianzen's treatment of Basil is more "traditional" or "Platonic" than that of Nyssan's, as has been suggested, he arrived at a similar conclusion. The episcopate needed more men like Basil—theologically orthodox, experienced in the ascetic life, but willing to sacrifice contemplative solitude to serve the church. Gregory Nazianzen places greater emphasis on Basil's education or intellectual formation, his *paideusis.* As noted above, he is quick to criticize Christians who belittled or scorned this quality. Bishops could and did function with limited education, he suggests, but such leaders would be only mediocre.[90] Upholding Basil as an example, he stresses the importance of learning in the bishop's struggles for the cause of orthodoxy. Though Gregory of Nyssa never dismissed the value of *paideusis* for a leader in the church, he emphasizes the *abandonment* of pagan education as the first major stage in the career of a model bishop. Both men, however, insist on lengthy training in asceticism and contemplation as the proper preparation for episcopal ministry. Moreover, in addition to the general praise of Basil's attributes that makes up the large part of Nazianzen's oration, a long section toward the end of the speech develops more systematically his particular virtues of poverty *(aktēsia),* self-control *(enkrateia),* virginity *(parthenia),* and support of the poor *(ptōchotrophia).*[91] These are not just moral but characteristically philosophic and monastic virtues. Indeed the qualities both orators praised and sought in bishops were supremely those of the monk.

Gregory's continuing preoccupation, if not near obsession, with the character and functions of bishops at the time he composed Oration 43 is attested by a poem dating from the same period, soon after his departure from Constantinople and while the ecumenical council was still in session. *De se ipso et de episcopis* evinces Nazianzen's state of mind during this turbulent time. It also reveals his conviction that bishops were best chosen from among monks, though it is more the eremitic holy man than the Basilian cenobite that Gregory has in view. To be sure, it is sometimes difficult to separate his ascetic from his aristocratic ideals of leadership; while he advocates contemplative withdrawal, a feature of monastic life, he also expresses disdain for those from the lower classes—farmers, laborers, and the like—who had apparently risen to the office of bishop. His statement that a bishop should be "from among the best" clearly included social as well as spiritual credentials.[92] In general, the poem bemoans the deplorable state of the episcopate, a characteristic theme in Nazianzen's writings. Bishops are described as hastily chosen, untrained, and often the very worst of men. While some protest that saintly men do not make good leaders because they have no aptitude for affairs, Gregory demonstrates the folly of this objection, concluding that "a man's character is the most persuasive thing of all."[93] Likewise the bishop's personal example is more important than his education or eloquence in teaching. Even proper hierarchical ascent, for which Gregory expresses concern in other writings, pales into insignificance beside the importance of the bishop's sanctity. In fact, the very grace of episcopal ordination is called into question when conferred on impure or evil men.[94]

Who, then, is the shepherd worthy of his calling? Gregory vividly depicts the bishop of his choice:

> You have this man who sleeps on the ground and is all befouled with dust. He has worn his body away keeping vigils, with psalmody, with standing night and day. He has drawn his mind away from all crassness toward the heights . . . He has washed away all the stains with rivers of tears, and any tiny speck he retained of that mud of life which spatters even the wise. He bears the noble seal of flesh that has been worn by prayers and countless hardships . . . In cold, in hunger, and in wretched garments, he yearns to put on the clothing that is imperishable. With insufficient food he does violence to the belly's pride . . . Once he was a rich man, but now he is poor . . . From cities, from the plaudits of the mob, from the whirl in which all public life is tossed, he is a fugitive. His fair soul he has molded towards God, and in his absolute solitude partakes of heavenly things only . . . To him the Spirit has disclosed the deeper meaning of the Holy Writ, uncovering all that is sealed to the understanding of the multitudes.[95]

An ascetic and contemplative life had clearly become Nazianzen's ideal for episcopal office by the later years of his life. Similarly, in reflections on his own episcopal career he describes his ministry in terms that recall the life of a monk. As bishop in Constantinople, he writes, he determined to fulfill the commandments "by ministering to the poor, exercising hospitality, tending the sick, persevering in psalmody, prayer, groaning, mortifications of the senses, of impulse of laughter, control of the tongue, lulling the flesh by the power of the spirit."[96] Several later letters reveal his continued dissatisfaction with the ongoing rivalry and low level of spirituality among bishops.[97] Throughout his career Gregory struggled to embody the monk-bishop ideal he so admired in others. He alternately resisted and succumbed to the ecclesiastical call on repeated occasions.[98] Despite personal ambitions and familial expectations, he often intimates that his sensitive, contemplative spirit made it difficult for him to realize his *via media*. For examples of the balanced contemplative and active life, Gregory looked back to biblical figures like Moses and the apostle Paul. In his own generation he found a model primarily in Basil of Caesarea. But we should not too hastily dismiss Nazianen's own career, as he seems to do in his autobiographical reflections. Recent scholarship has shown that Gregory was quite purposeful in shaping his identity as a bishop and theologian and that he was much more of a theoretician of episcopal office than has hitherto been recognized. Thus, in repeatedly stressing the conflict between contemplative and active life, between ascetic ideals and episcopal office, he was perhaps suggesting that for the model bishop this was a necessary, indeed a healthy tension.

Like his colleagues Basil and Gregory of Nyssa, Gregory Nazianzen was deeply concerned about episcopal leadership in the Christian East. He was particularly acrimonious in condemning the alleged evils of contemporary bishops. It would be easy to reduce his acerbic descriptions to the realm of rhetoric, inflamed by a mercurial temperament; and certainly Gregory's penchant for exaggeration should not be overlooked. But most bishops, even those he greatly admired, had treated him badly. Moreover, we must not forget the seismic shift that had taken place since Constantine in the status of bishops and its ambivalent consequences for church office as a whole. As a result, Gregory and his Cappadocian confreres addressed the subject of the episcopate from the viewpoint of crisis, both theological and moral. Nazianzen's starting point was generally the contemporary situation, and he drew heavily from personal experience of the decadence of the clergy as a counterpoint to his episcopal ideal. This may account for the fact that he says very little about the liturgical function of the priest or bishop. We find no detailed discussion of the proper administration of baptism or the role of the priest in celebrating the Eucharist. Perhaps Gregory viewed these as accessory functions, as part of the exercise or outward manifestation of true spiritual authority that he found so lacking among bishops of his day.[99] In light of this larger concern, proper preparation and character were the most important requirements for church leaders, and for these qualities Gregory looked primarily to the example of the monk. It is not surprising, therefore, that he showed the greatest satisfaction with the election of his cousin Eulalios as his replacement in Nazianzus in 383, for the man was experienced in ministry, noted for virtue, and committed to the monastic life.[100]

Nazianzen was not directly involved in the selection of bishops to the same extent as Basil or even Gregory of Nyssa. Nevertheless, his writings attest to his influence in propagating the ideal of a monastic episcopate. Despite his conflicts with fellow bishops, in his own lifetime Gregory of Nazianzus became well known and much revered for his orthodox

teaching and for his eloquent sermons and poems. He was a public figure who intended his letters to be read by a larger audience.[101] Scholiasts
from at least the sixth century onward commented on his writings, primarily on his orations but also on his poetry. In fact Gregory is the most
frequently cited and commentated church writer in the entire corpus of
Byzantine ecclesiastical literature. His speeches were read in churches
and used as models in schools of rhetoric. Parts of them may even have
been learned by heart.[102] As we have seen, Gregory repeatedly addressed
the problem of ecclesiastical abuses and the consequent need for a new
breed of leader in the church. The popularity of his writings is particularly significant in light of this preoccupation with the subject of church
office. He who was dubbed the Theologian devoted nearly as much writing to this theme as he did to the trinitarian problem.[103]

Among the orations that deal most extensively with the theme of ecclesiastical leadership, we have already referred to the role of Oration 2
as a model for Chrysostom's treatise on the priesthood. Gregory also influenced Jerome's linkage of the priesthood with asceticism, and Gregory the Great would draw deeply from Nazianzen in his own *Pastoral
Rule*.[104] Oration 43, "probably the greatest piece of Greek rhetoric since
the death of Demosthenes," certainly contributed to emerging ideals of
episcopal leadership.[105] In this speech Gregory claims that Basil's life
inspired many imitators. His own portrayal of the Cappadocian in the
funeral oration would do the same for later generations. At least in
the sixth century Gregory's panegyric of Basil was still being read in
churches.[106] Byzantine hagiography, particularly lives of bishops,
abounds with citations and unacknowledged borrowings from this famous oration. Finally, iconographic representations of Basil draw primarily from Nazianzen's descriptions.[107]

The ideal of ecclesiastical leadership that emerges in Gregory's writings is that of episcopal authority empowered and enhanced by ascetic
virtues. We have seen that Nazianzen himself struggled to combine
these variant modes of life in the course of his own career. Indeed his
own life may provide the clearest example of some of the tensions inherent in this paradigm of authority in the church. Yet his descriptions of
the episcopal ideal or of particular praiseworthy leaders show no such
ambivalence. Lifestyles once considered incompatible are made to co-
alesce harmoniously in the monk-bishop of Caesarea, who would set
the tone for upcoming generations of ecclesiastical leaders. Nazianzen's

model may well have derived from a Greco-Roman political ideal that he Christianized and adapted to the leader in the church. In the Platonic tradition, the ruler-philosopher prepared himself for public service through periods of withdrawal characterized by *otium* or *apragmon*.[108] Notwithstanding these Hellenic roots, future readers of Gregory's works would see in his ideal bishop the outlines of the philosopher of their own day, namely the cenobitic monk. For evidence, we need only look to the fifth century, by which time a large number of episcopal candidates in Asia Minor were being recruited from monastic communities.

6

John Chrysostom:
The Model Monk-Bishop
in Spite of Himself

Despite a certain ambivalence he expressed about both the status of monks and the qualifications of bishops, perhaps no one better exemplifies the spread and influence of the monk-bishop ideal in the generation after Basil the Great than John Chrysostom. The notion of the model bishop that John himself delineated did not precisely coincide with later developments or with the emphases of those who appealed to John as an example. Nevertheless, his own writings and the depictions of his life and ministry by later admirers served to advance a monastic model of leadership in the church.

To a great extent John's life followed the pattern of the famous monk-bishops of Cappadocia. Born in Antioch to a fairly wealthy and educated family, John studied for a time under the famous rhetorician Libanius. Despite extraordinary gifts and the potential for a promising career in law or the civil service, in his late teens John abandoned pagan learning and chose instead to study the Scriptures and theology. He was baptized in 368, was singled out by Meletius of Antioch for his admirable character, and served in some capacity as an assistant to the renowned bishop for a period of approximately three years.[1] Palladius, John's fifth-century biographer, says nothing about the precise nature of John's responsibilities or connection with Meletius, but a brief account of this period in Socrates' Church History offers some interesting and relevant information that is corroborated in John's own writings. The fifth-century historian does not mention the influence of Meletius at this point in John's life. Rather, he reports that when John was on the verge of entering the legal profession he was put off by "reflecting on the restless and unjust course" of those who pursue such careers. As a result, Socrates continues,

> he was turned to the more tranquil mode of life, which he adopted, following the example of Evagrius . . . Accordingly he laid aside his legal habit, and applied his mind to the reading of the sacred scriptures, frequenting the church with great assiduity. He moreover induced Theodore and Maximus, who had been his fellow-students under Libanius the sophist, to forsake a profession whose primary object was gain, and embrace a life of greater simplicity. Of these two persons, Theodore afterwards became bishop of Mopsuestia in Cilicia, and Maximus of Seleucia in Isauria. At that time being ardent aspirants after perfection, they entered upon the ascetic life, under the guidance of Diodorus and Carterius, who then presided over a monastic institution [asketerion]. The former of these was subsequently elevated to the bishopric of Tarsus . . . Now John was then living on the most intimate terms with Basil, at that time constituted a deacon by Meletius, but afterwards ordained bishop.[2]

I have cited this passage at some length because of its particular bearing on John's early exposure to models of asceticism and leadership. Reflecting back on this period in his De sacerdotio, John describes his intention "to pursue the blessed life of solitaries and the true philosophy" along with his friend Basil.[3] However, he also reveals that he was living at home with his mother at this time, for her entreaties dissuaded him from his plan to lodge with his fellow student and friend. On the one hand, then, the word asketerion in Socrates' account should not be understood as any kind of monastery; on the other hand, it clearly encompassed more than the necessary academic training for those aspiring to careers in the clergy.[4] Nor should this period be viewed merely as a natural step for John in his pursuit of a clerical career, a socially acceptable and financially remunerative profession.[5]

Though a career in the church by the end of the fourth century was a respectable alternative for educated, well-born young men, we must not overlook the distinctively ascetic component of the community of disciples gathered around Diodore and Carterius. J. N. D. Kelly has argued that the group to which John belonged resembled the characteristically Syrian bnay qyama, literally "sons of the Covenant," discussed in Chapter 1.[6] These young men might live with the clergy of a local church or remain at home, but members of such brotherhoods committed themselves in a covenant to Christ and to a life of celibacy, prayer, and renunciation. They served the clergy in various pastoral and liturgical functions and therefore formed a natural pool from which local bishops might draw to fill clerical vacancies in the church. We find hints of the kind of life John's ascetic circle pursued in his letter *Ad Theodorum lapsum,* probably written c. 368 to entreat his young friend Theodore to return to the brotherhood he had recently abandoned for more worldly pursuits. The community was clearly committed to ascetic life as well as serious study of the Scriptures. John refers to a register or enrollment list of brothers (*katalogos tōn adelphōn*) from which Theodore has blotted out his name, and he speaks of a covenant made with Christ (*pros ton Christon sunthēkas katepatēsas*) involving prayer, celibacy, and various forms of self-denial.[7] Though there is no mention of a vow of any kind, several passages in the letter describe the common values and elements of the daily routine of the young men that are reminiscent of monastic life. Reminding his lapsed friend of his former manner of life, John writes:

> Delicacy of food was disregarded and extravagant attire disdained, all pride was put down, and all zeal for profane wisdom was wholly transferred to the divine oracles; whole days were spent in reading, and whole nights were devoted to prayers; no mention was made of the glory of your patrimony, nor any thought taken of wealth. You knew that to clasp the knees and run to the feet of the brothers is superior to all high birth.[8]

While Diodore of Tarsus is best known as a biblical scholar, particularly for his emphasis on a more literal and historical interpretation of Scripture that characterized Antiochene exegesis, he was also a noted ascetic. Indeed he was so austere in his practice of ascetic disciplines that he harmed himself physically through excessive rigor, a fact that provoked the scornful chastisement of Emperor Julian and a pattern that would be followed by John himself.[9] Evidence that Diodore had been John's teacher and spiritual mentor for some time is supplied not only by Socrates but also by John himself in a speech given in Diodore's honor some years later. Preaching to his congregation in Antioch c. 392 John refers to Diodore, at that time already a bishop, as his teacher and spiritual father.[10] Reflecting on their earlier relationship while John was still serving as a deacon in Antioch, he remembers that Diodore himself used to call him the "staff of Moses," a phrase suggesting that both men, like the Cappadocians, viewed the Old Testament patriarch as a model of ecclesiastical leadership. John describes the bishop's previous praise of him, for which he now seems to be returning the favor, as a demonstration of Diodore's *philoteknia*. He goes on to praise his mentor's ascetic virtues and teaching of the Scriptures, comparing him with such biblical figures as Elijah and John the Baptist.[11] Finally, it should be borne in mind that at the time of their early association Diodore was already celebrated as an ascetic and a biblical scholar and was an ordained priest of the church at Antioch, where he had assumed additional pastoral and administrative duties during the absences of the exiled Bishop Meletius.

Thus, although some of the details remain blurred, John seems to have passed his earliest formative years as a committed Christian in the context of a group of like-minded ascetics who were both ardent students of Scripture and highly involved in service to the church. One of the mentors of these devoted young men was a master of asceticism and a teacher of the biblical text. This same Diodore, who corresponded amiably with Basil of Caesrea,[12] was closely connected with both Bishop Meletius of Antioch and his successor, Bishop Flavian. He served actively as a priest during John's youth and young adulthood and would later become bishop of Tarsus (378). Moreover, John himself, as well as each of the other three young men mentioned by Socrates as forming part of Diodore's scholarly, ascetic coterie—Theodore of Mopsuestia, Maximus of Seleucia, and Basil (most likely) of Raphanea—would all eventually rise to the episcopal dignity.

Toward the end of this three-year period during which Chrysostom was both studying and serving as the bishop's personal assistant, Bishop Meletius ordained him lector. Before receiving any further promotions, however, the young man retreated to the neighboring mountains to pursue a life of strict ascetic discipline under the tutelage of an aged Syrian hermit. So much we learn from Palladius, though the facts remain sketchy at best.[13] Judging from some of John's own reflections on this period, his environment might best be described as semi-eremitic, for he was clearly in contact with other monks besides his elderly ascetic mentor.[14] After four years in this setting, John retreated into even greater solitude, living for another two years alone in a cave. During this time his ascetic rigors so damaged his health that he was forced, according to

Palladius, to return to the city. Thus, after approximately six years of monastic withdrawal in the mountains and caves, John returned to Antioch, where he continued to serve the church under Bishop Meletius. In 381 he was ordained deacon, in 386 priest, and in 398 he reluctantly accepted consecration as bishop of Constantinople. His tenure in episcopal office would be quickly overshadowed by imperial and ecclesiastical intrigues in which he was involuntarily enmeshed. Throughout his ecclesiastical career, however, Chrysostom was renowned not only as a great preacher but as also a zealous reformer and a strong advocate of the monastic life.

Before examining Chrysostom's magisterial work *On the Priesthood,* we would do well to consider a few earlier writings that reflect directly on his premonastic and monastic experience and that will help to illumine our consideration of his later, mature treatment of church leadership. Two of his earliest writings, *A Comparison between a King and a Monk* and *Against the Opponents of the Monastic Life,* deal extensively with the subject of monasticism.[15] In fact their themes and emphases are so similar that despite a considerable difference in style between the two treatises, they have often been ascribed to the same period of John's career, the years immediately following his return from monastic solitude.[16] In view of John's very technical use of the *synkrisis,* one of the progymnasmatic forms traditionally taught in schools of rhetoric, as well as his use of phrases from the speeches of Libanius, Kelly has argued that the *Comparatio* belongs to John's premonastic period, when he had just completed his study of rhetoric and while he was still under the influence of Diodore's ascetic school. Both works express a broader apologetic against contemporary paganism in Antioch.[17] John defends Christian monasticism against its pagan despisers, presenting monastic life as a heavenly *politeia* rivaling the Hellenic ideal of the city and the benefits of Greek culture. Especially in the *Comparatio,* the monk rather than the pagan emperor represents the ideal of the true philosopher. John clearly views the ascetic life as the ideal for all leaders, civil as well as ecclesiastical. In *Against the Opponents,* for example, he notes that "even in government you will see that those who become famous are not the ones who live in wealth, luxury, and abundance, but rather those who live a life of poverty, simplicity and modesty."[18] Finally, both treatises also present monasticism as the angelic life, therefore as the Christian way of life par excellence.[19] They function as protreptic works inciting Christians and pagans alike to abandon the pursuit of wealth and worldly success and to embrace the true philosophical life of the monk.

Against the Opponents is particularly relevant to our discussion of ascetic ideals and the church, for besides revealing his esteem for ascetic life, which persisted throughout his career despite certain caveats, it also gives indications of John's early association of monks with the broader Christian community. The treatise was obviously written in the context of some opposition and hostility toward monks on the part of pagans and even Christians in Antioch. In response to this antimonastic spirit Chrysostom portrays monasticism as the authentic life of all true Christians. Instead of being persecuted, monks should be the subjects of imitation, he argues. Not only are they paragons of Christian perfection against a backdrop of urban corruption, but they represent the highest ideals of Hellenic culture as well, for they embody the virtues of the noblest pagan philosophers.[20] They also exemplify the true goals of Hellenic *paideia*. Even many great pagans despised or belittled the study of rhetoric, devoting their lives instead to "the branch of philosophy concerned with behavior."[21] The end of *paideia* is to form young people in virtue, Chrysostom suggests, a goal supremely promoted by monastic training and all too often undermined by contemporary rhetorical education. Indeed a liberal arts education, so cherished by cultured Christians as well as pagans, is unnecessary and often invidious to faith. Parents should therefore entrust their children to monks for their nurture and training.[22]

John does not believe the monastic life is the only means of salvation, but the type of life the monks lead is the standard for all Christians. "You deceive yourself and are greatly mistaken if you think that there is one set of requirements for the person in the world and another for the monk . . . Nor do the Scriptures know anything like this, but they want everyone to live the life of monks."[23] Considering the tremendous difficulty of living virtuously in the world, the good parent dares not spare his child the aid of a monastic upbringing. Realizing, no doubt, the hardness and impracticability of such a recommendation, later in the treatise John softens this proposal by suggesting that children be so committed only for a time, with the assumption that they will eventually return to their church and community ready to serve.

This concession also reveals the close connection already present in

John's thinking between monks and Christians living in the world. "Therefore, let us call them back only when they have become strong and able to render service to others," he advises. "Then you will see the benefits of philosophy, when they heal people suffering with incurable diseases, when they are hailed as benefactors, patrons and saviors to all, when they live like angels among people on earth, when everyone turns to look at them." Elsewhere in the treatise he presents a similar vision of monks as patrons and advisers of emperors, comforters of those who suffer, and models for Christians living in the world.[24] In fact he assumes that many would live and serve actively in the city were it not for the persecution they faced there on account of their righteousness and the threat that urban evils posed to their philosophy.[25] John's convictions about the necessary involvement of monks in the life of the church are by no means limited to this early tract. He is explicit in many later homilies about the crucial roles monks have to play, upholding the church in prayer, engaging in charitable work, evangelizing, serving as witnesses to God's salvation and coming kingdom and as models for all Christians.[26] In fact, it is noteworthy that Chrysostom devoted no single work to monasticism as a separate institution. He treats the concerns of monastic life only with reference to the life and mission of the church as a whole.

It may be precisely because of the failure of monks to serve the broader Christian community as he envisioned that John became slightly disillusioned or at least sobered with respect to the monastic vocation. While he maintained his enthusiasm for monastic ideals throughout his life, fairly early in his ecclesiastical career he expressed disappointment about certain characteristic foibles of monks. Several passages of his treatise *De compunctione,* probably composed shortly after *Against the Opponents* and likely during John's diaconate (381–386), offer hints of his concerns.[27] His criticisms center on a disengagement from the world, or more specifically from the church, that John finds reprehensible. In particular he censures monks who decline ecclesiastical responsibility or complain about the constraints such ministry might impose: "For generally all the monks, if someone asks them to perform any [ecclesiastical] ministry, will immediately ask first of all whether they will find time for repose or whether the petitioner can secure them rest, and to and fro the word *rest* is bandied about. Why do you speak this way, oh man? Why do you who travel the steep path ask about rest, and you who command that one enter through the narrow gate seek the wide? What could be worse than such distortion?"[28] He goes on to confess his own petty preoccupations when he first embarked on the monastic course, in light of the far more ponderous needs of the church and the world.

In the second book of this treatise he appeals to the examples of the apostle Paul and King David as models of the love of God and the contrition of heart that ought to characterize all Christians. While *Against the Opponents* lavished unmitigated praise on monks, his descriptions of biblical saints in *De compunctione* reveal a slightly tempered perspective. Isolation and solitude are no guarantee of virtue or sanctity, he suggests: only a heart inflamed with love produces such godly character. Such was the heart of Paul, who was truly "crucified to the world." While "moving about amidst cities, he was as absent from things present as we are absent from the bodies of the dead."[29] In a similar vein Chrysostom compares David explicitly with monks. Although he lived in the city and was burdened with the cares of administering the kingdom, "he maintained his yearning for Christ more ardently than those who live in solitude."[30] Solitude of purpose superseded solitude of place in John's thinking. This internalization of the monastic ideal of withdrawal, similar to what we have seen in the writings of the Cappadocians, enabled him more easily to transfer monastic principles to the Christian community as a whole and to the ecclesiastical hierarchy in particular.

Though John's experience with monastic factions in Constantinople would moderate his praise for monks, his admiration for the monastic way of life, rightly pursued, never subsided. Even before his rise to the episcopate, however, his increasing preoccupation with life in the city as a deacon and priest in Antioch caused him to focus attention on the needs of the church in a very secular setting. Combined with the ascetic values nurtured during his training under Diodore and his monastic experience on Mt. Silpios, the context of the city, as much as the virtues of the monk, shaped his model of leadership for the church. Similarly, his experience in church office came to influence his perception of monks and monasticism. In particular, he saw ever more clearly the importance of monks actively serving the Christian community and its leaders. Developing themes and concerns expressed in *De compunctione,* at one point John breaks off his lofty reflections in *The Incomprehensible Nature of God* to comment on the proper relation of monks to the church, and particularly to the church hierarchy. His comments reflect a growing concern about potential flaws or inadequacies of monastic life and a simultaneously strong emphasis on ecclesiastical authority, shifts in perspective that would increasingly mark his priestly and episcopal career:

> Let all monks, those who have taken possession of mountain peaks and who have crucified themselves to the world in every respect, hear these words. Let them, according to the power that is theirs, assist those in positions of leadership in the church; let them anoint those men with prayers in loving unity, being aware that if they do not assist in every way those who have been elevated by God's grace and have taken up cares of so many kinds, they have lost the total reward of their way of life and vitiated all their religious devotion.[31]

Chrysostom's fullest treatment of church office is undoubtedly his celebrated treatise *De sacerdotio*, or *On the Priesthood*. Written c. 390, when he had already been serving as a priest in Antioch for several years, the work purports to be an apology for his resistance to ordination some twenty years earlier.[32] In the first of six books that comprise the dialogue, John recounts how he and his boyhood friend Basil had heard rumors of a plan to ordain them and agreed to act in unison if such an advance were made.[33] Despite this pledge, John was convinced of his own unworthiness for the priesthood and certain of his friend's perfect suitability for the office. Thus, when the bishop came to consecrate the two young men, John fled while Basil unwillingly submitted to the yoke in the belief that his friend had done likewise. John later justified his deception by claiming that he was acting out of the highest interests of the church. Until recently most Chrysostom scholars have been highly skeptical of this mise-en-scène for the treatise, denying its historical basis. While the dialogue form of the work indeed gave John freer play with events, more recent scholarship has reestablished the underlying historicity of his autobiographical allusions.[34] It seems, then, that at the time of writing, John still faced some resentment about his earlier refusal of church office and wanted to defend his motivation for initially avoiding ordination.

Like the three Cappadocians, John was deeply troubled by the poor quality of ecclesiastical leadership in his day.[35] He shared with Gregory Nazianzen a lofty view of church office along with a sense of his own unworthiness for this charge. But in *De sacerdotio*, inspired at least in part by Gregory's Oration 2, Chrysostom's treatment of the priesthood is broader in scope.[36] Both authors were motivated by the desire to justify their flight from the burden of ecclesiastical responsibility. John, however, sought also to deter the many who were overly ambitious for church office. The hurried selection and ordination of unfit leaders lay at the root of the great troubles in the church, John affirms in his treatise.[37] Ecclesiastical authority itself is not bad, he declares, but rather the thirst for domination and power that has so infiltrated the clergy. Indeed bishops are often no better than civil rulers who distribute honors not according to virtues but on the basis of wealth, seniority, or prestige. As a result, men who are "evil and completely unworthy" are entrusted with the most holy and fearful things of God while those who are truly qualified are expelled from their offices.[38]

In such passages John refers to what he considered the scandalous process of choosing priests and bishops in his day. Like Basil of Caesarea and Gregory Nazianzen, he decries the factionalism, favoritism, and scheming that characterized episcopal appointments as much as the envy and ambition of those who vied for the highest offices. Moreover, if the Constantinian regime had transformed the status of priests and bishops, their rank and privileges only increased with the Theodosian triumph. In his farewell address in Constantinople Nazianzen had lamented the pomp and ceremony that accompanied episcopal elections. Chrysostom feared that such high honors would provoke the clergy to pride and vainglory and would adversely affect the motivation of potential episcopal candidates.[39] Expressing these concerns in his commentary on Acts, he wrote, "We run after this [the episcopate] just as we do after the dignities of the world. That we may have glory with men, we lose ourselves with God."[40]

While condemning such abuses and presenting his own defense in his treatise *On the Priesthood,* John also gives a detailed and eloquent exposition of the duties, demands, and dignity of the sacerdotal office. Chrysostom uses the word *hierosunē* (priesthood) to encompass both priests and bishops, though he sometimes employs the term *episkopos* to emphasize the extent of responsibilities incumbent upon a bishop alone.[41] He viewed the priesthood as an exalted calling, surpassing the rank of royalty and even superior to the monastic vocation.[42] The responsibilities of the priest are diverse, requiring a wide range of practical skills as well as the "virtue of angels," a lifestyle John often identified with monastic life.[43] Elsewhere in the treatise also he describes the priesthood in angelic terms, for while Nazianzen and others viewed the ordained clergy as a type of the priests and prophets of Israel, Chrysostom saw the Christian priesthood as a divine or heavenly order, a ministry instituted by the Holy Spirit: "For the priestly office is discharged on earth, but it ranks among heavenly ordinances. And this is very fitting, for no human being, nor angel, nor archangel, nor any other created power, but the Paraclete himself instituted this order and persuaded men, while still remaining in the flesh, to represent the ministry of angels."[44] Unlike Nazianzen, John devotes considerable attention to the liturgical functions of the clergy. He speaks of the holy and awe-inspiring sacraments over which the priest presides, particularly baptism and the Eucharist, as evidence of the great dignity of this office and demanding of the most pure and holy life.[45] His treatment of the minister's priestly role, as well as his prophetic and pastoral duties, may reflect an intention to offer a fuller theological exposition of church office in contrast to Nazianzen's more extempore responses to contemporary episcopal ills. In any case, John spares few details in describing the manifold tasks and burdens of ecclesiastical office—from the diligent preparation of effective sermons to the visitation of widows and virgins, patronage of the poor, care for the sick and needy, administration of justice, and careful management of church finances.[46]

Since *De sacerdotio* was written by a priest who was also intimately acquainted with monastic life, it is not surprising that ascetic ideals often enter into his discussion of church office. However, John does not present monastic virtues as the only requirement or even the main one for priestly or episcopal ministry. In fact in several sections of the treatise he describes the piety and discipline of the monk only to show the inadequacy of such virtues for the demands of ecclesiastical leadership. Reflecting on Christ's exchange with Peter in John 21, Chrysostom remarks that Christ does not say to this apostle, If you love me, practice fasting, sleeping on the ground, prolonged vigils, or any particular deeds of justice or mercy. Rather, he instructs his disciple, "Tend my sheep."[47] In a similar vein John argues that mortification of the body and other ascetic rigors are insufficient to produce the discernment and vigilance required of a leader in the church. Indeed the isolated and inactive life of monks may hide the defects of some men, while those who serve the church in public must expose their souls to all.[48] In another passage he points out that even the example of an apostolic life is of no avail in disputing heresy and false doctrine, yet this is the constant struggle of the priest.[49]

Scattered references to the ascetic life occur throughout *De sacerdotio,* but John devotes all of Book 6 to a series of comparisons between clergy and monks. He gives numerous examples of how priests and bishops face greater temptations, trials, and demands than do monks who dwell in solitude. For this reason, John argues, priests need even greater purity, discipline, and virtue.[50] Not only is the ascetic life alone inadequate preparation for leadership in the church, but John expresses serious misgivings about ordaining monks to such positions. He considers most monks ill-prepared for the tasks of the priesthood. Living in isolation and attending only to their own progress in virtue, they lack the experience and training to ward off worldly temptations, to serve the diverse needs of the multitude, and to govern the church.[51]

One might easily conclude from such passages that John had lost his enthusiasm for monastic life, but this would be an overstatement of his sentiments. Within a year of completing his dialogue on the priesthood, Chrysostom would be lauding monks as "beacons who give light to the entire world."[52] He encouraged his congregation in Antioch to visit monks in the nearby wilderness, and he specifically urged fathers to visit holy men with their adolescent sons.[53] Moreover, despite his reservations about monks in church office, he admits in *De sacerdotio* that some who had been chosen from the ranks of monks had shone in the exercise of ecclesiastical authority.[54] His concerns in this treatise reflect convictions already expressed earlier—both positively, in *De oppugnatores,* and negatively, in *De compunctione.* Monks ought to be involved in the life of the Christian community and not obsessed with their own solitude or preoccupied with thoughts of their own salvation. As he puts it in *De sacerdotio,* "Training oneself [in virtue] results only in one's own advantage but the benefit of the pastoral function extends to all the people."[55] While not denying the benefits of monastic life, in such passages he clearly places a higher value on the function of the priest.

Nevertheless, John describes paradigmatic priests and bishops in terms that reflect ideals of the contemplative or monastic life. First of all, their pastoral role as ecclesiastical leaders demands qualities and strategies of the spiritual father, or the abba of the desert. They must set a consistent saintly example, like that of the apostle Paul. They must possess discernment, discretion, and intuition so as to provide individualized guidance and apply gradual, gentle, and apt correction to disciples under their direction.[56] Moreover, those who receive the dignity of ecclesiastical office are "as if they had surpassed human nature, as if they had been released from our passions." As we have seen, he compares them with angels, a metaphor he often uses for monastics, demanding of church leaders even greater purity, virtue, and self-mastery than that expected of monks.[57] What is needed, John insists in response to the perplexity of his friend Basil, are men who demonstrate the attributes of monks yet manage to maintain those qualities while living in the world: "When examining candidates for the priesthood one should not even consider those [worldly ones] but rather one, if such a one exists, who while living and associating with the crowd is able to keep unharmed and unshaken the purity, serenity, holiness, steadfastness, sobriety and all the other virtues which distinctively belong to monks to an even greater degree than those who live in solitude." In a passage describing the diverse and burdensome duties of the priest or bishop, John expresses a similar sentiment: "He must know all the affairs of life no less than those who live in the world, but he must be free from all these affairs even more than the monks who occupy the mountains."[58]

Chrysostom hoped that church office would be reformed by the introduction of leaders committed to the ascetic life who were also able to teach, lead, and maintain their sanctity in a demanding role as well as a corrupt and provocative environment. For John this ideal was not merely theoretical. Bishop Flavian of Antioch, who ordained him to the priesthood and whom he eulogized in his first homily delivered on the day of his ordination, served as a model of the type of bishop John endorsed. Though not a monk, Flavian had pursued an ascetic life in the world before being elevated to ecclesiastical office. Despite an opulent upbringing, he exercised self-control, mastered his appetite, scorned the easy life, and embraced a life of poverty.[59] He compares Flavian with Abraham and especially with Moses, a favorite model of leadership for the Cappadocians.[60] Once raised to the episcopal dignity, and even in his old age, the bishop continued to practice ascetic disciplines. Yet he always exercised moderation, John explains, so as not to impair his ability to serve the church. While he carefully guarded his own life, Flavian spared no effort to join in the struggles of others and to help those who navigate to steer their ships safely.[61]

Such a man was Chrysostom's ideal for the office of bishop. Neverthe-less, he was well aware of the crucial roles that monks could play in po-sitions of ecclesiastical authority. As bishop of Constantinople John re-served primarily for monks the leadership of the church's missionary activity since he viewed their lives as symbols of salvation and as pecu-liarly suited to this vital apostolic task. He sent monks as missionaries to the Goths, to Phoenicia, and to various other locations.[62] He involved monks and nuns in the work of charitable institutions in Constanti-nople.[63] He also employed many monks as personal advisers and close collaborators. As noted above, even in *De sacerdotio,* which exalts the priesthood as higher or more valuable than the monastic state, John ac-knowledges that several monks who had been ordained had fulfilled their charge and served the church brilliantly. He himself ordained some as deacons and priests and gave them pastoral tasks. It seems that he also consecrated several monks to episcopal office. We know for certain of Heraclides, in Ephesus, whom he ordained in the wake of his deposi-tion of thirteen simoniac bishops in Asia Minor, but there were very likely others.[64] Prominent among those monks he influenced and possi-bly ordained was his deacon Palladius, the future bishop of Helenopolis, who was devoted to Chrysostom and would write the main account of his mentor's life.[65]

Unfortunately for John, neither his employment of monks nor his ex-perience and general advocacy of monastic life endeared him to the monks under his jurisdiction as bishop of Constantinople. The story of his heavy-handed efforts to control monastic life, on the one hand, and his persecution by monks, on the other, has been recounted in some de-tail.[66] Indeed some scholars have attributed John's attempted ordinations of monks to an endeavor to control the movement by clearly subordinat-ing monks to his episcopal authority. Though he had earlier complained of the isolation and inactivity of monks, their disengagement from soci-ety and from a church that badly needed their services, in Constantino-ple John encountered monks of a very different sort. Isaac the Syrian, the leader of monks and monasteries in Constantinople during his episco-pate, is the main representative of a distinctive type of monasticism that characterized the movement in the capital and that proved to be a thorn in the flesh for John.[67] As Gilbert Dagron has demonstrated, early Con-stantinopolitan monasticism, connected with the foundational activities of such theologically suspect figures as Eustathius of Sebaste and Marathonius, had semi-Arian roots, was primarily an urban phenomenon, and was marked by a series of conflicts with the hierarchy of the church.[68] Thus, while John's contemporary and nemesis, Bishop Theophilus of Alexandria, had at his disposal a disciplined cohort of monastic shock troops, Chrysostom was faced with a wandering, loosely organized, independently minded, international community of monks. These monks took an extremely active role in affairs of the city and the church, functioning as a kind of intra-urban lobby that frequently resisted episcopal authority. Confrontations with monastics of this type, particularly with the archimandrite Isaac, lie behind Sozomen's description of John's perspective on monasticism and his relations with Constantinopolitan monks:

> He highly commended those who remained in quietude in the monasteries and practiced philosophy there . . . But the monks who went out of doors and made their appearance in cities, he reproached and regarded as insulting philosophy. For these causes, he incurred the hatred of the clergy, and of many of the monks, who called him a hard, passionate, morose, and arrogant man. They therefore attempted to bring his life into public disrepute, by stating confidently, as if it were the truth, that he would eat with no one, and that he refused every invitation to a meal that was offered him.[69]

Dagron has duly emphasized the opposition between desert and city in John's monastic thought and suggests that he could not conceive of monasticism other than as a *desert* tradition.[70] Given the opposition he faced from monks in Constantinople, one can better understand John's apparent desire to keep monks on their mountaintops or otherwise far removed from the cities of the empire. But in light of his frequent praise for ascetic ideals in general and his expressions of esteem for the life of monks in particular, we ought not to conclude too quickly that John had become ideologically or systematically opposed to urban asceticism. First of all, his general ambivalence and apparent inconsistencies on issues such as monastic life have been shown to be less whimsical and more methodical than has often been assumed. Typical is his homily on the statues, where John congratulates monks for interceding on behalf of the citizens of Antioch in the aftermath of their treasonous acts, and then praises them even more highly for quickly withdrawing from the city after their intervention.[71] Moreover, although Dagron affirms that

there were no monks who actually supported the bishop in Constantinople, there was at least one urban ascetic circle that John admired and
that supported the bishop's ideals and reforms, namely the circle of virgins around the wealthy widow Olympias.[72] Here we find the kind of ascetics that John wished would characterize the monastic movement as a
whole: self-sacrificing, unobtrusively involved in service to the church,
and firmly committed and submitted to the authority of the bishop—
that is, to John himself. It would seem, then, that it was not so much the
residence of monks near cities that bothered Chrysostom, for from his
earliest writings he implied that ascetics should be constructively involved in the life of the church. It was the unruliness, independence,
and rebelliousness of monks, their lack of respect for the ecclesiastical
hierarchy, that John decried.

Whatever his personal concerns about monks or his expectations of
leaders in the church, the portrayal of Chrysostom's life, as much as his
actual career and writings, demonstrates the new image of the bishop
that had begun to take root in Asia Minor by the beginning of the fifth
century. If John himself was somewhat ambivalent about monks in
church office, his disciple Palladius was certainly not. The immediate
aim of his *Dialogue on the Life of St. John Chrysostom,* written shortly after John's death in 407, was to vindicate his hero from the false and
highly derogatory charges of his enemies.[73] However, Palladius's broader
objective was to present him as a model Christian bishop. He maintains
that this was the way John himself viewed his ministry, namely, "that he
was sent to serve as a model [*typos*] for bishops to follow in regard to his
manner of life."[74] This affirmation is followed by one of several descriptions of John's abstemious habits. The Deacon in the *Dialogue* explicitly
states that this account should be of help "for those who are ambitious
for the episcopate." Such men, he continues, "should be like the holy
John," who imitated the way of martyrs and coupled his management of
the churches with a rigorous ascetic life.[75] Particularly the last part of the
Dialogue is devoted to a description of John's exemplary way of life in
contrast to the evil and ambitious bishops who persecuted him. He is
compared with Moses both in his withdrawal from the world and in the
suffering he endured at the hands of men in authority.[76]

The image of John that emerges in the pages of the *Dialogue* is that of
the monk-bishop par excellence. Since his primary purpose was to reha-
bilitate John from false accusations leveled against him during his epis-

copate, Palladius devotes relatively little attention to the bishop's youth or the period of his priesthood. He does not, however, fail to mention John's early commitment to a life of asceticism. Describing his years of monastic solitude, Palladius recounts that John managed to suppress his bodily temptations during his first four years of austere self-discipline.[77] The young man then withdrew into a cave in complete isolation. There, over the course of another two years, he deprived himself of sleep in order to devote his energy relentlessly to the study of Scripture. So severe were John's habits, Palladius explains, that he damaged his gastric organs and kidneys. As a result of this sickness and as evidence of the Savior's providence, he was compelled to abandon his caves for the benefit of the church.

Though he left the mountains and caves for the city, he did not relinquish his ascetic way of life. He ended his days in a frail and emaciated body. In fact, Palladius has a great deal to say about John's abstemiousness with regard to food and drink, defending his much maligned eating habits as particularly appropriate to the study of Scripture.[78] He identifies John's predilection for solitude with John the Baptist's flight from the crowds and Jesus' withdrawal from the multitudes to a mountain. He points out that the prophets also withdrew from the crowds and stayed in the deserts.[79] Virtually ignoring John's acrimonious dispute with the monastic leader Isaac and the general resistance to his reforms on the part of Constantinopolitan monks, Palladius mentions Isaac only once, as "that street idler, the guide of false monks who wandered about saying bad things about the bishop."[80] He presents Chrysostom as a patron of monks, supporting and interceding for the monastic party in the controversy with Theophilus of Alexandria. Moreover, following the example of St. Paul, John's life was a model of temperance, simplicity, and piety for all men and women. Accordingly he is shown to have led even the common people to a stricter manner of life.[81]

Having himself dwelt among the monks of Alexandria, Nitria, and the Cells, Palladius exalts virtues and powers in the life of the bishop that were normally ascribed to the desert abba. Along with ascetic disciplines, he draws attention to John's unusual spiritual discernment or insight. In one instance the holy bishop is said to have known full well of a shameful plot against him.[82] Similarly, in exile outside Comana, John received a vision of the martyred bishop of the city foretelling his death. He accepted this oracle peacefully and prepared for his end, which came to pass the next day as predicted. He was buried in a martyr's shrine in the presence of a multitude of virgins, ascetics, and other holy men and women.[83] Alongside the sufferings he endured, John's life was accompanied by miraculous signs. For example, on the event of his exile "the angel of the church accompanied him as he left," unable to bear the evil wrought by the principalities and powers who had forced him to depart. What is more, the church itself was miraculously consumed in flames, starting with the throne on which John used to sit. "The flame looked for the expounder of the Word," Palladius explains, and "not finding him it consumed the church furnishings."[84] He attributes the conflagration to God's judgment and warning to evildoers. John's enemies, meanwhile, met with divine punishment through a variety of strange diseases and afflictions. The description of divine vengeance on the persecutors of the saintly monk-bishop is reminiscent of Nazianzen's account of God's chastisement of Emperor Valens for his decree of banishment against Basil.[85] In both cases the bishop's reputation as an ascetic and a holy man is linked to an endowment of extraordinary power or vivid manifestations of divine approval.

Finally, John's ascetic practices in no way vitiated his oversight of the churches or his diligent performance of pastoral duties. He is portrayed throughout the *Dialogue* as an ardent reformer, a just arbiter, and an indefatigable preacher and teacher of the Word. In addition to his efforts to reform the clergy, he designated the use of church funds to build hospitals and hospices paralleling the philanthropic institutions of Basil in Caesarea. According to Palladius, John's social endeavors, coupled with his condemnations of laxity, licentiousness, and avarice among clergy and laity alike, were the source of the many false charges trumped up against him. Nonetheless, as a result of his many reforms the church flourished and the city itself became marked by piety, sobriety, and Psalm singing.[86] In the closing pages of his biography Palladius eulogizes Chrysostom with a comparison that encapsulates the monk-bishop model he found in his mentor: "O blessed John, with what kind of words shall I weave an unfading crown to bring you? . . . Shall they be those words in the law spoken by Moses when he blessed the active Joseph and the contemplative Levi the priest (for I see them both in you)?"[87] He replies by quoting the blessing of Moses on the tribes of these two brothers, whom he uses to represent the active and contemplative life, respectively. The harmonious admixture of these two seemingly dissonant

modes of life, embodied in John Chrysostom, was Palladius's ideal for
the office of bishop.

In addition to portraying John as the model monk-bishop, the *Dialogue* also gives evidence for the growth of the monastic episcopate during this period, as does the author's more popular *Lausiac History*. Along
with seven or eight disciples of a certain monk Isaac who were ordained
by Theophilus "when he was still a lover of God," writes Palladius,
many disciples of another monk Isaac were also raised to the episcopate.[88] Outside Egypt a number of Chrysostom's supporters, whose trials
on his account are enumerated, were also monk-bishops. Palladius recounts how they endured imprisonment, beatings, tortures, and banishment for the sake of Christ.[89] The sufferings, ascetic disciplines, and charisma attributed to these bishops recall the extraordinary personalities
among the desert monks in his *Lausiac History* and in the *Apophthegmata
Patrum*. Like these more popular ascetic works, Palladius's *Dialogue* suggests a broader intention on the part of the author. He hoped not merely
to vindicate his friend and mentor but to present both John Chrysostom
and other monk-bishops as episcopal heroes, models for leadership in
the church.

Though John's ideal leader remained the ascetic living in the world,
monks themselves, rather than monastic virtues, were increasingly making their way into the episcopate. In spite of his reservations about the
ordination of monks, expressed most clearly in *De sacerdotio,* his own
words as much as his example were invoked in support of this practice.
After praising Chrysostom as "truly a bishop by his works" and noting
his special solicitude for monks, Callinicus, author of the mid-fifth-century *Vita Hypatii*, refers to an exhortation that John allegedly addressed
to the community of monks at Rouphinianai near Chalcedon: "You must
give account for the fact that you are hiding and not putting your lamp
on the lampstand. By refusing ordination you are causing others, whom
we do not know, to be ordained." Callinicus goes on to explain that one
of the brothers had bitten off his finger to disqualify himself for church
office.[90]

This is a rather surprising work in which to find a positive assessment
of John's episcopal authority vis-à-vis monks, for the monk Hypatius
himself resisted ordination, showed considerable independence from
the hierarchy of the church, and repeatedly undermined the authority of
his own bishop.[91] In short, he represented a form of monasticism that

John had denounced and that would soon be severely curtailed by the legislation of Chalcedon. Moreover, the laudatory words about John's relation to monks are immediately preceded by an equally praiseworthy description of his rival Isaac the Syrian, who used to regularly visit the monastery of Hypatius.[92] Writing some forty years after Chrysostom's episcopate but prior to the Council of Chalcedon, Callinicus discreetly avoids mention of their dispute. He did not wish to discredit his hero, a monk in the tradition of Isaac, nor did he want to highlight tensions between monks and the hierarchy of the church. But his juxtaposition of Isaac's leadership of the monasteries with the rebelliousness of some monks whom John hoped to ordain seems more than coincidental. In any case, whatever views John himself expressed, and however much or little he did to elevate monks to the priesthood or episcopate, he was remembered by future generations as a paradigmatic monk-bishop and a promoter of monks in church office.

III

The Triumph of an Ideal

7

From Nuisances to Episcopal Ideals: Civil and Ecclesiastical Legislation

The decades following Basil of Caesarea's episcopate were a period of gradual but steady progress in relations between the monastic movement and the church hierarchy. We have already examined the role of influential late fourth-century bishops and theologians in disseminating similar notions of spiritual authority. While they did not uphold a monolithic model and expressed different concerns and emphases with regard to episcopal leadership, in various ways they contributed to the increasing strength of a distinctly monastic episcopate in the churches of the eastern Roman Empire. Nevertheless, the writings of prominent bishops do not alone suffice to explain the changing perception of the monastic movement, the change in status of monks vis-à-vis the church hierarchy, and the influx of monks into the episcopate. These developments not only reflect the theological ideals of a monastic and ecclesiastical elite, but they also necessarily involved both the sanctions of imperial authority and the pressure of popular piety.

Imperial and ecclesiastical decrees of the fourth through sixth centuries documented developments between monasticism and the hierarchical church and also played a distinctive role in the increase of monastic bishops. In his writings on the interpenetration of church and state and the formation of secular and ecclesiastical law in late antiquity, Jean Gaudemet has noted several difficulties for the historian wishing to trace developments in the episcopate during this period. First, there has been relatively little research devoted to legal history in the period between the classical apogee and the Justinianic renaissance.[1] Fortunately, several more recent works have treated this period in greater depth.[2] Yet in mat-

163

ters pertaining to the episcopate we face the added problem of scanty information concerning the recruitment and social origin of bishops. Moreover, if imperial and conciliar decrees provide few details on issues of importance for the episcopate, they have even less to say about monks and monasticism prior to the Council of Chalcedon, although this reticence itself may have some bearing on our subject. Despite such limitations in considering the legal sources, we will proceed cautiously to try to discern the concerns and intentions of civil and ecclesiastical authorities in legislating on monks and monasticism, and particularly their view of the proper relation of monks to bishops.

In an important survey of Chalcedonian legislation regarding monasticism and the clergy, Leo Ueding remarked that prior to Justinian what is said about monasticism in Roman law amounts to a few details without synthesis.[3] The relative lack of attention to monasticism in the *Codex Theodosianus* reflects a broader reality suggested by the very structure of the text, namely that the subject of religious authority and belief was not traditional in Roman law and was therefore included as a new topic at the end of the compilation.[4] While there is certainly no systematic treatment of monasticism in the Code, a closer look at the details yields more than Ueding might lead us to believe. The earliest references to monks in imperial legislation are brief and scattered but primarily negative in tone. First, a decree of Emperors Valentinian and Valens in 370 censured "certain devotees of idleness [who] have deserted the compulsory services of the municipalities, have betaken themselves to solitudes and secret places, and under the pretext of religion have joined with bands of hermit monks [*monazontes*]."[5] The Count of the Orient is ordered to pursue these offenders and bring them back to their cities to fulfill their municipal obligations. A similar decree issued the previous year denounced those who had falsely donned the garb of philosophers to escape compulsory municipal duties.[6] In 398 a law forbade anyone "involved in public or private accounts" from being ordained after taking refuge in a church, insisting that such persons, "decurions, indeed, and all others who are called by a customary function to the duty that they owe," be returned immediately to their former condition.[7] None of these decrees occurs in Book 16, which treats affairs of the church, but they were rather directed against "fugitive decurions," a frequent and problematic phenomenon in the late empire, owing to the sinking social esteem of the curial order and its increasing financial burden.[8] In fact a novella of Valentinian III in 452 indicates that the monastic state continued to be used by some to escape their social status or evade compulsory public service. These persons—whether slaves, coloni, guildsmen, or decurions—were expressly forbidden to undertake clerical duties or to join with monks or monasteries.[9]

Monks, then, were not the explicit subject of the 370 decree and were described only as religious men who live in isolation. Nevertheless, they were seen to provide a refuge for delinquent civil servants. Emperor Valens, who came to power in 364, considered the monks of Egypt to be religious fanatics and agitators of sedition. His tribunes and their soldiers ravaged the monasteries of Nitria, killing many of the inhabitants; he condemned many monks to mines and quarries in distant provinces; and, according to Jerome, he passed a law constraining them to perform military service on pain of being clubbed to death.[10] The emperor's concerns about ascetics were not without justification, for even Cassian, an ardent supporter of the monastic movement, admitted that some monks of Egypt were actually frauds falsely living as solitaries and feigning humility to avoid discipline and responsibility.[11] But the emperor was probably less concerned about lazy or fraudulent monastics who gave the movement a bad name than about bands of pro-Nicene monks who conspired together against the Arian bishops, whom he favored.[12]

The next mention of monks chronologically in the Theodosian corpus occurs in Book 16 in a section entitled *De monachis,* the only title of the Code devoted explicitly to monks. It contains only two laws, the second a repeal of the first, yet both express concern about monks' involvement in urban affairs. In great cities of the East, the opposition of monks to social and political injustices, as well as the role they played in incidents of antipagan, antiheretical, and anti-Jewish violence, won them popularity with the masses and a reputation for inciting riots. The turbulence they inspired lies behind the first decree under this title, a constitution of Theodosius I in 390 requiring monks to remain in solitude and forbidding them to enter cities.[13] Though issued before the notorious destruction of the Serapeum in Alexandria, this decree followed an especially tumultuous period in Syria that saw the destruction of the pagan temple of Zeus in Apamea (c. 386), the razing of the Callinicum synagogue (388), the pillaging of temples and shrines around Antioch, and the demolition of a magnificent temple on the Persian frontier, most likely in Edessa.[14] As is made particularly clear in Libanius's famous oration *Pro templis,* composed in 386, such acts of religious violence often involved overzealous monks, that "black-robed tribe, who eat more than elephants and, by the quantities of drink they consume, weary those that accompany their drinking with the singing of hymns, [and] who hide these excesses under an artificially contrived pallor." It was members of this "scattered rabble" who ravaged temples and the estates on which they were situated.[15] These incidents occurred under the prefecture of the rabidly antipagan Spaniard Maternus Cynegius, whose wife, Libanius alleged, colluded with the monks in perpetrating such heinous crimes and bamboozling the emperor into betraying his own moderate character.[16] The antimonastic protests of notables like Libanius would have likely been countenanced by the new praetorian prefect of the East, the pagan Tatianus, who succeeded Cynegius in 388. It was under Tatianus's prefecture that the edict limiting the access of monks to cities was promulgated. Even the pious antipagan and generally promonastic emperor Theodosius, who issued the decree, must have recognized the dangers of fanatical bands of monks wreaking havoc in the populous cities and towns of the eastern Roman Empire. As he was already forced to admit to Ambrose concerning the Callinicum affair, the monks "commit many crimes."[17]

Not surprisingly the decree of 390 was revoked less than two years later, allegedly owing to the abuse of the earlier rescript by civil and military officials who had treated monks unjustly, but combined, no doubt, with the popularity of monks and their influence at the court of Theodosius I. Even in the abrogation of the law, however, the wording suggests a negative stance toward monks. They are now permitted ingress into towns not because of a new burst of favor or goodwill toward monks but to prevent their maltreatment at the hands of judges. Persecution could well turn monastic victims into martyrs, thereby increasing their popularity with the masses whose causes they often championed.[18] Similar concerns would be expressed again in subsequent years in both imperial and ecclesiastical sources, attesting to the growing presence and influence of monks in the urban setting. In 439 monks were barred entry to Constantinople unless duly furnished with a letter from their bishop.[19] Monastic factions in the capital were notoriously turbulent as well as influential. The Council of Chalcedon, which will be discussed more fully below, was especially harsh toward excommunicated monks who came to Constantinople to disturb the peace of the church. They were constrained to return to their solitude, forcibly if necessary.[20] Imperial legislation addressed this theme once again in 472. In a constitution of Leo included in the Justinianic corpus, monks were forbidden to leave their monasteries or to sojourn in cities, especially Antioch.[21] Should they be authorized to enter a city, they were expressly prohibited from discussing religion and provoking the people to revolt.

Another indication of annoyance, if not disfavor, with monks concerned their alleged vindication, detention, or harboring of condemned criminals. Clerics were also warned against such offenses, but monks in particular were taken to task. "It shall redound to the discredit of the bishops," warned a decree of 398, ". . . if they should learn that any of those acts which We prohibit by this law have been perpetrated by the monks in that part of a district in which they, the bishops, guide the people by instilling the doctrine of the Christian religion, and if they should not punish such violations."[22] This pronouncement, which occurs in a section of the Code devoted to criminal law, legal procedures, and appeals, reveals that monks were suspected by the temporal powers of lawless or disorderly behavior. At the same time it clearly placed them in subjection to episcopal authority, a factor that may account for the relative silence of imperial rulers with respect to monasticism. Even prior to the legislation of Chalcedon, which would more clearly define relations between monasticism and the church hierarchy, they considered monks, like clerics, to be the responsibility of bishops and therefore generally outside their direct sphere of jurisdiction.[23] In fact, one of the few laws touching on monastic life during the long reign of Theodosius II (408–450), and the only one actually included in his Code, placed monasticism squarely in the ecclesiastical realm. This constitution of 434 concerned the estates of monks, nuns, and clergy who died intestate.[24] Though the property of a deceased monk was to be incorporated into the decedent's monastery, characteristically, in light of imperial fiscal concerns, the law excepted those who were registered on the tax roles, were subject to the rights of a patron, or were obligated to the status of decurion. Expressing similar concerns about the illegitimate appropriation of property by ascetic communities, certain earlier decrees on heretics may have also had a broader target. It has been suggested that the *apotaktikoi* and *solitarii* condemned in the laws against the Manichees promulgated by Theodosius I in 381 and 382 actually included all Christian ascetics, whether orthodox or heterodox, who espoused radical doctrines or practices deemed socially dangerous to the rigid economic order of the empire.[25]

Much of this legislation suggests that the civil authorities of the late fourth and early fifth century regarded monks as little more than public nuisances who were to be tolerated whenever possible and controlled whenever necessary. Given the negative tenor of these decrees, it is surprising to find another, seemingly contradictory, side to imperial legislation on monks. The same law denouncing clerics and monks who attempted to protect criminals concludes with the suggestion that monks be ordained to church office: "From the number of these monks the bishops shall ordain clerics more suitably when, perchance, they think that they are in need of them."[26] Another law from this period urged the same practice of ordaining monks to fill the ranks of clergy. It added a sentence of warning, however, that helps to explain the motive of imperial authorities in issuing such a decree: "They [bishops] shall not incur disfavor by holding those persons who are bound by public and private accounts but shall have those already approved."[27] It has been suggested that this rescript of Arcadius and Honorius reflects intensified monastic influence at court after the death of Theodosius I, and this factor may well have played a role in the ruling.[28] However, considered together with the laws discussed above condemning fugitive decurions, we can surmise that the main concern of emperors was the attempt to evade compulsory public service or fiscal responsibilities by either attachment to a monastery or ordination to the priesthood.

By encouraging the ordination of monks, emperors could fulfill several objectives at the same time. They could better control unruly monks by placing the monastic movement squarely under the authority of the church hierarchy. They could stay the rising tide of curial flight by filling the clerical order with monks rather than illegal decurions. Finally, they could help meet the real needs of bishops who, if we believe the complaints of the Cappadocians, faced a lack of suitable candidates for ordination and themselves increasingly turned to monks for the priesthood and episcopate. While imperial legislators may not have been concerned to place more worthy candidates in positions of ecclesiastical authority, their decrees nonetheless sustained and even contributed to the spread of monks in church office.

Though it does not address the subject of monks at all, another decree in the Theodosian corpus is particularly revealing with regard to developing relations between the monastic movement and the church hierarchy. On the ascension of Theodosius I to the imperial throne, the Nicene cause finally triumphed. The new emperor soon published a series of laws intended to root out heresy and paganism in the empire. To set the standard for orthodoxy, in 381 he decreed that all churches must be in communion with a prescribed list of Nicene bishops.[29] Dissenting bishops would be expelled from their churches as heretics. It has been duly noted that Theodosius's enumeration of acceptable bishops corresponded to the recent decisions of the Council of Constantinople (381), for the eastern bishops had just approved a particular organization of the ecclesiastical hierarchy. Less apparent in this list, however, and surely not intentional in the emperor's nomination of bishops, is the close connection of many of them with the monastic movement. Of the eleven bishops named as the measure of orthodoxy for the Christian East, at least seven were either themselves former monks or else strong advocates of the monastic movement: Gregory of Nyssa, Amphilochius of Iconium, Diodore of Tarsus, Pelagius of Laodicea, Timothy of Alexandria, Optimus of Antioch, and Otreius of Melitene.[30] Thus, only a few years after the death of Basil of Caesarea the phenomenon of monks in the episcopate was clearly on the rise and implicitly sanctioned by imperial legislation.

In ecclesiastical law we find very little treatment of monasticism prior to Chalcedon.[31] A few earlier councils referred to consecrated virgins, and the Council of Laodicea (possibly c. 365) mentioned a distinct order of ascetics (*tou tagmatos tōn askētōn*) who were listed together with, but distinct from, the clergy.[32] Following the condemnation of ascetic abuses at the Synod of Gangra, however, few church councils contain any legislation directly pertaining to monks. Rules served as the earliest legal documents for the movement, and despite the tendency of imperial legislation to subject monks to their bishops, normally bishops exercised little or no authority over the life of the monastery. In fact we find hardly any suggestion in the sources that the establishment of monasteries necessitated even the prior acknowledgment of the bishop.[33] The few references to monks we do find in church law, however, attest the same tendencies with regard to monks and the church hierarchy that we have already seen in imperial legislation. They also foreshadow the decisions of Chalcedon and subsequent ecclesiastical legislation. The sixth Synod of Carthage (13 September 401) assumed or at least anticipated the ordination of monks, for it forbade bishops to ordain a monk from a monastery outside the bishop's own diocese.[34] The decisions of the Synod of Seleucia Ctesiphon (c. 410), connected with Bishop Maruta of Maipherqat and originating from Syria, had a great deal to say about monasticism.[35] The canons of this council decreed that a bishop must elect a chorepiscopus from the order of monks, and that monks were to be made priests to fill vacancies in villages where there were no *bnay qyama* who could be ordained to the priesthood. Canon 25 provided clear guidelines: "The bishop shall elect a man from the order of the monks, who is of (good) conversation, educated and has beautiful manners."[36] Several canons, however, emphasized the subordination of monks to the chorepiscopi of the region, who were in turn responsible for regular visitation of the monasteries.[37]

It is the bishop's authority over monks that is prominent in the canons of the Fourth Ecumenical Council, called by Emperor Marcian in 451 in the hope of bringing religious unity to the empire. In contrast to most earlier councils, the legislation of Chalcedon devoted considerable attention to the monastic movement. The increasing social, political, and theological engagement of monks in connection with Cyril of Alexandria and the Nestorian controversy, soon followed by the subversive activity of the archimandrite Eutyches, particularly escalated tensions between monks and the church hierarchy in Constantinople. These decades of turmoil, so graphically depicted for us in Dagron's masterful study "Les moines et la ville," set the stage for the monastic legislation of Chalcedon.[38] Monks or monasteries are at least mentioned, if not the primary subject, in ten of the thirty canons.[39] Echoing the tenor of imperial decrees that condemned monastic abuses, the Council of Chalcedon censured those who used monastic life as a pretext for causing disturbances in both church and state. This is the focus of canon 4 in particular.[40] It decreed that no monastery could be established without the consent of the bishop, that monks were subject to the bishop, that monks could not be involved in ecclesiastical or temporal affairs, and that monasteries could not admit a slave without the permission of his master. After censuring those who wandered indiscriminately from one city to the next, the canon stipulated that monks could not leave their monastery unless expressly requested to do so by the bishop in a case of necessity. Bishops, meanwhile, were charged to exercise careful oversight of the monasteries within their jurisdiction. Behind these decrees lay the specter of the archimandrite Eutyches, who had not only personally opposed his bishop and a synod of bishops but had also instigated a whole group of monks against the hierarchy in Constantinople. Insisting on the principles of *stabilitas loci* for monks, requiring their abstention from both secular and ecclesiastical affairs, and emphasizing the submission of monks to bishops, canon 4 of Chalcedon clearly defined the monastic state and became the foundation of all successive civil and canonical legislation regarding monasticism.[41]

Unruly and conspiratorial monks were the subject of several other canons. Canon 8 condemned clerics and monks who dared to rebel against their bishops, while canon 18 forbade them to form secret societies. Specifically it warned those who swore allegiances or plotted together against their bishops.[42] The organization of lawless and heretical monks was also in view in canon 23. Rebellious monastics could be particularly dangerous in the cities, especially in Constantinople, where they could incite the masses and upset the affairs of the church. Accordingly the council condemned clergy and monks who, without the permission of their bishop, came to Constantinople from distant provinces and stirred up trouble.[43] Such offenders were to be warned by the church and, if necessary, forcibly driven out of the capital city. As for monasteries, the subject of canon 24, once consecrated "in accordance with the will of the bishop," they must always remain monasteries and could no longer become lay habitations.[44] For ecclesiastical as well as secular authorities, then, the solution to actual or potential unruliness of monks was to affirm their subjection to the church hierarchy and to delegate to bishops the supervision of monastic institutions.

A superficial reading of the Chalcedonian legislation suggests that monks were perceived as nuisances not only by the state but also by the church. Closer inspection, however, reveals another aspect of relations between monks and the church hierarchy. Because of the primarily disciplinary nature of the canons, what is less obvious in this legislation is the degree to which monasticism was already integrated into the life of the church as a whole and into the hierarchy in particular. Along with consecrated virgins, monks were forbidden to marry. Alongside clergy and laity, they were warned against intervening in cases of simony.[45] Together with clergy, they were privileged with exemption from military and civil service, and they were subject to the same warnings against rebellion and conspiracy noted above.[46] Monks were also listed with bishops and clerics as those for whom involvement in temporal affairs was prohibited.[47] The tacit assumption in all these canons is that monks were a recognized and respected part of the church.

Canon 6 of Chalcedon goes further in this regard, pointing to the growing incidence of monks in church office. The canon denounced the practice of "absolute" ordinations and decreed that one could be ordained only to a particular church, martyrium, or monastery.[48] The reference to monasteries in this context indicates that the custom of ordaining a monk-priest to celebrate the divine service in large monasteries was already accepted. No less indicative of this practice are the references to ordained monks in other conciliar documents of the fifth century. Among the signatories of the deposition of Eutyches at the Synod of Constantinople in 448 there were twenty-three archimandrites, eighteen of whom were priests and one a deacon. While this is a particularly prominent example of this development among monastic leaders, it is by no means an exception.[49] Indeed, while Chalcedon officially made monasticism a canonical organ of the church, it actually served more to sanction earlier developments than to establish a legal basis for the movement.[50] Later ecclesiastical legislation provides further indications of the spread of ordained monks. We find several attempts to restrict bishops' rights to ordain monks and an emphasis on the necessary consent of the abbot.[51]

If the late fourth to early fifth century often saw "the collusion between episcopal power and the civil authorities, both held suspect by the monastic party,"[52] the Council of Chalcedon provided the basis for a new and long-lasting alliance between monasticism, the church, and the empire. On many counts the monastic legislation of Chalcedon echoed the canons of Gangra from a century earlier. Both condemned irregular, private meetings of monks; their abandonment of churches and regular liturgical gatherings; their formation of large ecclesiastically independent communities; their seditious intervention in the social order; the turbulence they inspired in the cities and towns by their excessive zeal; and their scorn for bishops and the church hierarchy. Though Gangra temporarily clipped the wings of certain ascetic enthusiasts who were particularly prevalent in Armenia, a chain of Eustathian-inspired monastic communities continued and thrived in the cities of the East, especially in Constantinople. However, Chalcedon pushed forever to the heretical fringes the popular, if ecclesiastically irreverent, forms of monastic life represented by the Eustathians, Macedonians, and Marathonians, and the partisans of Isaac the Syrian. Monasticism by no means retreated from the great cities of the eastern Roman Empire, where it was deemed particularly troublesome. But in place of the influential, largely independent monastic factions of previous decades, Chalcedon legislated a disciplined and stable monastic institution, respectful of the church hierarchy and acceptable to imperial authorities.[53] This kind of monasticism, now officially regulated by the church and sanctioned by the state, would be a vast, legitimate pool from which to draw future bishops and patriarchs. Indeed this process had already begun, and even the bishops of Constantinople who took the brunt of monastic factionalism in the early decades of the fifth century were themselves often monk-bishops. Especially after Chalcedon, however, civil, ecclesiastical, and monastic authorities tended to converge, if from somewhat different motives, in support of this paradigm of leadership.

Returning to the civil authorities, in the *Codex Justinianus* and the *Novellae* of Justinian, affairs of the church, including monasticism, received pride of place. In fact, Justinian eventually incorporated into civil law the canons of the first four ecumenical councils,[54] and his own legislation confirmed and expanded on the ecclesiastical decrees of Chalcedon concerning monasticism. The emperor legislated in great detail on monasteries and monastic life in keeping with his general enthusiasm for monasticism. It was also under Justinian (527–565) that decrees concerning the priesthood and the episcopate defined the legal status of church leaders for centuries to come. Since the time of Constantine, the late antique bishop operated increasingly in the sphere of the state as well as the church, embodying the mutual interaction of religious and secular spheres of interest. Thus, the political, social, and economic dimensions of the episcopate are evident in imperial edicts. What we find in Justinianic legislation is a sixth-century picture of the bishop from the viewpoint of the state.[55] Imperial pronouncements on the status of monasticism and on the requirements for higher church office reveal the increasing interconnection, both philosophical and official, of monastic and episcopal ideals.

The Justinianic legislation regarding monastic life is found primarily in the *Novellae*, a compilation of new laws passed by the emperor himself subsequent to the main work of codification. These decrees clarified and built on the canons of Chalcedon and earlier imperial edicts. However, it was Justinian who first gave monasticism its official and uniform character as well as its full institutional significance in state life.[56] On the one hand we find in imperial utterances a high regard for the monastic way of life. In 535 Justinian issued *Novella 5*, which is devoted exclusively to monasticism. The preface to this *novella,* Justinian's first ruling on the subject, described the monastic vocation in the following terms: "Monastic life is so honorable and can render the person embracing it so acceptable to God, that it removes from him every human blemish, declares him to be pure and conformed to natural reason, greatly enriched in understanding, and superior to human beings by virtue of his thoughts."[57] Within the same laudatory preface, the monastic life was explicitly linked with the offices of the bishop and the clergy, concerning which regulations were given immediately following those set forth for monks.[58] The same law also referred to monks deemed worthy of ordination to the clergy, instructing them to continue as priests in their monastic way of life and forbidding them to marry, even though marriage was still permitted for the secular clergy.[59]

A novella of 539 made it clear that monks were to be especially honored and protected by law. The preface explains that some ascetics, both monks and nuns, had been vexed by civil and military officials, forcefully removed from their monasteries, and obliged to appear before civil tribunals. As a response to these complaints the law decreed that civil judges had no right to hear the cases of monks and would be fined and censured for such action, for imperial officials ought to promote rather than hinder monastic life. Similarly, civil and military judges, as well as bishops and clergy, were to ensure that no one, especially actors and actresses, put on the monastic habit in jest or otherwise ridiculed the manner of life pursued by monks and nuns. Offenders of this law would be subject to corporal punishment or even exile.[60]

The monastic state was clearly held in high esteem throughout the Justinianic corpus. At the same time, however, there is no ambivalence about the status of monasticism as an institution. Monks, monasteries, and monastic life were definitely subordinated to the church hierarchy in this legislation, even surpassing the emphasis we have observed in the Chalcedonian canons. The relegation of monasticism to the oversight of bishops was clearly articulated already in the *Codex Justinianus*, but several later *novellae* expanded on the practical implications of this relationship.[61] Thus, for example, accusations and legal proceedings against monks were to be brought before local bishops rather than civil courts.[62] The founding of a new monastery, as well as a new church, required the approval of the bishop, and the bishop had to ascertain that any new institution had a sufficient endowment for its continued maintenance.[63] Men's and women's monastic houses were to be strictly separated, and the maintenance of discipline fell ultimately under the bishop's sphere of jurisdiction. Even the choice of an abbot required the examination and approbation of the bishop, a stipulation that did not appear in earlier legislation.[64] The bishop was also responsible for the installation of the new abbot.

The large majority of laws concerning the episcopate delineate the functions or duties of the bishop.[65] Those that outline the bishop's responsibilities vis-à-vis monastic life echo the legislation of Chalcedon and reaffirm the bishop's authority over the monastic institution. There is, however, at least one new element in the Justianianic legislation on requirements for episcopal office that suggests the increasing influence of monastic ideals on the conception of the model bishop. For the first time in civil or ecclesiastical legislation we find the stipulation that those ordained to the episcopate could not be married or have living children or grandchildren.[66] The motives underlying these decrees are diverse, not least of which are fiscal concerns. Since the time of Constantine, the wealth of bishoprics, especially in some large urban areas, had steadily increased. As a result, ecclesiastical legislation already required that the bishop's personal property be clearly distinguished from the property of the church.[67] Though the Justinianic decrees on episcopal celibacy did not treat these financial matters explicitly, the requirement of unmarried bishops with no heirs would clearly alleviate such concerns.[68] Other pastoral and theological reasons for this legislation were mentioned in the decrees themselves. No one burdened with everyday affairs, particularly the care of children, could devote himself fully to the divine liturgy and the affairs of the church. Moreover, the bishop was "the spiritual father of all the faithful." He had embraced the church as his wife, and all orthodox Christians were his children.[69] This idea was not new with Justianian, for the notion of the bishop's mystical bond with his church, comparable with the marriage relationship, had already been articulated by several theologians and churchmen of the patristic period.[70] Some eastern bishops appealed to this idea to support the prohibition of episcopal transfers, which had been decreed by canon 15 of Nicaea. But Jus-

tinian was the first to draw out its implications in such a way that episcopal celibacy was not only desirable but required by law.

None of the decrees prohibiting the marriage of bishops obliged the
episcopal candidate to take monastic vows. However, the same legislation shows strong links between the monastic vocation and episcopal office. Most obvious in this regard are the laws delineating prerequisites
for episcopal candidacy. To preclude overly hasty ordinations, it was decreed that a potential bishop had to have served as a cleric for at least six
months or else have made a monastic profession.[71] Indeed the monastic
state was the only route to the episcopate for some men. *Curiales* and *of-
ficiales,* frequently banned from church office in the past because of
obligatory municipal duties and financial responsibilities, now became
eligible for episcopal consecration, but only after a tenure of fifteen years
in a monastery.[72] Such laws indicate that the monastery was not only an
acceptable source of candidates for episcopal office but in fact a typical
one, at least by the mid-sixth century and probably earlier. Finally, if the
predominant influence of the monastic movement behind the requirement of episcopal celibacy has been questioned, certainly the Justinianic
prohibition of married bishops, which strictly delimited the pool of acceptable priests, strengthened the influence of monasticism in the future
of episcopal leadership. Such laws could have only increased an already
growing tendency to choose bishops from the ranks of monks.

Though imperial legislation was deemed an integral part of church
law in the Byzantine East, especially by the reign of Emperor Justinian,
the Council of Trullo (691–692), also known as the Quinisext Council,
set the ecclesiastical seal on the Justinianic decrees concerning clergy,
bishops, and monks.[73] Extremely conservative in its approach to earlier
canons, the council took for granted the legislation of Justinian and provided no further explanation for the decrees contained in the corpus. It
merely offered procedural regulations for the accession of married men
to the episcopal dignity. Not least of these was the reminder that the
bishop had to cease cohabiting with his wife.[74] Likewise the wife of the
prospective bishop had to be separated from her husband "by their mutual consent" and enter a convent, where she would be provided for by
the bishop.[75] Again there is no requirement here that the prospective
bishop take monastic vows. However the Trullan canons set the tone for
all future ecclesiastical legislation pertaining to bishops in the Christian

East, and the ordination of monks to the episcopate steadily increased, in practice if not by decree.[76]

Whatever difficulties the monastic movement had posed for earlier civil and ecclesiastical authorities, the Council of Chalcedon paved the way for a new working relationship between monks and the church hierarchy. Combined with ever-growing enthusiasm and esteem for monks throughout the eastern Roman world, the stringent social, fiscal, moral, and marital requirements for episcopal office defined by Justinian and confirmed by later ecclesiastical legislation made monks not only legitimate but ideal candidates for the office of bishop.

8

Normalizing the Model:
The Fifth-Century Church Histories

Outside the legal sources, a great variety of ecclesiastical writers from the late fourth through the sixth century testify to closer relations between monks and the church hierarchy. Historical as well as hagiographical accounts illustrate the growing acceptance and esteem for bishops who had come from the monastic life. Clearly the ordination of monks became more common in the decades leading up to Chalcedon. Late fourth-century visitors to monastic sites in Egypt and the Holy Land observed the presence of monk-priests among the holy ascetics, and Palladius's *Lausiac History,* written c. 420, abounds with examples of ordained monks.[1] Nor was this phenomenon restricted to Egypt and Palestine. Writing during the period of Basil's episcopate, Epiphanius of Salamis, himself a monk-bishop, suggests that it was already customary to choose priests and bishops from among virgins if not monks.[2] Egeria's account of her travels in Mesopotamia and the Sinai reveals that the practice of ordaining monks was well established there by the end of the fourth century. In fact, it seems that it was exclusively monks who were chosen as bishops of some cities.[3] In Syria the work of monks in the conversion of pagans increased their contact with the church hierarchy as well. In Asia Minor, as we have noted, Basil ordained his brother Peter to direct the monastery on the Iris and on his deathbed ordained a group of disciples who were likely monks. The monk-priest Sacerdos, a close friend of Gregory Nazianzen, had oversight of the monks of Caesarea and administered a refuge for the city's poor.[4] The sermon *De renunciatione saeculi,* mistakenly attributed to Basil but originating from a Basilian monastery of early date, assumes the elevation of some monks to the priesthood. The author warns of the temptations to pride and the need for even greater humility that come with ecclesiastical office.[5]

The ordination of monks to all ecclesiastical ranks inevitably brought them into closer relations with their bishops. Conversely, monks who became bishops naturally maintained contact with their monasteries. From them they often drew assistants or advisers, who sometimes became their successors, thereby perpetuating a monastic paradigm of leadership. We find scattered references to monk-bishops as well as monk-priests well before Chalcedon. One of the earliest and best known of these references appears in Athanasius's letter of exhortation to Dracontius, a monk fleeing his episcopal consecration. He reminded Dracontius that he was not the first monk to be ordained to the office of bishop. Both here and in his *Festal Letter* 40, written in 368, Athanasius actually listed several Egyptian monks who had been raised to the episcopal dignity.[6] In *Festal Letter* 40 he named the monk Isidore as the successor to Bishop Dracontius, an indication that his earlier appeal to the renegade monk had been effective. Athanasius himself ordained a number of pro-Nicene monks, hoping both to ensure the success of orthodoxy against its rivals in Egypt and to strengthen links between monks and the church hierarchy. In correspondence he was careful to affirm the necessary submission of monks to their bishops, but he also portrayed the bishop as an ascetic adviser who, like himself, both shared and protected many ideals and practices of the monk.[7] Echoing the legal sources we have surveyed, some of these letters emphasized episcopal control of the monastic movement. However, at least two other types of sources from the fifth and sixth centuries throw a different light on the spread of monks in church office, and it is to the first of these genres that we now turn.

Like the legislation examined in the preceding chapter, the ecclesiastical histories of the fifth century both documented and helped to sanction and encourage the spread of monk-bishops in the eastern church. The legal documents surveyed spanned a period of approximately two centuries, from the late fourth to the late sixth century, and the hagiographical texts we will consider next cover a similar period. Here, however, we will focus on a shorter period toward the middle of the fifth century during which three great church historians composed their works. In their writings one can already discern subtle but definite changes in the presentation of episcopal leadership as compared with the fourth-century sources we have hitherto examined. The preface to the Church History of Evagrius Scholasticus makes it clear that by the late sixth century the Church Histories of Eusebius, Socrates, Sozomen, and Theodoret were recognized as the great classics of this genre.[8] While each of the major fifth-century church historians had his own peculiar perspectives and objectives in chronicling the history of the church subsequent to the account of Eusebius, their portrayals of bishops bear significant similarities.[9] In fact their very focus on the clerical elite in their histories, to the exclusion of details as seemingly central to church history as the development of Christian worship and the life of the broader Christian community, testifies to an increasingly clericalized understanding of the church or what really mattered in the church. Although the relative lack of attention to social, economic, and even liturgical developments in the church leaves unfortunate gaps in their presentation, it makes their treatment of bishops all the more significant.

In studies of the fifth-century church historians, we have been duly warned about the disingenuousness of their accounts, especially as regards heresy and schism,[10] and this caution may be extended to their treatment of good and bad bishops as well. Moreover, reflecting on the frequent appeal to the miraculous to bolster both orthodox theology and politics, Arnaldo Momigliano commented that, "There is only one step from the stories of miracles and ascetic feats which spice the ecclesiastical histories to the lives of saints which have nothing but miracles and ascetic feats." Indeed he warned of "the vanity of any attempt at separating hagiography from ecclesiastical history."[11] He may have overstated his point in this instance, for elsewhere both Momigliano and others have emphasized the reasonably critical use of documentary evidence by Eusebius and his fifth-century continuators.[12] Nonetheless, his discussion of the late Roman ecclesiastical historians points to two factors about these writers and their audience that make them particularly valuable for our inquiry. First, these Christian intellectuals, unlike their pagan predecessors, both transmitted to the masses and shared with the common people many of their views about miracles, heresy, paganism, and the right ordering of society and the church in the Christian Roman Empire. Indeed the very attention to the lives and deeds of holy men in their works suggests changes in the character of ancient society as well as developments in the writing of history.[13] Second, in keeping with their abolition of boundaries between the cultured or learned and the popular, the church historians strove to influence a courtly audience as well as a broader readership; specifically they hoped to have the ear of the scholarly emperor Theodosius II, who in many ways shared the distinctively Christian culture of his subjects.[14] Robert Markus speaks of the wider reading public for ecclesiastical history in Constantinople, an audience "presumably not confined to pious emperors and court officials . . . , readers who snatched each installment eagerly from the press."[15] Finally, if we hear the tone of hagiography in some of their descriptions of bishops, it is one of the factors that interests us in their accounts, for we would like to know which bishops were exalted or idealized and for what reasons their leadership was positively appraised.

Despite their consciousness of standing in an established historiographical tradition and their general adherence to characteristic themes and subjects of their fourth-century predecessor, one new development since the account of Eusebius that the fifth-century historians included was the rise of the monastic movement.[16] Sozomen explicitly listed monasticism among the major topics to be covered in his history, explaining that an account of the monastic pioneers and their successors was not foreign to an ecclesiastical history and expressing his hope that the record of their deeds and manner of life might serve as an inspiration to others. After acknowledging that this enormous subject required a work of its own, Socrates nonetheless indulged himself in a lengthy digression on the lives of monks.[17] Before examining the historians' treatment of bishops it will be helpful to consider their general perceptions of monasticism, particularly its relation to the church hierarchy. Though there are some discrepancies between their accounts, my concern is less with the accuracy of particular facts than with the way in which details were construed to convey a particular notion of episcopal authority. If Momigliano is right about the largely common Christian culture and beliefs shared by upper and lower classes, by the educated as well as the uneducated, in the first half of the fifth century, then descriptions of episcopal leadership and assumptions about what makes a good bishop as much as a good emperor will often reflect a broader cultural consensus.

Although tensions between rival monastic groups were not overlooked, for the most part all three church historians spoke of monks and monasticism in praiseworthy terms. Perhaps no passage better reveals their general esteem for the movement and its penetration into the culture of the eastern Roman world than a passage from Socrates' encomiastic description of Theodosius the Younger. The ascetic emperor himself observed regular fasts and "rendered his palace little different than a monastery."[18] Monks held great sway over the broader population as well, especially in Egypt, where their opinions were "always adopted by the people" and their testimony was "universally received" because of their reputation for virtue and philosophical living.[19] Our historians presented the monastic movement primarily as a positive force of the orthodox church in the struggle against heresy. Socrates explained, for example, that Basil of Caesarea established monasteries in Pontus as part of a definite strategy for counteracting the spread of Arianism. He also described the outrages perpetrated against Egyptian monks, who suffered harassment, persecution, and exile for defending the "homoousian" faith.[20] Sozomen, who was especially interested in monasticism and devoted considerable attention to the phenomenon, actually interrupted his treatment of the Arian crisis in Book 3 to insert a eulogy of great ascetics and holy men, many of whom were also staunch supporters of Nicaea.[21] Later in his account he commended the "philosophers" of Syria, Cappadocia, and the surrounding region for their faithful adherence to the Nicene faith. In areas where Apollinarianism and Eunomianism particularly threatened the population, Sozomen maintained that the monks turned the people away from these heresies by their virtuous example and right beliefs. In like manner, he affirmed, the monks led the Egyptians in the battle against Arianism.[22] Regarding the origins of monasticism in Constantinople, which was linked with a form of semi-Arianism, our historians are either silent or, in the case of Sozomen, the movement is treated as part of the history of the capital city rather than the church.[23]

Theodoret's Church History has less to say about monasticism than one might expect from the pen of a monk-bishop. Though he did include biographical sketches of several celebrated ascetics, at several points he excused his brevity in treating this theme by noting that he had discussed particular monks in greater detail in his *Philotheus*.[24] His Church History presents the most focused attack on the Arian movement, though behind this target lay more immediate and localized Antiochene christological concerns.[25] In his treatment of the Arian heresy he placed monks in the vanguard of the battle. Egyptian holy men actively defended Athanasius and propagated the orthodox doctrines of

Nicaea. Reflecting on the role of Antony, who "abandoned the desert and went up and down that city" (namely Alexandria) preaching against the Arians, Theodoret praised monks for their active engagement in affairs of the church. "Those godly men," he affirmed, "knew how to adapt themselves to each particular opportunity, when to remain inactive, and at rest, and when to leave the deserts for the towns."[26] He also described the concord between bishops and ascetics in Egypt on the appointment of the pro-Nicene bishop Peter as the successor of Athanasius. In Syria and Asia Minor a number of monks were raised to the episcopal dignity precisely because of their faithfulness to the Nicene cause.[27] Theodoret's *Historia religiosa* provides still other examples of the services monks rendered on behalf of the orthodox church and its leaders. They helped combat heresies, mediated conflicts, and advised bishops who sought their counsel or assistance.[28]

Not only were monks presented as champions of Nicene orthodoxy by the fifth-century church historians but they were also shown to have played an important role in the task of evangelization. Monks, Sozomen claimed, "were instrumental in leading nearly the whole Syrian nation, and most of the Persians and Saracens, to the proper religion"; they were similarly involved in evangelizing pagan areas around Palestine.[29] Monks who were banished under the reign of Emperor Valens brought Christianity to the pagan lands where they were sent. In this connection we learn of the ministry of the monk-priests Eulogius and Protogenes during their exile in Thebes and of Egyptian monks who were banished to islands uninhabited by Christians.[30] When the Nicene party held sway, monks often worked hand in hand with the ecclesiastical hierarchy and even under imperial aegis.[31] Less salacious aspects of the Christianizing zeal of monks and bishops were not neglected by our historians, who recounted in straightforward, even approving tones the collaboration of these parties in the closure and violent destruction of pagan temples and shrines, but it is the resistance of pagans rather than their persecution by Christians that is emphasized.[32] Describing a short period of peace and prosperity in the church, Sozomen encapsulated the spirit of cooperation between monks and clergy that all three historians idealized: "Religion daily progressed, by the zeal, virtue, and wonderful works of the priests, and of the ecclesiastic philosophers, who attracted the attention of the pagans and led them to renounce their superstitions."[33]

Even more indicative of a growing harmony between the monastic movement and ecclesiastical leadership is the obvious integration of monks into the hierarchy of the church. All three historians refer to or assume this phenomenon with no hint of surprise. While both Sozomen and Socrates included accounts of monks fleeing ordination, it was not the norm in any of the church histories. Socrates even included Evagrius's mild rebuke to the monk Ammonius, who had cut off his ear to disqualify himself for the episcopate.[34] In fact, monk-bishops were more of a commonplace than a rarity in the fifth-century chronicles of the church. Along with famous monk-bishops like the three great Cappadocians, John Chrysostom, and Epiphanius of Salamis, we hear of many lesser-known ascetics who ascended the episcopal throne. A few examples from each of the historians must suffice.

Among the many accounts of bishops and patriarchs in Socrates' Church History, he describes the brief episcopate of Maximian of Constantinople, an ascetic who succeeded Nestorius. Though "rude of speech," he was highly regarded for his sanctity and ordered well the affairs of the church.[35] In contrast to the apparently less educated Maximian, the bishop Silvanus had been trained in the school of Troilus the Sophist but had abandoned a rhetorical career for the ascetic life. Noting his elevation to the see of Philippolis and later transfer to Troas, Socrates emphasized his ascetic austerities and recounted the miracle ascribed to him as bishop of the city.[36] The desert monk Moses was similarly eminent for both piety and miracles. When sought by Queen Mavia of the Saracens to serve as bishop over her nation, Moses initially resisted ordination. This was clearly not because of his longing for solitude, an excuse commonly alleged for refusing the episcopate, but rather because the Arian bishop Lucius of Alexandria was to perform the consecration. Moses' friends therefore took him to the mountains to be ordained by Nicene bishops in exile, and in turn Queen Mavia fulfilled her promise to terminate the Saracen war.[37] In keeping with his Novatian sympathies, Socrates presented several Novatian bishops in a positive light. Noteworthy among them was Bishop Paul, a former teacher of Latin, an ascetic, the founder of a monastery, and a lover of the poor. In fact the church historian devoted three chapters to the career of this monk-bishop, whose piety was affirmed by supernatural discernment and miraculous deeds.[38] Esteemed by all for his moral rectitude, and faithful to the end in his ascetic discipline, Paul chose as his successor an ascetic priest whom he had personally trained.

In keeping with the general connection between monks and Nicene orthodoxy, Sozomen sketched the life of the western monk-bishop Martin of Tours.[39] In addition to his philosophical life and his persecution at the hands of Arian bishops, he is praised for his performance of miracles and signs as wonderful as those of the apostles. In Palestine it was pagans rather than heretics who harassed the monks Ajax and Zeno in the maritime city of Maiouma. Both, however, zealously defended their faith, persevered in their monastic practices, and faithfully administered the churches under their episcopal jurisdiction. They were approximate contemporaries with the monk-bishop Acacius of Beroea, whom Sozomen describes in the same chapter.[40] He singled out several bishops in his long lists of celebrated monks of Egypt, Palestine, Syria, and Asia Minor. The monastery of Rhinocurura in Egypt is said to have consistently produced exemplary bishops, and the clergy of the church resided together in a kind of clerical monastery.[41] The description of Epiphanius of Salamis highlights his attainments in "monastic philosophy" and particularly his ability to maintain his asceticism and virtue while governing the church of a large seaport city on Cyprus and even conducting civil affairs.[42] Prominent among the ascetics of Syria were Vitus and Protogenes, who became successive bishops of Carrhae, while from the region of Edessa we find the monks Barses and Eulogius who, Sozomen claimed, were not ordained bishop of a particular city but were given the title as an honor in recognition of their excellent conduct.[43] Later in this chapter he distinguished the "ecclesiastical philosophers" of Galatia, Cappadocia, and the neighboring provinces from their largely eremitic Syrian counterparts, explaining that they lived in communities due to the harsh, cold climate. The most renowned of these monks, Leontius and Prapidius, were later made bishops, the former in Ancyra and the latter over several villages. Prapidius is also noted for presiding over the poorhouse established by Basil in Caesarea.[44]

From Theodoret we learn the background of Pelagius of Laodicea, whom Socrates and Sozomen mentioned only in passing. In his bridal chamber on the very day of his wedding, wrote the bishop of Cyrrhus, Pelagius "persuaded his bride to prefer chastity to conjugal intercourse, and taught her to accept fraternal affection in the place of marriage union." On account of his continence and cultivation of all the other virtues, he was "unanimously chosen for the bishopric."[45] Theodoret attributed healings and miracles to the monk-bishops James of Nisibis, Barses of Edessa, and Moses of the Saracens. He also ascribed prodigious

acts to the exiled monk-priests Eulogius and Protogenes, whom we encountered in Sozomen's list of prominent Syrian monks and who were
later raised to the episcopate.[46] After the death of Valens, Theodoret recounted, Bishops Eusebius of Samosata and Meletius of Antioch ordained several monks in Asia Minor and Syria.[47] Though he does little
more than list them here, many monk-bishops in Theodoret's Church
History are described in greater detail in his *Historia religiosa*. There we
learn of their extraordinary deeds and also of their faithful adherence
to an ascetic regimen alongside their performance of episcopal duties.
Theodoret himself continued to pursue an ascetic life as bishop, stayed
in close contact with monks, and promoted monasticism in his region.[48]

Exaltation of their monastic pedigree, ascetic accomplishments, and
ongoing ascetic commitment does not seem out of place in describing
bishops of monastic origin. It is in fact the almost prosaic inclusion of
this species of bishop that may be particularly worth noting in these histories. Nor does the bold defense of Nicene orthodoxy, now the legal religion of state, seem a peculiar trait to attribute to late Roman bishops,
even monastic bishops. However, another feature in the portrayal of
bishops by the fifth-century church historians is more extraordinary. It is
the ascription to bishops of unusual power as holy men in their societies. The descriptions of Basil in the funeral orations of the two Gregorys
already contained elements of this new aspect of episcopal authority,
but Socrates, Sozomen, and Theodoret projected the image much more
forcefully. Discussing the portrayal of the emperor by the successors of
Eusebius, Glenn Chesnut has noted thirteen examples of confrontations
between Christian holy men and emperors in the church histories of
Socrates and Sozomen.[49] In each of these incidents the holy man is said
to have warned or rebuked the emperor for his misbelief or for a specific
misdeed, and in each case the ruler is humbled and forced to succumb
to the will of the holy man. The bold and virtuous Vetranio, for example, publicly defended the Nicene faith before Emperor Valens, who
had come to Scythia in an attempt to win the bishop over to Arianism.
Affronted by Vetranio's staunch opposition, the emperor immediately
banished the holy man but was soon obliged to recall him for fear of
insurrection, for the Scythians highly esteemed their bishop and were
offended at his absence. "Thus," concludes Sozomen, "was the intention of the ruler openly frustrated by Vetranio."[50] Theodoret's Church
History includes similar confrontation accounts, some of which involve

miracles confirming the holy man's authority. For example, during the siege of Nisibis by the Persian king Shapur II, the prayers of the holy bishop Jacob brought down a plague of mosquitoes and gnats upon the Persian soldiers and their animals, who were forced to abandon the city and flee.[51]

Echoing Peter Brown, Chesnut explains that the late antique holy man was expected to embody *parrēsia,* that is, a divinely endowed boldness that enabled him to speak forthrightly and fearlessly to anyone, including the most powerful rulers. "These human bearers of the divine had power that could be felt even politically," he comments, "and before that power even an emperor had to bow his will."[52] What Chesnut fails to mention regarding the confrontation stories in Socrates and Sozomen is that eleven of the thirteen Christian "holy men" in these accounts were actually bishops.[53] Most were ascetic bishops or, like Athanasius, strong advocates of the monastic movement. If, as Chesnut suggests, these motifs reveal the late antique notion of the good Christian emperor who humbly submits to the power of holiness, they present just as vivid a picture of the ideal Christian bishop. He is an ascetic who, by virtue of his reputation as a holy man, wields considerable authority in the political realm as well as in the church. Together these vignettes provide vivid evidence of the merging of ascetic and episcopal authority in the first half of the fifth century.

There was, of course, a wider variety of episcopal types described in the works of Socrates, Sozomen, and Theodoret. In keeping with Theodoret's fixation on Arius and Arianism in his Church History, he particularly praised those bishops who had struggled or suffered for the cause of Nicene orthodoxy. Though many of these prelates were in fact ascetics, they are praised for their involvement in crushing heresy, irrespective of their connection to the monastic movement.[54] Alongside his anti-Arian polemic Theodoret's regional interest in the patriarchate of Antioch caused him to pay special attention to three particular bishops of the city—Eustathius, Meletius, and Flavian—all of whom he represented in near hagiographical terms.[55] Bishop Flavian of Antioch was his particular hero. Though an ascetic eulogized by John Chrysostom and closely connected with the Syrian monks who are the subject of Theodoret's *Historia religiosa,* Flavian's valiant stance against heresy is primary in his Church History.[56]

Socrates' consistent condemnation of episcopal rivalry and his fervent devotion to Origen and Origenism led him to describe the same three Antiochene bishops in rather different terms. Eustathius, for example, is listed among those "worthless characters" who reviled his beloved Origen.[57] Socrates also censured harshly the anti-Origenist bishop Theophilus of Alexandria, and even presented Epiphanius of Salamis in a negative light for conspiring with Theophilus in the condemnation of Origen. He excused this monk-bishop several times, however, explaining that he was a man of extraordinary piety but simple-minded and therefore easily deluded by Theophilus.[58] Meanwhile Socrates esteemed Bishops Eusebius of Caesarea, Gregory Thaumaturgus, Basil of Caesarea, and Gregory of Nazianzus, as well as a number of other monks, priests, and theologians who embraced Origenist teachings.[59] Most of those whom he praised for faithfulness to the Origenist tradition happened to be ascetics as well.

Socrates, and to a lesser extent Sozomen, also commended bishops who exemplified a spirit of moderation or a measure of religious tolerance in their exercise of episcopal authority.[60] Yet in descriptions of humanist bishops, an ascetic element was often present as well. Bishop Proclus, for example, was praised for his learning, his irenic temperament, and his moral excellence, traits not necessarily connected with asceticism. Yet Socrates also affirmed that he possessed all the virtues of his mentor, Atticus of Constantinople, who was himself both an ascetic and a bishop of moderate inclination. Socrates emphasized the prudence and tolerance as well as the asceticism of Bishop Atticus, who originally hailed from Sebaste and was seemingly shaped by Eustathian ideals.[61] In an interesting account of another moderate bishop, we hear of a group of Egyptian prelates during the reign of Constantine who wished to proscribe conjugal intercourse for all bishops, priests, and deacons, even if they had married prior to their ordination. Paphnutius, a one-eyed miracle-working bishop in Upper Thebes, vehemently opposed this measure.[62] Addressing an assembly of bishops, Paphnutius urged them "not to impose so heavy a yoke on the ministers of religion," defended the honor of marriage, and even designated the intercourse of a man with his lawful wife "chastity." After presenting Paphnutius's argument for leniency, to which the assembled bishops assented, Socrates explained that the bishop himself had never been married, was renowned above all men for his chastity, and had even been brought up in a monastery (askētēriō). In short, the commendation of bishops for temperance, prudence, or a broader range of deeds and attributes did not contradict or supersede the ideal these historians found in the monk-bishop. Indeed it had become almost de rigueur to describe a Christian leader in ascetic terms, whether or not he had ever lived the life of a monk, a good indication of the pervasive influence of monastic ideals in late Roman culture as a whole.

Let us conclude our examination of the fifth-century church historians with a closer look at their portrayal of Basil of Caesarea in particular. Basil himself espoused ascetic ideals in the episcopate and sought directly to influence the choice of monks or committed ascetics for bishoprics in Asia Minor. His two close associates presented Basil's life as a model of episcopal leadership and a pattern for aspiring ecclesiastics. It remains for us to consider how the Cappadocian was perceived by succeeding generations and in what sense his portrayal typifies the emergence of a new episcopal ideal. The church historians are instructive in this regard. Socrates described Basil's excellent education, his abilities in rhetoric, and his abandonment of profane studies to embrace the monastic life. Similarly Sozomen pointed to the dual source of Basil's fame, "his extreme addiction to the philosophic life and astonishing powers of eloquence."[63] Theodoret related nothing specific about Basil's background but praised the holy man's virtue and piety, by which he had become celebrated throughout the empire.[64] In a similar fashion, then, these historians highlighted the moral character and asceticism that complemented the Cappadocian's intellect and enhanced his leadership of the church.

Especially intriguing, however, is the particular incident in Basil's life that all three church historians chose to recount in greater detail. It is the story of the bishop's confrontation with Emperor Valens. First related in Gregory Nazianzen's funeral oration, the use of this episode by all three historians serves as a testimony to the great influence of this speech.[65] With a few variations, the account proceeds as follows. At the command of Valens, his prefect was sent to Caesarea to persuade Basil to renounce the Nicene faith and embrace the emperor's religious convictions.[66] Though threatened with banishment and even death, the bishop stood firm. Shortly thereafter, the emperor's son was stricken with a dangerous illness, whereupon Valens summoned Basil to pray for the boy's recovery. Following the emperor's refusal to turn to the orthodox position, or his appeal to the Arians on his son's behalf, the boy died.[67] Sozomen noted that the boy had actually rallied briefly on Basil's arrival, before the emperor solicited the prayers of the heretics. He remarked in conclusion that the details of this incident "are quite inadequate to convey an idea of the wonderful endowments of Basil."[68]

Theodoret's rendition of the affair includes an equally dramatic aftermath. Though Valens felt deep remorse at the death of his son and actually came to admire Basil's character, he soon forgot what had come to pass between them. On a later occasion, having again endeavored unsuccessfully to lure Basil into communion with the Arians, he determined to issue an edict for the bishop's banishment. When he attempted to carry out his plan, however, the following occurred:

> When he tried to affix his signature to it he could not even form one tittle of a word, for the pen broke, and when the same thing happened to the second and to the third pen, and still he strove to sign that wicked edict, his hand shook; he quaked, his soul was filled with fright; he tore the paper with his hands, and so proof was given by the Ruler of the world that it was He Himself who had permitted these sufferings to be undergone by the rest, but had made Basil stronger than the snares laid against him, and, by all the incidents of Basil's case, had declared His own almighty power . . . Thus Valens was disappointed in his attack.[69]

Given such displays of divine power on behalf of bishops, little wonder that emperors feared them and attempted to elicit their support! As Henry Chadwick has observed, emperors had no experience dealing with this new combination of institutional authority and charismatic power.[70] The type of authority exercised by bishops in late antiquity has been described as a "novelty" and a "potentially explosive compound." Indeed "the emperor's willingness to listen to bishops, as he had once listened to philosophers, implied his recognition of new forms of local power."[71] While these observations refer to the role and function of the bishop in general, they are all the more poignant in light of the increasing asceticization of the episcopate in this period. Episcopal authority came to be based on the bishop's "spirituality as an ascetic and holy man."[72] Moreover, while the Cappadocians had exalted and sought monastic ideals in the lives of ecclesiastical leaders, by the middle of the fifth century a subtle shift has occurred in the portrayal of the model bishop. As we will see in some of the ascetic and hagiographical writings of the period, and as is graphically illustrated here in Theodoret's description of an episcopal-imperial encounter, it is no longer simply monastic ideals that are emphasized; more often it is the manifestation of spiritual power proceeding from ascetic virtues that comes to the fore.

Confrontations like that of Basil and Emperor Valens are not unusual in the fifth-century histories of the church. In his groundbreaking work on the role of the holy man in late antiquity, Peter Brown suggested that it was not only secular rulers who were forced to cope with the spiritual power of these "God-bearing men." In the East the holy man often stood in opposition to the ecclesiastical hierarchy itself.[73] More recently Brown has proposed a model of cooperation or alliance between the monk as holy man and the bishop as patron of the poor, both men of *parrēsia* who together could sway the will of emperors and powerful urban elites.[74] These scenarios offer insight into the multifaceted relations between bishops and emperors in the late Roman world. What we see in fifth-century portrayals of monk-bishops, however, is neither rivalry nor cooperation but the unusual coalescence of two distinct types of power. The institutional authority of the triumphant Nicene church and the spiritual power of the holy ascetic are embodied in the same man.

What Basil advocated and sought in church leaders, what Nazianzen found so rare, was presented as almost effortless and commonplace by the next generation. Ascetic ideals had become the prized handmaiden of episcopal office for a new generation of bishops. Beginning in the last quarter of the fourth century the ordination of monks was sanctioned, if not actually encouraged, by imperial as well as ecclesiastical authorities. The fifth-century church histories attest to the acceptance or normalcy of monks ordained to priestly and episcopal functions. At the same time, they present an ascetic model of leadership as a positive paradigm, if not an ideal, for the exercise of authority in the church, praising even nonmonastic bishops in terms congruent with monastic life. In contrast to the suspicion with which monks were viewed in previous generations, by the middle of the fifth century ascetic ideals have been accepted by society as a whole and assimilated by the church hierarchy, and the monastic movement has contributed to a reframing of the episcopal image. Increasingly, fifth- and sixth-century churchmen found in the monk-bishop the quintessence of episcopal authority.

9

The Broadening Appeal:
Monastic and Hagiographical Literature

An intriguing account from the *Apophthegmata patrum* explicitly connected Basil of Caesarea with the practice of ordaining monks. Gradually compiled from the mid-fifth century, based on earlier oral tradition, the *Apophthegmata* includes the following entry under Basil the Great:

> One of the old men said, "When Saint Basil came to the monastery one day, he said to the abbot, after the customary exhortation, 'Have you a brother here who is obedient?' The other replied, 'They are all your servants, master, and strive for their salvation.' But he repeated, 'Have you a brother who is really obedient?' Then the abbot led a brother to him and Saint Basil used him to serve during the meal. When the meal was ended, the brother brought him some water for rinsing his hands and Saint Basil said to him, 'Come, here, so that I also may offer you water.' The brother allowed the bishop to pour the water. Then Saint Basil said to him, 'When I enter the sanctuary, come, that I may ordain you deacon.' When this was done, he ordained him priest and took him with him to the bishop's palace because of his obedience."[1]

This is the only story related about Basil in the popular collection of sayings and anecdotes of the desert fathers. Interestingly, one of the two passing references to the Cappadocian's ministry in the *Lausiac History* also has the bishop involved in the ordination of a monk. Several centuries later both a pseudo-Amphilochian account of the life and miracles of St. Basil and the Syriac Vita tradition of Ephrem the Syrian preserved a similar representation of Basil's episcopal activity in a legendary meeting of the two holy men. In both texts Ephrem is depicted as a monk; the former describes Basil ordaining him to the priesthood and the latter to the diaconate.[2]

However much Basil may have actually placed monks in positions of authority in the church, the tradition about the bishop's life singles out this aspect of his ministry. The more obedient the monk, the more worthy Basil deemed him of ecclesiastical office. Not only does the *Apophthegmata* account testify to the growing reality of ordained monks, but it suggests as well that the example of Basil continued to play a role in encouraging or at least sanctioning this practice.[3] It also serves here as an introduction to other genres of literature that tell us more about common perceptions of monks and bishops and the shaping of those perceptions by monastic and ecclesiastical writers. Even more than the Church Histories surveyed in Chapter 8, a variety of hagiographical writings from the fifth and sixth centuries helped to popularize a model of monastic-episcopal leadership and to ensure its eventual dominance throughout the Christian East.

Until now we have focused primarily on texts read as well as written by Christian elites. The literature to be examined in this chapter represents the broadening appeal of the monk-bishop both geographically and socially. Though not aimed exclusively at the lower classes, hagiography was certainly a popular genre. Those who wrote the Lives of saints in late antiquity, often less educated than the classical authors whose style they adapted to their own monastic experience, tried to shape ideals of holiness for a broader community. Toward this end they passed on anecdotes and stories of holy men and women to a wide audience for whom the accounts communicated a way of life to be imitated and perpetuated.[4] To be sure, hagiographical literature is complex, and recent scholarship has questioned the very existence of hagiography as a genre, since it is subject matter rather than rules of style or literary form that defines hagiography.[5] Moreover we will be considering not only full-length Lives of saints, in which the focus is the lifelong sanctity and posthumous miracles of the deceased holy man, but also biographical collections of living holy men that were aimed at promoting their lives and ideals and forming a community around individual exponents of a particular written tradition.[6] Charged with religion and emotion, these collective biographies present not the life *(bios)* of the saints they so vividly depict but their paradigmatic "way of life" *(politeia)*.[7] For these reasons the title of this chapter refers to monastic and hagiographical sources rather than simply "hagiography." The mimetic quality of this literature, its offer of ideological and literary exemplars, its appeal to the heart, its distinctive use of paradox, and its broad diffusion among readers of all social and educational levels throughout the eastern Roman and later Byzantine world are factors that make these sources especially valuable for understanding the ideals of a broader spectrum of society.[8]

There are many Lives, monastic collections, and different forms of ascetic literature that might have been included here, and I have had to be selective in choosing both texts and the material within each of the texts considered. In keeping with our focus on ideals of leadership in general and the portrayal of bishops in particular, we will look at texts that feature bishops or that include a significant number of bishops, even if episcopal personalities or intervention seem peripheral to the main account of monks and holy men. The legislation examined in Chapter 7 shows that the Council of Chalcedon was a watershed with respect to the legal status of monasticism. It also proved a pivotal event for the identity of eastern monastic communities and was a crucial subtext in the representation of monks and bishops in hagiographical literature for more than a century. For these reasons this chapter is divided into an examination of pre-Chalcedonian and post-Chalcedonian literature. We will examine texts from a wider geographical representation in the East, where a monastic episcopate spread and thrived, and attempt to discern in these writings the diverse social, political, and theological reasons for the appeal of monks as bishops. Despite distinctive monastic and ecclesiastical traditions, ascetic and hagiographical sources from Egypt, Syria, and Palestine, as well as Asia Minor, converge in their portrayal of the monk-bishop as an ideal and increasingly a norm for leadership in the church.

Fifth-Century Ascetic and Hagiographical Literature

The tradition of ordaining monks to both the priesthood and the episcopate, which we observed already during the episcopate of Athanasius, persisted in Egypt and is clearly attested by hagiographical literature. In the *Lausiac History*, the frequent descriptions of monks "deemed worthy of the priesthood"[9] suggest the author held ordained ministry in high regard. A monk-bishop himself, Palladius was quite purposeful in his ef-

forts to win allegiance to the monastic life and to influence its organization.[10] His advocacy of the growing custom of placing monks in church
office reflects a similar intentionality. Palladius's *Dialogue on the Life
of St. John Chrysostom* reveals that Theophilus of Alexandria ordained
many monks of Nitria and the Cells.[11] Likewise his *Lausiac History* includes a number of monk-bishops alongside the many monk-priests.
Some resistance to ordination continued, as is apparent in the famous
case of Ammonius, who cut off his ear and threatened to cut out his
tongue to disqualify himself for the episcopate.[12] Equally telling in this
account, however, is the fact that the people of a neighboring city actually sought out the pious and learned ascetic to have him ordained as
their bishop. Though Ammonius thwarted their plan, the account shows
that holy monks were highly regarded by the people and considered
suitable, if not favorable, candidates for leadership in the church. The
alacrity of Bishop Timothy's response also suggests that ordaining a
monk to episcopal office was a relatively unremarkable event, at least by
the time Palladius composed his popular collection. Confirming this
supposition from a very different source, a study of episcopal lists in late
antique Egypt affirms that the appointment of monks as bishops had become "a general custom in Egypt" by the fifth century.[13]

A close association between asceticism and church office has an even
longer history in Syria, as was suggested in Chapter 1. In the fifth century the tradition of placing monks in the episcopate is attested in diverse sources of Syrian provenance. One of the best examples of this
practice, showing both the perpetuation of a monastic ideal of episcopal
leadership and new dimensions in its growing popularity, is provided by
the career of Rabbula of Edessa. Born to a wealthy family in Chalcis
(Qenneshrin) near Aleppo, Rabbula served as bishop of Edessa from
412 until his death in 436. Our chief source on his life and career is
an anonymous vita composed largely as a propaganda piece before the
Latrocinium Ephesenium, better known as the Robber Synod of 449.[14]
Testifying directly to his monastic and ecclesiastical ideals, we also possess Rabbula's own canons for the conduct of clergy, monks, and the
bnay and *bnat qyama*.[15] These rules indicate that the indigenous Syrian
ascetic life of the Covenant persisted alongside the newer Greek models
of monasticism that were by now firmly rooted in northern Syria as
throughout the empire.

In the *Life of Rabbula* three major themes evince the author's idea of the model bishop, clearly embodied by his heroic protagonist. The first is the bishop's asceticism. The son of a pagan father and a Christian mother, Rabbula was educated in Greek literature and remained a pagan throughout his youth and young manhood. Though exposed to Christianity through the efforts of his mother and his wife, Rabbula was finally converted through a series of events connected with monastic life in the region of Chalcis and particularly with a group of ascetics who figure prominently in the writings of Theodoret of Cyrrhus. Impressed by a miracle of healing performed by the hermit Abraham, Rabbula began to question his pagan beliefs. His mother brought him to the nearby bishops Eusebius of Chalcis and Acacius of Beroea, bishops who had been instructed in the same monastery. Acacius was a former monk and disciple of the hermit Marcianus, and all three of these men came from aristocratic Syrian families.[16] Under their influence Rabbula was convinced of the truth of Christianity and made a pilgrimage to the Holy Land to be baptized in the Jordan River. On his return he unburdened himself of his riches, freed his household slaves, committed his widowed mother, wife, and children to monasteries, and went out to the desert to dwell in a monastery near the aforementioned recluse Abraham. Lengthy passages of the *Life* describe Rabbula's ascetic discipline, comparing him with St. Anthony and presenting him as a kind of *alter Christus*.[17]

Before long, however, a group of bishops in Antioch, including the monk-bishop Acacius of Beroea, elected Rabbula to the episcopal see of Edessa. Rabbula did not resist ordination and even admitted to himself that he harbored a "longing for this dignity."[18] Nonetheless, the *Life of Rabbula* insists on his humility and details his consistent ascetic lifestyle and involvement in monastic affairs throughout his episcopal career. Not only did he continue his habits of abstinence, regular fasting, and nightly prayer, striving as bishop "even to double the harsh mortifications of his monastic life," but each year he withdrew from Edessa to his former monastery near Chalcis for a forty-day period of solitude and tearful intercession before God.[19] Rabbula's understanding of Christian faith and practice, then, was nurtured in an environment in which the life of the church was entwined with monasticism and monastic bishops were an unremarkable if not common phenomenon.

Closely connected with the bishop's ascetic life was his concern for the urban poor, another theme that dominates the vita.[20] This link is established immediately in the account of Rabbula's conversion. In what had already become a hagiographical trope, the saint immediately sold all his possessions and distributed his gold and silver to those in need. By the secret ordering of God, his alms managed to benefit the saints and the poor of Edessa, his future episcopal see.[21] Once bishop of the city, Rabbula devoted himself to their cause. He modeled a simple lifestyle, preached against the accumulation of riches, taught about the Christian's responsibility for widows, the indigent and the needy, and even sold the gold and silver dishes of the church to give their value to the poor. Rabbula was also involved in establishing or renewing foundations for the city's poor and sick.[22] Like Eustathius of Sebaste and Basil of Caesarea, he had hospitals built with the funds of the church and committed their administration to zealous deacons and monks. Though care of the poor was a recognized episcopal duty, Rabbula's hagiographer presents his concern for the poor as an expression of his ascetic principles.[23]

The bishop also condemned the luxury and worldliness of the clergy, a third major motif of the *Life*. Rabbula is portrayed as a tireless reformer who exhorted his clergy to righteous, ascetic living. He warned both clergy and monks against a broad range of transgressions, from involvement in worldly affairs to cohabitating with female relatives, associating with women, receiving bribes or gifts, eating meat, and taking baths. We know from Rabbula's own rules that he was concerned about the maintenance of strict order and discipline and determined to rout out some of the very abuses described in his vita. In keeping with these alleged abuses, the *Life* emphasizes his extreme caution and painstaking, prayerful deliberation over the ordination of clergy. Rabbula strove to ensure that his priests "would be as similar to the heavenly angels as human nature allowed."[24]

So far there is nothing radically new in this presentation of an ideal bishop. A similar ascetic background and ongoing concern for monastic life, the plight of the urban poor, and the reformation of the clergy dominated the careers of Basil of Caesarea, John Chrysostom, and other monk-bishops we have examined. But the *Life of Rabbula* only hints at what other sources make plain about the holy bishop: he was a man of excessively severe and even violent temperament. Indeed he did not hesitate to resort to violence when he believed such force was warranted. As a young monk Rabbula's asceticism and piety were already linked with violence. Accompanied by his friend and fellow monk Eusebius, he had set out for the city of Baalbek (Heliopolis) to destroy the pagan temples and idols there. Though they anticipated and even longed for martyrdom, "God preserved them from this for the sake of their future appointment as excellent administrators of the episcopate."[25] As bishop, Rabbula ordered pagan temples in Edessa destroyed and used the stones to construct a special women's hospital.[26] He was characteristically severe toward heretics and dissenters, though we hear more about his tremendous, no doubt exaggerated success in converting the city's Jews and pagans than about displays of episcopal force against them. The details of his own theological *volte face,* his treacherous efforts to safeguard his own position in a sea of ecclesiastical enemies, and his venom toward his former friend and episcopal successor Ibas (Hiba) of Edessa are known to us through other sources but hardly mentioned in the vita. In the *Life of Rabbula* the full strength of the bishop's aggression is reserved for his own clergy and monks. On several occasions it seems that the bishop himself applied physical force. Following an account of a series of admonitions to his clergy, the biographer explains that those who were not persuaded by his love were subdued by fear of his power. Rabbula's exhortations and harsh warnings, threatened suspension of priests, "punishments" and "threats of punishments" fill many pages of his *Life.*[27] Little wonder, then, that clergy, monks, and laity alike are described repeatedly as living in fear before the holy bishop, a bishop who gained the title the Tyrant of Edessa.[28]

The role of bishops in instigating violence against paganism as well as in the theological controversies of the late fourth and fifth centuries has been discussed in several recent studies.[29] Here it comes to the fore in the Life of a bishop noted for his asceticism. Indeed, praise for the bishop's humility, holiness, and rejection of worldly values is placed side by side with accounts of his austere regulations, punishments, and threats. As Averil Cameron has suggested, ascetic discourse can express both rejection of conventional authority and authoritarianism itself.[30] The juxtaposition of these motifs in the *Life of Rabbula* reflects some of the reasons why ascetic discourse was so well suited to the official church in whatever beliefs or causes it endeavored to promote or combat. Such discourse could be used to sanction violence as much as nonviolence, nonconformity as much as the imposition of uniformity. Since the monk-bishop himself inherently embodied a number of paradoxes— at once the countercultural holy man and the official representative of the hierarchical church—he was uniquely positioned to mediate the ideology of empire. A connection between the ascetic goal of self-mastery, intolerance of others, and violence is particularly prominent in the *Life of Rabbula,* but it would play itself out in the Lives of other bishops as well. The support of such figures could be useful to the state in bringing potentially divisive or disruptive factions into harmony with imperial ideology.

Drawing from a slightly different genre of the same period and the same region, the writings of Theodoret of Cyrrhus, particularly his *Philotheus,* more commonly known by its Latin title, *Historia religiosa,* provide added insights into relations between monks and bishops and evidence of the growing appeal of the monk-bishop model. Unlike the *Historia Lausiaca* and other popular ascetic collections, the *Historia religiosa* was not translated into Latin until the sixteenth century. Its influence was therefore limited to the Christian East, and it is particularly representative of Syro-Byzantine ideals of monastic life in the fifth century. Indeed Theodoret may have focused on the holy men and women of Syria, both deceased and still living, precisely to demonstrate their equality with the better known ascetics of Egypt and Palestine.[31] Written around 440, Theodoret's history of Syrian monks displays submission and respect of monks toward their bishops, a position of subordination that would shortly be formalized by the canons of Chalcedon. He describes many instances when bishops visited monks and several cases in which bishops intervened in monastic life, urging specific ascetics to moderate excessively rigorous practices.[32] Much more prominent in the *Historia religiosa,* however, is evidence of harmony and cooperation between monks and the church hierarchy. Monks serve as helpers or advisers to bishops, they intervene for the cause of orthodoxy, they pray for bishops and in turn request their blessings.[33] Especially those who serve as abbots or overseers are involved in many of the same tasks as bishops. We also encounter ordained monks who demonstrate the author's belief that "it is possible even for those who move about the crowds to attain the summit of virtues."[34] This conviction is best exemplified by the lives of the monk-bishops whom Theodoret describes throughout the text.

Monks ordained to the episcopate are shown to be pillars of orthodoxy, arbiters of justice, and men of great or even miraculous power. But what is consistently characteristic of these monks is their ongoing faithfulness to ascetic ideals and practices even after having assumed the responsibilities of episcopal office. James or Jacob of Nisibis, the first holy man to appear in Theodoret's account and one whom the author knew only through legend, is representative of all these qualities. Alongside his ascetic virtues, Jacob performed a variety of miracles. He dried up and restored the source of a river; caused a stone to shatter into a thousand pieces, convincing a judge to revoke his unjust verdict; and sent a plague of mosquitoes on the armies of the Persian king.[35] Rendered conspicuous by such prodigies, which placed him in the center of local and imperial politics, and loved by all the people, he was made bishop of his native city. Though never formally a monk, in Syro-Byzantine historical memory Jacob functioned as both monk and bishop par excellence. More than half of Theodoret's account of his life is devoted to the monk's episcopal career, especially his spiritual leadership in the struggle against Arianism. But no less important than his great deeds is the bishop's consistent way of life:

> Though he abandoned the life he had led in the hills, and chose against his will to live in the city, he did not change his food or clothing, but rather changed his location without modifying his way of life. His labors increased and became much more numerous than before because to his regimen of fasting, sleeping on the ground and clothing himself in sackcloth, he added the complete care of those in need; that is to say, he concerned himself with widows, protected orphans, reproved those who acted unjustly and offered just aid to their victims.[36]

Jacob of Nisibis did not stand alone in his example of loyalty to a monastic regimen while fulfilling his episcopal vocation. Similar descriptions of bishops recur in Theodoret's history. During twenty-eight years of service as a bishop, Acacius of Boerea did not neglect his ascetic way of life but rather "mixed ascetic and civic virtue, guarding the rigor [akribeian] of the one with the practical management [oikonomian] of the other."[37] This is the same Bishop Acacius who was instrumental in Rabbula's conversion, ascetic commitment, and election as bishop of Edessa. As bishop of Zeugma the monk Aphthonius relinquished neither his ascetic routine nor the care of his monastic flock; likewise the monk-bishop Helladius of Cilicia did not abandon his former "philosophy" but "added each day to those labors the exertions of the episcopate."[38] This dual vocation is particularly prominent in the life of Abraham of Carrhe. Though "constrained to exchange his position, he did

not change his life," the account begins. After a lengthy description
of his episcopal duties, hospitality, just arbitration of disputes, and his
appearance at the imperial court, Theodoret reminds us of Abraham's
lifelong consistency. Far from neglecting or lessening his regimen, as
bishop of Carrhe the monk even "increased his ascetic labors."[39]

The final chapter of the *Historia religiosa,* entitled "On Divine Love,"
was actually written several years later and appended to the text.[40] In
this postscript Theodoret provided a more concrete theological foundation for the monastic way of life. The heroism of the ascetics recounted
throughout his history is due to nothing less than love for God. The author appeals to a number of Old and New Testament illustrations of such
self-sacrificial love. His most protracted example is that of the apostle
Peter. In an exegesis of John 21:14–19 Theodoret shows that care for
one's brethren is the greatest love of all.[41] His treatment of this passage
seems to reflect his personal preoccupations around the time he was
writing. According to his own testimony, he had not desired the episcopate when he was first called away from monastic life to serve the
church. Eventually he would endure a temporary exile and be prevented
from attending to his flock, at which point he considered it his highest
duty. Through the diffusion of the *Historia religiosa* with its epilogue,
"On Divine Love," Theodoret not only attested and sanctioned the
growing custom of choosing bishops from monasteries but encouraged a
monastic spirituality for the priesthood and episcopate.[42]

The influence of Theodoret on the intersection of ascetic and episcopal ideals is also evident in certain writings of Palestinian provenance.
The editors of the fifth-century *Life of Porphyry,* bishop of Gaza, attributed to Mark the Deacon, have demonstrated that the early redactor of
this text incorporated several sections of the *Historia religiosa* into the
life of this monk-bishop.[43] However, while Theodoret's accounts of ascetic heroes unfold primarily in remote areas of the Syrian desert, the
Life of Porphyry revolves around the urban setting of Gaza, an ethnically,
linguistically, and religiously diverse city that served as an economic and
cultural center for the Roman province of First Palestine. Most of the biography recounts the bishop's efforts to convert the pagans and destroy
the pagan temples of Gaza, for which purpose he went as far as the court
of Emperor Arcadius in Constantinople.[44] Porphyry eventually gained
the necessary support from Arcadius's wife, Eudoxia, by accurately pre-
dicting the birth of a son to the imperial pair. At the emperor's command

and under the oversight of the imperial officer Cynegius, a host of military and civilian troops tore down, burned, and plundered the many temples of Gaza. They searched the villages and even private homes of pagans and consigned to flames their idols and sacred books. The holy bishop's ultimate victory over paganism in Gaza was marked by the razing of the Marneion and the construction of a glorious Christian church over the charred debris of the former temple of Zeus.[45]

The account of Porphyry's ecclesiastical ministry includes dreams, visions, powerful prayers, and miraculous deeds that led to the conversion of numerous pagans and heretics. Easily overlooked in this extremely engaging narrative, however, is the fact that the zealous and enterprising bishop had started his career as a humble monk. Leaving his illustrious and wealthy family in Thessalonica, the young Porphyry had set sail for Egypt, settling first in the desert of Scetis and then in a cave near the Jordan River.[46] When he fell mortally ill he moved on to Jerusalem, where he earned his keep as a lowly cobbler, daily visiting the holy places in spite of a serious, painful affliction of the liver. After a miraculous cure, Porphyry was entrusted by the bishop with the task of guarding the wood of the Holy Cross and was eventually ordained priest. Echoing a major theme of Theodoret's *Historia religiosa,* the *Life of Porphyry* describes his steadfast adherence to his ascetic regimen even after ordination to the priesthood. On his forced election as bishop of Gaza the monk wept bitterly, protesting his unworthiness,[47] but he soon embarked on what was to be an extremely active career as the leader of the church and the champion of orthodoxy in this tumultuous region. In keeping with deeply ingrained habits of monastic life, even the destruction of the Marneion was accompanied by fasts, prayers, miraculous signs, the chanting of Psalms, and a holy procession through the city, all led by the monk-bishop.[48] As the congregation of pious clergy, laity, and soldiers began to clear away the rubble of the once celebrated pagan temple, they zealously shouted, "Christ has conquered!" Indeed the constant juxtaposition of ascetic and military imagery is striking. As in the *Life of Rabbula,* the *Life of Porphyry* reveals links between ascetic rigor, intolerance, and violence. The immoderate behavior of the bishop and his followers seems a far cry from the connection between asceticism and tolerance that characterized some of the bishops in Socrates' Church History, and certainly ascetic ideals were only one of several motivating factors behind Porphyry's actions.[49] Nonetheless, his *Life* demonstrates once again the malleability of ascetic rhetoric, which could help to sanction even contradictory ideals and practices.

Chalcedonian and Non-Chalcedonian Lives

A crucial source for Palestinian monasticism in the post-Chalcedonian period are the biographies of Cyril of Scythopolis. Written in the late 550s and spanning the careers of famous monks from 405 to 558, Cyril's *Lives of the Monks of Palestine* represents the monastic movement in Palestine at its height in size and influence.[50] Links between Palestine and Egypt are well known, and Cyril drew heavily from collections like the *Apophthegmata Patrum* and the *Lausiac History*. Also prominent is the influence of the *Historia religiosa*.[51] But unlike Theodoret and other monastic biographers, Cyril of Scythopolis was not himself a monk-bishop, indeed not a bishop at all. Written in part to heighten the prestige of Jerusalem and the Holy Land through the extraordinary lives of their monastic inhabitants, this work presents monks, rather than bishops, as successors of the apostles and hails one monk as "our new Moses."[52] Cyril's intention in recounting the lives of great holy men was not primarily didactic. He wanted his readers to be impressed by the sanctity and authority of his ascetic heroes, to trust in the continuing efficacy of their power, in short, "to pray to—or through—the saints rather than to imitate them."[53] This is not to deny his conscious appeal to a powerful urban elite, mirrored by the cosmopolitan collection of monastic leaders who came to inhabit the desert of Palestine and form the subject of his *Lives*.[54] Nevertheless, what we find in Cyril's writings is the perspective of monastic figures as distinct from civil or church officials. For this reason they provide a crucial counterbalance to any discussion of monk-hierarchy relations or ideals of leadership in the century following Chalcedon.

Cyril's *Lives* reveals a degree of ambivalence about the appointment of monks to church office. In fact, there seem to be more reservations than we find expressed in Theodoret's writings. Neither of the two main holy men featured in Cyril's biographies, Euthymius and Sabas, became bishops. Sabas in particular expressed hesitancy about ordination, though he honored and employed the priests who visited his first laura. He postponed consecrating the church he had built in the cave, "for he did not wish to be ordained priest or in any way to be appointed a cleric; for he said that the desire to be made a cleric is the origin and root of thoughts of love of power."[55] Similarly Theognius, under pressure from the whole community on the Mount of Olives to lead the church there, fled to the desert "in fear of the danger of wielding authority." The very same phrase is used to account for Theodosius's flight to the desert on his unanimous election as superior of the church of the Chrisma.[56]

Despite such concerns, the *Lives of the Monks of Palestine* abounds with monks ordained to the episcopate. Raised by Bishop Otreius of Melitene, a friend and correspondent of Basil of Caesarea, and educated by two learned ascetics and future archbishops of the city, Euthymius, "despite his reluctance," was ordained a priest in his homeland.[57] Though he left the city because of his hatred of glory and longing for the desert, as a famed monastic leader in Palestine Euthymius approved the appointment of his monks to the office of bishop. Martyrius and Elias, whom he had personally trained in the ascetic life, became patriarchs of Jerusalem. The monk Stephen was ordained bishop of Jamnia, Gaianus bishop of Medaba, and Cosmas bishop of Scythopolis.[58] Euthymius himself requested a bishop for the newly converted Saracens and, on gaining patriarchal consent, chose the monk Peter to be ordained to the post.[59] Indeed it seems that Euthymius's gift of clairvoyance was especially reserved for episcopal appointments, as he accurately predicted the consecration of a number of future patriarchs and bishops.[60] Even Sabas, who had voiced reservations about church office, was eventually ordained priest and became an archimandrite responsible for all the monasteries of Jerusalem and at the imperial court. In this supervisory capacity he did not object when monks under his jurisdiction were raised to episcopal office.[61] Finally, alongside Euthymius and Sabas, Cyril includes brief biographies of five other holy men of Palestine, three of whom were monk-bishops: John the Hesychast, referred to repeatedly as "bishop and solitary"; Abraamius of Cratea, a "lover of solitude"; and Theognius, "the dazzling light of the desert and brilliant luminary of the episcopacy" who, Cyril affirms, distinguished himself in both orders, the monastic and the episcopal.[62]

Several common themes emerge in the relation of monks to the episcopate in these *Lives*. First, the reluctance of monks to serve in positions of ecclesiastical authority has become something of a commonplace. At times such unwillingness entails flight from ordination, as in the cases of Theognius and Theodosius, but more often it is mentioned only in passing.[63] In some instances a monk is summoned by the bishop "as if on some other business," then ordained before he has an opportunity to object.[64] The practice of choosing bishops from Palestinian monasteries had clearly become customary by the mid-sixth century, and for that very reason a note of caution seemed warranted. What is also evident are some reasons why monks were popular choices for the episcopate—from the viewpoint of clergy, laity, and civil officials alike. Ascetic rigor, moral character, and knowledge of Scripture continued to play a large role in qualifying a man as worthy of this office. Moreover, Cyril's monks all managed to maintain an ascetic regimen even after episcopal consecration, perfectly combining monastic virtues with their pastoral duties as bishops.

Perhaps equally significant, their ascetic life frequently issued in demonstrations of power—dreams, visions, supernatural discernment, predictions of the future, exorcisms, cures, and miraculous feats.[65] Theodoret had attributed similar deeds to his monastic heroes, but the theme of miracles is even more prominent in Cyril's biographies. The lives of these holy monks rendered them more powerful than metropolitans and patriarchs, and they could even prevail upon emperors and empresses.[66] As in other hagiographical texts, the ascription of miracles to monks was also used to support their positions in theological debates.[67]

This changing relation to power on the part of monks is somewhat paradoxical. On the one hand, monks clearly placed themselves under the authority of bishops in keeping with the decrees of Chalcedon and the legislation of Justinian. Sabas himself yielded to the will of his patriarch and instructed Abba Abraamius to do likewise.[68] Bishops frequently visited monasteries, chose abbots, and consecrated monastic churches. These practices reflect the supervisory role of bishops required by both ecclesiastical and imperial decrees. On the other hand, evidence from the *Life of Sabas* in particular shows that Chalcedonian and Justinianic legislation on monasticism was not always strictly kept in practice. We find numerous examples of Sabas founding monasteries without the approval of the bishop and several instances of the appointment of a superior without any mention of episcopal consent.[69] More important, the authority of the saintly Sabas had become so great that he was less often called to submit to his bishop than he was sought out by bishops and patriarchs to represent their causes at the imperial court. Emperors Anastasius and Justinian both promptly granted the requests of this monastic patron.[70] The increasing diplomatic role of monks is indicative of their growing influence in society as a whole and their full integration into the life of the church and the empire.

A related theme helped to popularize the choice of monks for church office. Rather than isolated from society and the church, monks are consistently portrayed as defenders of orthodoxy against the prevailing heterodoxies of their region. Long sections of Cyril's *Lives* present Euthymius and Sabas in the struggle against a variety of anti-Chalcedonian factions and Sabas's intervention in the condemnation of Origenism, culminating in the Fifth Ecumenical Council (553) and the expulsion of the Origenist monks.[71] The shorter Lives also show monks battling pernicious teachings that had infiltrated the desert, for as is clearly stated in the Life of Theodosius, the monk's "strict asceticism [is] linked to true and orthodox faith."[72] Similarly, Theodoret's *Historia religiosa* suggests that there were monastic factions on both sides of major doctrinal disputes, each maintaining the truth of its cause and each currying the favor of the reigning imperial and patriarchal authorities. Indeed it has been argued that theological divisions among the monks are Cyril's primary concern.[73] Certainly the increasing association of monks with "orthodoxy," beginning in the fourth and fifth centuries, contributed to their status as particularly worthy candidates for the episcopate in the Christian East. Paragons of virtue, champions of orthodoxy, and mediators of divine power—who would not want such a patron as bishop of his city, and what emperor would not want such a bishop on his side?

The contemporaneous *Lives of the Eastern Saints* by John of Ephesus, to which we will shortly turn, represents an intriguing Miaphysite counterpoint to Cyril's Chalcedonian biographies, showing that the connection between monastic life and orthodoxy cut both ways.[74] Indeed strong links between asceticism, orthodoxy, and episcopal authority are already apparent in non-Chalcedonian texts composed a generation earlier. Particularly revealing are the writings of John Rufus, bishop of Maiouma in the early sixth century. John Rufus consistently associated his episcopal heroes with both ascetic rigor and anti-Chalcedonian "orthodoxy," the former often serving as proof of the latter. His *Plerophoriae* (Testimonies) was ostensibly a tract against the Christological "heresies" propagated by the Council of Chalcedon and its "renegade bishops," but it also served as a justification for the true spiritual authority of his mentor, the Georgian monk-bishop Peter the Iberian (c. 409–488).[75] In fact much of the text presents a rivalry between bishops: on the one hand, Peter the Iberian, bishop of Maiouma, and Timothy Aelurus (the Weasel), archbishop of Alexandria, both champions of non-Chalcedonion "orthodoxy"; on the other hand, the long-deceased Nestorius of Constantinople and Juvenal of Jerusalem, the latter a kind of reincarnation of the former, both villains and betrayers of the true faith.[76] Of course, terms like orthodoxy, heresy, and true faith in these texts express the *non*-Chalcedonian perspectives of their authors.

To make his case for the theological errors of Chalcedon and the truth of the non-Chalcedonian opposition, throughout the *Plerophoriae* John Rufus appealed to a long list of monastic fathers who foresaw, prophesied, or attested the apostasy of the council and the prevarication of its bishops. As displays of power frequently attested the spiritual authority of monks in Cyril of Scythopolis's biographies, so visions and signs confirmed the orthodoxy of John's monastic heroes and the falsehood of their opponents, largely bishops who had signed the "godless" Tome of Leo and the equally pernicious Definition of Chalcedon.[77] Two brief stories from successive chapters provide graphic examples. First we hear about two monastic factions, the former followers of the "diophysite bishops" and the latter a group of "orthodox monks," who decided to put their opposing doctrinal views to the test by throwing the anti-Chalcedonian Encyclical along with the profession of Chalcedon and Leo's Tome into an ardent fire. The latter Chalcedonian documents were immediately reduced to ashes while the Encyclical emerged from the flames untarnished. At this sign the partisans of the renegade bishops repented, abandoned their error, and became orthodox. In the next chapter, an analogous account related by the anti-Chalcedonian monk Basilide, the hands—rather than the documents—of the opposing parties were exposed to the flames. The hand of the heretical (Chalcedonian) priest was immediately consumed while that of the ignorant but orthodox (non-Chalcedonian) laic remained unharmed.[78]

Amid these testimonies of faithful monastic witnesses, John conveniently neglects to mention the fact that Patriarch Nestorius, the demonic root of the diophysite apostasy, had himself been a monk. And as for Patriarch Juvenal, though once a monk and even the head of a monastery, after his change of sides at Chalcedon, as if by a stroke of God's anger his monastery became a desert waste and was abandoned by all its inhabitants.[79] This false monk and two-faced archbishop is repeatedly compared with Judas and even with the Antichrist. Meanwhile John Rufus accentuates Peter the Iberian's orthodox monastic pedigree. Extolled for his ascetic rigor, his faithfulness to the anti-Chalcedonian cause, and his continued encouragement of his flock while in exile, John refers to him consistently as "Abba Peter," "Abba Peter, the bishop," or simply "our father."

In an interesting interlude concerning the author's own background, we learn that John Rufus, formerly a law student in Beirut, had been ordained priest by Patriarch Peter the Fuller of Antioch "during the time of the Encyclical."[80] When Emperor Zeno came to power in 476 Peter was sent into exile, and John himself left Antioch and settled among the monks of Palestine under a new spiritual director, Peter the Iberian. However, in 482 Zeno circulated his Henoticon, a document intended to ignore Chalcedon and unite the warring Christological factions around the first three ecumenical councils.[81] He recalled Peter the Fuller from exile in exchange for support of this new ecclesiastical policy. Peter in turn sent to John Rufus two messengers, one a former *synkellos* of John, to encourage his priest to rejoin him in Antioch. Supported by John Rufus's friends and family in Arabia, the envoys tried to persuade him to return to Antioch and to his former mentor. Unsure of what to do, John consulted Peter the Iberian and received in response a letter from his spiritual father warning him to stay away from the Syrian capital. Soon after receiving this letter the envoys of Peter the Fuller fell gravely ill and begged John for mercy because they had sinned against him. One of them, a certain Bishop Peter, tearfully admitted that he had once been the spiritual disciple of the anti-Chalcedonian archimandrite and bishop Pamprepios, but that "he had been seduced by the desire for the episcopate" and had transgressed the true faith by his partisanship of Chalcedon.[82] These signs of divine disfavor toward the envoys, together with the discouraging letter from Peter the Iberian, convinced John Rufus to refuse the invitation to Antioch. Preferring the desert of Gaza to the allure of an ecclesiastical career in the great Syrian capital, John chose to remain with his new spiritual director, whom he would eventually succeed as bishop of the less prestigious see of Maiouma. Ultimately, then, it was not episcopal office that defined spiritual and even doctrinal authority for this monk and future bishop as much as the pious life and deeds of his spiritual director and abba, the monk Peter the Iberian.

The importance of monastic pedigree is equally apparent in John Rufus's vita of his spiritual father. The son of a Christian king of Georgia, Peter the Iberian was born at a time when the Iberian kingdom was the object of both Roman and Persian ambitions. According to his Life, while Peter was still a boy he was taken as a hostage to Constantinople, where he was raised and loved like a son by Emperor Theodosius II.[83] As a youth he already lived an austere ascetic life and longed to retire from the world. Rejecting his royal lineage and renouncing opportunities for advancement in the imperial capital, the young prince managed to escape his guards, and he fled to the city of Jerusalem to become a monk. He settled in a monastic community between Gaza and the seaside town of Maiouma, where he would eventually serve as bishop. The transition to church office was not simple, however, for Peter resisted ordination. While still living in the Holy City prior to the Council of Chalcedon, Peter had successfully avoided ordination at the hands of Juvenal of Jerusalem, despite many attempts.[84] Though finally ordained to the priesthood in Maiouma, he refused to celebrate the liturgy for seven years. Then, when Juvenal revealed his apostasy at Chalcedon, the clergy and monks of Jerusalem elected the monk Theodosius as a rival archbishop of the Holy City. Zealously devoted to monasticism and a champion of non-Chalcedonian orthodoxy, Theodosius in turn "chose pious men from among the holy monks" to consecrate as bishops.[85] The citizens of Maiouma carried Peter the Iberian to the Holy City for this purpose. Though Peter again attempted to flee, the voice of God gently rebuked him and urged the monk to accept his ecclesiastical charge.

With divine sanction, then, Abba Peter was consecrated to the episcopal see of Maiouma. As bishop he continued to live as a monastic, and during his long exile he was involved in ordaining monks to serve the churches that had remained faithful to Dioscorus and anti-Chalcedonian orthodoxy.[86] Far from advocating new teachings or new practices of monastic or ecclesiastical life, Peter the Iberian considered himself and was described by his biographer as standing in the tradition of the Cappadocian Fathers. Traveling back to Palestine on one occasion, the holy bishop received a vision redirecting his path through Beirut. The meaning of his vision, Peter realized, was that God desired "that some of the lawyers be offered to him as a holy sacrifice, those who could bear the cross and follow his example, in the manner of Basil and Gregory and John [Chrysostom]."[87] Responding to this divine guidance, he went to

Beirut, where he so influenced a group of devout law students in the city that many converted and several abandoned the world to become monks, both before and after Peter's death. A few members of this remarkable circle later became bishops as well, imitating even more closely the pattern set by their mentor, Peter the Iberian, and his own Cappadocian models. On his deathbed Peter bid his followers, John Rufus among them, not only to remain steadfast in the "orthodox" faith and to curse all heresies, namely those promulgated by Chalcedon, but also to attain purity of soul and body and avoid inflaming the passions. Specifically he urged them, "Always read and meditate on the books composed by the saintly bishop Basil concerning the ascetic life . . . and direct your conduct and manners according to his holy precepts and legislation."[88] For Chalcedonian and non-Chalcedonian alike, then, the teachings as well as the life of Basil of Caesarea remained paradigmatic for monks and bishops.

Some of the heroes of John Rufus's *Plerophoriae* and *Vita Petri Iberi* reappear in John of Ephesus's *Lives of the Eastern Saints,* written almost a half century later. In fact several protagonists of these later *Lives* were disciples of Peter the Iberian. A few monk-bishops figure prominently in John's biographies, laying the groundwork for what would become a separate non-Chalcedonian ecclesiastical hierarchy; but they are also representative of the merging of ascetic and episcopal authority in the non-Chalcedonian context. With the ascension of Justin I in 518 and the abrogation of the Henoticon came a massive expulsion of non-Chalcedonian bishops and monks. Many regrouped in Egypt; some settled near the Persian frontier. Now officially deemed "heretics" by the imperial church, Miaphysites had to organize for survival.[89] When a crisis of leadership arose, John of Tella stood in the gap. First distinguished in the solitary life, John was elevated to the episcopate of Tella, where he continued to pursue a strict ascetic life both before and after being driven from his see.[90] Though most Miaphysite bishops feared that ordinations would increase persecution, John stressed the needs of the faithful and gained special permission to ordain. He is said to have ordained an astounding 170,000 men from cities as far away as Armenia, Arzanene, and Cappadocia, as well as the frontier.[91] Ascetic ideals were not his only concern, for he also insisted on proof of literacy and some knowledge of the Scriptures. But there is little doubt that monks were primary among his ordinands. In one night alone he ordained to the diaconate some seventy monks of Amida, including John of Ephesus's entire monastery.[92] Severus of Antioch wrote to John of Tella praising his asceticism as well as his service to the non-Chalcedonian churches. He compared the exiled bishops on the hill of Marde to Elijah the Tishbite on Mt. Horeb. As Elijah was rewarded with the revelation of God and initiation into more perfect knowledge, so these bishops who imitated his zeal and asceticism would "be gratified with the conversation and sight of God" and would render the hill of Marde more glorious still by their ministry.[93]

Eventually imprisoned and martyred, John of Tella was succeeded in his efforts by John of Hephaestopolis, a monk from Gaza who had lived in the monastery of Peter the Iberian and was made a bishop in Egypt after the expulsion of the Palestinian monasteries. With the onset of persecutions in Egypt in 536, this John traveled to Constantinople, where a non-Chalcedonian community continued to worship under the protection of Empress Theodora. Refugees flooded into the city both for the support of their brethren and to seek ordination.[94] So numerous were the ordinations John of Hephaestopolis performed, this time in the imperial city itself and at the risk of almost certain death, that even the sympathetic empress warned him to be careful.[95]

The monastic life was not merely a step en route to high church office for these bishops. For them as for their biographer, John of Ephesus, ascetic living was expected of the laity in general and was an integral part of the episcopal vocation. Nor was the monastic calling disconnected from the duties of the bishop, since in *Lives of the Eastern Saints* many nonordained monks were actively involved in caring for the needy; providing spiritual oversight for their communities, both in and out of exile; and serving as models for the imitation of all.[96] Defending his inclusion of the lives of these two bishops (John of Tella and John of Hephaestopolis) among his biographies of the eastern saints, largely simple ascetics with no worldly or ecclesiastical status, John of Ephesus explained: "Since the purpose of our work and the course of our history aims at showing and describing the circumstances of the perfect lives which the saints lived, therefore . . . we will insert spiritual pastors, and will also in our work state the circumstances of their activity in God's church, since they also were complete and perfect in both forms of beauty [the pastoral and the ascetic]."[97]

Another bishop to appear in *Lives of the Eastern Saints* was Severus of Antioch, who figured in Cyril's *Lives* as an archrival of the saintly

Sabas. We know much more about Severus through two other vitae and through an extensive corpus of his own sermons and letters.[98] Born c. 465 in Asia Minor, Severus, like Basil of Caesarea, came from a wealthy landowning family of political and religious prominence, and like Gregory Nazianzen he had a bishop in the family, for his grandfather had served as bishop of Sozopolis and participated in the Council of Ephesus. Like his two fourth-century predecessors Severus received an excellent education. He studied Greek and Latin grammar in Alexandria, then moved on to Beruit to study law. In that cosmopolitan cultural and intellectual center Severus shone among his pagan and Christian colleagues. Though still not baptized, in Beirut Severus became part of a circle of aspiring ascetics who studied law by day and devoted themselves to prayer and Christian philosophy by night. They were also well known for their opposition to idolatry, the magic arts, and other pagan practices that apparently still flourished in the city. The group identified with the monk-bishop Peter the Iberian, who visited the city in 488 and whose anti-Chalcedonian stance would permanently mark Severus's own theology.[99] But in Zacharias Rhetor's references to Peter and his connection with this avid group of Christian law students, the Iberian's monastic life was principally in view and was seemingly adduced as a proof of his orthodox faith.[100]

Following an already familiar pattern, the promising young student of jurisprudence abandoned worldly pursuits for the humble life of a monk. Severus entered Peter the Iberian's monastery, where he was ordained priest, lived for a time as an anchorite, and eventually founded his own monastic house near Maiouma. Known for rigorous asceticism and theological acumen, Severus was consecrated Patriarch of Antioch in 512. With the change of theological tides in 518 he found himself among the many Miaphysite exiles in Egypt. There in the desert, wrote John of Ephesus, he "carried out to the full the monastic model in which he had before also lived" while at the same time serving the anti-Chalcedonian churches of the East.[101] Severus engaged in an extensive correspondence tackling both urgent practical concerns and difficult theological issues. Modern scholars have noted his indebtedness to the trinitarian theology of the Cappadocians, a link that was also stressed by his biographers and by Severus himself.[102] As a student he had been introduced to the writings of Basil and Gregory and "was entirely won over by them." His reading of their works may have led to his conversion, and they certainly motivated him toward a major shift in his choice of career.[103] His ecclesiastical ideas were built on Cappadocian models as well. Severus repeatedly turned to them for support in the precarious situation the Miaphysites faced regarding ordinations.[104] Also in keeping with his Cappadocian predecessors, more important to his biographers, and equally part of the Severan legacy was the merging of ascetic and episcopal authority that he both embodied and promoted.

The juxtaposition of Cyril's *Lives of the Palestinian Monks* with the anti-Chalcedonian texts just surveyed shows that the ideal of the monk-bishop was equally strong in the non-Chalcedonian and Chalcedonian contexts. But there are important contrasts, as well as similarities, between Cyril's Chalcedonian *Lives* and the *Lives of the Eastern Saints*. While *Lives of the Palestinian Monks* aimed at an elite cosmopolitan milieu, John of Ephesus wrote primarily for a poorer, provincial audience. His *Lives* express a more earthy spirituality, though it may be an exaggeration to assert that Cyril's monastic heroes took no real interest in affairs of the world.[105] The very fact that they assumed positions of hierarchical authority suggests that leadership of the Christian people was deemed a worthy, if not always desirable, vocation for a monk. Considered together with Cyril's *Lives,* these contemporaneous non-Chalcedonian accounts show that the model of the monk-bishop not only appealed to a broad theological base, used to sustain non-Chalcedonian as much as Chalcedonian polemics, but also had widespread social support—from the disenfranchised lower classes to ecclesiastical dignitaries to powerful circles at the imperial court. Finally, if Cyril's *Lives* are set primarily in a remote desert environment, his monks were never far from cities or towns and, like the Cappadocian Fathers, were often well connected with ecclesiastical and imperial elites of the great cities. John of Ephesus described a more engaged urban asceticism. In different ways, then, these texts reveal important connections with urban life, an aspect of eastern monasticism that increased interaction with the hierarchical church and the tendency to recruit bishops from the ranks of monks.

We have seen that an older tradition of Syrian protomonasticism, introduced in Chapter 1, linked asceticism with Christian living as a whole and expected—indeed assumed—it of Christian bishops. This indigenous Syrian asceticism may well lie in the background to the spiritual ideals of John of Ephesus and his eastern saints. But by the fifth century we more often see influences flowing in the opposite direction, from Asia Minor to Syria, Palestine, and Egypt along a kind of ascetic trade route. One noteworthy example is the impact of Cappadocian models on the life and thought of Severus of Antioch, who would play such an important role in the ecclesiastical structure as well as the theology of the non-Chalcedonian churches.

Admittedly Palestine was unique in the Christian East with regard to the dominance of monastic life in the church. The presence of the holy sites in Jerusalem and the geography of the surrounding desert made it a continual place of pilgrimage and monastic settlement for the international community as well as a hotbed of imperial and ecclesiastical politics. One might also argue that the non-Chalcedonian texts surveyed here are anomalies representing a narrow spectrum of persecuted marginal groups. If taken alone, then, one could make the case that these hagiographical works were unreflective of broader trends in the church. But the infiltration of monks into positions of high ecclesiastical authority that we have seen in diverse geographical and theological contexts is evident even in Constantinople, where monastic bishops gained ascendancy later than in other eastern sees. One of the best examples is provided by the *Life of Eutychius,* the biography of a sixth-century monk who twice became patriarch of Constantinople.[106] This is an especially appropriate text with which to conclude our consideration of hagiographical literature. Though composed in the generation after the collections just examined, this *Life* had a related apologetic intent. Likely delivered as a panegyrical oration before Emperor Maurice in the 580s, perhaps on an anniversary of Eutychius's death, it was intended to justify the patriarch's role in the Fifth Ecumenical Council and the ensuing religious controversies that involved both his deposition and his eventual reinstatement as patriarch.[107] Its author, the presbyter Eustratius, was highly dependent on Cappadocian sources and shows the ongoing influence of their legacy of leadership. Finally, the *Life of Eutychius* suggests the extent to which monastic ideals have been assimilated even in the highest office in the eastern church, showing that the movement has gained political as well as ecclesiastical prominence. Far from being an outsider or an episcopal anomaly, the monk-bishop has become a typical player on the imperial stage.

Eutychius himself is known to us from several other texts, which give mixed reviews of his life depending on the author's purpose or theological stance, but certainly Eustratius offers the most detailed account.[108] Eutychius's career followed what was already a fairly typical episcopal trajectory. Born to a pious family in Phrygia, he received his primary education under the tutelage of his grandfather, the priest Eutychius. Showing promise of a future ecclesiastical career, at the age of twelve Eutychius was sent to Constantinople to continue his studies. He excelled in both sacred and profane learning, but already as a youth he had set his heart on a monastic course. He entered a monastery in Amasea and was soon given charge of monastic organization for the entire metropolis.[109] When his bishop fell ill, Eutychius was sent to Constantinople as his representative for the upcoming council. The monk impressed both Patriarch Menas and Emperor Justinian with his knowledge of the Bible and its application to controversies of the day. Indeed it seems to have been solely on the basis of his biblical argumentation that he became Justinian's candidate of choice for the patriarchate on the death of Menas in 552, just prior to the start of the council.[110] In his account of the council itself, Eustratius emphasizes the new patriarch's harmonious cooperation with the emperor rather than any details of debate. Shortly afterward, however, Eutychius fell foul of the imperial will, for he refused to support Justianian's aphthartodocetist decree.[111] Deposed and eventually banished to his former monastery, after the death of John Scholasticus in 577 Eutychius was recalled to Constantinople by popular demand under the new emperors Justin II and Tiberius. Hailed like Athanasius on his return to Alexandria, Eutychius served another four and a half years as patriarch until his death in 582.[112]

Several scholars have discussed the importance of the *Life of Eutychius* for the theological and political setting of the Fifth Ecumenical Council and the ongoing doctrinal divisions that the council notoriously failed to resolve.[113] Eustratius's persistent appeal throughout the text to a canon of approved authorities, that is, orthodox church fathers, represents an approach to authority that would reach its height in the war of florilegia that marked the iconoclastic controversies. For example, in a passage defending Eutychius's teaching on bodily resurrection, an issue on which he had published certain controversial writings, Eustratius defended his hero by affirming that "he breathed the words and teachings of Basil, the Gregorys, and the great Dionysius, and the rest of the holy doctors, prophets and apostles no less than the very air."[114] Perhaps more subtle but nonetheless consistent is the appeal to certain fathers as models of leadership in the church. Again the Cappadocians were primarily in view. Already in the opening paragraphs of the prologue Eustratius cites "the great Basil," and he concludes the *Life* with a description of Eutychius as "this new Basil," praising his virtues in the very words of Nazianzen's panegyric. He calls on men and women of all ranks and stations in life to join him in his eulogy, for Eutychius, like Basil, was a protector of widows, a father to orphans, a friend of the poor and strangers, a doctor to the sick, and a guardian of health for the healthy; indeed "he became all things to all people in order to win all or almost all."[115] Though Basil is the primary model in the *Life of Eutychius,* Athansius also served as a paradigm for leadership. Here too, however, Eustratius's references to the Alexandrian bishop are based primarily on Nazianzen's oration on Athanasius.[116]

Alongside general comparisons with the teachings and lives of the Cappdocian Fathers, a specific career pattern is revisited in the *Life of Eutychius.* As a student in Constantinople, Eutychius determined to abandon earthly ambitions and "to run toward the mountain of virtues, that is, to the angelic choir of the monks." A high-level education renounced for the monastic vocation followed the well-trodden path of the Cappadocians, and like them Eutychius embraced the ascetic life in imitation of Elijah and John the Baptist.[117] His "desert" was a monastery in Amasea, where before long Eutychius was made a "catholicos" and given supervisory responsibility over monastic life in the entire metropolis, a dignity that did not in any way lessen his humility.[118] He was eventually called to Constantinople to serve the church in a new capacity. Though resistant to ordination, like so many of his monastic predecessors, Eutychius was persuaded by a vision that his assumption of the patriarchate was the will of God.[119] With due emphasis on canonical order, then, Eustratius described the monk's ascension to the patriarchal throne at the age of forty. This is the occasion of one of his important borrowings from the Cappadocians, for like them Eustratius divided the bishop's life into three forty-year periods following the pattern of Moses: education in the world, ascetic withdrawal culminating in the vision of God, and return to lead the people of God. Elsewhere as well, comparisons of Eutychius with Moses abound.[120] As we have seen in the encomia of Basil, Athanasius, and Gregory Thaumaturgus, as well as in Nyssan's *Life of Moses,* the Cappadocians frequently appealed to the Mosaic paradigm as an ideal for a leader of the church. By borrowing this tripartite typology, Eustratius identified his hero not only with Moses but also with great monk-bishops of past centuries, implicitly promoting their pattern of life as well. In a passage connecting leadership, orthodoxy, and asceticism—largely a pastiche of quotations from Nyssan's *Life of Moses*, Nazianzen's orations on Athanasius and Basil, and Basil's own sermon *Attende tibi ipsi*—Eustratius exalted Eutychius's governance of the church, affirming that "his life and character were a norm for the episcopate, his teachings the rule of orthodoxy."[121]

Besides its clear reflection of Cappadocian ideals of leadership, several themes in this text show developments in the episcopal image in keeping with some of the Lives examined in this chapter. Eustratius is at best laconic about the Fifth Ecumencial Council, the major event of Eutychius's patriarchate, and even inexplicit about Eutychius's specific ascetic practices. Yet he spares no detail in recounting the miraculous deeds that flowed from the bishop's monastic life. In exile in Amasea the monk and former patriarch is said to have performed a series of miracles demonstrating the power of his holy life and confirming the orthodoxy of his faith.[122] Such wondrous deeds continued after his return to Constantinople and restoration to his patriarchal see. As in the Lives of increasing numbers of late antique monk-bishops, asceticism is linked with both spiritual power and institutional authority, which even emperors ignore at their peril.

Other aspects of Eutychius's career also harmonize with the hagiographical accounts we have considered here. Though an "obscure monk" whose elevation to the patriarchate by Justinian was due more to political expedience than to theological ideals, his family and monastic background help explain his very presence in Constantinople at the propitious moment and make the emperor's choice less surprising than our sources might lead us to believe.[123] Not only did Eutychius hail from an ecclesiastical family, the grandson of a priest on his mother's side, but also his father had been an army officer under Belisarius.[124] The family apparently had connections in Constantinople, for they were able to send the youth to the imperial capital for his education. Moreover, his monastery was located in the city of Amasea, and he had oversight of what appears to have been a large number of monastic institutions in the region. There are, then, clear connections with urban life in Eustratius's description of the future bishop's upbringing and monastic vocation. Eutychius's career represents a typical pattern of episcopal recruitment during this period, already evident in fifth- and sixth-century monastic biographies we have surveyed. Monks chosen for the episcopate were generally *not* isolated hermits but monastic leaders already serving in pastoral and administrative roles. In such positions of authority and oversight their monastic duties corresponded in many ways to their future tasks as bishops. We must acknowledge that Eustratius's objective in the *Life of Eutychius* was not merely to eulogize the bishop, much less to offer a treatise on the episcopate, but rather to defend the patriarch's orthodoxy, for Eutychius was a controversial figure in his day.[125] Yet written in the highest rhetorical style and delivered before the emperor and his court in St. Sophia,[126] his encomium advocated a pattern of life that would typify episcopal leadership for the remainder of Byzantine history.

Along with the descriptions of Basil by his Cappadocian colleagues and the treatment of Chrysostom in the *Dialogue,* the increasing number of monastic bishops included among the Lives of saints proliferating in the East from the fifth century through the end of the Byzantine era indicate the role played by ascetic and hagiographical literature in reframing the episcopal image. Bishops took their place alongside ascetics and virgins as heirs of the honors once reserved for Christian martyrs alone.[127] Hippolyte Delehaye long ago noted the following progression in the formation of hagiographical literature:

> The cult of martyrs had its complement in the cult of confessors, among which were first of all the ascetics, or virtuosos of penitence, then the ecclesiastical leaders who were especially worthy of the religion. Parallel to these developments, the Acts of martyrs appeared first, then the Lives of saints, monks chief among them, and finally the biographies of several great bishops.[128]

While the canons of Chalcedon emphasized the subordination of monasticism to the hierarchy of the church, these other ecclesiastical sources stressed the high esteem for monks that made them desirable candidates for the episcopate. The importance of such texts for our consideration of bishops lies in the role they played in shaping as well as reflecting late antique ideals, even in institutionalizing modes of thought and models of leadership.[129] It was the paradigm of the monk-bishop, sanctioned and fostered by its representation in the diverse literature of the period, that ultimately prevailed in the churches of the East as the monastic state became the normal prerequisite for episcopal office.

Epilogue: The Legacy of the Monk-Bishop in the Byzantine World

To speak of the monk-bishop in Byzantium as a legacy from an earlier era may seem odd to some readers. In fact, I conclude this study where most references to the monastic episcopate begin. The reigning assumption seems to be that the victory of the monastic party in the iconoclastic controversies of the eighth and ninth centuries marked the rise of this phenomenon in the Byzantine world. To be sure, an actual monopoly over the episcopate was not attained until after these struggles had ended, and in Constantinople itself monks did not gain predominance in the patriarchate until even later. Nonetheless, as we have seen, well before Iconoclasm a monastic ideal of episcopal authority had spread widely in the Christian East, and a corresponding trend was set in motion with regard to episcopal appointments. How that ideal fared and some of the forms it took in later Byzantine history, from Iconoclasm to Hesychasm, is the primary subject of this epilogue. A few concluding reflections on a combination of hagiographical and spiritual writings introduced in these pages will also show some of the ways in which the Cappadocian legacy of leadership was transmitted and adapted in later centuries of Byzantine history and will perhaps suggest why it continues to leave its imprint today on the church in the Orthodox world.

Bishops and Hagiography during and after Iconoclasm

Though few have offered more than cursory comments on these developments, standard treatments of Byzantine history have expressed the view that the eighth century in particular marked the rise of a monastic

219

episcopate, or that the victory of the iconophiles, led largely by a rigorist monastic party in Byzantium, was the touchstone for this great influx of monks into positions of ecclesiastical power and influence.[1] In his study of the institutions of the Byzantine empire, Louis Bréhier could not conceal a tinge of remorse in his description of this phenomenon with regard to the recruitment of patriarchs: "With the eighth century a large number of monks, simple and often uneducated ascetics, attained to the patriarchate . . . Since the dispute over images an antagonism enduring to the end of the Empire opposed the secular clergy, which encompassed an elite of erudites and theologians, to monks who despised ancient learning."[2] Others are more nuanced in their accounts of this trend, but the notion of a monastic episcopate arising in conjunction with if not as a direct result of the iconodule triumph is fairly typical. At the same time we see a tendency to portray bishops as supporters of imperial policy in theological as well as social matters, over against the holy men and women of the Byzantine world. In the context of Iconoclasm it was the bishops who succumbed to the theological whims of the reigning emperors, whereas simple monks are shown to have led the resistance to heretical emperors and compromising bishops alike and to have suffered persecution and even martyrdom for their efforts.[3]

While we have seen several examples of the merging of holy man and church office bearer in the period from the mid-fourth century to the late sixth, there is little doubt that by the seventh century the majority of eastern bishops stood on the side of imperial authorities in contradistinction to the Byzantine holy man, who served as a patron of the disenfranchised masses.[4] The causes of this episcopal shift in allegiance away from the people and toward the ruling classes have to do with broader social and economic developments of the period, not the least of which was the decline of urban life precipitated by the Arab raids of the seventh century. Bishops were among the *dunatoi* of their cities. They fulfilled important functions in municipal government and were not infrequently called upon by emperors to serve as political advisers or mediators in crises of the day.[5] At the same time that bishops were rising in status and importance, monks and holy men "suffered a real setback within the highest social and political circles of the capital."[6] In this light, given the civil and administrative functions of bishops, their role as defenders of the ideological interests of the state as well as the church, and their general identification with a class of social and economic elites in early Byzantine society, we might expect popular monastic writings of the iconoclast period to exalt holy men or monks while denigrating the political schemes of contemporary clergy and bishops; and there are certainly examples of such an opposition in the literature of this era. The *Vita Stephani Iunioris,* probably the best-known example of iconodule hagiography, refers to iconoclast bishops as *episkotoi* in contrast to *episkopoi.* These "bishops of darkness" were clearly the pawns of the evil emperor, fulfilling his impious commands in opposition to the faithful and especially the holy monks.[7] The writings of Theodore Studites describe the nefarious deeds of these compromising prelates in a similarly reproachful tone.[8] Alongside such unflattering representations of church officials, however, the ideal of the holy ascetic bishop—both spiritual patron of the common people and powerful ecclesiastical mediator in the face of imperial authority—would continue to win the hearts and command the esteem of the faithful. If Iconoclasm evoked the profound gulf that had developed in seventh- to early eighth-century Byzantium between bishop and holy men, as Peter Brown has so keenly observed, the model of the monk-bishop, revived in the outpouring of hagiographic texts of the ninth to tenth century, embodied the perfect resolution of the tension.

The portrayals of monks and bishops in saints' Lives of this period attest to an ideal that persisted from an earlier age and promoted the continuation of a particular ecclesiastical pattern. For this reason, in my brief discussion of Iconoclasm I will focus not on the conflict over visual images but on a particular hagiographic text.[9] Most of the protagonists in the hagiography of the period are iconodule heroes, though a few are ambivalent in their stance toward icons. Hagiography was a genre that both sides of the iconoclastic divide valued. Though they rejected pictorial representations, iconoclasts had high regard for the biographies of saints whose lives and virtues, as living images, were deemed worthy of imitation.[10] In defense of this ethical or spiritual theory of images, they drew on excerpts from the writings of the church fathers, not least of which was a passage from Letter 2 of Basil of Caesarea: "The study of the God-inspired writings constitutes the best path toward the discovery of what is proper, for they provide a guide for our actions together with the lives of blessed men handed down to us in written form; they are set before us as living images of the way of life according to God through the imitation of godly deeds." A florilegium comprising this and similar patristic quotations was cited by the iconoclasts at their Council of Heireia in 754 and reflects their positive view of saints' Lives as legitimate counterparts to the icons whose veneration they denounced.[11]

Of the relatively few hagiographical accounts dating from the iconoclastic period (730–843) and its immediate aftermath, even fewer can be identified as iconoclast or noniconodule Lives. This has nothing to do with an antipathy for hagiography on the part of iconoclasts and very much to do with a political and ecclesiastical climate that was at best volatile and at worst unfavorable to the expression of iconoclast sentiments. Moreover, Ihor Ševčenko has shown that even iconodule Lives are relatively scarce from the era of Iconoclasm itself; most of the hagiography we associate with this period is actually of a later date.[12] The *Life of George of Amastris* is among these rare noniconodule hagiographic texts composed during the second iconoclastic period (815–843).[13] Though the authorship of the *Life* is still debated, strong arguments have been presented for Ignatius, the deacon and skevophylax of the Great Church and former metropolitan of Nicaea who died shortly after 845. In his later career he composed two better-known vitae of the patriarchs and iconodule heroes Tarasius and Nicephorus. While the first modern editor of the *Life of George* rightly attributed it to Ignatius, he overlooked the iconoclastic character of the text largely because he was ignorant of the author's earlier iconoclastic sympathies.[14]

Written some time between 829 and 842, the *Life of George* is surprisingly silent or at least not explicit about issues related to Iconoclasm, and it seems likely that the author was an iconoclast by necessity rather than conviction.[15] For these reasons the text has been described as a noniconodule rather than a strictly iconoclast vita, yet certain features distinguish the *Life of George* from a typical iconodule counterpart. Material icons are absent from the account but the saints are depicted as "living images," and the author refers to an iconoclast rather than an iconodule council. Old Testament allusions preponderate among the biblical citations in this and other noniconodule Lives, and the distinctive eucharistic theology of the text suggests an iconoclast origin.[16] Thus, if its authorship is still open to debate, the noniconodule character of the *Life* is hard to contest.

Many features of the *Life of George of Amastris* show the enduring legacy of a monastic ideal of episcopal leadership and the specific influence of Cappadocian models. Most obvious is the fact that even in this iconoclast *Life,* which one might expect to denigrate or at least belittle monasticism, given the antimonastic tendencies of some iconoclast rulers, the monastic life is presented as an ideal preparation for the episcopate. Rather than gloss over George's monastic background, the author devotes special attention to his ascetic training and the resulting formation of his character. Praising the saint's virtues, he captures in a series of metaphors the scope of George's life and ministry: he was "the model for ascetics," the "adornment of the priesthood," and the "support of the *migados,*" that is, of those who lived the mixed life.[17] Following a description of his miraculous birth and noble parentage, we hear of the youth's academic prowess, which he rejected for a deeper knowledge of God. Similarly he renounced worldly pleasures and even ecclesiastical honors in preference for an austere and dedicated religious vocation. He longed for the wilderness, having in his mind the examples of Elijah, Moses, and John the Baptist.[18] George was not content simply to pursue the ascetic life in the world, for he chose to live for some time both as a semieremitic monk and then as a member of a cenobitic monastic community. In a monastery at Bonyssa he devoted himself to a rigorous ascetic discipline, spending large parts of his day and night in meditation on the Scriptures and the Lives of saints. Among the brothers he lived the angelic life, "on the boundary of both human and bodiless nature."[19] But he was not to remain in this peaceful retreat, explained his biographer, for his virtuous life "could no longer be concealed just as a lamp cannot hide on a mountaintop nor a pearl conceal its own brilliance."[20]

Before long an embassy from Amastris arrived at George's monastery to persuade the holy monk to take the place of the city's recently deceased bishop. The envoys seemed to regard the episcopal vocation as a higher calling. They exhorted George to imitate the saints and apostles of old, who had carried the message of God's mighty deeds to all people, "for the perfection of virtue is not characterized by providing for oneself but rather . . . in the care and salvation of the many."[21] The suggestion that monastic life benefits only one's own self as opposed to a larger community seems almost antimonastic in tone. But George himself rebuffed the entreaties of the envoys and countered their arguments. He considered the episcopate a high and worthy aspiration, but, alluding to his own monastic vocation, he feared lest "the better" be dragged down by "the worse" and said he wished to remain unenslaved by intercourse with what was inferior. Likewise he referred to ecclesiastical ministry as the extension of good works, but he insisted that his own path led to the highest of goods *(pros to eschaton tōn agathōn)*, and he in no way wished to be deterred from it.[22] At this point the Amastrin delegation recognized the monk's resolve and felt compelled to resort to force to carry out its intentions. Ignoring his vigorous refusal, the envoys took hold of George against his will and dragged him off to Constantinople for consecration.

Once he had assumed the episcopal dignity, George fulfilled his commission with diligence. He was as "an archetypal list," providing "indelible images of virtue" and teaching by deed as much as by word.[23] Nor did the bishop abandon his monastic ideals. His continuing advocacy of the ascetic life appears in an interlude regarding Emperor Nicephorus I (802–811), whom George had served as a spiritual adviser prior to Nicephorus's reign. Inspired by the saint, the emperor himself is said to have aspired to an ascetic life. He secretly donned George's coarse tunic and threadbare cloak, regarding these garments as "the safeguard and strength of his kingdom." Moreover, he scorned his luxurious bed, spent sleepless nights on the ground, and allegedly considered as nothing the imperial diadem and his very rule over the Romans compared with his association with the holy man.[24] Though the hagiographer's motives are unclear in depicting this characteristically antimonastic emperor as a secret ascetic and friend of the saintly monk-bishop, Ignatius reveals in this passage the continuing priority of asceticism in George's episcopal career.[25] Admittedly it is not ascetic feats but powerful prayers and miraculous deeds that fill most of the remaining pages of the *Life*. As we have seen, however, such acts were common manifestations of the spiritual authority of a holy ascetic-turned-bishop, and George proved no exception. Whether repulsing barbarians, stilling the water and the wind, miraculously producing the required eucharistic elements, or posthumously healing the blind, the lame, and the sick, he repeatedly demonstrated the power of holiness as he prevailed against evil forces threatening the people of God.[26]

We also see throughout the *Vita* the prevalence of Cappadocian models—not only figuratively, as the monk-bishop ideal was embodied in the person of George of Amastris, but literally in actual borrowings from writings of Basil the Great and especially from the funeral oration on Basil. In the appendix to his article on hagiography of this period, Ševčenko lists several passages in the *Life of George*, as well as in the vitae of Patriarch Nicephorus and Gregory the Decapolite, where the hagiographer drew on Nazianzen's speech. Attempting to demonstrate Ignatian authorship of these Lives, Ševčenko even posited the following scenario: "Ignatios would have the Funeral Oration on Basil in mind, or on his table, whenever he composed the life of a Saint."[27] Borrowings from Nazianzen range from the use of similar metaphors or ideas to the literal copying of words or passages from the celebrated fourth-century oration. With regard to his studies, George, like Basil, "learned the entire curriculum, both theirs and ours."[28] Describing his pursuit of the monastic life, his hagiographer lifts phrases directly from Gregory's panegryic. The young George "embraced the desert along with Elijah and John," and the cave that served as his first semieremitic dwelling is deemed "a workshop of virtue." The future bishop of Amastris was also said to rival and surpass an array of biblical saints and even classical heroes with whom Gregory had compared his friend Basil.[29]

Some passages suggest parallel deeds or events. For example, the sudden blindness of the wife of the *strategos* of Trebizond on George's arrival to intervene for Amastrin merchants who had been unjustly condemned recalls the illness of Emperor Valens's son on the very night that the infamous Arian ruler had published an edict for Basil's banishment.[30] But amid such intriguing similarities and the many passages copied literally from Nazianzen's oration, the most significant parallel for our topic is the careers of the two saints. Both held promise of worldly success, both retreated to the wilderness to pursue a monastic life, and both relatively quickly returned to their native cities to serve the church. This progression marked the lives of increasing numbers of bishops in the early Byzantine period. Indeed while the stylistic qualities of Nazianzen's funeral oration rendered it worthy of imitation, and borrowings from the speech have been noted in writings throughout the Byzantine era, the subject matter of the panegyric is often overlooked. Gregory represented his friend Basil as the epitome of the Christian leader, a monk-bishop par excellence. It is this model, encased in all its exalted rhetoric, that became the standard for bishops like George of Amastris—both a paradigm for their actual lives and a pattern for the portrayal of their lives in the proliferation of episcopal vitae in ensuing centuries.

Connected with this enduring monastic-episcopal ideal are two final observations on this text. First, if Ignatius the Deacon is the author of the *Life of George of Amastris*, then the same model of leadership is operative in his iconoclast *Life* and his later iconodule vita of Patriarch

Nicephorus. Nicephorus, too, is said to have renounced the world (in his case, a successful career in the imperial service) for a solitary ascetic and contemplative life, reluctantly accepting the patriarchate only on the condition that he first be permitted to take monastic vows.[31] From both perspectives, then, the complementarity of monastic life with a future ecclesiastical career is taken for granted or even idealized. Thus the *Life of George* provides one of several examples of the fact that iconoclasm did not necessarily mean monachomachy. Supporting this hagiographical evidence is the simple fact that two of the three iconoclast patriarchs of Constantinople in the ninth century were themselves monks and even abbots before their promotion to the episcopal throne.[32] Though the ideal of the monk-turned-bishop was certainly not distinctive to the iconoclastic milieu, neither was it unique to the iconophiles. As illustrated by non-Chalcedonian texts examined in Chapter 9, the model of the monk-bishop might well be embraced by both sides of theological controversies. Indeed the monastic life was often deemed a surer mark of the true spiritual authority of a Christian leader than episcopal office itself. Also worth noting is a distinction about timing. The *Life of George of Amastris* is an example of relatively rare hagiography dating from the iconoclast period itself. Evidence from this non-iconodule *Life,* then, helps to dispel the assumption that a monastic episcopate arose in the aftermath of Iconoclasm or principally as a result of the monastic triumph in that struggle.

If extant hagiography from the iconoclast era is relatively scarce, the genre abounds in the next two centuries of Byzantine history.[33] Hagiographers now had a host of new heroes to commemorate, and many of the saints who were the subjects of this new outpouring of texts were champions and martyrs of the iconodule cause. Though the majority of ninth- and tenth-century saints were male monastics, less often observed is the significant number of new Lives of bishops, as opposed to simple iconodule martyrs or holy ascetics. Wolfgang Lackner describes some ten new episcopal vitae from this period, in addition to six Lives of patriarchs.[34] He refers to these texts as evidence of a new type of saint who worked in the world and undertook tasks on behalf of society, in contrast to the world-denying ascetics who dominated the hagiography of previous centuries. Though he does not discuss their origins, most of the energetic bishops he lists came out of the monastic milieu.

Of the six patriarchs of Constantinople Lackner names as the subjects of new Lives, five were at one time monks.[35] His list of new, more socially active bishops includes such episcopal personalities as Theophylact of Nicomedia, Peter of Argos, and Nicephorus of Miletus. Theophylact headed a monastery in Propontide, where he was said to have lived a quasi-angelic life, wholly removed from the affairs of the world. On discovering this luminary, however, Patriarch Tarasius "added to his monastic light the light of the episcopate."[36] Indeed Theophylact became renowned not only for resisting the iconoclast regime of Leo the Armenian but also as a merciful bishop who cared personally for the unfortunates of his city.[37] Peter of Argos was a wandering monk who was elected bishop of Argos later in life. In this capacity he was involved in ransoming Christian captives, missionary work with pagan Slavic tribes, and feeding and caring for his people after an Arab raid into the Peloponnese. Though no monastic foundation was associated with him during his lifetime, Peter of Argos was remembered as a great monastic patron and founder. Nicephorus of Miletus was yet another monk-bishop known for his love of the poor and his role as a monastic founder. After serving for several years as bishop of Miletus, Nicephorus retreated again to a monastery and eventually came to oversee two houses.[38] All three of these bishops were well born, well educated, and heavily involved in social, philanthropic, and pastoral activity. Lackner has rightly discerned a distinction between these highly engaged churchmen and many of the more remote holy men of an earlier era. But their monastic pedigree and ongoing commitment to monastic life and ideals formed an important part of their identity. It likely influenced their own selection as bishop as well as the tasks they undertook in the church and the world. Such figures show the continuing vibrancy of a monastic ideal of leadership that had evolved several centuries earlier but had gained new strength with the rising fortunes of the monastic party following the iconoclastic controversies. They also reveal the tremendous breadth and appeal of the monk-bishop paradigm, for it joined contemplative and active vocations, putting holy men, hermits, and virtuous monks in the service of the church and society at large.

In addition to a plethora of new Lives celebrating recent heroes of the faith, the literary history of the eighth to tenth century witnessed the rewriting, revision, and collection of older saints' Lives. Though Symeon Metaphrastes is best known for this work, the process actually began as early as the seventh century, in part reflecting a sense that the age of the great saints had passed and the hope that their image and their cult could be revitalized for contemporaries.[39] The writings of Nicetas David the Paphlagonian provide a prominent example of such hagiography in the late ninth to early tenth century. Educated at the patriarchal school of Constantinople, where he was later to win the coveted chair of rhetoric, Nicetas himself became a monk and eventually the bishop of Dadybrae. But he is best known for his composition of more than fifty panegyrics of the saints, principally biblical and patristic figures but also near contemporaries, among which his vita of the monk-bishop Patriarch Ignatius is most famous.[40] One of his earlier hagiographical works was an encomium of Gregory Nazianzen for which his main literary models were Nazianzen's own writings, prominent among them his funeral oration on Basil of Caesarea.[41] Indeed the *Encomium of Gregory Nazianzen* is replete with direct quotations, copied forms and figures of speech, and many other subtle borrowings from its namesake. A letter to Nicetas from a contemporary actually criticized the piece for precisely such stylistic imitations.[42] As a result of such usage, however, Gregory's eulogy of Basil continued to serve as a stylistic paradigm for writers of vitae and panegyrics in Byzantium, and Basil's life continued to serve as a model of the episcopal career.

Nicetas's objective in his encomium of Gregory was to portray his hero neither primarily as a bishop nor as a monk but rather as the consummate theologian.[43] The route to this exalted title was the path of asceticism and contemplation. Only through a time of purification and illumination in the wilderness was Gregory equipped for the supreme role he was to play as a leader and teacher of God's people. Thus, in concluding his treatment of this preparatory period, Nicetas remarks that Gregory became an example "of the sort of man one ought to be who is going to preside over a bishopric."[44] In addition to its extensive use of Nazianzen's writings, Nicetas's retelling of Gregory's life followed the typical Cappadocian threefold progression for the model bishop: high achievements in the intellectual realm, abandonment of those aspirations for the monastic life, and ultimate return to the world in the service of the church. Not surprisingly, amid the host of biblical figures with which Gregory is compared in this encomium, the longest *synkrisis* is devoted to Moses.[45] Like Moses, Gregory was "naturally suited" for the secular wisdom in which he was so well trained as a youth, but he fled its "baseness and superstition." Similarly, Nicetas continues, "Not migrating to a mountain of Midian as Moses had, but ascending to the height of the holy state of freedom from passions, and not, like Moses, having wed himself to a mortal wife, but having fallen in love with the perfect wisdom . . . Gregory, if any man, saw the Invisible One. And, looking with unveiled face upon the glory of the Lord as in a mirror, he was filled with contemplation and power and was sent off to this pleasure-loving Egypt of ours."[46] We have seen how prominently this Old Testament patriarch figured in the writings of the Cappadocians as a model for episcopal leadership, in particular the three stages of his career that are outlined in this passage. The Mosaic pattern was clearly impressed on future generations as well, and we find it presented once again in this text by Nicetas, exalting Gregory of Nazianzus as the model Christian leader—ascetic, theologian, and bishop.

The Slavic Context: An Example from Medieval Serbia

Jumping ahead several centuries, a final hagiographic subject, St. Sava of Serbia (1175–1235), illustrates the transition of a monastic episcopate to the broader Byzantine commonwealth and points to distinctive ecclesiastical developments in the Slavic Orthodox traditions. While both the actual and the literary life of St. Sava show the lasting impress of the late antique ideal of the monk-bishop, there are also variations on that ideal suggesting the flexibility of the model that so facilitated its transmission to posterity. Long before the emergence of autocephalous orthodox churches or even a native Slav clergy, Byzantine missions in the recently converted lands beyond its borders were largely monastic in composition.[47] Monks also served as the first priests and filled other positions of authority within the hierarchy of the newly established churches. Byzantine and gradually indigenous Slavic monks became the primary teachers, writers, and translators as well as the church leaders, passing on the culture, traditions, and ecclesiastical ideals of the Byzantine church to its daughter churches in the emerging Slavic lands.[48] But as social and political realities changed with time, and elements of Byzantine cultural and intellectual life adapted to new geographical and ethnic settings, so too were episcopal ideals and patterns modified to suit their new contexts.

Sava of Serbia, whose unique mythopoetic sway in eastern Europe has been said to rival that of Alexander the Great, epitomized the new model bishop in the Byzantine Slavic world.[49] Born Rastko, Sava was the third son of Stefan Nemanja, the grand župan of Serbia and the first head of a dynasty that would reign until 1371. When Rastko turned fifteen his father made him governor of a western province, an area that included a significant stretch of the Adriatic coast that would later be known as Herzegovina. The boy's tenure as a provincial governor was short-lived, however, for less than two years later, in 1191 or 1192, Rastko fled from his home and his father's court to Mt. Athos. He took the name Sava for the sixth-century monastic St. Sabas of Palestine and joined the Greek monastery of Vatopedi. The Holy Mountain at this time already had Georgian, Russian, Bulgarian, and Italian monasteries in addition to Greek houses and was a truly international religious community. Through the monks' reading, copying, and translating of Byzantine texts in the scriptoria of these monasteries, Mt. Athos became a major center for the diffusion of Byzantine culture, secular as well as religious, to the lands of Orthodox eastern Europe.

Athonite monasticism shaped Sava's spiritual vision and provided the models he would later use in organizing the monasteries and governing the churches of his native Serbia. At least partly under Sava's influence, toward the end of his life his father abdicated his throne to his son Stefan Nemanjić, became a monk at Studenica monastery, which he had founded, and eighteen months later joined Sava on Mt. Athos, where the grand župan turned lowly monk died in 1198. After his father's arrival, together they planned for the foundation of Hilandar monastery, which under Sava's leadership would begin to play its incomparable role in the religious and cultural history of Serbia. In the next few years Sava pursued a more rigorous and isolated ascetic life on Athos while at the same time becoming a figure of increasing spiritual and institutional authority. He was ordained deacon and priest, and at some point between 1200 and 1204 he traveled to Thessalonica to be consecrated archimandrite. Sava returned to Athos, where he was present during the capture of Constantinople by crusading armies in 1204 and the subsequent Latin incursion onto the Holy Mountain. Soon afterward, however, he returned to his homeland and in 1207 was appointed abbot of Studenica, the leading monastery in Serbia. From there he put his administrative talents to work in advancing monastic and liturgical life and promoting in various ways the intimate link between church and ruling dynasty that so characterized medieval Serbia. Little wonder, then, that Sava became the obvious candidate for the first archbishop of an independent Serbian church, an honor he attained from the Byzantine emperor and patriarch in Nicaea in 1219.[50]

Besides presenting this basic outline of his career, the two main hagiographic sources on St. Sava give us a picture of the ideal bishop in the context of medieval Serbia. Both Lives were composed by monks: the first by Domentijan, an Athonite monk and disciple of Sava who wrote shortly after Sava's death in 1235; the second, a major revision of Domentijan's work by Teodosije, another Athonite monk who wrote in the early fourteenth century.[51] Both Domentijan and Teodosije devoted considerable space in their vitae to Sava's pursuit of the monastic vocation. From the very start of his biography Teodosije's long title attests to this primary interest: "The life and exploits in the desert with his father . . . of our holy father Sava, first Serbian archbishop and teacher."[52] The desert *(pustinje)* here is Mt. Athos, the main locus of both Lives. Both authors describe the youth's escape from his homeland to the Holy Mountain for which he had longed. We are given detailed accounts of Sava's activities and development on Mt. Athos: his rigorous ascetic practices, his refusal to be swayed from his monastic vocation despite persistent pressure from his royal family, his devotion to prayer and *hesychia* *(ćutanje),* and his increasing stature and influence among fellow monks and hermits. We learn too of his initial rejection of ecclesiastical honors both prior to his ordination as deacon and priest on Athos and again in the face of the patriarch's proposal in Nicaea. Both narratives also emphasize his continuing love and beneficence toward the monasteries of Athos. Even amid the pressing duties of his episcopate, including extensive travel and diplomatic missions on behalf of the state as well as the normal responsibilities of oversight, Sava still found time to return repeatedly to the Holy Mountain. The link between his monastic and episcopal vocations is made explicit in one passage in particular. Reflecting on Sava's ascetic feats in Serbia and anticipating his imminent elevation to the office of archbishop, Teodosije commented that "even more than when he lived in the desert, with great effort, through fasts and nocturnal watches he was putting the body to death, and not that he would gain prestige or be only the lawgiver to monks, but rather even before his consecration [to the episcopate] by his works he showed himself to be an apostle."[53]

We find in these Lives familiar themes and even the familiar threefold pattern for the model episcopal career—renunciation, retreat to the wilderness, and return to service in the church and the world—a paradigm we have seen with the Cappadocians as well as other Byzantine hagiographical texts discussed above. There are, however, modifications of the ideal, subtle twists and shifts of emphasis in the presentation of the life of a holy bishop. Whereas earlier writings often stressed lofty intellectual achievements that the future bishop abandoned for the life of a monk, in the vitae of Sava there is little mention of learning or intellectual pursuits and no hint of academic prowess. Instead, the comforts, wealth, and esteem of the royal household and the temptations of worldly glory are what Sava rejected for the humble monastic vocation. These descriptions of the monk's renunciations reflect new realities on two levels. First, for medieval Slavs the high level of secular as well as religious education that so characterized learned monk-bishops of late antiquity was severely limited.[54] Second, we find in the Slavic context the general tendency, particularly pronounced in Serbia, for high church officials to be members of the royal household.[55] It is thus less often the prestige of education than the lure of wealth and power that must be abandoned by the prospective monk and future bishop of such pedigree.

Though he had certainly renounced personal wealth, as archbishop Sava was in a position to exploit the riches of the state for his monastic ambitions. One of his main preoccupations, an emphasis in his Lives far outweighing its importance in late antique vitae or panegyrics of bishops, was the foundation and decoration of new monasteries. Funds for these Serbian monastic houses, as well as for monasteries on Mt. Athos, in Constantinople, and in the Holy Land, were abundantly provided from the royal treasury of Sava's brother Stefan Nemanjić and his two sons who succeeded him. The lavish gifts and immense amount of gold donated for the construction and enhancement of monasteries, even allowing for the exaggerations of Sava's hagiographers, raise questions about the apparent wealth of the Serbian state. But such generous endowments also point to the important role these institutions played as royal monasteries, serving to strengthen the important partnership between church and state that typified the medieval Serbian dynasty and that Archbishop Sava, son of Grand Župan Stefan Nemanja, himself embodied.[56]

The Lives of Sava also show his monastic orientation in other aspects of his leadership of the church. A principal obligation of the new archbishop was to provide much needed bishops and clergy for the Serbian churches, and monastic candidates were his obvious choice. The first native bishops of Serbia were monks whom Sava brought back with him from Hilandar on Mt. Athos, and on several occasions thereafter the Lives recount his choosing of new bishops, priests, and deacons from the leading monasteries of Serbia.[57] Sava also selected monks for missionary work to un-Christianized or still largely pagan areas of Serbia, ordaining them as archpriests and sending them out to evangelize, teach doctrine, and regulate the moral life of the church in these regions.[58] His choice of his own successor was a monk as well: his disciple Arsenije, who had been serving as hegumen of Studenica monastery. Sava appointed Arsenije to replace him and consecrated him to the archiepiscopal throne before leaving on his final pilgrimage to the Holy Land.[59] All these examples demonstrate the persistent tendency of monastic bishops to choose church leaders from their own ranks.

Alongside such important administrative tasks as the foundation of monasteries and the appointment of bishops, Domentijan and Teodosije describe Sava's personal ascetic practices, continued and occasionally even intensified despite his new ecclesiastical position.[60] They also stress his special love and care for the poor, an ongoing philanthropic duty of Byzantine bishops but a virtue specially connected with monastic life as well. From the start of his sojourn on Mt. Athos Sava is compared with St. Thomas ministering to the Indians. Barefoot, he traveled from monastery to monastery and among the solitary hermits, dividing between them the gold he had been sent by his parents.[61] His first sermon in Serbia expounded the lesson of the rich man and Lazarus (Luke 16:19–31), with his late father, Stefan Nemanja, serving as the counterpoint to the merciless rich man.[62] Both before and after his episcopal consecration, Sava preached often about the duty of almsgiving and generosity to the poor, asserting that prayer and fasting alone were not enough if one neglected those in need. Commenting on one of these homilies, Dimitrije Bogdanović suggests that it summarized Sava's social ethic. In this connection he makes one of his only references to the patristic foundations of Sava's ideas, specifically the teachings of Basil the Great and John Chrysostom. Even Sava's posthumous mercies show particular concern for the less fortunate.[63]

Indeed Sava's miraculous deeds, often reenactments of Christ's own miracles, are among those features connecting him with great monk-bishops of the past. In addition to healing the sick, calming storms at sea, and miraculously producing the fish needed for his own nourishment, his God-given powers clearly benefited his native Serbia. Describing some of the many miracles of Sava and his father, Teodosije commented that "other rulers, hearing about the awesome wonders that the saints performed, sought favor with the monarch Stefan [Nemanjić] and dared not undertake anything against his state."[64] One example of Sava's influence on behalf of this "new Israel," as Serbia is often called throughout the Lives, is his interaction with King Andrew II of Hungary. By his words, prayers, and prodigious deeds the bishop allegedly persuaded the king to cease his hostilities toward Serbia, to renounce the Latin faith and to embrace "true orthodoxy."[65] In another moment of crisis Sava raised his brother Stefan from death, enabling the ruler to abdicate the throne to his son and become a monk before finally expiring less than a year later.[66] Moreover, as had become commonplace in hagiographical accounts of Byzantine bishops, such extraordinary powers were not limited to the saint's earthly career. The final pages of both Lives of Sava, as in that of George of Amastris, are almost exclusively devoted to his posthumous miracles.

It comes as no surprise that these texts owe much to Byzantine hagiographical and spiritual traditions. Among the most influential writings of the patristic period, hagiographical works were copiously translated, propagated, and imitated by the Slavs of the Middle Ages. The Lives of bishops like Gregory Nazianzen, Basil the Great, and John Chrysostom were especially well known and highly regarded. Singling out the Lives of the three hierarchs among the best-known texts to medieval Slavs, Ivan Dujčev cites the late tenth-century Bulgarian Cosmas the Presbyter, who instructed his audience of monks and priests as follows: "Imitate the holy fathers and bishops who exercised your functions before you, I mean Gregory, Basil, John, and all the others, whom it suffices only to name in order to frighten the demons."[67] Despite differences in emphasis and style from earlier vitae, the model of the late antique monk-bishop and even some of the forms and language of such patristic writings persist in medieval Serbian biographies. Like Sava himself, Domentijan and Teodosije had access to the rich store of Greek theological, monastic, hagiographic, and literary texts on Mt. Athos. More recent Byzantine literature served as the primary models for our Serbian authors, particularly the rhetorical Byzantine Metaphrastic hagiography and, in

Teodosije's case, probably Byzantine secular historiography as well.[68] But the influence of earlier patristic writers, whether used directly or mediated through later Byzantine authors, should not be overlooked and is especially important for understanding episcopal ideals. As might be expected, both of Sava's hagiographers drew heavily from the sixth-century *Life of Sabas* by Cyril of Scythopolis in introducing his Serbian namesake.[69] Not only was this particular monk chosen by Sava as his patron saint, but Cyril's *Lives of the Palestinian Monks* was particularly popular among the Slavic communities on Mt. Athos and was among the main sources on which the Slavs modeled their monastic life.[70]

More closely related to our narrower focus on leadership of the church are passages that directly reflect on the character or role of the ideal bishop. We have already noted the threefold pattern of the episcopal career that is evident in the Lives of Sava. Despite medieval Slavic variations on these three stages, they are recognizable here just as they were presented by the Cappadocians and embodied particularly in Basil of Caesarea. Several passages also suggest the more direct influence of Nazianzen's funeral oration on Basil. Many of the same *synkriseis* recur comparing Sava with biblical heroes, most prominently Elijah and John the Baptist.[71] Teodosije describes Sava's rise to the archiepiscopal throne in terms that echo Gregory's appraisal of Basil's ecclesiastical advancement almost word for word: "He did not steal authority by bribery, nor as a thief, he did not seize it by force, not pursuing honor but rather being pursued and barely persuaded by honor, not having received human favor but divine favor from God."[72] Though the author would have had access to Gregory's influential oration in the scriptoria of monasteries on Mt. Athos, such encomiastic passages, like the *synkriseis,* were common stock in Byzantine hagiography and panegyrics and need not reflect direct borrowing from Nazianzen. But they do reveal the continuation of Cappadocian ideals of leadership, both rhetorical *and* actual models that were passed on through such texts from one generation to the next in the Christian East.

Finally, both Serbian hagiographers appealed to the life of Moses as a model for the episcopal career, comparing Sava favorably with the biblical patriarch. There was more reason than in most other hagiographic texts to draw such a comparison, for Sava had compiled and codified for the needs of his church what was to become the most authoritative Slavonic body of Byzantine law, constituting the basis of Serbian civil as well as ecclesiastical legislation. In this sense Sava was indeed a great lawgiver like Moses, and this specific analogy between the two men was drawn.[73] But it was far from the only or even the primary point of comparison. Teodosije spoke of Moses mainly as a model of prayer, so Sava, like the Old Testament patriarch, gained victory over evil forces and wrought miracles on behalf of his people through his prayerful intercessions.[74] But it was Domentijan who developed the Mosaic analogy to the utmost. The Moses-*synkrisis* in his *Life of Sava* is by far the longest in the text, presenting parallels stretched to near absurdity between almost every incident in the two leaders' careers.[75] In most cases Sava is shown to have in some way surpassed his biblical predecessor. For example, whereas Moses led "thousands" of Israelites out of slavery in Egypt, Sava is said to have brought "myriads of people" to the true faith, having delivered them from the deception of idols. And while Moses fed the Israelites in the desert with manna sent from God, Sava loved the desert from his youth, feeding and caring for those who inhabited it and serving all their needs both spiritually and physically.[76]

Most striking throughout the *synkrisis* is a single term that is repeatedly used to describe these two men of God. It is not their role as rulers or prophets or lawgivers that is singled out for praise, though all of these functions are included in the lengthy comparison. What is emphasized is that each of the two leaders was a *bogovidac,* literally a divine visionary or "God-seer." On descending from Mt. Sinai during his final pilgrimage to the Holy Land, Sava is described as "having become like the great God-seer [Moses], not only bearing God himself within him and on him but also adorned with his favor. And this one [Sava] became a second God-seer, and he was deemed worthy to see not only God's back, but by the favor granted him from above he was deemed worthy to serve the Lord himself through holiness and righteousness before him all the days of his life."[77] The whole *synkrisis* is structured around this formula: the God-seer (Moses) did a wonderful deed while this new visionary (Sava) performed a similar but even greater feat. Whether Domentijan intended to show that Sava was truly greater than Moses is arguable, but he certainly viewed the Serbian archbishop as a *bogovidac,* one who had had a vision of God and been uniquely prepared to lead through this theophany. We have already examined the significance of such a divine encounter in the Cappadocians. Both in their writings and in this *Life of Sava* it seems to have been required or simply assumed of the bishop worthy of his calling.

The Contribution of the Byzantine Prophetic Tradition

What is reflected in the hagiographical texts we have considered here—both middle Byzantine Lives and the medieval Serbian Lives of St. Sava—is the growing reality of an episcopate dominated by monks. Already by the eighth century hagiography was largely silent about married prelates unless it was to magnify in some way the misogyny of monks.[78] The formal status of clergy and bishops had not changed since the legislation enacted at the Council of Trullo (691–692), but monastic ideals increasingly overshadowed the strictly legal expectations for bearers of church office.[79] Young clerics were not forced, but were certainly strongly advised, to remain celibate, and renunciation of all familial attachments and obligations was again prescribed for bishops. Meanwhile the ordination of monks became increasingly commonplace, and monks who held no ecclesiastical office were implicitly regarded as a separate if not inferior class. Alongside social, political, and ecclesiastical factors governing these developments, the further progress and near institutionalization of such patterns had to do with the popularity of particular spiritual movements in the Byzantine world from the eleventh to the fourteenth century. As spiritual ideals helped to generate a predominantly monastic episcopate in the Christian East, we will end by reviewing developments in the Byzantine prophetic and mystical tradition that, whether intentionally or not, contributed to the permanence of this model of leadership.

The triumph of an exclusively monastic episcopate in the East was due at least in part to individuals who were neither completely sympathetic to, nor regarded sympathetically by, the hierarchy of the church. Chief among these influential figures was St. Symeon the New Theologian (949–1022). We are well informed about the career of this charismatic monk and spiritual director, owing to a detailed Life composed by his disciple Nicetas Stethatos.[80] Though this portrayal of his life followed many of the standard Byzantine *topoi*, in the case of Symeon they were largely true to fact and substantiated by many of his own autobiographical comments.[81] Born to noble and wealthy parents in rural Paphlagonia, Symeon was sent to Constantinople at age eleven to be educated. His intellectual ability and academic success is attested by the significant corpus of his writings. Symeon's paternal uncle, to whose care he had been entrusted, recognized the boy's gifts and persuaded him to enter the imperial service as an official of the bedchamber in the court of the brother emperors Basil II and Constantine Porphyrogenetes. But after his uncle's sudden death, at age fourteen Symeon left the palace to manage the household of a patrician while pursuing a life of asceticism and prayer in the evenings. He began to frequent the monastery of Studios, where he found a spiritual father, the monk Symeon Eulabes, also known as Symeon the Studite.

The young Symeon eventually became a monk of Studios, but his continuing devotion to his spiritual mentor was considered scandalous in this highly regulated community. Symeon Eulabes was not the hegumen of the monastery but simply one monk among many, not the most highly regarded and apparently considered a charlatan by some of the brothers. Though Symeon eventually relocated to the monastery of St. Mamas, where he was ordained priest and became hegumen on the death of his predecessor, his troubles did not cease. When Eulabes died (c. 986), Symeon organized his cult and began to celebrate his memory "like that of all the other saints."[82] Much of Nicetas's *Life* focuses on the cult of Symeon's spiritual father, a lifelong obsession for Symeon that provoked a rebellion of some of his monks, a clash with the episcopate, and his temporary forced exile. He was eventually recalled by Patriarch Sergius, who affirmed Symeon's purity of faith and life and allegedly offered him an important archbishopric by way of compensation for the wrongs inflicted on him.[83] Instead the monk chose to retire to a small oratory, where he guided others and gathered a community of disciples who continued to commemorate Eulabes. Though still viewed with suspicion by some, thirty years after Symeon the New Theologian's death his relics were translated to the Studios monastery, where the young monk had begun his volatile career.

If his life was controversial, Symeon's teachings were no less provocative. There are at least two related areas of Christian thought on which he left a definitive mark: the doctrine of the vision of God and the idea of spiritual direction or, more specifically, spiritual fatherhood.[84] Neither one of these notions or emphases lay outside the sphere of Orthodox theology, and both were the particular concern of mystics. But Symeon's distinctive perspective on these ideals got him into trouble with the ecclesiastical authorities of his day, since his teachings challenged the very hierarchical structure they represented. Concerning the vision of God, Symeon taught largely out of his living experience of what he believed to be the truths of Scripture and the theology of the Fathers. Even before becoming a monk Symeon had had his first of many mystical experiences, a vision of God as light. On his consecration to the priesthood he had a similar vision of the Holy Spirit descending upon him as an immense light, and he continued to have such divine encounters throughout the remainder of his monastic and priestly career.[85] Little wonder that his biographer described him at one point as the divine visionary or God-seer *(ho theoptikōtatos)*,[86] the exact equivalent of the Slavic term *bogovidac* that Domentijan ascribed to Moses and Sava in his *Life of Sava*. In keeping with his personal experience, Symeon preached the importance, indeed the necessity, of a conscious vision of God. To see God, he believed, was the essence of Christian perfection and the hope of the Christian's beatitude in the life to come. For Symeon it was a great travesty to profess to be a spiritual guide without a conscious apprehension of this vision or to affirm that one had received the gift of the Spirit unconsciously, by faith and intellect alone, and not by mystical experience. Indeed he considered it blasphemous to deny the possibility of such direct operations of the Holy Spirit in the lives of believers who, through prayer and repentance, ardently sought the vision of God.[87]

It was Symeon's integration of these ideas with his teachings on spiritual direction that perplexed representatives of the church hierarchy. His emphasis on the experiential knowledge of God indirectly, and at times directly, posed a challenge to worldly bishops and clergy of his day. For example, he warned his readers against imagining that they were spiritual before they had actually received the Holy Spirit. Do not rush "to receive the confessions of others, to rise to the position of hegumens and authorities, to dare to accept the priesthood without fear, to put yourself forward shamelessly by countless intrigues for metropolises and episcopates," Symeon admonished would-be ecclesiastical leaders.[88] Elsewhere he warned against meddling in divine affairs, "as if ordaining ourselves before being called from above."[89] Indeed the very notion of ordination came into question in Symeon's writings, for even an unordained monk could receive the "baptism of the Spirit," serve as a director of souls, and be more efficacious spiritually than those who possessed only human ordination. Likely Symeon's own spiritual father lay in the background of such teachings, for Eulabes "had no ordination from men" yet had received an ordination from above.[90] It was also increasingly common for laymen, particularly (though certainly not exclusively) wealthy and influential aristocrats in Constantinople, to choose monks as spiritual directors. These monks might well be unordained, yet by virtue of their *parrēsia,* their direct access to God, they were sought out in ways that the secular clergy were not. Beyond their spiritual functions, such monastic fathers might also play important social and political roles in the Byzantine state.[91] The threat, of course, was that charismatic figures like Symeon would usurp the authority of the sacerdotal hierarchy or even subvert the powers of the ruling imperial dynasty.

Though some of his writings seem to suggest antisacramental or even antisacerdotal views, Symeon managed to avoid such extremes. He was himself an ordained priest, and his highest experience of the vision of God as divine light occurred repeatedly during the consecration of the eucharistic elements.[92] Symeon had no desire to undermine the institutions of the hierarchical church, but he did want to expose what he considered the decadence of clergy and bishops of his day as well as the relative laxity of contemporary monastic life. To counteract an increasing abstraction in theology and formalism in worship and prayer, Symeon called both monks and laity back to the necessity of personal mystical experience, which he believed was available to all baptized Christians. But for leaders in the church, a divine encounter was indispensable, its absence unthinkable. A living experience of God was the very purpose of the monastic life and the only adequate preparation for leading and serving fellow Christians. Thus, while he instructed monks to follow the examples of St. Thecla, the apostles, and others who had in solitude sought the divine illumination, in a passage that recalls Nazianzen he went on to commend the example of Moses as well. Moses went up to the summit of the mountain alone and encountered God in the cloud, but he did not remain there. Likewise, after hearing God's voice and being initiated into the heavenly mysteries, Symeon explains, he who imitates this patriarch "will give the laws to others; he will be illumined, and he will illumine others with the light of knowledge; he will be pardoned, and thereafter he will pardon. This one asks and receives, and having received, he distributes to those who ask him."[93]

Although Symeon escaped any condemnation for or even long-lasting suspicion of heresy, he was a controversial figure in his day, and some churchmen clearly resisted and resented his appeals as a one-man crusader for reform.[94] But his spiritual influence was widespread, and his followers, both monastic and lay, advanced many of his teachings. Nicetas Stethatos, Symeon's professed disciple and himself a Studite monk, certainly echoed some of his mentor's sentiments on the episcopate. In a passage of his *Treatise on the Hierarchy,* which closely follows the Pseudo-Dionysian scheme, Nicetas suggests that the wisdom of the Word of God might appear to shine more brightly in the lives of lower clergy or monks than in the lives of bishops.[95] Without denying the validity of the institutional hierarchy, he explains that he who has been given the power to manifest the Spirit by his word—whether priest, deacon, or monk—also shines forth the brilliance of the episcopal dignity even if he has not been ordained by human hands.[96] Far from anti-sacerdotalism, however, this treatise attests to the interpenetration of monastic and ecclesiastical ideals. On the one hand, the true bishop is cast in the role of a monk who has throughout his life overcome the desires of the flesh. Indeed the whole ecclesiastical hierarchy should manifest the purity and detachment of the "angelic life," and not surprisingly, married clergy are tacitly excluded from the scheme. Thus, a monastic model of leadership had clearly come to shape Nicetas's notion of church office. But his description suggests the opposite phenomenon as well, that is, the imposition of ecclesiastical models on the monastic order. In his hierarchical scheme, in which the ecclesiastical ranks mirror the celestial hierarchy, unordained monks occupy the lowest level of all, even below that of subdeacons and lectors.[97]

However much his monastic disciples perpetuated his ideals, it has been suggested that Symeon's greatest influence was felt in the lay milieu, particularly among the Constantinopolitan aristocracy. Symeon served as a spiritual father to many noble families in the capital, and even while living in exile under patriarchal ban he continued to receive frequent visits from patricians and middle-ranking court officials.[98] Representing precisely this level of society in the generation after Symeon, the Byzantine general Catacalon Cecaumenus wrote in his *Strategicon* advice on the episcopate in which more than one scholar has heard the clear echo of Symeon:

> If you are headed for holy orders to become, for example, a metropolitan or a bishop, do not accept this dignity as long as you have not received, by means of fasts and vigils, a revelation from above and the perfect assurance that comes from God; and if the manifestation of God tarries, take courage, persevere, humble yourself before God and you will see it, provided that your life is pure and surmounts the obstacles of the passions. And why do I say metropolitan? If it is even for the patriarchal throne that you have been chosen without a divine vision, do not have the temerity to take in hand the management of the holy Church of God.[99]

While this statement does not explicitly affirm that only monks should serve as bishops, it provides yet another example of a contemplative or monastic ideal of ecclesiastical authority, this time from the pen of a lay aristocrat. The popularity and influence of the spiritual writings of Symeon who, according to Dagron, "dominates not only his epoch but the whole religious history of Byzantium,"[100] helps to explain the reasons why a monastic paradigm of leadership persisted and ultimately prevailed in the Christian East.

The late eleventh century is generally viewed as a turning point for the Byzantine state. For monks and monasticism, closely tied to the fortunes of the empire, it marked the beginning of a downward spiral in prestige and influence. Holy men, especially practitioners of more eccentric ascetic feats or miraculous predictions and cures, were increasingly regarded with suspicion in aristocratic and ecclesiastical circles.[101] Hagiography, like the lives of the saints it portrayed, was pressed to conform to standard patterns, and individuality was discouraged. Oddly enough, however, criticism of ascetic extremes and denunciation of specific holy men in the twelfth and thirteenth centuries did not diminish the influx of monks into positions of ecclesiastical authority. This may well have to do with the types of monks who were chosen for church office, in what has been referred to as a process of "politicization" of the Byzantine saint that started in the eleventh century.[102] The continued choice of monks as bishops during this period was partly due as well to the relatively high level of education that many managed to achieve. But also, as Paul Magdalino has so aptly put it, "All Byzantines had a soft spot for a holy man." By way of example he cites the emperor Manuel I Comnenus, certainly no great patron of monks or monasteries; yet even Manuel appointed to the patriarchal see of Jerusalem a one-time holy fool who had become a monk at Patmos, where his ascetic practices included self-flagellation and weeping naked in the tombs of dead monks.[103] More prosaic choices were the norm, of course, but the ideal of the holy ascetic bishop clearly prevailed through this period of relative monastic and spiritual decline.

While the fate of the empire worsened in the fourteenth century, Byzantium experienced yet another monastic revival. Hagiography flourished, and ascetics once again played dominant roles as prophets, advisers, and ecclesiastical mediators. This monastic recovery was associated with the spiritual movement known as Hesychasm, most often identified with its leading representative, the monk of Mt. Athos and eventual archbishop of Thessalonica, Gregory Palamas.[104] The controversy in which he was embroiled and the spiritual revival that followed on the hesychast triumph had long-lasting ramifications for both the Slavic and the Greek churches. Hesychasm was not a new idea but a recovery of deep traditions of Orthodox spirituality, particularly a reaffirmation of the experience of deification or *theosis,* human participation in divinity. In response to the accusations of Barlaam the Calabrian, an Italian monk of the Greek rite who had criticized the spiritual practices of certain monks on Mount Athos, Gregory Palamas stressed the knowability of God and defended the possibility of *theosis,* a belief that lay at the heart of Christian life in the eastern church. In particular the Athonite monks claimed that one could experience the divine light that had shone around Christ on Mt. Tabor, an affirmation that echoed the teachings of Symeon the New Theologian on the vision of God.

In what is probably their most representative document, the "Hagioretic Tome," Palamas and the hesychasts reflected on the special role of monastics in the church. In statements pregnant with implications for the exercise of spiritual authority, they compared the monks of their day with the prophets of the Old Testament. The Tome ascribed to contemporary monastic saints spiritual senses that allowed them a clearer vision of God and a special prophetic role in the church.[105] Through the course of a protracted controversy interwoven with diverse political and ecclesiastical issues, Barlaam's views were condemned and the teachings of Gregory Palamas affirmed as true Orthodox doctrine and spirituality. The final resolution of this controversy in favor of the hesychast position at a synod in 1351 helped to reestablish the prestige and influence of monks.

Long before this period, monks had already come to monopolize most of the bishoprics in Byzantium, with Constantinople standing out as the notable exception to the rule. But even in the capital the situation was steadily changing. During the period between 705 and 1204 forty-five of the sixty-seven patriarchs of Constantinople were monks, and even before the final resolution of the hesychast controversy, the large majority of fourteenth-century patriarchs were monks in the hesychast tradition.[106] But the Palamite victory marked a decisive turning point. After that time the ecumenical patriarchate, which had far longer and more often than any other eastern see resisted the allure of monks in favor of the prestige of humanists, finally succumbed to complete monastic dominance of this highest ecclesiastical office.

*   *   *

In the context of a chapter on Basil the Great and leadership of the church, the Byzantine scholar John Meyendorff discussed both Symeon the New Theologian and Gregory Palamas.[107] This connection brings us full circle in our examination of the monastic-episcopal ideal. Though Basil may have been more successful in balancing sources of spiritual authority, these later Byzantine prophetic figures shared with the great Cappadocian a commitment to personal experience of God as well as obedience to superiors, freedom alongside authority. "The institutional and sacramental authority of the bishops and the spiritual authority of the saints coexist in the catholic Church," Meyendorff explained, "and the tensions which occasionally arise between them cannot justify the suppression of either one."[108] But he neglected an important dimension of that coexistence, for in the Byzantine church from Basil of Caesarea to Gregory Palamas these two forms of authority came increasingly to reside in the same person. Ideally the monastic bishop represented both the institutional authority of the church *and* the charismatic experience of the holy man. Though individual bishops might fall short of the ideal, it was this Basilian legacy that shaped the leadership of the eastern church for centuries.

To be sure, it was a peculiar assortment of churchmen who fell into the category of monk-bishops. They were educated elites, wealthy aristocrats, royal dignitaries, and simple peasants by background. They stood on opposing sides of theological disputes. They resisted imperial policies, cooperated with the state, and even served as patrons and protectors of their homeland. They were holy fools, great theologians, and leaders of prominent spiritual movements. Some even condoned or perpetrated acts of violence. And of course, as we have seen, a confluence of social, political, and legal factors also contributed to the emergence of a monastic episcopate in the Christian East. But alongside, or perhaps underlying, these diverse backgrounds and circumstances was a theological ideal that must not be ignored. The ascetic bishop had seen God; he was a *bogovidac*. He had purged his passions, contemplated divine truths, and ultimately, like Moses, encountered the living Lord on Mt. Sinai. This vision, the fruit of the bishop's monastic vocation, was the true source of his authority in the church and the world. Whatever abuses or perversions of this ideal took place, the belief persisted in the Orthodox churches that only such an individual was suited to lead the people of God.

Abbreviations

AB	*Analecta Bollandiana*
ACO	*Acta Conciliorum Oecumenicorum*
ACW	Ancient Christian Writers
BZ	*Byzantinische Zeitschrift*
CH	*Church History*
CHR	*Catholic Historical Review*
CJ	*Codex Justinianus*
Courtonne	Basile de Césarée: Lettres, ed. Y. Courtonne, 3 vols. (Paris, 1957– 1966)
CSCO	Corpus Scriptorum Christianorum Orientalium (Louvain, 1903–)
CTh	*Codex Theodosianus*
DACL	*Dictionnaire d'archéologie chrétienne et de liturgie*
DOP	*Dumbarton Oaks Papers*
FOC	Fathers of the Church
Gallay	Saint Grégoire de Nazianze: Lettres, ed. P. Gallay, 2 vols. (Paris, 1964)
GCS	Die griechischen christlichen Schrifsteller der ersten drei Jahrhunderte (Berlin, 1897–)
GNaz	Gregory of Nazianzus
GNO	Gregorii Nysseni Opera, ed. W. Jaeger, 10 vols. (Leiden, 1952–1990)
GNyss	Gregory of Nyssa
GOTR	*Greek Orthodox Theological Review*
HE	*Historia ecclesiastica*
HR	*Historia religiosa*
HTR	*Harvard Theological Review*
JAC	*Jahrbuch für Antike und Christentum*
JECS	*Journal of Early Christian Studies*
JEH	*Journal of Ecclesiastical History*
JHS	*Journal of Hellenic Studies*
JÖB	*Jahrbuch für österreichischen Byzantinistik*
JRS	*Journal of Roman Studies*
JTS	*Journal of Theological Studies*
LCL	Loeb Classical Library

Mansi	Sacrorum conciliorum nova et amplissima collectio, ed. J. D. Mansi, 31 vols. (Florence and Venice, 1757–1798)
NPNF	Nicene and Post-Nicene Fathers (translation series)
OCA	Orientalia Christiana Analecta
OCP	*Orientalia Christiana Periodica*
PG	Patrologia Graeca, ed. J. P. Migne (Paris, 1857–1866)
PL	Patrologia Latina, ed. J. P. Migne (Paris, 1844–1864)
PO	Patrologia Orientalis
RAC	*Reallexikon für Antike und Christentum*
RAM	*Revue d'ascétique et de mystique*
RB	*Regulae brevius tractatae = Short Rules*
REA	*Revues des études augustiniennes*
REB	*Revue des études byzantines*
REG	*Revue des études grecques*
RF	*Regulae fusius tractatae = Long Rules*
RHE	*Revue d'histoire ecclésiastique*
RHR	*Revue de l'histoire des religions*
RM	*Moralia = Moral Rules*
RSR	*Revue des sciences religieuses*
RTAM	*Recherches de théologie ancienne et médiévale*
SC	Sources chrétiennes (Paris, 1942–)
SP	*Studia Patristica*
SVQR	*Saint Vladimir's Seminary Quarterly Review*
TU	Texte und Untersuchungen zur Geschichte der altchristlichen Literatur (Leipzig, 1882–)
VC	*Vigiliae Christianae*
VSM	*Grégoire de Nysse: Vie de Sainte Macrine,* ed. P. Maraval, SC 178 (Paris, 1971)
ZKG	*Zeitschrift für Kirchengeschichte*

Notes

Introduction

1. On Nitria and its surroundings, see Derwas J. Chitty, *The Desert a City* (Crestwood, N.Y.: St. Vladimir's Seminary Press, 1966), pp. 11–13. Chitty's description is largely based on the important archeological discoveries of H. G. Evelyn-White, *The Monasteries of the Wadi'n Natrun, 2: The History of the Monasteries of Nitria and Scetis* (New York, 1932).

2. The account of Ammonius that follows is based primarily on Palladius, *Historia Lausiaca* 11 and 46, in Cuthbert Butler, ed., *The Lausiac History of Palladius,* Texts and Studies 6, vol. 2 (Cambridge: Cambridge University Press, 1898), pp. 32–34, 134–135; English trans., Robert T. Meyer, *Lausiac History* (Westminster, Md.: Newman Press, 1965). On Ammonius see also Socrates, *HE* 6.23; Sozomen, *HE* 6.30; and Palladius, *Dialogus de vita S. Joannis Chrysostomi,* ed. P. R. Coleman-Norton (Cambridge: Cambridge University Press, 1928), 6 and 17.

3. *Historia Lausiaca* 11.1. Another account relates that three brothers cut off their ears because "they were under compulsion to become bishops." *Historia Monachorum in Aegypto* 20.14, in André-Jean Festugière, ed., *Subsidia Hagiographa* 53 (Brussels: Société des Bollandistes, 1971), pp. 122–123; Norman Russell, trans., *The Lives of the Desert Fathers: The Historia Monachorum in Aegypto* (Kalamazoo, Mich.: Cistercian Publications, 1981), pp. 106–107.

4. Leviticus 21:16–24 excludes those with physical defects from the priesthood. Canon law became increasingly stringent in this regard, emphasizing voluntary mutilation as cause for exclusion. On ecclesiastical legislation regarding physical qualities requisite for ordination, see Jean Gaudemet, *L'Église dans l'Empire Romain (IVe–Ve siècles),* Histoire du droit et des institutions de l'église en Occident 3 (Paris: Sirey, 1958), pp. 127–128.

5. For the connection of Ammonius and the Tall Brothers with Theophilus's anti-Origenist campaign, see Elizabeth Clark, *The Origenist Controversy: The Cultural Construction of an Early Christian Debate* (Princeton: Prince-

249

ton University Press, 1992), especially pp. 45–49, 105–108. Clark's insightful reconstruction of texts and events suggests that Ammonius's act of self-mutilation was integral to broader anti-Origenist polemics.

6. On the unsuccessful resistance of Dracontius and the successful avoidance of ordination on the part of Pachomius, see David Brakke, *Athanasius and the Politics of Asceticism* (Oxford: Clarendon, 1995), pp. 99–110 and 113–120, respectively.

7. See Theodoret, *HR* 15.4 in Theodoret of Cyrrhus, *A History of the Monks of Syria,* trans. R. M. Price (Kalamazoo, Mich.: Cistercian Publications, 1985), p. 115. For another example of resistance to ordination in this work, this time after the fact, see the account of Macedonius in *HR* 13.4.

8. The monk in question was Peter the Iberian. See John Rufus, *Plerophories,* ed. F. Nau, PO 8/1 (Paris: Firmin-Didot, 1911), XLII, p. 93, and John Rufus, *Vita Petri Iberi,* ed. R. Raabe, *Petrus der Iberer* (Leipzig: J. C. Hinrichs'sche Buchhandlung, 1895), pp. 50–52.

9. Callincus, *Vita Hypatii* 11.8–9, ed. G. J. M. Bartelink, *Callincos, Vie d'Hypatios,* SC 177 (Paris: Éditions du cerf, 1971), p. 114.

10. GNaz, Orations 2 and 42.

11. For patristic exegesis of Old Testament passages interpreted in support of the ascetic life, see Elizabeth Clark, *Reading Renunciation: Asceticism and Scripture in Early Christianity* (Princeton: Princeton University Press, 1999), pp. 104–113.

12. The word *apotassō* in Luke 14:33 originally meant "to set apart" but later connoted renunciation. See G. W. H. Lampe, *A Patristic Greek Lexicon* (Oxford: Clarendon, 1961). It would be a major motif of early Christian ascetic movements and monastic developments.

13. 1 Timothy 3:1–7; cf. Titus 1:6.

14. For Paul's descriptions of his own ascetic discipline and call to ascetic living, see 1 Corinthians 9 and 1 Corinthians 7, especially vv. 29–35.

15. A foundational treatment of these themes is Peter Brown, *The Body and Society: Men, Women and Sexual Renunciation in Early Christianity* (New York: Columbia University Press, 1988). The formation of the Asceticism Group in 1985 as a working group of the American Academy of Religion inspired a series of conferences and publications related to biblical texts and their interpretation or reception by the late antique ascetic milieu. See especially Vincent L. Wimbush, ed., *Discursive Formations, Ascetic Piety and the Interpretation of Early Christian Literature* (Atlanta: Scholars, 1992), and Leif E. Vaage and Vincent L. Wimbush, eds., *Asceticism and the New Testament* (New York: Routledge, 1999).

16. Transformed from its original military and athletic connotation by the Sophists, *ascesis* continued to denote training or prolonged effort but ex-

panded to include interior moral exertion and discipline. See Hermigild Dressler, *The Usage of* Askeō *and Its Cognates in Greek Documents to 100 A.D.* (Washington, D.C.: Catholic University of America Press, 1947); James A. Francis, *Subversive Virtue: Asceticism and Authority in the Second-Century Pagan World* (University Park: Pennsylvania State University Press, 1995), pp. 11–19.

17. Werner Jaeger, *Early Christianity and Greek Paideia* (Cambridge, Mass.: Harvard University Press, 1961), p. 90. On the ideal of *ascesis* see Pierre Hadot, *Philosophy as a Way of Life: Spiritual Exercises from Socrates to Foucault,* trans. Michael Chase (Cambridge, Mass.: Blackwell, 1995), especially pp. 126–144 on an important distinction between modern and Christian uses of the word *asceticism* and the notion of *ascesis* in ancient Greek philosophy.

18. Alison Keith and Leif E. Vaage, "Imperial Asceticism: Discipline of Domination," in Vaage and Wimbush, eds., *Asceticism and the New Testament,* pp. 414–419.

19. For asceticism as a virtue of rulers in the thought of Marcus Aurelius, see in particular *Meditations* I.7 and 16.

20. See especially Michel Foucault, *The History of Sexuality,* 3: *The Care of the Self,* trans. Robert Hurley (New York: Random House, 1986), pp. 67–68, 235–240. However, Foucault also spoke of "asceticism in a very broad sense," or "the self-forming activity" *(practique de soi),* as one of four major aspects of the relationship to oneself that he called ethics; see the interview with Foucault, "On the Geneaology of Ethics," in Herbert L. Dreyfus and Paul Rabinow, *Michel Foucault: Beyond Structuralism and Hermeneutics,* 2nd ed. (Chicago: University of Chicago Press, 1983), p. 239. An emphasis on asceticism in this broader sense would be common to the ethics of both Greco-Roman and early Christian society.

21. See Kurt Weitzmann, ed., *Age of Spirituality: A Symposium* (New York: Metropolitan Museum of Art, 1980), especially Ihor Ševčenko, "A Shadow Outline of Virtue: The Classical Heritage of Greek Christian Literature," pp. 53–73.

22. See, for example, Peter Steinfels, "Greek Orthodox Group Backs Married Bishops," *New York Times,* 14 July 1990, p. 25L; Peter Hullier, "Episcopal Celibacy in the Orthodox Tradition," *SVQR* 35/2–3 (1991): 271–300, and idem, "Mandatory Celibacy as a Requirement for Episcopacy," *GOTR* 40/1–2 (1995): 213–219.

23. Garcia M. Colombas, *El monacato primitivo,* vol. 1 (Madrid: Biblioteca de autores cristianos, 1974), pp. 333–334, borrowing from J. Pargoire, *L'Église Byzantine de 527 à 847* (Paris: Librairie Victor Lecoffre, 1905), p. 66. A few scholars have rightly noted that this process developed earlier in some

areas. See, for example, Heinrich Bacht, "Die Rolle des orientalischen Mönchtums in den kirchenpolitischen Auseinandersetzungen um Chalkedon (431–519)," in *Das Konzil von Chalkedon, 2: Entscheidung um Chalkedon* (Würzburg, 1953), p. 303.

24. The model of the senator-turned-bishop was much more prominent in the West than in the East. On the elite status of bishops and various episcopal career patterns, see Claudia Rapp, "The Elite Status of Bishops in Late Antiquity in the Ecclesiastical, Spiritual, and Social Contexts," *Arethusa* 33 (2000): 379–399, and idem, "Bishops in Late Antiquity: A New Social and Urban Elite?" in J. Haldon, ed., *Elites Old and New in the Byzantine and Early Islamic Near East,* Studies in Late Antiquity and Early Islam 6 (Princeton: Darwin Press, 2003), pp. 144–173.

25. For example, Peter Brown, *Power and Persuasion in Late Antiquity: Towards a Christian Empire* (Madison: University of Wisconsin Press, 1992), and Rita Lizzi, *Il potere episcopale nell'oriente romano: Rappresentazione ideologica e realtà politica (IV–V sec. d.C.)* (Rome: Edizioni dell'Ateneo, 1987).

26. See Max Weber, *Sociology of Religion* (Boston: Beacon Press, 1963), pp. 166–183. Nevertheless Weber's ideas on economic and political implications of asceticism and his reflections on processes of institutionalization are foundational. See the collection of Weber's writings in S. N. Eisenstadt, ed., *On Charisma and Institution Building: Selected Papers* (Chicago: University of Chicago Press, 1968), especially "The Nature of Charismatic Authority and Its Routinization," pp. 48–65.

On asceticism, politics and power see Richard Valantasis, "Constructions of Power in Asceticism," *Journal of the American Academy of Religion* 63 (1995): 775–821, and part 5 of Vincent L. Wimbush and Richard Valantasis, eds., *Asceticism* (Oxford: Oxford University Press, 1997). Also relevant is the older work of Hans von Campenhausen, *Ecclesiastical Authority and Spiritual Power in the Church of the First Three Centuries,* trans. J. A. Basker (Stanford, Calif.: Stanford University Press, 1969), which raised important questions about the interrelation of different modes of authority in the early church.

27. Louis Bréhier, *Le monde byzantin, 2: Les institutions de l'empire byzantin* (Paris: Éditions Albin Michel, 1949), p. 512, explains that from the ninth century large numbers of monks began to enter the episcopate in Constantinople, and that after the triumph of the Hesychasts in the fourteenth century they gained a monopoly.

28. See Aline Rousselle, "Aspects sociaux du recrutement ecclésiastique au IVe siècle," *Mélanges de l'école française de Rome—Antiquité* 89 (1977): 333–370. On the monk-bishop in a slightly later western context, see also Simon J. Coates, "The Bishop as Pastor and Solitary: Bede and the Spiritual

Authority of the Monk-Bishop," *JEH* 47/4 (1997): 601–619. For a more systematic treatment of clerical celibacy in the western context, see Roger Gryson, *Les origines du célibat ecclesiastique* (Gembloux: J. Duculot, 1970).

29. In particular Philip Rousseau, *Ascetics, Authority and the Church in the Age of Jerome and Cassian* (Oxford: Oxford University Press, 1978), and idem, "The Spiritual Authority of the 'Monk-Bishop': Eastern Elements in Some Western Hagiography of the Fourth and Fifth Centuries," *JTS* n.s. 23 (1971): 380–419. On related issues in the West, see Conrad Leyser, *Authority and Asceticism from Augustine to Gregory the Great* (Oxford: Clarendon, 2000).

30. Henry Chadwick, "The Role of the Christian Bishop in Ancient Society," Protocol Series of the Colloquies 35 (Berkeley: Center for Hermeneutical Studies, 1980). The publication includes responses of Peter Brown, Robert M. Grant, Ramsey MacMullen, and Massey H. Shepherd. See also Lizzi, *Il potere episcopale*.

31. *Vescovi e pastori in epoca teodosiana, XXV Incontro di studiosi dell'antichità cristiana*, Studia Ephemeridis Augustinianum 58 (Rome: Institutum Patristicum "Augustinianum," 1997).

32. Peter Brown, "The Rise and Function of the Holy Man in Late Antiquity," *JRS* 61 (1971): 80–101; idem, "The Rise and Function of the Holy Man in Late Antiquity, 1971–1997," *JECS* 6/3 (1998); and John Howard-Johnston and Paul Anthony Hayward, eds., *The Cult of Saints in Late Antiquity and the Middle Ages: Essays on the Contribution of Peter Brown* (New York: Oxford, 1999). On individual figures of spiritual authority see also Jan Willem Drijvers and John W. Watt, eds., *Portraits of Spiritual Authority: Religious Power in Early Christianity, Byzantium and the Christian Orient* (Leiden: Brill, 1999).

33. Gilbert Dagron et al., eds., *Évêques, moines et empereurs (610–1054)*, Histoire du christianisme 4 (Paris: Desclée, 1993).

34. H. A. Drake, *Constantine and the Bishops: The Politics of Intolerance* (Baltimore: Johns Hopkins University Press, 2000).

1. Monks and Bishops in the Christian East from 325 to 375

1. John Cassian, *De coenobiorum institutis* XI.17.

2. Peter Brown, "The Rise and Function of the Holy Man in Late Antiquity," in idem, *Society and the Holy in Late Antiquity* (Berkeley: University of California Press, 1982), p. 110. For a critique of the representation of Pachomian monasticism as a "desert movement" see James E. Goehring, "Withdrawing from the Desert: Pachomius and the Development of Village Monasticism in Upper Egypt," *HTR* 89 (1996): 267–285, reprinted in his

collection of essays, *Ascetics, Society and the Desert: Studies in Egyptian Monasticism* (Harrisburg, Pa.: Trinity International Press, 1999).

3. Ewa Wipszycka, "Le monachisme égyptien et les villes," in idem, *Études sur le christianisme dans l'Égypte de l'antiquité tardive,* Studia Ephemeridis Augustinianum 52 (Rome: Institutum Patristicum Augustinianum, 1996), pp. 281–336.

4. Goehring, *Ascetics, Society and the Desert,* p. 7. The processes of institutionalization of accepted orthodox norms examined by Goehring parallel in many ways the findings of Susanna Elm, *"Virgins of God": The Making of Asceticism in Late Antiquity* (Oxford: Clarendon, 1994), regarding varieties of women's ascetic life in late antiquity.

5. First to reevaluate the meaning of the term *apotaktikoi* on the basis of the documentary evidence was E. A. Judge, "The Earliest Use of Monachos for 'Monk' *(P. Coll. Youtie 77)* and the Origins of Monasticism," *JAC* 10 (1977): 72–89, and idem, "Fourth-Century Monasticism in the Papyri," in Roger S. Bagnall et al., eds., *Proceedings of the Sixteenth International Congress of Papyrology* (Chico, Calif.: Scholars Press, 1981), pp. 613–620. See also Goehring, *Ascetics, Society, and the Desert,* pp. 53–72.

6. For the "antithesis" see Brown, "Rise and Function," p. 110. See Goehring, *Ascetics, Society and the Desert,* pp. 45–46, for a series of examples from the *Apophthegmata Patrum* of anchoritic interaction with the world.

7. See *Vita Prima* cc.27, 28, 29, 32, 39, 43, 44, 67, 112. For the Greek text and an English translation of the *Vita Prima,* the best of the Greek versions of the *Life,* see *The Life of Pachomius,* trans. Apostolos N. Athanassakis, Early Christian Literature Series 2 (Missoula, Mont.: Scholars Press, 1975).

8. Philip Rousseau, *Pachomius: The Making of a Community in Fourth-Century Egypt* (Berkeley: University of California Press, 1985), especially chap. 8. For social and economic links between monasticism and Egyptian society beyond the strictly Pachomian setting, see Goehring, *Ascetics, Society and the Desert,* pp. 39–52.

9. Rousseau, *Pachomius,* pp. 156–159.

10. *Vita Antonii* c.67.

11. *Vita Antonii* c.91. Regarding Antony's relationship with Athanasius see also the Prologue. On his connection with Serapion see c.82.

12. See, for example, *Vita Antonii* c.90, where Antony is said to have frequently asked a bishop to instruct the people about proper Christian burial procedures.

13. Samuel Rubenson, *The Letters of Antony: Monasticism and the Making of a Saint* (Minneapolis: Fortress Press, 1995). The book includes a translation of the seven letters. For Rubenson's comparison of the letters with the *Vita Antonii,* see pp. 126–144; for comparison with the *Apophthegmata Patrum,* pp. 152–162.

14. For references to the church, see Letters II.10, IV.1, and VI.85 in Rubenson, *Letters,* pp. 203, 210, 222.

15. See, for example, *Vita Antonii* cc.68, 69, 89, 91.

16. Robert C. Gregg and Dennis E. Groh, *Early Arianism: A View of Salvation* (Philadelphia: Fortress Press, 1981), pp. 131–161. See Rubenson, *Letters,* pp. 78 and 79 n. 1, which counters Gregg and Groh's suggestion that monastic theology lay behind the Arian view of salvation. For a reevaluation of Athanasian authorship of the *Vita Antonii,* see Bernadette McNary-Zak, *Letters and Asceticism in Fourth-Century Egypt* (Lanham, Md.: University Press of America, 2000), pp. 88–93.

17. The need for monastic support would be all the more urgent if Arians themselves were attempting to win the allegiance of monks. See Gregg and Groh, *Early Arianism,* p. 137. On Melitian monastic organization see Goehring, *Ascetics, Society and the Desert,* pp. 187–195, especially 194 n. 29. On the Melitians' ecclesiastical threat to Athanasius, see Elm, *"Virgins of God,"* pp. 342–347.

18. *Ad Dracontium* 7, PG 50, 532A. See also his *Apologia contra Constantium* c.28, PG 25, 632, for reference to monks and ascetics who had been bishops from the time of his predecessor, Alexander, and who were banished when the Arians gained ascendancy.

19. *Ad Dracontium* 9, PG 25, 532D; and 8, 532C, for Athanasius's perspective.

20. *Ad Dracontium* 7, PG 25, 532A. On the bishop's tasks of teaching and preaching, see also *Ad Dracontium* 10.

21. Throughout this letter Athanasius referred to episcopal ministry as a charge imposed or entrusted by God. Similarly, several times he referred to the "grace" or "gift" of God or even to the "grace of the episcopate" (*tēn tēs episkopos charin*). *Ad Dracontium* 2, PG 25, 525. Cf. section 1 (where "grace" is used twice in this sense) and section 4, PG 25, 524A and B and 528A.

22. *Ad Dracontium* 10, PG 25, 534C. The two verbs *didaskein* and *proistasthai* are used here to signal major functions of bishops who lead the church and monk-priests who serve in monasteries. On Athanasius's strategy in the appeal to Dracontius, see David Brakke, *Athanasius and the Politics of Asceticism* (Oxford: Clarendon, 1995), pp. 99–110.

23. For example, fasting is discussed in section 9 (PG 25, 532D–533C), but it is described more as an option than as a requirement for bishops.

24. Though Brakke, *Athanasius and Asceticism,* p. 100, acknowledges that "Athanasius did not run roughshod over . . . monastic values," he argues that "political necessity was a prime motivation for Athanasius' programme of placing monks in the Egyptian hierarchy." Charles Kannengiesser, "Athanasius of Alexandria and the Ascetic Movement of His Time," in Vincent L. Wimbush and Richard Valantasis, eds., *Asceticism*

(Oxford: Oxford University Press, 1997), pp. 479–492, provides balance for purely political interpretations but may go too far in pitting political goals against piety, as though the one necessarily undermines the other.

25. *Ep. fest.* 40, translated from the Coptic text in Brakke, *Athanasius and Asceticism,* p. 334.

26. See Goehring, "Pachomius's Vision of Heresy: The Development of a Pachomian Tradition," in *Ascetics, Society and the Desert,* pp. 137–161.

27. Leo Ueding, "Die Kanones von Chalkedon in ihrer Bedeutung für Mönchtum und Klerus," in *Das Konzil von Chalkedon,* ed. Alois Grillmeier and Heinrich Bacht (Würzburg: Echter, 1953), 2, p. 575 n. 19, citing the Coptic *Lives* 169, c.101 (ed. Louis-Théophile Lefort; CSCO 99). For examples of Pachomius's respect for episcopal authority see *Vita Prima* cc.29, 31, 99. On his attitude toward the church hierarchy see Ueding, "Die Kanones," pp. 580–588; Rousseau, *Pachomius,* pp. 161–162 and 169–173; and Brakke, *Athansius and Asceticism,* pp. 111–120. The last section of the *Vita Prima* (cc.120–150), devoted to Pachomian communities under his successors Horsisius and Theodore, shows similar respect toward bishops and the church. On the complexity of the sources for this period of Pachomian history, see James Goehring, "The Fourth Letter of Horsiesius and the Situation in the Pachomian Community Following the Death of Theodore," in *Ascetics, Society and the Desert,* pp. 221–240.

28. *Vita Prima* c.30.

29. *Vita Prima* c.27: Athanassakis, pp. 33–35. See also *Vita Prima* c.37 and c.42. Horsisius (c.126) and Theodore (c.135) express similar reservations about ordaining monks.

30. This incident is recorded only in *Vita Prima* cc.112–113. On the trial's significance see Philip Rousseau, "Spiritual Authority of the 'Monk-Bishop,'" *JTS* n.s. 22 (1971): 387.

31. *Vita Prima* c.112: Athanassakis, p. 153. These same two former monks, Muitus and Paul, were later listed by Athanasius among those who had accepted episcopal ordination. *Ad Dracontium* 7, PG 25.532A.

32. *Vita Prima* c.112: Athanassakis, p. 155.

33. See Rousseau, *Pachomius,* p. 173. For the commercial activity of monks in local villages, see James Goehring, "World Engaged," in *Ascetics, Society and the Desert,* pp. 139–144.

34. See Derwas J. Chitty, *The Desert a City* (Crestwood, N.Y.: St. Vladimir's Seminary Press, 1966), pp. 11 and 29–35, and for what follows, Philip Rousseau, "The Spiritual Authority of the 'Monk-Bishop': Eastern Elements in Some Western Hagiography of the Fourth and Fifth Centuries," *JTS* n.s. 23 (1971): 397–402.

35. Such images of late fourth- and fifth-century Syrian asceticism were popu-

larized particularly by Peter Brown, "Rise and Function" and idem, *The Body and Society: Men, Women and Sexual Renunciation in Early Christianity* (New York: Columbia University Press, 1988), pp. 229–35. On the use of these and other later sources for interpreting early Syrian asceticism see Sidney Griffith, "Asceticism in the Church of Syria: The Hermeneutics of Early Syrian Monasticism," in Wimbush and Valantasis, eds., *Asceticism,* pp. 220–223. Though I use the terms Syria and Syrian here, Greater Syria was a land of cultural confluence and bilingualism. My focus is Mesopotamia and the northeastern province of Osrhoene, the principal cultural centers of the Syriac-speaking people, and secondarily the predominantly Greek-speaking area of western Syria with its cultural center of Antioch.

36. For an overview of Syrian protomonasticism, including discussion and critique of the relevant literature, see Griffith, "Asceticism in the Church of Syria."

37. See Judge, "The Earliest Use of Monachos," pp. 72, 86–87; F. E. Morard, "Monachos: Une importatation sémitique en Égypte?" *SP* 12 (1975): 242–246; idem, "Encore quelques reflexions sur Monachos," *VC* 34 (1980): 395–401; and Griffith, "Asceticism in the Church of Syria," pp. 229, 238.

38. Griffith, "Asceticism in the Church of Syria," pp. 224–225. On three primary meanings of the Syriac term *ihidaya* see Robert Murray, "Exhortation to Candidates for Ascetical Vows at Baptism in the Ancient Syriac Church," *New Testament Studies* 21 (1974/1975): 59–80, especially pp. 67 and 79. For other examples of the use of *ihidaya* by Aphrahat and Ephrem see Edmund Beck, "Ein Beitrag zur Terminologie des ältesten syrischen Mönchtums," in *Antoninus Magnus Eremita, 356–1956: Studia ad antiquum monachismum spectantia,* ed. B. Steidle (Rome: Herder, 1956), pp. 254–267. Unlike the Syriac *ihidaya,* the Greek *monachos* is a nonbiblical term.

39. For example, after describing the religious importance of celibacy Aphrahat concludes, "For so it is fitting for Christ's disciples to emulate Christ their Lord." Similar Christological significance is evident in Ephrem's hymn to St. Julian Saba, 2.13: "Because he had seen the glory of the *ihidaya,* he too became an *ihidaya.*" Passages cited in Griffith, "Asceticism in the Church of Syria," pp. 225, 228.

40. On Ephrem's self-identification as an ascetic see also *Carmen* 31.37 and the editor's note in *Carmina Nisibena,* (German) trans. Edmund Beck, CSCO 219 (1961), pp. 95–96. On Ephrem and the church see Sidney H. Griffith, "Ephraem, the Deacon of Edessa, and the Church of the Empire," in Thomas Halton and Joseph P. Williams, eds., *Diakonia: Studies in Honor of Robert T. Meyer* (Washington, D.C.: Catholic University of America Press, 1986), pp. 22–52.
    Aphrahat's formal position in the church has been a subject of debate.

Marie-Joseph Pierre, ed. and trans., *Aphraate le Sage Persan: Les exposés,* SC 349 (Paris: Les Éditions du Cerf, 1988), p. 40, thinks that Aphrahat was indeed a bishop. Shafiq AbouZayd, *Ihidayutha: A Study of the Life of Singleness in the Syrian Orient. From Ignatius of Antioch to Chalcedon 451 A.D.* (Oxford: ARAM Society for Syro-Mesopotamian Studies, 1993), pp. 56–58, believes he was not a cleric but only the spiritual leader of the *bnay* and *bnat qyama.*

41. *Carmina Nisibena* 19.1. *Carmina Nisibena,* 13–21, treats Bishops Jacob (303–338), Babu, Vologeses (356–361), and Abraham (361–363), all of whom Ephrem knew and served. On his portrayal of their lives see Jean M. Fiey, "Les évêques de Nisibe au temps de saint Éphrem," *Parole de l'Orient* 4 (1973): 123–135. On Ephrem's view of bishops and the church see I. Ortiz de Urbina, "L'Évêque et son rôle d'après saint Éphrem," *Parole de l'Orient* 4 (1973): 137–146.

42. *Carmina Nisibena* 19.3.

43. See ibid. 17.3 and 21.5. "Fold of herdsmen" is Griffith's translation of the Syriac *dayra d'allane* in 17.3; see "Asceticism in the Church of Syria," p. 237.

44. Ibid. 21.2–8.

45. Ibid. 18.1. Cf. 17.4–5 for another comparison of Abraham with Vologeses.

46. Ibid. 15.9.

47. Ibid. 14. Cf. Theodoret, *HR* 1, for the much more extreme portrayal of the bishop's ascetic pursuits and miracles that became standard. On Jacob see David Bundy, "Jacob of Nisibis as a Model for the Episcopacy," *Le Muséon* 104 (1991): 235–249.

48. See Arthur Vööbus, *History of Asceticism in the Syrian Orient* 2, CSCO 197, Subsidia 17 (Louvain, 1960), pp. 326–330.

49. Edmund Beck, ed., *Des Heiligen Ephraem des Syrers Hymnen auf Abraham Kidunaya und Julianos Saba,* CSCO 322–323 (1972). Griffith, "Asceticism in the Church of Syria," pp. 235–238, suggests that when monastic practices from Egypt and Palestine were adopted by Julian Saba and his followers they appeared as a kind of reform movement among the *bnay qyama.*

50. Sozomen, *HE* 6.33. For Ephrem's description of Barses' character see especially *Carmen* 29.5–10. From *Carmen* 33.8 we know that Barses was the first bishop of Harran, though Sozomen reports that the monk Barses was ordained bishop not of any particular city but as an honorary gesture because of his excellent conduct (*HE* 6.34). See also the chapter on anchoritic colonies and "monk-bishops" in the vicinity of Harran in Stephan Schiwietz, *Das morgenländische Mönchtum, 3: Das Mönchtum in Syrien und Mesopotamien und das Asketentum in Persien* (Mödling bei Wien: Missionsdruckerei St. Gabriel, 1938), pp. 49–56.

51. Ephrem alludes to this conflict in *Carmen* 31. See also Schiwietz, *Das morgenländische Mönchtum* 3: 51.
52. Basil, Letters 225 and 267.
53. George E. Gingras, trans., *Egeria: Diary of a Pilgrimage,* ACW 38 (New York: Newman Press, 1970), Chapters 19–20.
54. *Carmina Nisibena* 29, 31, and 33 deal extensively with the cities of Edessa and Harran and Bishops Barses and Vitus. On the ascetic terminology Ephrem employed see *Carmina Nisibena:* Beck, pp. 90 n. 2, 95 n. 36, and 99, n. 5.
55. For the significance of Syrian geography and climate in the rise of the late antique holy man see Brown, "Rise and Function," especially pp. 111–114. For more detailed descriptions of Syrian villages and the surrounding landscape see Georges Tchalenko, *Villages antiques de la Syrie du Nord,* 1 (Paris: Librairie orientaliste Paul Geuthner, 1953), especially pp. 377–421. The climate in cities like Edessa and Nisibis, more northerly and further inland, was probably not as mild as in the Syrian desert areas described in these works. Nevertheless, speaking of the region between the Tigris and Euphrates Rivers, Ammianus Marcellinus acknowledges that the winters were moderate: "clementia hiemis ibi mollissimae," *Res gestae* 18.7.5.
56. Susan Harvey, "The Stylite's Liturgy: Ritual and Religious Identity in Late Antiquity," *JECS* 6/3 (1998): 524. Though Harvey, like Brown, focuses on a later period, the description of the Syrian landscape is apt.
57. PG 47, 321B; loosely translated in Sebastian Brock, "Early Syrian Asceticism," *Numen* 20/1 (1972): 1.
58. See Brown, "Rise and Function," pp. 112–115. For an example of Libanius's judgment of monks see Oration 30.8–11 and 48.
59. See Brown, "Rise and Function," especially pp. 115–133. Numerous examples of the exercise of power and patronage by Syrian monks can be found in Theodoret's *Historia religiosa.*
60. See Bacht, "Die Rolle des orientalischen Mönchtums," pp. 298, on the role of Syrian monks in events leading up to and including Chalcedon. However, Bacht's description of the relative independence of Syrian monastic communities draws principally from fifth- and even sixth-century sources.
61. Griffith, "Asceticism in the Church of Syria." See also Joseph Amar, "Byzantine Monachism and Greek Bias in the *Vita* Tradition of Ephrem the Syrian," *OCP* 58 (1992): 123–156.
62. See George Nedungatt, "The Covenanters of the Early Syriac Speaking Church," *OCP* 39 (1973): 191–215, 419–444, especially pp. 200–204.
63. For the distinction between the monastic milieu of Syria and that of Basilian monasticism see Mario Mazza, "Monachesimo basiliano: Modelli spirituali e tendenze economico-sociali nell'impero del IV secolo," *Studi*

storici 21 (1980): 51. Like Mazza, I am using the terms *urban* and *city* loosely to contrast the centers of population, even if only towns or large villages, with the many truly rural areas of Asia Minor.

64. *Vita Antonii* c.14.

65. Sozomen, *HE* 6.34; trans. Hartrfanft, NPNF, 2nd ser., vol. 2, p. 371. Cappadocia was in fact renowned for its excessive cold. See Angelo di Berardino, "La Cappdocia al tempo di Basilio," in *Mémorial Dom Jean Gribomont (1920–1986)* (Rome: Institutum Patristicum "Augustinianum," 1988), p. 171.

66. Gilbert Dagron, "Les moines et la ville: Le monachisme à Constantinople jusqu'au Concile de Chalcédoine (451)," *Travaux et Mémoires* 4 (1970); 229–276; here especially pp. 253–256.

67. Ibid., pp. 240, 261f. In this connection Dagron describes the controversies surrounding Gregory Nazianzen, Chrysostom, Nestorius, and Eutyches.

68. See the chapter on Cappadocia in A. H. M. Jones, *The Cities of the Eastern Roman Provinces,* 2nd ed. (Oxford: Clarendon, 1971), pp. 174–190. See also Berardino, "La Cappadocia," and Ramon Téja, *Orangización economica y social de Capadocia en el siglo IV, según los padres capadocios* (Salamanca: Universidad de Salamanca, 1974), pp. 169–188.

69. Basil describes the city as *poluanthropos* (*Homilia in Gordium*, PG 31, 496C), and Gregory Nazianzen calls Caesarea "the metropolis of eloquence" in Oration 43.13, lines 7–8, SC 384. For other allusions to the size of the city in the Cappadocians' writings see B. Gain, *L'Église de Cappadoce au IVe siècle d'après la correspondance de Basile de Césarée, 330–379* (Rome: Pontificium institutum orientale, 1985), pp. 228–230.

70. For references to this hospice see GNaz, Oration 43.63; Sozomen, *HE* 6.34; Theodoret, *HE* 4.16; and Basil, Letter 94. See Chapter 3 for further discussion of the Basileiados.

71. For examples see RF 37, 38, 39, 42, and RB 155, 207, 285, 292. On the social and economic significance of these emphases in Basilian monasticism see Mazza, "Monachesimo basiliano," pp. 55–58. Emmanuel Amand de Mendieta, "Le système cénobitique basilien comparé au système cénobitique pachômien," *RHR* 152 (1957): 41–42, argued that the decentralized structure and strategic placement of monasteries were part of Basil's plan to channel the sometimes tumultuous and enthusiastic ascetic fervor of the region into the service of the church and the cause of Nicene orthodoxy. For another perspective on Basil's organization of monastic communities see Elm, *"Virgins of God,"* pp. 210–211.

72. Eustathius's influence on Basil and his role in the origins of the monastic movement in Asia Minor were emphasized in E. Amand de Mendieta, *L'ascèse monastique de Saint Basile: Essai historique* (Éditions de Maredsous, 1949), pp. 52–61. Several articles, especially those of Jean Gribomont,

treat the relationship of the two pioneers in greater depth. For Eustathius's influence in Greater Armenia, particularly on the charitable foundations that Nerses the Great established in the towns and villages, see Nina G. Garsoïan, "Nerses le Grand: Basile de Césarée et Eustathe de Sébaste," *Revue des études arméniennes* n.s. 17 (1983): 145–69, especially 164–169.

73. There are no extant works of Eustathius of Sebaste, and the chronology of his career remains obscure. What we know of him has been gleaned from the following primary sources: Sozomen, *HE* 3.14, 4.24–26, 5.14, and 6.10 and 13; Socrates *HE* 2.43; Epiphanius of Salamis, *Panarion,* 75; the acts of the Synod of Gangra; and Basil's correspondence. On his life and ascetic ideals see especially Jean Gribomont, "Eustathe de Sebaste" in idem, *Saint Basile, Évangile et Église: Mélanges,* (Bégrolles-en-Mauges: Abbaye de Belle-fontaine, 1984), 1, pp. 95–106, which combines several of Gribomont's earlier dictionary entries. Charles Frazee, "Anatolian Asceticism in the Fourth Century: Eustathios of Sebastea and Basil of Caesarea," *CHR* 66 (1980): 16–33, also offers a reconstruction of Eustathius's career.

74. Socrates, *HE* 2.43, and Sozomen, *HE* 4.24.

75. Regarding Eustathius's journey to Egypt and the influence of Arius see Basil's Letters 130.1, 244.3 and 9, 263.3. Basil implies that Eustathius sat directly under Arius's teaching in Alexandria. Athanasius placed Eustathius squarely in the Arian camp in both *Historia Arianorum ad monachos,* 4, and *Epistola ad episcopos Aegepti et Libyae,* 7, though one must bear in mind the polemical dimension of these writings. Regarding Antioch, Athanasius included Eustathius's name at the end of a list of Arians who had been raised to the episcopate despite the earlier refusal of Bishop Eustathius of Antioch to allow them into the ranks of the clergy (*Historia Arianorum* 4; PG 25, 700A). Gribomont, "Eustathe de Sébaste," p. 96, questions the likelihood of an Antioch connection, suggesting that his name was simply added to the end of Athanasius's list at a later date. We know nothing certain of Eustathius's whereabouts until after 330.

76. Sozomen, *HE* 4.24.9; Basil, Letters 244.8, 263.3.

77. Sozomen, *HE* 4.24.9. On his organization of ascetics see *HE* 3.14.31–37.

78. The collection was compiled in Antioch prior to 379 in an anti-Nicene milieu. See Jean Gribomont, "Le monachisme au IVe s. en Asie Mineure: De Gangres au Messalianisme," in *SP* 2, TU 64 (Berlin, 1957), p. 402, who draws from E. Schwartz, "Die Kanonessammlungen der alten Kirche," *Zeitschrift der Savigny-Stiftung für Rechtsgeschichte,* Kanonistische Abteilung 25 (1936), pp. 33–36. The acts of Gangra survive in full in several Latin versions, in Georgian, and in Greek; the canons alone, in Syriac, Armenian, Arabic, and Old Church Slavonic.

79. Despite ongoing debate, many scholars continue to uphold a date around 341, proposed more than a century ago by Friedrich Loofs, *Eustathius*

von Sebaste und die Chronologie der Basilius-Briefe (Halle: Max Niemeyer, 1898), p. 79f. See Gribomont, 'Le monachisme au IVe s. en Asie Mineur," p. 401; Frazee, "Anatolian Asceticism," p. 19; Dagron, "Les moines et la ville," p. 249; Elm, *"Virgins of God,"* pp. 106–107. Paul Jonathan Fedwick, *The Church and the Charisma of Leadership in Basil of Caesarea* (Toronto: PIMS, 1979), pp. 134 and 158, supported 341/342 in 1979 but in 1981 suggested the mid-360s or even 370s. See Fedwick, "A Chronology of the Life and Works of Basil of Caesarea," in Fedwick, ed., *Basil of Caesarea: Christian, Humanist, Ascetic* (Toronto: PIMS, 1981), nn. 14 and 81. Philip Rousseau, *Basil of Caesarea* (Berkeley: University of California Press, 1994), pp. 74–75, hesitatingly suggests a date as late as the mid-350s in keeping with T. D. Barnes, "The Date of the Council of Gangra," *JTS* n.s. 40 (1989): 121–124. Though Barnes presents convincing evidence for 358 or 359 as a terminus *ante quem* for the council, his brief inquiry hardly does justice to the arguments of Gribomont for the earlier date. He does not mention the connection of Eustathius and his party with Eusebius of Nicomedia in Basil's letters and in Sozomen, nor does he offer an explanation for Basil's complete silence about this council.

80. Jean Gribomont, "Saint Basile et le monachisme enthousiaste," *Irénikon* 53 (1980): 126–127. The identification of the Eusebius who presided at Gangra with the Arian bishop Eusebius of Nicomedia, later bishop of Constantinople, assumes the earlier venue for the council.

81. Sozomen, *HE* 4.27 and 4.20.

82. On the various stages of this conflict over Constantinople see Gilbert Dagron, *Naissance d'une capitale: Constantinople et ses institutions de 330 à 451* (Paris: Presses universitaires de France, 1974), pp. 419–425, 431–433.

83. Mansi, 2, pp. 1095–1122; C. J. Hefele and H. Leclercq, *Histoires des conciles d'après les documents originaux* (Paris: Letouzy et Ané, 1907), I/2: 1029–1045. For an English translation of the acts of the council see Vincent L. Wimbush, ed., *Ascetic Behavior in Greco-Roman Antiquity: A Sourcebook* (Minneapolis: Fortress Press, 1990), pp. 448–455. See Dagron, "Les moines et la ville," pp. 249–252, for the connection of these canons with monastic developments in Constantinople.

84. For a fuller discussion of these canons in the context of the whole see Elm, *"Virgins of God,"* pp. 108–111.

85. Mansi, 2, pp. 1104–1105; Hefele-Leclercq, *Histoires des conciles,* I/2: 1042–1043; trans. O. Larry Yarbrough in Wimbush, ed., *Ascetic Behavior,* p. 454. In some early manuscripts this epilogue appears as canon 21.

86. Sozomen, *HE* 3.14. In "Saint Basile et le monachisme enthousiaste," pp. 130–135, Gribomont connects the Eustathians condemned at Gangra with the followers of Macedonius. Condemnations of Eustathians, then,

must be seen in light of the anti-Macedonian and generally anti-ascetic spirit of Eusebius and the bishops who supported him.

87. Epiphanius, *Panarion* 75: PG 42, 504–516. We know from Athanasius, *Epistola ad episcopos Aegypti et Libyae,* 7, composed between 356 and early 357, that Eustathius was elected to the metropolitan see of Sebaste before 357, probably in 356.

88. On Eustathius's doctrinal emphases and the origins of the heretical *pneumatomachi* see Gribomont, "Eustathe de Sebaste," especially pp. 100–102. For suggestions of a connection between Eustathian asceticism and the later Messalian movement see Gribomont, "Saint Basile et le monachisme enthousiaste," 129–144.

89. Letter 223.3.

90. Letter 119.

91. Letter 207.2 and 3.

92. GNaz, Oration 2.7, lines 19–21, in SC 247, pp. 96–98.

93. GNaz, Oration 18.18. This incident was provoked by Gregory the Elder's allegedly unwitting subscription to an unorthodox creed. See Jean Bernardi, *La prédication des pères cappadociens: La prédicateur et son auditoire* (Paris: Presses universitaires de France, 1968), pp. 102–103. Here and in Oration 6, Gregory implied that the monks were overly hasty in their reaction, since his father had simply been deceived.

94. GNaz, Oration 6.2. The description refers to both communal and solitary monastic life, suggesting that both forms were practiced in the vicinity of Nazianzus by the early 360s. See 6.2, lines 27–32, in *Grégoire de Nazianze: Discours 6–12,* ed. Marie-Ange Calvet-Sebasti, SC 405 (Paris: Éditions du cerf, 1995).

95. GNaz, Oration 6.3, lines 16–17. The exhortation to unity takes up most of sections 12–18. The overzealousness of some monks is a recurring theme in his orations. See 6.11 and 20; also Orations 4.10, 18.18, 21.25, 22.5.

96. GNaz, Oration 43.28–29.

97. Gribomont, "Le monachisme au IVe s. en Asie Mineur," p. 402.

2. Asceticism and Leadership in the Thought of Basil of Caesarea

1. *De judicio dei* 1, PG 31, 653A; Letters 204.6, 210.1, 223.3.

2. GNaz, Oration 43.5–8, in *Grégoire de Nazianze, Discours 42–43,* ed. and trans. Jean Bernardi, SC 384 (Paris: Éditions du cerf, 1992). See also in this regard, *Grégoire de Nysse: Vie de Sainte Macrine* (hereinafter *VSM*), ed. and trans. Pierre Maraval, SC 178 (Paris: Éditions du cerf, 1971), 2 and 20. Maximinus's persecution lasted from approximately 306, while he was still a caesar, until his death in 313.

3. GNaz, Oration 43.9, 10, 12.

4. See D. Amand de Mendieta, "La virginité chez Eusèbe d'Emèse et l'ascétisme familial dans la première moitié du IVe siècle," *RHE* 50 (1955): 777–820, and Marcella Forlin Patrucco, "Aspetti di vita familiare nel IV secolo negli scritti dei padri cappaddoci," in Raniero Cantalamessa, ed., *Etica sessuale e matrimonio nel cristianesimo delle origini* (Milan: Vita e pensiero, 1976), especially pp. 173–179. On Basil's family in particular see Maraval's introduction to *VSM*, pp. 47–49, and Susanna Elm, *"Virgins of God": The Making of Asceticism in Late Antiquity* (Oxford: Clarendon, 1994), p. 78f.

5. On Eustathius's early influence in this area see Frazee, *CHR* (1980), especially pp. 17–20. Paul Jonathan Fedwick, *The Church and the Charisma of Leadership in Basil of Caesarea* (Toronto: PIMS, 1979), p. 160 n. 15, notes that Eustathians were running hospices and schools in the region. Basil's family owned estates in Cappadocia, Armenia Minor, and Pontus (*VSM* 20) increasing the likelihood of his exposure to various ascetic groups. In Letter 244.1 Basil refers to his early contact with Eustathius.

6. In both *VSM* 21 and GNaz, Oration 43.12, Basil the Elder is allegedly known throughout Pontus as a teacher of rhetoric. Regarding Musonius see Letters 28.1 and 210.3.1–5.

7. *VSM* 7 and 11. The initial decision of Emmelia and Macrina to retreat from the city to the family's country estate was not out of the ordinary for wealthy aristocrats of the day and did not signify a conscious adoption of an ascetic life. Elm, *"Virgins of God,"* pp. 78–91, retraces the stages by which the family gradually became an ascetic household and ultimately an ascetic institution.

8. *VSM* 6. Though Gregory may have exaggerated Macrina's role, Basil, who never mentioned the existence of his sister, surely minimized it. According to *VSM* 12, Macrina raised her brother Peter and gave him a monastic education. The reason for Basil's complete silence about Macrina is not entirely clear. Philip Rousseau, *Basil of Caesarea* (Berkeley: University of California Press, 1994), pp. 24–26, attributes his general reticence about family to his conviction that ecclesial pedigree counted far more than family associations. See also Rousseau, "Basil of Caesarea: Choosing a Past," in Graeme Clarke, ed., *Reading the Past in Late Antiquity* (Rushcutters Bay: Australian National University Press, 1990), pp. 37–58. Later, Macrina's close connections with Eustathius, whose doctrinal aberrations were to prove so embarrassing for Basil, likely reinforced his silence about her.

9. Naucratius retreated from the world in 352 and died in a hunting accident in 357, the year Basil arrived in Annesi. See *VSM*, chaps. 8–10. Naucratius has frequently been overlooked in treatments of Basil's ascetic formation.

Elm's discussion of both Naucratius and Macrina, *"Virgins of God,"* pp. 78–105, provides a helpful corrective to the tendency to minimize their roles.

10. On Macrina the Elder see Letter 204.6. For references to the tradition of Gregory see Letters 204.6, 207.4, 210.3; *De spiritu sancto* 74. On oral traditions about Gregory Thaumaturgus and their transmission see Robin Lane Fox, *Pagans and Christians* (New York: Alfred A. Knopf, 1987), pp. 528–539, and Raymond Van Dam, "Hagiography and History: The Life of Gregory Thaumaturgus," *Classical Antiquity* 1 (1982): 272–308. Jean Gribomont, "L'origénisme de Saint Basile," in *L'homme devant Dieu: Mélanges H. de Lubac* (Paris: Aubier, 1963), p. 281, points to Gregory Thaumaturgus's influence in mediating a form of Origenism to Basil.

11. Letters 204.6, 207.4, 210.1 and 5, 223.3; *De spiritu sancto* 72 and 74. Rousseau, *Basil of Caesarea*, pp. 11–14, emphasizes Basil's increasing identification of his family with the tradition of Gregory Thaumaturgus.

   Gregory's life is known to us through four main sources: Eusebius, *Historia ecclesiastica* 6.30; Jerome, *De viris illustribus* 65; Gregory's "Canonical Letter" (PG 10, 1020–1048); and a letter to Origen, allegedly written by Gregory himself on the completion of his studies (c. 238). For a summary of his life and the text of this letter see Henri Crouzel, ed., *Grégoire le Thaumaturge, Remerciement à Origène suivi de la lettre d'Origène à Grégoire*, SC 148 (Paris: Éditions du cerf, 1969). Crouzel, pp. 22–23, notes that the five extant Lives of Gregory Thaumaturgus are mostly legendary, recounting his famous miracles for the purpose of edification. Only the biography of Gregory of Nyssa, *De vita Gregorii Thaumaturgi*, GNO X.1.3–57 (= PG 46, 893–958), has some historical value. See also Lane Fox, *Pagans and Christians*, pp. 517–545, and Van Dam, "Hagiography and History."

12. *De vita Gregorii Thaumaturgi*, GNO X.14 (= PG 46, 908C).

13. An edition and translation of Origen's "Letter to Gregory" appear in the same volume as Gregory's *Remerciement*. P. Nautin, *Origène, sa vie et son oeuvre* (Paris: Beauchesne, 1977), pp. 183–197, argues that Origen's reply was actually sent to another Gregory. Crouzel, *Remerciement*, pp. 79–87, followed by Lane Fox, *Pagans and Christians*, pp. 516–517, maintains that Gregory Thaumaturgus was in fact the recipient. The letter is also in J. Armitage Robinson, ed., *The Philocalia of Origen* (Cambridge: Cambridge University Press, 1893), pp. 1–4; George Lewis, trans., *The Philocalia of Origen* (Edinburgh: Clark, 1911). Nazianzen alludes to his collaboration with Basil on the *Philocalia* in Letter 115.3: Gallay 2, 10.

14. Letters 28.1–2, 204.2; *De spiritu sancto* 72 and 74.

15. *De spiritu sancto* 29.74, in Basile de Césarée, *Sur le Saint-Esprit*, ed. Benoît Pruche, SC 17 bis, 2nd ed. (Paris: Éditions du cerf, 1968), pp. 510–512.

16. GNaz, Oration 43.19. For the Cappadocians, "philosophy" or "philosophic life" most often referred to ascetic or monastic life. See Basil, Letters 4 and 210.1. See also Gustave Bardy, "'Philosophie' et 'philosophe' dans le vocabulaire chrétien des premiers siècles," *RAM* 25 (1949): 97–108; and for a thorough treatment of developments in the use of these terms, A.-M. Malingrey, *"Philosophia": Étude d'un groupe de mots dans la littérature grecque des Présocratiques au IVe s. après J.-C.* (Paris: Klincksieck, 1961).

17. Along with rhetoric, in Oration 43.23 Nazianzen mentions philosophy, astronomy, and geometry among the subjects Basil studied. On Basil's studies in Athens see Rousseau, *Basil of Caesarea,* pp. 27–60, and Yves Courtonne, *Un Témoin du IVe siècle oriental: Saint Basile et son temps d'après sa correspondence* (Paris: Belles Lettres, 1973), pp. 46–51. On Homer's continuing centrality in literary studies see H. I. Marrou, *A History of Education in Antiquity,* trans. George Lamb (Madison: University of Wisconsin Press, 1982), pp. 10–13, 162.

18. Robert Kirschner, "The Vocation of Holiness in Late Antiquity," *VC* 38/2 (1984): 105, describes this philosophy as "an amalgam of Platonic metaphysics and Pythagorean ascetic piety associated with Neoplatonist succession." On pagan attitudes toward asceticism in the third and fourth centuries see Garth Fowden, "The Pagan Holy Man in Late Antique Society," *JHS* 102 (1982): 33–59. On Christian responses to non-Christian asceticism see Gregorio Penco, "I padri della Chiesa di fronte all'ascetismo non cristiano," in *Oikoumene: Studi paleocristiani pubblicati in onore del Concilio Ecumenico Vaticano II* (Università di Catania, 1964), pp. 77–92.

19. For examples of Plotinus's ascetic practices see Porphyry, *Vita Plotini* 1–2 and 8. These passages are put into the broader framework of the biography of Plotinus in Patricia Cox, *Biography in Late Antiquity* (Berkeley: University of California Press, 1983), pp. 102–133.

20. On the portrayal of Theodosius and other emperors in the fifth-century Church Histories see G. F. Chesnut, *The First Christian Histories: Eusebius, Socrates, Sozomen, Theodoret and Evagrius* (Macon, Ga.: Mercer University Press, 1986), pp. 231–251. See also Claudia Rapp, "Comparison, Paradigm and the Case of Moses in Panegyric and Hagiography," in *Panegyric in Late Antiquity,* ed. Mary Whitby (Leiden: Brill, 1998), pp. 281–285.

21. Ammianus Marcellinus, *Res gestae,* LCL (Cambridge, Mass.: Harvard University Press, 1940), trans. John C. Rolfe, II, 22.9.2 and 25.4.3–4; see also 25.2.2.

22. Ibid., 24.4.27. On Julian's "inviolate chastity" see also 25.4.2–3. Such an association was not unique to the fourth century. James A. Francis, *Subversive Virtue: Asceticism and Authority in the Second-Century Pagan World* (University Park: Pennsylvania State University Press, 1995), pp. 21–52,

shows how Marcus Aurelius's Stoicism incorporated a form of asceticism that was politically and socially acceptable. Even the more radical asceticism of the pagan Apollonius of Tyana was "rehabilitated" in Philostratus's early third-century *Vita Apollonii* and put to the service of traditional religious, cultural, and social norms. Francis, *Subversive Virtue,* p. 118.

23. Eunapius, *Lives of the Philosophers and Sophists,* trans. Wilmer Cave Wright, rev. ed., LCL (Cambridge, Mass.: Harvard University Press, 1952), 492, p. 507. Eunapius said almost nothing about Prohaeresius's Christian faith. Nazianzen was silent about his influence on Basil, but he devoted an epitaph to Prohaeresius on his death in 367. Basil's other famous teacher of rhetoric, Himerius, was a pagan. For Eunapius's brief description see *Lives,* 494, pp. 516–518. Socrates, *HE* 4.26 and Sozomen, *HE* 6.17, mention both Prohaeresius and Himerius.

24. M. L. W. Laistner, *Christianity and Pagan Culture in the Later Roman Empire* (Ithaca, N.Y.: Cornell University Press, 1951), p. 15. On the moral object in philosophy, see Marrou, *Education in Antiquity,* p. 206; on rhetoric, pp. 169 and 196.

25. *Ad adolescentes* 4: PG 31, 573C; see also 2: 568CD, and 3: 569D–572A.

26. Konstantinos G. Bonis, "Basilios von Caesarea und die Organisation der christlichen Kirche in Vierten Jahrhundert," in Jonathan Fedwick, ed., *Basil of Caesarea: Christian, Humanist, Ascetic, a Sixteen-hundredth Anniversary Symposium* (Toronto: Pontifical Institute of Mediaeval Studies, 1981), 1, pp. 295–296. See Gregory's description of the evils of Athens in Oration 43.21, and Eunapius, *Lives,* 483, p. 468, on the bitter feuds between citizens and students of the city.

27. See GNaz, Oration 43.20–22.

28. See F. Loofs, *Eustathius von Sebaste und die chronologie der Basiliusbriefe* (Halle: Niemeyer, 1898). More recent treatments include Jean Gribomont, "Eustathe le philosophe et ley voyages du jeune Basile de Césarée," *RHE* (1959): 115–124; idem, "Saint Basile et le monachisme enthousiaste," *Irenikon* 53 (1980): 123–144; and Charles Frazee, "Anatolian Asceticism in the Fourth Century: Eustathios of Sebastea and Basil of Caesarea," *CHR* 66 (1980): 16–33.

29. For Basil's portrayal of the Eustathians see especially Letter 223.2, 3. Compare his own ascetic ideals in Letter 2 (c. 358), written during the same period. On connections between Eustathian ideals and the ascetic household of Basil's sister and mother, see Elm, *"Virgins of God,"* pp. 106–111.

30. A draft of the *Moralia* may have been the "written rules and regulations" to which Gregory refers in Letter 6. See Rousseau, *Basil of Caesarea,* pp. 228–232, on the content and early dating of this text. According to Gribomont, "Saint Basile," *Théologie de la vie monastique: Études sur la tradition*

patristique (Paris: Aubier, 1961),p. 100, in Basil's *Moral Rules* New Testament citations number more than 1,500.

31. For Basil's contact with Eustathius and Eustathian ascetics during this period see Letter 223.5. For his description of these years of retreat see Letters 14 and 2; for Gregory's perspective, GNaz, Letters 4–6, especially 6.3.
32. Epiphanius of Salamis, *Panarion* 75.1: PG 42, 504C.
33. See RF 7; RF 20, 38, 39. See also Letter 150 to Amphilochius, a protreptic for the cenobitic life. On the significance of the urban context in Basil's monastic system, see Mazza, "Monachesimo basiliano: Moelli Spirituali e tendenze economico-sociali nell'impero del IV secolo," *Studi storici* 21 (1980): 51–57. On the importance of solitude see Letters 2.2, 14, 22.1, 207, 210.1, and RF 5, 6 and 7: PG 31.920–933.
34. Socrates, *HE* 2.43; Sozomen, *HE* 3.14. Jean Gribomont, "Eustathe de Sebaste," in *Saint Basile, Évangile et Église: Mélanges* (Bégrolles-en-Mauges: Abbaye de Bellefontaine, 1984), 1, pp. 95–96, surmises that Eustathius was born c. 300 and entered the clergy some time before 325.
35. Epiphanius, *Panarion* 75.2: PG 42, 505A; trans. Williams, p. 494; also Sozomen, *HE* 3.14.
36. For the events surrounding Aerius see Ephiphanius, *Panarion* 75: PG 42, 504–516; 3 GCS 37.333–336. Aerius was allegedly moved by jealousy, for he himself desired the episcopal dignity (*Panarion* 75.1).
37. On Eustathius's participation in councils and other church affairs see Letters 263.3 and 223.5.
38. See Letters 79,99.3 and 119; on Tyana, Letter 67.
39. Letters 244.3 and 263.3. On Eustathius's links to Arius see also Athanasius, *Hist. arian. ad mon.* 4 (PG 25, 700). Interestingly, in Letter 79 Basil thanked Eustathius for working together with him against the Arian heresy. For further mention of the doctrinal differences that came to divide the two friends, see Letters 138.2, 226.2–3, 237.2.
40. Gribomont, "Eustathe de Sebaste," p. 97, suggests that the Arian leadership of the council exploited his ascetic practices as a pretext for his condemnation. Eustathius was subsequently restored to his see.
41. RB 310: PG 31, 1304C; *De baptismo*: PG 31, 1601 B; Jeanne Ducatillon, ed. and trans., *Basile de Césarée: Sur le baptême*, SC 357 (Paris: Éditions du cerf, 1989), p. 250.
42. RF 19: PG 31, 968–969, and PG 55, 1044–1052; RB 139: PG 31, 1176A, and PG 238, 1241C. RF 1–3: PG 31, 905–917, focus on the greatest commandment, love of God and neighbor. The remaining rules, Basil suggests, simply describe the practical outworking of this commandment.
43. In Letter 1 Basil explains that after hearing of Eustathius's "philosophy" he left Athens and returned to Cappadocia but did not find him there. In this context he describes his travels to Syria, Egypt, and Alexandria. See

Gribomont, "Eustathe le philosophe," p. 116. Basil visited solitaries and ascetic communities in the east (Letter 223.2, 3), but this must have been on his return trip, after recovering from an illness that beset him in Alexandria. On the originality of Basil's monastic system see Emanuel Amand de Mendieta, "Le système cénobitique basilien comparé au système cénobitique pachômien," *RHR* 152 (1957), and J. Gribomont, "Obéissance et Évangile selon saint Basile le Grand," *Supplement de la vie spirituelle* 5 (1952): 193, 214. In contrast see the older studies that assume Pachomian influence: W. K. Lowther Clarke, *St. Basil the Great: A Study in Monasticism* (Cambridge: Cambridge University Press, 1913); E. E. Morison, *St. Basil and His Rule: A Study in Early Monasticism* (Oxford: Oxford University Press, 1912); Margaret Gertrude Murphy, *St. Basil and Monasticism,* Patristic Studies 25 (Washington, D.C.: Catholic University of America, 1930).

44. See especially Letter 80, in which Basil expressed his desire to meet him.

45. Nazianzen was amazed that his friend so readily accepted promotion to the episcopate and, with it, the tumult of worldly affairs. See GNaz, Letter 40: Gallay 1, pp. 49–50.

46. See Basil's comments on his retreats to Annesi in Letter 210.1: Courtonne 2, 190. In Oration 43.29 Nazianzen explains that Basil established "rules" for monasteries in Pontus during a period of retirement there.

47. On Dianius, see Letter 51.2, written c. 370, toward the beginning of Basil's episcopate; on Gregory the Elder see GNaz, Oration 18.18: PG 35, 1005C–1008A.

48. Theodoret, *Historia ecclesiastica* 5.21.3–4, in *Theodoret: Kirchengeschicthte,* ed. Leon Parmentier, 3rd ed., GCS N.F. 5 (Berlin: Akademie Verlag, 1998), 317.21–22; English trans., Blomfield Jackson, NPNF, 2nd ser., vol. 3 (Grand Rapids, Mich.: Eerdmans, 1892), p. 146. See also GNyss, *Contra Eunomion* I: PG 45, 288–296B, for Valens's reign of terror followed by the achievements of Basil.

49. Letters 91, 92.2, 242.1, 243.4. For other images of the "tempest" besetting the churches see Letters 80, 82, 203.1, 244.8, 256, and *De spiritu sancto* 30.76–7. For references to "shipwreck" see Letters 82, 90.1, 92.3, 243.4; *De spiritu sancto* 30.76–77.

50. For descriptions of the West see Letters 92.3 and 243.1. Yet compare his earlier requests in Letters 90 and 92, written in 372, with Letters 242 and 243.1,4, written four years later. Letter 239 to Eusebius of Samosata also complains of the West's unhelpfulness.

51. Letter 92.2, Courtonne 1: 200.8–20.

52. Letter 90.2, Courtonne 1: 196.7–9; Letter 239. For evidence of the continuing strength of the Arian persecution in Syria see Letters 220–222, written in 375 to the churches of Berea and Chalcis. See also Letter 242.

53. Letter 243.2: Courtonne 3, 69. Basil's friend Eusebius of Samosata was ap-

prehended and exiled under similar circumstances. See Theodoret, *HE* 4.13.

54. For examples of the former see Letters 264, 265, 267, 268; for the latter, Letters 256 and 257. Similarly, several of Basil's homilies include words of encouragement to the faithful in the face of Arian persecution. See especially *Hom.* 18: PG 31, 496B, and *Hom.* 19: 521B.

55. Letter 82: Courtonne 1, 184.14–17; written in 372. See also Letter 92.3: Courtonne 1, 202.30–32.

56. Letter 258.1: Courtonne 3, 101.16–20. See also Letter 226.1.

57. See Letters 66, 67, 69, 82. The many letters Basil devoted to this affair suggest its centrality during his episcopate. For an analysis of the correspondence related to its various phases see Robert Pouchet, *Basile le Grand et son univers d'amis d'après sa correspondence,* Studia Ephememeridis Augustinianum 36 (Rome: Institutum Patristicum "Augustinianum," 1992), pp. 405–438, 509–553.

58. Letter 210.4. See also Letters 204 and 205; compare Letter 188, canon 1.

59. Letter 244.9: Courtonne 3, 82. On the confusion among bishops see Letters 263 and 265. On the heresy of Marcellus see Letters 69 and 125.

60. Bishop Theodotus of Nicopolis is a prominent example of suspicion of Basil. Accusations that Basil had betrayed his former friend are implied in Letters 244 and 250 to Bishop Patrophilus of Aegae, Letter 251 to the people of Evaesae, and Letter 263.2 to the westerners. In response Basil insisted that the Eustathian party had changed its doctrinal position while he himself had always remained faithful to the Nicene creed. See Letters 251.4 and 223.3, 5.

61. Letter 226.2.

62. See especially Letters 90.2 and 239.1.

63. *De spiritu sancto* 30.76–79.

64. *De judicio dei* 1: PG 31, 653B. This account of internal dissension bears a marked resemblance to the description in *De spiritu sancto* 30, written in 377. This would suggest a similar dating for *De judicio dei.*

65. For specific cases and Basil's reservations see Letters 190, 121, and 122. For the complaint to Eusebius see Letter 237.2: Courtonne 3, 56.22; see also 190.1 and 239.1 to Eusebius for other concerns about church leadership.

66. *De spiritu sancto* 30.77: PG 32, 213D; Pruche, 524.

67. Letter 92.2: Courtonne 1, 200.14–17. Cf. Letter 243.2.

68. Letter 53.1: Courtonne 1, 137.7–8. On chorepiscopi see E. Kirsten, "Chorbischof," *RAC* 2 (1954): 1105–1114, and the older but more detailed article of H. Leclercq, "Chorévêques," *DACL* 3/1 (1913), cols. 1423–1452. On chorepiscopi in Basil's letters see B. Gain, *L'Église de Cappadoce au IVe*

siècle d'aprés la corresondance de Basile de Césarée, 330–379 (Rome: Pontificum institutum orientale, 1985), pp. 94–100, and Clemens Scholten, "Der Chorbischof bei Basilius," *ZKG* 103/2 (1992): 149–173.

69. Letter 54: Courtonne 1, 140.21–25.

70. On these and other titles for bishops see Gain, *L'Église de Cappadoce,* pp. 75–77.

71. Similarly, in *Ad Dracontium* 10 (PG 50, 534C) Athanasius used a verbal form of this word to designate the function of both bishops and monastic leaders. In keeping with Basil's variation, I use an assortment of expressions to refer to positions of leadership in the church and the monastic community but consistently employ the term *bishop* when Basil himself designated this office. On Basil's terminology for leadership see also Fedwick, *Church and Charisma,* pp. 47–50; Gain, *L'Église de Cappadoce,* p. 75 n. 65, for specific references; and Piero Scazzoso, *Introduzione alla ecclesiologia di san Basilio* (Milan: Vita e pensiero, 1975), pp. 310–312. For historical and theological background on the term *proestōs* see J. P. Fedwick, "The Function of the *Proestōs* in the Earliest Christian *Koinōnia,*" *RTAM* (1981): 5–13.

72. On the purpose and intended audience of the work see J. Gribomont, "Les Règles Morales de Saint Basile et le Nouveau Testament," *SP* 2, TU 64 (Berlin, 1957), pp. 416–426, and the discussion below.

73. These include Letters 18, 106 (to a soldier), 116 and 117 (to a decurion), 277 (to a student), 299 (to a tax assessor), 289 (concerning a slandered woman). See also Gain, *L'Église de Cappadoce,* pp. 119–120, regarding consecrated women, or *kanonikai.* W. K. Lowther Clarke, *The Ascetic Works of Saint Basil* (London: S.P.C.K., 1925), 46, points out that the reference in RB 312 (PG 31, 1305A) to certain laity who join the monks for prayer implies those who live the ascetic life outside the monastic community.

74. See RF 25–55, PG 31, 984–1052. See also Gribomont, "Saint Basile," pp. 99–113, for an overview of Basil's development in this regard, and Rousseau, *Basil of Caesarea,* p. 232, for similar consideration of his ascetic writings.

75. On the development of Basil's ascetic corpus see Jean Gribomont, *Histoire du texte des Ascétiques de S. Basile* (Louvain: Publications universitaires, 1953). For summaries see A. de Vogüe, "Les Grandes Règles de Saint Basile: Un survol," *Collectanea Cisterciensia* 41 (1979): 201–226, and Rousseau, *Basil of Caesarea,* pp. 354–359. The earliest edition of the *Asceticon,* known as the *Small Asceticon,* is preserved only in the Latin translation of Rufinus. For a critical edition see Klaus Zelzer, ed., *Corpus Scriptorum Ecclesiasticorum Latinorum* 86 (Vienna: Hoelder-Pichter-Tempsky, 1986). The precise dates of composition of the *Short Rules*

(*Regulae brevius tractatae* = RB, PG 31, 1080–1305) and the *Long Rules* (*Regulae fusius tractatae* = RF, PG 31, 905–1052) are uncertain, but the latter were written during Basil's episcopate (i.e., after 370) and reflect a more advanced stage of monastic organization. Because both the *Asceticon* and the *Moralia* are in PG volume 31, I will henceforth cite only the relevant column and section.

76. RF 31: 993BC, 43: 1028BC; RB 152: 1181D, 171: 1193D, and 303: 1297. For more implicit allusions see RF 47: 1056CD; RB 303: 1297AB.

77. For examples see RF 31: 993BC and 43: 1028BC; RB 171: 1193D and 303: 1297B. According to Clarke, *Ascetic Works*, p. 39, *ho proestōs* occurs nearly fifty times in the *Asceticon*. On Basil's use of other terms for positions of responsibility in the cenobium as well as for "the rank and file," see Clarke, *Ascetic Works*, pp. 39–42.

78. *Proemium in RB:* PG 31, 1080. See also RB 303: 1297AB, and RF 45: 1032CD.

79. RB 235: 1240CD; Clarke, *Ascetic Works*, 316–317.

80. See RF 33 and RB 108–111, 153, 154. Because of Basil's predominant treatment of men's monasteries and male overseers, I use the masculine pronoun throughout this description.

81. On his concern for proper order and hierarchy see RF 49 (1037D–1040A) and especially 45 (1032C), where Basil fears that if a community remains deprived of a superior it could be transformed into a sort of "democracy," forgetful of the traditional rule and discipline. Gribomont, "Saint Basile," pp. 109–110, downplays the place of hierarchy and obedience to the superior in Basilian monasticism. Though the *Asceticon* does not stress any particular hierarchical structure, the overseer's position of authority and command is emphasized even in *Short Rules* 1–286, generally considered to represent an earlier stage in the development of Basil's ascetic corpus. For examples see RB 152, 171, 235.

82. RF 27: 988B, 48: 1037B, and implied in 54: 1044B.

83. See RF 7: 933C, 32: 996A, 35: 1008AB; RB 183:1204D–1205A.

84. K. Suso Frank, "Hinführung," in *Die Mönchsregeln* (St. Ottlien: EOS Verlag, 1981), p. 61. On Basil's appeal to the early church see Pier Cesare Bori, *La chiesa primitiva: L'immagine della communità delle origini—Atti 2,42–47; 4,32–37—nella storia della chiesa antica* (Brescia: Paideia editrice, 1974), pp. 97–105 and 159–165; and E. Amand de Mendieta, *L'ascèse monastique de Saint Basile: Essai historique* (Éditions de Maredsous, 1949) pp. 128–144.

85. RF 43: 1029AB; RF 43: 1028C–1029B; RB 104: 1153D–1156A.

86. For the more severe judgment of overseers see RB 231: 1236D–1237A; on their need for the fear of God, RF 24: 984AB, 25: 985BC, and RB 98: 1149D. For the allusion to Ezekiel 3:18 see RF 25: 984C and 29: 992C.

87. For the superior or a "proven brother" as an arbitrator see RF 49: 1037C–1040A. Concerning his role as distributor of tasks, RF 41: 1021A–1024C; RB 104: 1153D–1156A, 149: 1180D–1181A, 152: 1181CD. In most cases the superior would appoint an administrator to oversee distribution of necessities and assignment of duties within the monastery (RF 34: 1000B–1001D). The distributor should then exhibit the same fairness and sensitivity as the superior in discharging this duty (RB 149: 1180D–1181A).

88. RB 236: 1241A. For Basil's instructions and admonitions to those who taught the Scriptures see RF 25: 985AB, 45: 1032C–1033C; RB 235: 1240CD; and *Proem. in RB*: 1080AB. In RF 35: 1004A Basil listed the ability to speak alongside other requirements of an overseer, and he noted in RF 32: 996CD that the "gift of the word" *(to tou logou charisma)* was given only to a few.

89. On the need for counsel, RF 48: 1037B and RB 104: 1146A; on occasional meetings of superiors, RF 54: 1044B.

90. RF 29: 992BC, 30: 992D–993A; RB 113: 1157CD.

91. 1 Thessalonians 2:7, 8; quoted twice in RF 25: 985A and C, and once in RB 98: 1152A. On the need for mildness and compassion in exhortation and rebuke see also RF 50: 1040BC and RB 113: 1157CD.

92. For the former qualities see RF 35: 1008B and RB 152: 1181D; for the latter, RF 25: 984C–985C. For comparison of the overseer with a doctor applying appropriate treatment to his patients, see RF 28: 988CD, 51: 1040D–1041A; and RB 99: 1152B.

93. RF 43: 1028B; Clarke, *Ascetic Works,* p. 216.

94. RF 43: 1028C–1029B. See also RF 26: 985D–988A on the superior's duty to care for the weak with tenderness and sympathy.

95. RF 35: 1004B.

96. RF 41 presents a particularly good example of the connection between inner renunciation and outward deeds in Basil's discussion of work. On poverty, see RF 8 and 9: 988D–944B; RB 85: 1144A, 92: 1145C–1148A, 205: 1217CD. On chastity, RF 5: 920C–921A, 15: 956B. The theme of obedience receives by far the most attention and is woven into many of the Rules. See especially *Proem. in RF*: 889A–901A, RF 28: 988C–989C, 29: 992AC, 31: 993CD, 41: 1021A–1024D, 47: 1036C–1037A; and RB 1: 1081AC, 37–39: 1108AC, 114–117: 1160–1161C, 166: 1192C, 199: 1213D–1216A, 280: 1280B, 303: 1296D–1297D. Gain, *L'Église de Cappadoce,* pp. 140–142, notes that Basil did not speak specifically of vows, but his words evince the seriousness of monastic commitment in these areas.

On the necessity of solitude, see RF 5: 920B–924D, 6: 925A–928B. On silence, RF 13: 949BC; RB 173: 1197A, 208: 1221BC. On fasting, RB 128–130: 1168D–1169B, 138: 1173BD, 139: 1176A, 277: 1277C. On prayer, RF 37: 1009C–1016C; RB 43–44: 1109C–1112A, 138: 1173BD, 147: 1192D, 201: 1216C, 221: 1229A, 252: 1252B, 261: 1256C–1260B, 277: 1277AC.

97. *Himation trichinon:* RB 90: 1145AB; RF 16–19: 957A–969B. Clarke, *Ascetic Works,* p. 264 n. 2, points out that Cassian forbade the use of a "robe of sackcloth" because it promoted vanity and restricted the monk's ability to fulfill his duties. See Cassian, *Inst.* 1.2.

98. RB 238: 1241C, 258: 1253D–1256A; RF 18–19: 965B–969B.

99. RF 17: 964C; Clarke, *Ascetic Works,* p. 181. Cf. Letter 2.

100. PG 31, 1509D–1513A. On the nature and dating of this document see Gribomont, *Histoire,* p. 278f. Rousseau, *Basil of Caesarea,* pp. 354–355, also accepts this prefatory letter as genuine.

101. *Proemium ad hypotyposin:* PG 31, 1512D–1513A. The reference to those who teach seems to denote bishops, although it may include priests as well. The earlier quote is from 2 Timothy 2:2.

102. On the central place of the *Moralia* in Basil's ecclesiology see Klaus Koschorke, *Spuren der alten Liebe: Studien zum Kirchenbegriff des Basilius von Caesarea* (Freiburg: Universitätsverlag, 1991), pp. 39–49. On its dating see Gribomont, *Histoire,* p. 159f., who argues for its early composition. Fedwick, *Church and Charisma,* pp. 149–152, suggests that the *Moralia* represents an accretion of texts and revisions begun as early as 361 that reached their final form during the later years of Basil's episcopate (c. 377). Rousseau, *Basil of Caesarea,* pp. 228–229 and n. 211, proposes an early date for the text, between 359 and 361, during Basil's Pontus retreat. I concur with Rousseau for reasons he summarizes. For the text of the *Moralia* see PG 31, 700B–869C.

103. RM 60–69 (793–816) treat the variety of gifts in the church, showing Basil's conviction that all gifts should be equally respected. RM 70–80 (816D–869C) deal with positions of leadership as well as with the married state, widows, slaves, children, virgins, soldiers, and rulers. Gribomont, *SP* 2, TU 64 (1957), p. 148, suggests that Basil's approach here reflects a response to problems arising out of the Eustathian ascetic milieu.

104. See RM 70 (816D–845B) in contrast to RM 20 and 21 (736C–741A). Almost half of RM 80 (860C–869C), the second longest in the corpus (containing twenty-seven subpoints), is also devoted to those who lead in the church. Regarding the relative lack of attention to the cultic or sacerdotal function of the priest or bishop here and throughout Basil's writings see Koschorke, *Kirchenbegriff,* pp. 210–212.

105. RM 70.1: 816D–820A. Basil did not use the term *bishop* here but spoke more generally of those commissioned to preach the Gospel. However he made explicit reference to bishops, priests, and deacons in RM 71: 845BD.

106. Regarding qualifications for church office Basil repeatedly cited relevant passages from 1 Timothy 3 and Titus 1 (see especially RM 70.1: 816D–820A; 71: 845BD) as well as passages from the Gospels.

107. RM 72.1: 845D. Cf. RM 70.5: 821C and 40: 760C.

108. See RM 70.5–7: 821B–824B, 70.23: 836AC, 70.30: 841A, 70.36: 844D–845A.

109. On this practice see Irenée Hausherr, *Spiritual Direction in the Early Christian East,* trans. Antony P. Gythiel (Kalamazoo, Mich: Cistercian Publications, 1990). On Basil's views see Pierre Humbertclaude, *La doctrine ascétique de Saint Basile de Césarée* (Paris: Beauchesne, 1932), pp. 131–144.

110. On this central requirement of *Besitzlosigkeit* (propertylessness) for clergy in the *Moralia* see Koschorke, *Kirchenbegriff,* pp. 214–215. This emphasis foreshadows later civil and ecclesiastical legislation regarding the property and possessions of bishops.

111. Robert C. Gregg, *Consolation Philosophy: Greek and Christian Paideia in Basil and the Two Gregories* (Cambridge, Mass.: Philadelphia Patristic Foundation, 1975), p. 132 with reference to Letters 28, 29, 62, 227.

112. Letter 51: Courtonne 1, 132. Basil wrote this letter in self-defense, seemingly against charges that he had anathematized Bishop Dianius. This may account in part for his protracted adulation of the bishop's character.

113. On Elpidius see Letters 205 and 206; on Valerian, Letter 91. For other commendations of virtue in the lives of bishops see Letter 67 concerning Meletius of Antioch and Letter 161 congratulating Amphilochius of Iconium on his episcopal consecration.

114. Gregg, *Consolation Philosophy,* p. 144 regarding Letter 28. This intentionality was not limited to one letter of condolence.

115. Letter 246: Courtonne 3, 85; Letter 154. On this latter letter and the identification of Ascholius as already a bishop despite the lack of direct reference to his episcopal status, see Pouchet, *Basile le Grand,* pp. 452–456.

116. Letter 271: Courtonne 3, 143.

117. RM 70.37: 844D–845A.

118. On the integrity and sincerity of the preacher in Basil's thought see Thomas Špidlik, *La sophiologie de S. Basile,* OCA 162 (Rome: Pontificum institutum orientalium studiorum, 1961), pp. 254–257.

119. Letter 53.2. See also Letter 240.3 to the priests of Nicopolis and Letter 199, canon 27.

120. Letter 205: Courtonne 2, 181. See also Letter 252, in which Basil applauded the Pontic bishops for their lives of rigid discipline.

121. Letter 81: Courtonne 1, 183. For further discussion of this letter see Chapter 3.

122. Letter 146. On Antiochus see Wolf-Dieter Hauschild, ed., *Basilius von Caesarea: Briefe* (Stuttgart: A. Hiersemann, 1973), 2, nn. 141 and 187. Similarly, in his sermon *In psalmum* 33.8 (PG 29, 369D–372B), Basil recommended meditation on the judgment of Christ as a motivation to subdue evil desires.

123. See Letter 210.1.

124. Letter 291: Courtonne 3, 164.30–31, 163.11–16. Letter 24, at the end of which Basil defended this same chorepiscopus, Timothy, against apparent accusations of calumny, provides some clues about the context of Letter 291. See Pouchet, *Basile le Grand,* pp. 560–561.

125. RM 70.29: 840D.

126. Letter 2.2. Cf. *In ps.* 45.8: PG 29, 429B.

127. This is suggested by Gain, *L'Église de Cappadoce,* p. 108, reflecting on Letter 188, canon 10. Gain's discussion of Basil's views, however, may be making too much of too little evidence. On legislation regarding married clergy see Jean Gaudemet, *L'Église dans l'Empire Romain (IVe–Ve siècles)* (Paris: Sirey, 1958), pp. 140–141. The ordination of married priests has always been permitted in the eastern church.

128. On Eustathius see Letters 1, 34, 223.5, and on Basil's search for spiritual guides, Letter 204.6. Jean Robert Pouchet, "Eusèbe de Samosate, père spirituel de Basile le Grand," *Bullétin de litterature Ecclésiastique* 85/3 (1984): 179–195, examines Basil's use of the term *father* for Eusebius in Letter 27. Though Eusebius himself was not a monk, the nature of their relationship seems to have been based on a monastic model. See especially Pouchet's comments, p. 193.

129. On Basil's role as a spiritual guide to monks see *Proem. in RF:* 889A and *Proem. in RB:* 1080AB. For his instruction regarding spiritual direction see RF 15: 853B, 26: 985D–988A; RB 15: 1092BC, 113: 1157CD, 229: 1236A. On the need for ascetics to have spiritual trainers see also Letter 23.

130. See Pouchet, *Basile le Grand,* p. 57, for evidence.

131. Letter 150.4: Courtonne 2, 75. In Letters 161.2 and 176 Basil wrote of his relationship with Amphilochius as being that of a father and a beloved son. After Amphilochius was consecrated bishop of Iconium, he continued to seek Basil's advice, though now particularly on questions of biblical interpretation and canon law. For Basil's instructions to Amphilochius see Letters 188, 199, 217, 233–236.

132. Letter 127: Courtonne 2, 37.18–19; Letter 164.1. The recipient of Letter 164 has long been identified as Ascholius of Thessalonica, but Pouchet, *Basile le Grand,* pp. 460–464, shows that the addressee of both this and Letter 165 is actually Ascholius's close associate, the bishop and confessor Vetranius of Tomi. The context of the letter is the transfer of Sabas's relics from Scythia to Cappadocia.

133. *In ps.* 44.5: PG 29, 400D, and *In ps.* 28.2: PG 29, 284B and 33.8: 369AB, respectively. See also *Hom.* 12.15: PG 29, 417A–420B, in which the spiritual leader is called to govern well toward the goal of perfection. On the audience, dating, and some themes of Basil's sermons see Jean Bernardi, *La prédication des pères cappadociens: Le prédicateur et son auditoire* (Paris: Presses universitaires de France, 1968), pp. 17–91.

134. *In ps.* 33.8: PG 29, 369A.

135. Letters 226 and 262.1.

136. Letter 199, canon 19.

137. For example, Letters 138.2, 201, 213.2.

138. Letters 191 and 204.4; on collegiality see also Letter 70.

139. See RF 54: 1044AB.

140. Letter 222: Courtonne 3, 7.31–35. This parallels his description of the monastic superior: "One has the power of the eye, having been entrusted with the common care, both testing the things that have been done, and foreseeing and arranging the things that are to be done." RF 24: 984A; cf. RF 43: 1028AC. On the importance of experience in church office see Letter 81.

141. All three of these men were ascetics as well as bishops. See Fedwick, *Church and Charisma*, pp. 55–60, on the leader's role as defender of the faith and for discussion of Basil's own example.

142. *Ad adolescentes*, PG 31, 564–589. Basil said very little about the requisite education of clergy, but it seems that study of Scripture was its central component.

143. Letter 81: Courtonne 1, 183. On ignorance and neglect of the canons among the clergy see Letters 54, 90.2, 92.2.

144. See Letter 260 to Optimus of Antioch, the letters to Amphilochius, and *De spiritu sancto* 1.1, 2. Compare Letter 159.1 to Eupaterius and his daughter.

145. RB 95: 1148D–1149A, 235: 1240CD; Letter 2.3. RB 303: 1296D–1297D also assumes considerable knowledge of the Bible on the part of monks.

146. On psalmody in Basilian monastic communities see RF 37: 1009C–1016C; RB 43: 1109C, 147: 1180AB, 281: 1280B, 307: 1301B; and Letters 2.6 and 207.3. On mealtime Bible readings see RB 180: 1204A. For Basil's instruction on the teaching of Scripture see RF 45: 1032C–1033C and RF 15: 953D, where he prescribes biblical education for children in the monastery.

147. RF 32: 996C. Cf. RB 303: 1297A. This gift was not the domain of the superior alone, but Basil said it is accorded to very few and is associated with those particularly well-versed in the Scriptures. On those commissioned to instruct fellow monks see RF 45: 1032C; RB 235: 1240CD, and 236: 1241A.

148. Letter 226. Regarding ascetics' knowledge of the doctrinal struggles of the church see also Letters 258.1, 262, and Letter 52 to canonesses.

149. Letter 257.2: Courtonne 3, 99. In the East, in Egypt as well as Asia Minor, monks were increasingly perceived as defenders of orthodoxy. Their function as protectors of doctrine caused them to play an ever-expanding role in church politics. See Heinrich Bacht, "Die Rolle des orientalischen Mönchtums in den kirchenpolitischen Auseinandersetzungen um Chalkedon (431–519)," in *Das Konzil von Chalkedon,* ed. Alois Grillmeier and Heinrich Bacht (Würzburg: Echter, 1953), 2, pp. 193–314.

150. RF 3: PG 31, 917C; *In ps.* 29.5: PG 29, 317B; *In ps.* 33.12: 380A; 44.2: 392BC; *In ps.* 33.2: 356C.

151. RB 114: 1160A.

152. See Letter 28.1 for Musonius; Letter 81 for Innocent; Letter 241 for Eusebius; *De spiritu sancto* 29.73 for Gregory Thaumaturgus.

153. These sermons were probably preached during Lent, 378. On the date and occasion see Amand de Mendieta, "La préparation et la composition des neuf 'Homélies sur l'Hexaéméron' de Basile de Césarée," *SP* 16, TU 74 (Berlin, 1985): 349–367.

154. *Hex.* 1: PG 29, 5C; Basile de Césarée, *Homélies sur l'Hexaéméron,* ed. and trans. Stanislas Giet, SC 26 bis (Paris: Éditions du cerf, 1968), p. 90. See Giet's comment, p. 91 n. 4; also the insightful article by Marguerite Harl, "Les trois quarantaines de la vie de Moise, schéma idéal de la vie du moine-évêque chez les pères Cappadociens," *REG* 80 (1967): 407–412.

155. *Ad adolescentes* 2: PG 31, 568C.

156. PG 30, 129A. The ascription of this text to Basil is questionable, but Harl, "Les trois quarantaines," pp. 409–410, links it unquestionably with the fourth-century Cappadocian monastic milieu, specifically the milieu connected with Basil.

157. The use of Moses as a paradigm for Basil and for episcopal leadership in the writings of both Nyssan and Nazianzen will be discussed in Chapters 4 and 5, respectively. See also A. Sterk, "On Basil, Moses, and the Model Bishop: The Cappadocian Legacy of Leadership," *CH* 67/2 (1998): 227–253.

158. Fedwick, *Church and Charisma,* p. 36; see pp. 37–100 for extensive treatment of these two functions.

159. Peter Brown, "The Saint as Exemplar in Late Antiquity," in *Saints and Virtues,* ed. John Stratton Hawley (Berkeley: University of California Press, 1987), pp. 9–10. Compare Basil's instructions to Amphilochius in Letter 150.4.

160. Letter 2.3: Courtonne 1, 9.

161. Koschorke, *Kirchenbegriff,* p. 233.

162. Jean Gribomont, "Un aristocrate révolutionnaire, évêque et moine: Saint Basile," *Augustinianum* 17 (1977): 184.

3. Reframing and Reforming the Episcopate

1. On the function of the holy man as a patron see Peter Brown, "The Rise and Function of the Holy Man in Late Antiquity," in *Society and the Holy in Late Antiquity* (Berkeley: University of California Press, 1982). While Brown's study focuses on Syria, many factors apply to the Cappadocian milieu as well. On late antique patronage in general see L. Harmand, *Le patronat sur les collectivités publiques des origines au bas-empire* (Paris: Presses universitaires de France, 1957), and for the economic and social conditions in which patronage operated, Evelyne Patlagean, *Pauvreté économique et pauvreté sociale à Byzance, 4e–7e siècles* (Paris: Mouton, 1977). On Basil's practice of patronage see Barnim Treucker, *Politische und sozialgeschichtliche Studien zu den Basilius-Briefen* (Munich: Habelt, 1961), pp. 29–63, and M. Forlin Patrucco, "Social Patronage and Political Mediation in the Activity of Basil of Caesarea," *SP* 17 (1982): 1102–1107.

2. Harmand, *Le patronat*, p. 432, describes the great innovation of the late empire: "le patronat tend à prendre désormais le caractère d'une garantie *contre l'État*." On the church and patronage in Cappadocia see Mazza, *Studi Storici* (1980), pp. 57–58, and Gribomont, *Augustinianum* (1977), especially pp. 191–192. For the perception of the bishop's social duties during this period see Jean Gaudemet, *L'Église dans l'Empire Romain (IVe–Ve siècles)* (Paris: Sirey, 1958), pp. 350–356.

3. Letters 35–37, composed c. 363–365, concern the tax assessment of the country priest Leontius, a foster brother of Basil. On the burden of patronage see especially Letter 37; for similar complaints during his episcopate, Letters 309 and 311.

4. For example, Letters 63 and 84. On Basil's efforts to establish and nurse friendly relations with the imperium see Gerald F. Reilly, *Imperium and Sacerdotium according to St. Basil the Great* (Washington, D.C.: Catholic University of America Press, 1945), pp. 134–138.

5. For appeals on behalf of friends and relatives: Letters 32, 33, 107–109, 111, 112, 137, 280; for governors: Letters 96, 147–149; for the appointment of Elpidius: Letter 78.

6. Letters 84, 281, 313, 179, respectively.

7. Letters 74.1 and 3; 96 and 104. On Basil's mediation on behalf of Cappadocian curials see Thomas Kopeček, "The Cappadocian Fathers and Civic Patriotism," *CH* 43 (1974): 298–303.

8. Letter 143. Letters 142 and 144 address the same issue. See also Letter 35 for Basil's comments on patronage of the poor, and GNaz, Oration 43.35, for Nazianzen's description of his activity in this realm. On Basil's labors for the "malheureux," see Stanislas Giet, *Les idées et l'action sociales de*

Saint Basile (Paris: Librairie Lecoffre, 1941), pp. 400–423. On the response of Christian bishops to the problems of poverty in the fourth century see Peter Brown, *Poverty and Leadership in the Later Roman Empire* (Hanover, N.H.: University Press of New England, 2002).

9. Letter 104; Letter 284; Letters 88 and 110. For other requests on behalf of the poor or afflicted see Letters 303, 308, 309, 316, 317.

10. For example, *Hom.* 6: PG 31, 261–277, 7.2: 284A–C, 8: 304–328, 21.8: 553A–556B. On the themes of many of the homilies concerning the rich, the poor, and economic implications of the Gospel for creating "a Christian polity" see Philip Rousseau, *Basil of Caesarea* (Berkeley: University of California Press, 1994), pp. 175–82.

11. Letters 177, 178; 273–275; 307; 72, 73. In the case of the slaves, Basil advises that they be set free and that their master, a Christian, send them to Basil himself for suitable punishment. B. Gain, *L'Église de Cappadoce au IVe siècle d'après la correspondance de Basile de Césarée, 330–379* (Rome: Pontificum institutum orientale, 1985), p. 313, has pointed out that Letters 72 and 73 suggest the practice of *audientia episcopalis*.

12. See Letters 86 (to the governor) and 87 (without address), respectively. In Letter 87 (Courtonne 1, 192.8–9) Basil's language indicates that the recipient was a Christian. See also Robert Pouchet, *Basile le Grand et son univers d'amis d'après sa correspondance* (Rome: Insitutum Patristicum "Augustinianum," 1992), pp. 316–317.

13. Treucker, *Studien,* p. 63, citing S. Dill, *Roman Society in the Last Century of the Western Empire* (New York, 1958), p. 214. Nevertheless, with the rise to prominence of Christian bishops in late antiquity, love of the poor was increasingly becoming a public virtue; see Brown, *Poverty and Leadership,* pp. 1–44.

14. See Fragment of Letter to a Priest 290D–291A, trans. W. C. Wright, *The Works of the Emperor Julian,* LCL (Cambridge, Mass.: Harvard University Press, 1949), 2, p. 303, and Ep. 22 (to Arsacius), ibid., 3, p. 69. Both letters are discussed by Brian Daley, "Building a New City: The Cappadocian Fathers and the Rhetoric of Philanthropy," *JECS* 7/3 (1999): 435–37.

15. Peter Brown, *The World of Late Antiquity* (New York: Harcourt, Brace, Jovanovich, 1971), p. 110, notes this phenomenon even among great western spokesmen of monasticism like Jerome, comparing it to "a Latin aristocrat's enduring contempt for the *petite bourgeoisie.*" He contrasts this with the more socially engaged urban monasticism of the east.

16. For a particularly servile letter of petition see the opening of Letter 104 to the prefect Modestus, Courtonne 2, 4–5, written to request tax exemption for the clergy. For self-aggrandizing comments see Letter 112.3; also Letters 148 and 149. On the network of interests involved in patronage see Letter 280 to Modestus, discussed by Rousseau, *Basil of Caesarea,*

p. 161. Rousseau presents a more nuanced picture than others of Basil's struggles as both a patron and a Christian bishop working within a complex and idiosyncratic imperial system. See especially pp. 162–163 and n. 126.

17. The term *Basileiados* occurs in Sozomen, *HE* 6.34.9; Joseph Bidez, ed. revised Günther Christian Hansen, *Sozomenus Kirchengeschichte,* GCS n.F. 4 (Berlin: Akademie Verlag, 1995), 291.19. For the phrase "new city" and his detailed description of the complex see GNaz, Oration 43.63.

18. Epiphanius, *Panarion* 75.1: Frank Williams, trans., *The Panarion of Epiphanius of Salamis* (Leiden: Brill, 1987), p. 491. Also easily overlooked in the background to Basil's plans are models of clerical and ascetic life he encountered in the towns and cities of Mesopotamia and Syria. In Letter 223.2 Basil specifically mentioned modes of ascetic life he had found and admired in Palestine, Coele Syria, and Mesopotamia as well as Egypt. He mentioned the same areas in Letter 207.2.

19. See Letter 119, where Basil and Sophronius are mentioned by name as having been sent by Eustathius and later having returned to Armenia with a bad report about Basil. Rousseau, *Basil of Caesarea,* p. 141 n. 29 and p. 149, identifies these "shadowy figures" as the "sentinels and spies" of which Basil later complained in Letter 223.3 to Eustathius. Pouchet, *Basile le Grand,* p. 571, suggests the ascetics had been sent by Eustathius to help in the foundation of the new complex.

20. Sozomen, *HE* 6.34.9: Bidez, 291.20, described the Basileiados as a *ptōchōn katagōgion.* References to a soup kitchen derive from a phrase in GNaz, Oration 43.35.20, which actually described Basil's care for the Caesareans following the famine of 369, prior to the construction of the Basileiados. His description of the completed complex later in the same oration (43.63) stresses care for lepers. Writing in the 450s, the monk-bishop and church historian Theodoret, *HE* 4.16, also spoke of the Basileiados primarily in terms of a hospital. In Letters 150 and 176 to Amphilochius, Basil himself referred to it as a poorhouse *(ptōchōtrophein),* though he gives a much fuller description of the multipurpose complex in Letter 94.

21. Letter 94: Courtonne 1, 205.29–206.45. On the dating of this letter see Rousseau, *Basil of Caesarea,* pp. 148, 352–353. Letters 150 and 176 to Amphilochius, which mention the complex, date from 372 and 375, respectively.

22. See Letters 142–144. Letter 142 mentions a *ptōchōtrophia* (Courtonne 2, 65.10–11), and Letter 143 refers to several foundations: a *ptōchōtropheion* for which Basil requests financial assistance; a similar foundation in Amaseia that the recipient of the letter, a *numerarius,* himself supports; and a general reference to a *ptōchōtropheia* for which the man's colleague had already promised aid *(philanthropian).* Courtonne 2, 65.6–16.

23. GNaz, Oration 43.63, lines 38–39; Theodoret, *HE* 4.16; Parmentier, 4.19.13, p. 245.

24. GNaz, Oration 43.63, lines 5–6. For the relevant sermons see *Hom.* 6 (= 322), PG 31.261–277; *Hom.* 7 (= 323), PG 31, 277–304; and *Hom.* 8 (= 325), PG 31.304–28.

25. Daley, "Building a New City," details ways in which the Basileiados represented the broader efforts of the Cappadocians to reconstruct Greek culture and society along Christian lines. See also Kopeček, "Cappadocian Fathers," especially pp. 301–303; Stefania Scicolone, "Basilio e la sua organizzazione dell'attività assistenziale a Cesarea," *Civiltà classica e cristiana* 3 (1982): 353–372; Stanislas Giet, *Les idées et l'action sociales de s. Basile* (Paris: Gabalda, 1941), p. 420f.; and Rousseau's contextualization of the project in his chapter "City and Church" in *Basil of Caesarea*, especially pp. 139–144 and 170–171.

26. For example, Letters 142 and 143.

27. *Tois therapeutais tou theiou*. Letter 94: Courtonne 1, 205.34. See Pouchet, *Basile le Grand*, p. 301 n. 5. See also Pouchet's commentary on Letters 35–37, pp. 185–188. On the close connection between Basil's social activity and monastic vision in the Basileiados see also Klaus Koschorke, *Spuren der alten Liebe: Studien zum Kirchenbegriff des Basilius von Caesarea* (Freiburg: Universitätsverlag Freiburg Schweiz, 1991), pp. 306–311.

28. Sozomen, *HE* 6.34.8–9; GNaz, Oration 43.63.

29. Letter 150.1: Courtonne 2, 71.2–8, and for the bishop's customary visits to the hospice, 150.3: Courtonne 2, 74.4–6. For the later invitation to visit the complex see Letter 176.

30. Treucker, *Studien*, p. 63.

31. See the description of Basil's interaction with the emperor and the prefect in GNaz, Oration 43.54, 55.

32. GNaz, Oration 43.57.

33. Caesarea remained the capital of Cappadocia Prima, while Tyana became the capital of Cappadocia Secunda. Except for Caesarea, all the cities of the former province belonged to Secunda. For details on this and other partitions of Cappadocia, see A. H. M. Jones, *Cities of the Eastern Roman Provinces*, 2nd ed. (Oxford: Clarendon, 1971), pp. 182–187, and R. Teja, *Organización económica y social de Capadocia en el siglo IV, según los padres Capadocios* (Salamanca: Universidad de Salamanca, 1974), pp. 196–201. For a broader perspective on this affair see also Raymond Van Dam, "Emperor, Bishops, and Friends in Late Antique Cappadocia," *JTS* n.s. 37 (1986): 53–76.

34. Letters 74–76. Teja, *Organización económico y social*, pp. 198–200, notes that Basil's claims were somewhat exaggerated but explains that Valens's

measures did have serious consequences for the Cappadocian population. Both Jones, *Cities,* p. 183, and Teja, p. 198, suggest that Valens's transfer of many Caesarean *curiales* to Podandus indicates his initial intention to make this obscure village the capital. However, Giet, *Les idées et l'action sociales,* p. 367 n. 1, points out that neither Basil nor Gregory Nazianzen says anything about this. On the whole affair see also Kopeček, "Cappadocian Fathers," pp. 298–301.

35. On the emperor's respect for the office of bishop see Section B of Karl Leo Noethlichs, "Materialen zum Bischofsbild aus den spätantiken Rechtsquellen," *JAC* 16 (1973): 28–59.

36. Van Dam, "Emperor, Bishops, and Friends," p. 57. In Letter 94: Courtonne 1, 205, Basil wrote, "The great emperor . . . has allowed us to manage the churches by ourselves." In Letter 99 it seems that Basil was specifically charged to provide bishops for the province. See also Letters 102–103 and 227–230 regarding Basil's episcopal intervention in Armenia.

37. Jones, *Cities,* pp. 184–185. Cappadocia was also strategically located in the center of Asia Minor and at a central point on the axis of communication between Constantinople and Antioch. Teja, *Organización económico y social,* p. 208.

38. GNaz, *Carmen de vita sua,* II.I.xi, v.447, PG 37, 1060A; Denis Molaise Meehan, trans., *Saint Gregory of Nazianzus: Three Poems,* FOC 75 (Washington, D.C.: Catholic University of America Press, 1987), p. 89. Paul Jonathan Fedwick, *The Church and the Charisma of Leadership in Basil of Caesarea* (Toronto: PIMS, 1979), p. 53 n. 85, thinks chorepiscopi numbered only about fifteen, but Gain, *L'Église de Cappadoce,* p. 95 n. 146, argues that Gregory's figure is not so far off, estimating the number at 30–35. Gain, pp. 59–62 and 79–80, also estimates at least a dozen bishoprics under Basil's direct authority. On chorepiscopi in Basil's letters see Clemens Scholten, "Der Chorbischof bei Basilius," *ZKG* 103/2 (1992): 149–173.

39. Gaudemet, *L'Église dans l'Empire Romain,* p. 374, lists the canons of the eastern councils that deal with chorepiscopi. Despite limitations on their power enjoined by these councils, Basil's Letters 53 and 54 show that in practice they assumed authority beyond what was sanctioned canonically. Jones, *Cities,* p. 433 n. 20, notes that no less than five Cappadocian chorepiscopi participated in the Council of Nicaea. Chorepiscopi subscribed the councils of Ephesus and Chalcedon as well. See Gain, *L'Église de Cappadoce,* pp. 94–100, especially nn. 149 and 164, regarding the episcopal character of their office.

40. See especially "canonical letters" 188, 199, 217.

41. Letter 282.

42. Letter 55: Courtonne 1, 141–142. Pouchet, *Basile le Grand,* p. 215, places

this letter together with Letters 53, 54, 290, and 291 as part of a general reform of the clergy that Basil began to enact on his assumption of episcopal office.

43. See Letter 169. Along with Letters 170 and 171, which treat the same issue, this letter is mistakenly attributed to Basil. It is actually Nazianzen's; he brought this complaint before Basil, requesting his intervention. See W.-D. Hauschild, trans., *Basilius von Caesarea* (Stuttgart: A. Hiersemann, 1973), 2, p. 171 n. 188.

44. Letters 120–122, 126, 127, 216.

45. See Letters 95, 99, 125, 126, 244.2. Gain, *L'Église de Cappadoce*, pp. 393–395, describes the purposes and dates of Basil's journeys, both completed and projected voyages.

46. Letter 216: Courtonne 2, 207; see also Letter 217.1. Regarding Armenia see Letter 99.

47. See Gaudemet, *L'Église dans l'Empire Romain*, pp. 345, 380–382.

48. Letters 100, 176, and 252, respectively.

49. Letters 95, 98.1, 201; Letters 92, 204.4, 205.

50. Letter 202 to Amphilochius.

51. See, for example, Letter 100 and Letters 227–230 (regarding the replacement of Theodotus of Nicopolis).

52. RF 15: PG 31, 956BC, and Letter 199, Canon 19. For Basil's correspondence with monks see Letters 123, 226, 256, 257, 259, 262, 295.

53. Letter 119: Courtonne 2, 25.

54. Letter 207.2: Courtonne 2, 185. See also Letter 28.2. See Pouchet, *Basile le Grand*, pp. 344–347, 473–479, 481–482, for further discussion.

55. See J. Mateos, "L'office monastique à la fin du IVe siècle: Antioche, Palestine, Cappadoce," *Oriens christianus* 47 (1963): 53–88, especially pp. 69–74.

56. Jean Bernardi, *La prédication des pères cappadociens: Le Predicateur et son auditoire* (Paris: Presses universitaires de France, 1968), p. 376. On Basil's preaching in particular, see pp. 89–91. See also Rousseau, *Basil of Caesarea*, pp. 175–189.

57. On subduing the flesh and the passions, *In ps.* 28.8: PG 29, 304B–305A; *In ps.* 29.6: PG 29, 320C; and *In ps.* 32.9: PG 29, 345C. On detachment from worldly goods, *Hom.* 21: PG 31, 540–564; on abstinence, *In ps.* 29.6: PG 29, 320CD. Two sermons, *Hom.* 1 and 2, PG 31, 164–197, are devoted to fasting.

58. On withdrawal for prayer see *In ps.* 33.3: PG 29, 357B, and *In ps.* 45.8: PG 29, 428C–430C; on asceticism, *Hom.* 3: PG 31, 204C; *In ps.* 115: PG 30, 112B. On virgins, see *In ps.* 44.11: PG 29, 412CD; against sects, *In ps.* 28.3: PG 29, 288B, and *In ps.* 115: PG 30, 113C. Bernardi, *La prédication*, p. 29, places the homilies on the Psalms sometime between 368 and 375.

59. Letter 291. Cf. Letter 116 to Firminus, a young soldier and ascetic.
60. Letter 94. The precise identification of these *therapeutai* is unknown. They may have been lower clergy (Gain, *L'Église de Cappadoce,* pp. 69–70 n. 43) or monks (Hauschild 1, p. 219 n. 412).
61. GNaz, Oration 43.40. In 43.77 Gregory described people's efforts to imitate Basil.
62. On metropolitans see Gaudemet, *L'Église dans l'Empire Romain,* pp. 380–382. On much of what follows see also R. Gryson, "Les elections épiscopales en Orient au IVe siècle," *RHE* 74 (1979): 301–345.
63. The requirement of a synod for designating bishops was established by the Council of Antioch (330 or 341), canons 16, 19, 23. On the translation of bishops see Antioch, canon 21, and its repetition by the Council of Sardica (343). Sardica, canon 3, proscribed episcopal interference outside the bishop's own province.
64. See Basil's Letters 121 and 122 for his complaints about uncanonical ordinations.
65. Letter 190.1: Courtonne 2, 142. On the date and setting of this letter see Pouchet, *Basile le Grand,* pp. 410, 414; also Hauschild 2, n. 239.
66. Letter 216: Courtonne 2, 207.
67. See especially RM 70.37: PG 31, 844D–845A, and the discussion above, Chapter 2.
68. See Letter 121: Courtonne 2, 27.11–14, and Letter 122, respectively. On the complex relations between Cappadocia and Armenia in the background to Letters 120–122 see Rousseau, *Basil of Caesarea,* pp. 278–287, and Pouchet, *Basile le Grand,* pp. 276–279.
69. Letter 54: Courtonne 1, 140.
70. Van Dam, "Emperor, Bishops, and Friends," p. 63.
71. Letter 290: Courtonne 3, 161.10–13. Cf. Letter 53: Courtonne 1, 138.14–19, to chorepiscopi, in which Basil referred to the same biblical account of Simon the Magician (Acts 8:20) to support his argument about selling church office. Pouchet, *Basile le Grand,* pp. 559–561, puts Letter 290 in the same context of Basil's early episcopate.
72. See in this regard GNaz, Oration 43.59, and Gryson, "Les elections épiscopales," p. 338.
73. Regarding his independent appointment of bishops see Letters 81, 99.4, 102, 103; on the transfer of a bishop, Letters 227, 228; on his involvement in affairs beyond Cappadocia, Letters 99.3–4, 190, 216.
74. Letter 115, concerning the ordained slave, is misattributed (despite Gain, *L'Église de Cappadoce,* p. 65, and Hauschild 2, p. 160 n. 61). The situation is clarified in GNaz, Letter 79. Gregory himself, at the direction of his father, Gregory the Elder, performed the ordination. On the whole affair see Pouchet, *Basile le Grand,* pp. 564–567.

75. Letter 217, prologue: Courtonne 2, 209.28–32.

76. Letter 188.1: Courtonne 2, 124.

77. In Letter 188.1 Basil seems to have placed the Encratites in the category of schismatics, and he advised both caution and leniency in receiving them into communion. Fedwick, *Church and Charisma*, pp. 64–67, discusses this letter, though he does not mention Izoïs and Saturninus.

78. GNaz, *De vita sua* II.I.xi., vv.440–517, and Oration 43.58–59. Gregory's Letters 48, 49, 50, and Orations 9–12 also throw light on this incident. For a detailed analysis see Stanislas Giet, *Sasimes: Une méprise de saint Basile* (Paris: Librairie Lecoffre, 1941).

79. GNaz, Letter 50.5: Gallay 1, 65.

80. GNaz, Letter 50.4.

81. GNaz, Letter 49, and Oration 10.1–2.

82. *De vita sua* II.I.xi., vv.416–425; Letter 48.5 and 7–10; Letter 49; Oration 10.1–2; and Oration 11.3.

83. *De vita sua* II.I.xi, vv.440–449: Meehan, pp. 89–90. We will return to this incident in Chapter 5.

84. In *De vita sua* II.I.xi., vv.493–495, Gregory spoke of his inability to resist his father's anger at his flight. In Oration 10 he spoke of his longing for the philosophic life as the reason for his flight from episcopal responsibilities; here he renounced his anger toward Basil, but in Oration 43.59 he described Basil's action as an infidelity "of which not even time has effaced the pain." Elsewhere he described his forced consecration as "tyrannical" (*De vita sua* II.I.xi., v.393; Letter 63.6: Gallay 1, 83).

85. In *De vita sua* II.I.xi., vv.520–533, we learn that Gregory never took over the see of Sasima. In Oration 12 he accepted joint ministry with his father but reiterated his desire for spiritual calm and withdrawal.

86. In *De vita sua* II.I.xi, vv. 229–231, Gregory writes: "We had all in common, and a single soul, as it were, bound together our two distinct bodies." Meehan, p. 83. On the intimacy of their relationship see also GNaz, Oration 43.19, 20, 24, and *Basilii Magni Epitaphia* cxixf., PG 38, 72–82. Seven letters expose their mutual engagement to pursue the monastic life: GNaz, Letters 1, 2, 4, 5, 6; Basil, Letters 1 and 14. On their respective notions of monastic life in these letters see Giet, *Sasimes,* pp. 37–54.

87. Letter 48.2–3 and *De vita sua* II.I.xi., vv.391–399; E. Fleury, *Grégoire de Nazianze et son temps* (Paris, 1930), p. 236, cited by Giet, *Sasimes,* pp. 88. For other theories about Basil's motivation see Giet, pp. 83–93.

88. See especially Giet, *Sasimes,* pp. 93–103.

89. Letter 98.2: Courtonne 1, 213.

90. For a discussion of Basil's influence on Gregory based on the relevant sources see Michel Aubineau, ed., *Grégoire de Nysse: Traité de la virginité*

(= *De virginitate*), SC 119 (Paris: Éditions du cerf, 1966), pp. 56–61. In a letter to Gregory, Peter of Sebaste described Basil as "this one who led you toward the light by a spiritual childbirth." Letter 30.6 in *Grégoire de Nysse: Lettres*, ed. Pierre Maraval, SC 363 (Paris: Éditions du cerf, 1990).

91. For references to Gregory's use of *didascalos* for Basil see Aubineau, "Introduction," *Traité*, p. 59 n. 9. For other titles of respect attributed to Basil in Nyssan's writings see ibid., p. 56 n. 2, and *VSM*, SC 178, p. 162 n. 1. Basil's correspondence includes only two letters to his brother. Letter 38, a short theological treatise, is likely the work of Gregory himself; Letter 58 presents him in a negative light. See also Gerhard May, "Einige Bemerkungen über das Verhältnis Gregors von Nyssa zu Basilius dem Grossen," in *Epektasis: Mélanges Jean Daniélou* (Paris: Beauchesne, 1972), pp. 509–515; and below, Chapter 4.

92. Letter 11.4 (Gallay 1, p. 17) See, however, Maraval's comments on this letter, "Grégoire de Nysse, évêque et pasteur," *Vescovi i pastori en epoca teodosiana* (Rome: Institutum Patristicum "Augustinianum," 1997), 2, 384.

93. Aubineau, "Introduction," *Traité*, p. 81. See Letter 100 to Eusebius. On the forgeries see Basil's Letter 58 to his brother; also Letters 59, 60. This incident probably occurred early in 371.

94. See Aubineau, "Introduction," *Traité*, pp. 29–30. In Letter 100, probably written in 373, Gregory certainly holds episcopal office.

95. Letter 225: Courtonne 3, 22, written by Basil to Demosthenes on behalf of all the bishops of Cappadocia Prima. For what Letter 225 suggests about accession to the episcopate in this epoch see Maraval, "Grégoire de Nysse," 2, pp. 384–385.

96. See GNaz, Oration 11.3.

97. GNyss, *De virginitate,* ed. Aubineau, II.3. On Basil's intentions see Aubineau's comments, pp. 143–146.

98. Letter 215: Courtonne 2, 207; Letters 215, 231, 232. See also Letters 237.2 and 239.1 regarding Gregory's expulsion from his see. For Basil's defense of Gregory, see Letter 225.

99. Hauschild 2, pp. 165–166 n. 121, and Karl Holl, *Amphilochius von Ikonium in seinern Verhältris zu den grossen kappadoziern* (Tübingen: J. C. B. Mohr, 1904), pp. 16–17.

100. Letter 138.2: Courtonne 2, 56.

101. Letter 161.1: Courtonne 2, 92–93. Writing to Amphilochius's aggrieved father, Nazianzen denied his own involvement in the selection of his son and hinted at Basil's role. See GNaz, Letter 63.6: Gallay 1, 83. On the letters and the relationship between Basil and Amphilochius see Pouchet, *Basile le Grand,* pp. 405–438.

102. Much of what we know of Amphilochius's life and career in Constantino-ple is gleaned from passages in the writings of Gregory Nazianzen. For the following see Gregory's Letters 22–24, and *Carmina* I.II.ii, v. 102. In addi-tion to encouragement in ascetic life, Gregory also directed his cousin to-ward involvement with the church. See especially Letter 9.2: Gallay 1, 1.12.

103. Letter 150. References to "wandering in the desert" and "caves and rocks" in 150.4: Courtonne 2, 75.13–14, suggest that the friends were headed toward an eremitic vocation. This letter was written in the name of Hera-cleidas to his friend Amphilochius, expressing their common ambition; it also serves as a protreptic for the cenobitic life and for Basil as an ascetic teacher. Judging from its style, Basil himself was the author.

104. Letter 150.1 and 4; Courtonne 2, 71.11, 72.23–24, and 75.8–10.

105. Gregory Nazianzen wrote three letters to Amphilochius during this period that assume that his cousin had visited Basil and come under his influence (Letters 25–27, especially Letter 25). Amphilochius never became a monk in the strict sense, since he remained with his father until his episcopal consecration.

106. See especially Letters 161.2, 176.

107. See Letter 199: Courtonne 2, 154; also Letters 161.1, the beginning of 188, and 232. The so-called canonical letters—188, 199, 217—were written in response to Amphilochius's questions about moral and canonical issues. See also Letters 233–236, which "sum up in a remarkable and unusual way his theological position on almost every fundamental point he ever ad-dressed." Rousseau, *Basil of Caesarea,* p. 261. Amphilochius also seems to have made some personal visits to Basil.

108. Both chapters 1 and 30 of *De spiritu sancto,* the first and the last, were writ-ten as letters to Amphilochius. Regarding Basil's emphasis on the Holy Spirit in his writings to Amphilochius see Pouchet, *Basile le Grand,* pp. 429–436, and on the connection with Basil's image of the priesthood, Rousseau, *Basil of Caesrea,* pp. 153–154.

109. Jean Gribomont, "Saint Basile et le monachisme enthousiaste," *Irenikon* 53 (1980): 143–144, discusses Amphilochius's efforts to impose spiritual au-thority. See also Constantine Bonis, "What Are the Heresies Combatted in the Work of Amphilochius Metropolitan of Iconium (ca. 341/5–ca.395/ 400) 'Regarding False Asceticism'?" *GOTR* 9 (1963): 79–96. On the dif-ficulty of governing the church in Lycaonia see Holl, *Amphilochius von Ikonium,* pp. 20–24.

110. Rousseau, *Basil of Caesarea,* p. 283. For Basil's reference to this order see Letter 99.1: Courtonne 1, 214.1–2.

111. Letters 102 and 103. For the request to Basil see Letter 99.4: Courtonne 1,

217–18. For a reconstruction of the relations, events, and dates of Basil's journeys to Armenia see Pouchet, *Basile le Grand,* 276–289. Pouchet puts Basil's trip to Satala in the summer of 372, while Rousseau assumes the following year.

112. The Councils of Melitene (358) and Constantinople (360). Apparently Eustathius did not feel obligated to submit to the decisions of these councils because they emanated from heretical bishops.

113. Letter 122: Courtonne 2, 27–28. From the time of Gregory the Illuminator, who had been consecrated bishop of Armenia between 303 and 313 by the bishop of Caesarea, Leontios, it had become traditional for the *catholicos,* a kind of patriarch of Armenia, to be ordained by the metropolitan bishop of Caesarea. Pouchet, *Basile le Grand,* p. 276. See also Letters 120 to Meletius of Antioch and 121 to Theodotus of Nicopolis complaining about the affair. During his earlier journey to Satala, Basil himself had rehabilitated a certain Cyril, *catholicos* of Armenia, who had been calumniated by the Christians of Satala (Letter 99.4). In Letter 120 he described Anthimus's consecration of Faustus as an affront to Cyril and to his own authority and an act that filled Armenia with discordant factions.

114. Letter 102: Courtonne 2, 3. Hauschild 2, 157 n. 31, suggests that he was probably a priest in Caesarea or a chorepiscopus in the surrounding area.

115. Letter 103: Courtonne 2, 4; Letter 229.1.

116. In Letter 102 Basil said that the church of Satala had been long deprived of a leader. For further commentary on the selection of Poemenius see Pouchet, *Basile le Grand,* pp. 287–289.

117. See Letters 227 and 229.1.

118. In Letter 228: Courtonne 3, 32, Basil wrote: Nicopolis "will share with you a common father who will impart a portion of his grace to each of you." Cf. Letter 227. Regarding episcopal transfers see Antioch (330 or 341), canon 16, and the Council of Sardica (343); also Gryson, "Les élections épiscopales," pp. 306–310.

119. Letters 227: Courtonne 3, 30; 228: 33; and 229.1: 34.

120. Letter 230: Courtonne 3, 36.

121. Letter 238. On these occurrences, which caused Basil severe anguish, see also Letters 237.1, 239, 240.

122. Letter 81 is Basil's response. For the identification of "Innocent" with Faustinus of Iconium see Jean Robert Pouchet, "L'énigme des lettres 81 et 50 dans la correspondance de saint Basile: Un dossier inaugural sur Amphiloque d'Iconium?" *OCA* 54 (1988): 9–46, and Hauschild 1, p. 210 n. 358. Since Faustinus died in 373, Hauschild places the letter in 372.

123. See Letters 205 and 226.1 for references to the priest Meletius.

124. Letter 81: Courtonne 1, 183.24–26; Letters 244.9, 263.3. Hermogenes was

the predecessor of Dianius of Caesarea and had participated in the Council of Nicaea.

125. Letter 81: Courtonne 1, 183.28–33. Based on this description Pouchet, "L'énigme," (1988), 26–27, argues that he is none other than Meletius, Basil's beloved priest whose harsh ascetic discipline he described in Letter 205. See also Pouchet, *Basile le Grand,* pp. 405–407.

126. See GNaz, Letter 53. On the earliest collections and collectors and their motives see Pouchet, *Basile le Grand,* pp. 45–72. The foundational studies of Marius Bessières and Stig Yngve Rudberg on the manuscript tradition of Basil's correspondence have been updated and revised by Pouchet; see pp. 48–50 for a summary of his revisions. On Basil's letter writing see also Fedwick, *Church and Charisma,* pp. 169–173.

127. On Basil's correspondence see Photius, *Bibliotheca* 143; on his other writings, *Bibliotheca* 141 and 191.

128. Letter 294: Courtonne 3, 169. For other remarks on the written word, see Letters 135, 219.1, 297.

4. Gregory of Nyssa

1. *Res gestae* 22.5, in *Ammianus Marcellinus: The Later Roman Empire,* trans. Walter Hamilton (New York: Penguin, 1986), p. 361.

2. Werner Eck, "Der Einfluss der konstantinischen Wende auf die Auswahl der Bischöfe im 4. und 5. Jahrhundert," *Chiron* 8 (1978): 562. Eck refers to Cyprian, *Ep.* 80.1, regarding Valerian's decree. On the rising status of bishops and its significance for their selection see also Rita Lizzi, *Il potere episcopale nell'oriente romano: Rappresentazione ideologica e realità politca (IV–V sec. d.C.)* (Rome: Edizioni dell'Ateneo, 1987), pp. 12–32; H. A. Drake, *Constantine and the Bishops* (Baltimore: Johns Hopkins University Press, 2000), especially pp. 309–352; and Claudia Rapp, "The Elite Status of Bishops in Late Antiquity in the Ecclesiastical, Spiritual and Social Context," *Arethusa* (2000): 379–399.

3. Gregory's ascetic and theological treatises *De virginitate, Contra Eunomium, De hominis opificio,* and *In Hexaemeron* were all at least partly inspired by the thought of Basil of Caesarea. Even his late work *De instituto christiano* presents in exhortatory form the basic monastic doctrine and ideals expressed in the question-answer scheme of Basil's *Rules.* However, Gregory also modified Basil's legacy. See Gerhard May, "Einige Bemerkungen über das Verhältnis Gregors von Nyssa zu Basilius dem Grossen," in *Epektasis: Mélanges Jean Daniélou* (Paris: Beauchesne, 1972), pp. 509–515.

4. A notable exception is Pierre Maraval, "Grégoire de Nysse," in *Vescovi e pastori in epoca teodosiana* (Rome: Institutum Patristicum "Augustin-

ianum," 1997), 1, pp. 383–393. For an introduction to Nyssan's thought, see Anthony Meredith, *Gregory of Nyssa* (London: Routledge, 1999).

5. See for example Letters 53–55 to suffragans; Letter 286 to a civil official.

6. Letters 92.1 and 164.2.

7. Letter 99.1. See also Letters 98.1, 136.2, 248, 258.2.

8. Letters 119, 213.

9. Letter 204.4: Courtonne 2, 175. See also Letters 223.2 and 2.1.

10. Carole Straw, *Gregory the Great: Perfection in Imperfection* (Berkeley: University of California Press, 1988), p. 181, notes the same emphasis in the writings of Gregory the Great and interprets it as a transfer of monastic views to the church at large.

11. For the first explanation see Philip Rousseau, *Basil of Caesarea* (Berkeley: University of California Press, 1994), pp. 6–8; the second is suggested by May, "Einige Bemerkungen," p. 511, though he also mentions other factors.

12. These viewpoints are noted by Anthony Meredith, "Gregory of Nazianzus and Gregory of Nyssa on Basil," *SP* 32 (1997): 163–169.

13. See "Index des citations d'auteurs anciens" in *Grégoire de Nysse: Lettres,* ed. Pierre Maraval, SC 363 (Paris: Éditions du cerf, 1990), pp. 325–334. For references to titles ascribed to Basil in Gregory's writings see Michel Aubineau, ed., *Grégoire de Nysse: Traité de la virginité,* SC 119 (Paris: Éditions du cerf, 1966), p. 56 n. 2, and P. Maraval, ed., *VSM,* p. 162 n. 1.

14. *In Hexaemeron,* PG 44, 61A–64A.

15. *De hominis opificio,* PG 44, 125B; *De vita s. patris Ephraem Syri,* PG 46, 833C.

16. Gregory, *Contra Eunomium,* I, PG 45, 249AB. For further adulation of Basil in this work see PG 45, 424B, 272D, 288C–293B.

17. *In quadragintas martyres,* GNO X.1.2, 160.12–16 (= PG 46, 776A).

18. *De virginitate* II, 3, 15–17 in Aubineau, *Traité,* p. 270.

19. *De virginitate,* Pr. 2, 14–24.

20. This is expressed most clearly in chapter XV, in which Gregory explained that it is not right "to limit this perfection to bodies only, but it pervades and inspires in its purpose as many as are and are considered the perfections of the soul." *De virginitate* XV.1, 3–6. Chapter III.1 confirms that Gregory was married at the time that he wrote this treatise. Regarding his marriage, a subject of some debate, see Jean Daniélou, "Le mariage de Grégoire de Nysse et la chronologie de sa vie," *REA* 2 (1956): 71–78, and Paul Devos, "Grégoire de Nazianze témoin du mariage de Grégoire de Nysse," in Justin Mossay, ed., *II. Symposium Nazianzenum* (Paderborn: Schöningh, 1983), pp. 269–281. Nyssan was also married at the time of his episcopal consecration in 372. Celibacy was by no means required of bish-

ops in this period and the married state was fairly common among eastern bishops.

21. *De virginitate* XXIII, 1, 1–8. The "written instructions" (*eggraphoi didaskaliai*) that Gregory mentioned here most probably refer to Basil's first spiritual writings, the *Moralia*. See Aubineau, *Traité*, p. 522 n. 1.

22. *De virginitate* XXIII, 6, 9–10.

23. *De virginitate* Pr. 2, 17–20. See also Aubineau, *Traité*, p. 545 nn.8–10. Susanna Elm has argued that the very purpose of this treatise was to present Basil's model of ascetic life as the only acceptable one. See *"Virgins of God,"*: *The Making of Asceticism in Late Antiquity* (Oxford: Clarendon, 1994), pp. 197–199 and especially 213–214.

24. On the dating see Pierre Maraval's discussion, *VSM*, pp. 57–67.

25. *VSM* 6, 6–16.

26. Maraval, *VSM*, p. 163 n. 7, cites the following examples: Gregory of Nyssa, *In Bas.* (PG 46, 801D); Gregory of Nazianzus, Letter 5: Gallay 1, p. 6; Letter 6: p. 7. Likewise Basil himself insisted on the necessity of manual work for monks: RF 37: PG 31, 1009C–1016C. See also RF 38–42, and RB 61, 105, 142, 147, 207.

27. *VSM* 14, 2–4.

28. *VSM* 12, 22–27.

29. *VSM* 14, 4–6.

30. Jean Bernardi, *La prédication des pères cappadociens: Le prédicateur et son auditoire* (Paris: Presses universitaires de France, 1968), pp. 313–314, follows Jean Daniélou, "La chronologie des sermons de Grégoire de Nysse," *RSR* 29 (1955): 351–353, in assigning the date January 1, 381. However, Basil's death most likely did not occur on January 1, 379, the traditional date. Maraval, "Grégoire de Nysse," p. 390, now withdraws his earlier date (August 377) in favor of August 378, proposed by Robert Pouchet, "La date de l'élection épiscopale de Basile et celle de sa mort," *RHE* 87 (1992): 5–13.

    The text of Gregory's encomium is in GNO X.1.2, pp. 109–134; also PG 46, 788C–817D. For longer English quotations I cite James Aloysius Stein, ed. and trans., *Encomium of St. Gregory Bishop of Nyssa on his Brother St. Basil, Archbishop of Cappadocian Caesarea* (Washington, D.C.: Catholic University of America, 1928).

31. GNO X.130.7–10: Stein, p. 51. See also 109.4–6 and 110.19–20.

32. For Basil's comments on his brother's naïveté and political ineptitude see especially Basil's Letter 215; also Letters 58 and 60.

33. On structure and topics for various types of funeral orations see Menander Rhetor, *epid.* 211. Though fourth-century Christian orators did not claim to be following Menander's prescriptions, their speeches generally did conform to these rules.

34. Bernardi, *La prédication,* pp. 314–315. For the idealization of Basil's background see GNO X.132.5–14: Stein, p. 55.
35. See GNO X.111.8–16 for Gregory's summary of this argument. For a schema of the encomium see Stein, p. xli.
36. GNO X.114.10–11. The idolatry to which Gregory referred is primarily the Arian heresy, which he went on to describe in 114.119f.
37. GNO X.116.8–9: Stein, 19. Elijah is praised for his disdain for the body (112.24–113.6); John for the exercise of virtue (113.18–19); Paul for his transcendence of the body and consequent initiation into spiritual mysteries (113.26–114.5).
38. See especially GNO X.114.12–14.
39. GNO X.118.16–21. See 116.13–119.15 for the entire comparison with Paul.
40. GNO X.120.4–7. The title *ho didaskalos hemōn* is ascribed to Basil throughout the oration.
41. GNO X.120.7–21: Stein, p. 29.
42. GNO X.122.10–12; GNO X.124.14–17.
43. GNO X.125.3–5: Stein, p. 39.
44. GNO X.127.4–6: Stein, p. 43.
45. GNO X.127.13f.
46. GNO X.129.1.
47. Marguerite Harl, "Moïse figure de l'évêque dans l'Eloge de Basile de Grégoire de Nysse (381)," in Andreas Spira, ed., *The Biographical Works of Gregory of Nyssa,* Proceedings of the Fifth International Colloquium on Gregory of Nyssa (Philadelphia: Philadelphia Patristic Foundation, 1984), p. 100.
48. GNO X.129.5–9: Stein, pp. 47–49.
49. See GNO X.129.9–19.
50. GNO X.130.7–10.
51. GNO X.131.9–11: Stein, 53.
52. GNO X.133.19–134.21.
53. See Gregory's Letter 1, especially sections 17–20, 27, and 30–35, in Pierre Maraval, ed., *Grégoire de Nysse: Lettres,* SC 363 (Paris: Éditions du cerf, 1990). The probability that Nyssan delivered the encomium in Caesarea itself, where Helladius was at the time presiding as bishop, adds a subtly provocative dimension to the speech. Although Letter 1 may have been written after the encomium, it reflects a long-standing dispute.
54. Cf. Gregory's homily *In sanctum Stephanum,* GNO X.1.75–101 (December 386), where he placed Stephen, a deacon, on the same level as the apostles Peter, James, and John (X.1.97). Bernardi, *La prédication,* pp. 293–294, suggests that Gregory was challenging an increasing preoccupation with hierarchies within the episcopate itself.

55. GNO IX.1.441–457. On this oration see Basil Studer, "Meletius von Antiochen, der erste Präsident konzils von Konstantinopel (381), nach der Trauerrede Gregors von Nyssa," in Spira, ed., *Biographical Works*, pp. 121–144, and Bernardi, *La prédication*, pp. 315–318.

56. GNO IX.1.449.16–17. Curiously Meletius is compared with Moses in "goodness," an attribute not commonly ascribed to the patriarch.

57. For evidence of the later reworking of the text see Bernardi, *La prédication*, pp. 308–309. Bernardi places the oration on November 17, 380; see also Maraval, *VSM*, pp. 57–67. For the text see GNO X.1.3–57 (= PG 46, 893–958); English trans. Michael Slusser, *St. Gregory Thaumaturgus: Life and Works*, FOC 98 (Washington, D.C.: Catholic University of America Press, 1998), pp. 41–87.

58. See Raymond Van Dam, "Hagiography and History: The Life of Gregory Thaumaturgus," *Classical Antiquity* 1 (1982): 272–308. Regarding some of the dominant themes in the *Vita* see Lucas F. Mateo Seco, "El Cristiano ante la vida y ante la muerte," in Spira, ed., *Biographical Works*, pp. 206–209.

59. On these details of Gregory's background and the virtues of his youth see GNO X.8.6–9.8 (= PG 46, 900B–D). Most of these details, as well as many other events in the *Vita*, conflict with the Thaumaturge's own description of his life in his Letter to Origen.

60. GNO X.10.8–11 (= PG 46, 901C).

61. For the Egypt episode see GNO X.10.14–13.3 (= PG 46, 901D–905C), and Van Dam, "Hagiography and History," p. 280. Henri Crouzel, ed. and trans., *Grégoire le Thaumaturge: Remerciement à Origène, suivi de la Lettre d'Origène à Grégoire*, SC 148 (Paris: Éditions du cerf, 1969), p. 21, notes that the episode with the prostitute is almost a commonplace in hagiographical literature. Athanasius, for example, is said to have experienced and overcome the same temptation.

62. GNO X.13.9–12 (= PG 46, 905C–D). On the circumstances and content of Gregory's studies in Caesarea under Origen, see Robin Lane Fox, *Pagans and Christians* (New York: Knopf, 1987), pp. 519–528, and Crouzel, *Remerciement*, pp. 14–22.

63. GNO X.14.18–15.1 (= PG 46, 908CD). Notice in this passage that the married state which characterized Moses' career did not for Gregory detract from the ability to lead God's people.

64. GNO X.17.24–19.5 (= PG 46, 912C–913A). On this trinitarian creed attributed to Gregory Thaumaturgus see L. Abramowski, "Das Bekenntnis des Gregors Thaumaturgus bei Gregor von Nyssa und das Problem seiner Echtheit," *ZKG* 87 (1976): 145–66. The creed likely originated with Nyssan himself.

65. GNO X.19.14–19 (= PG 46, 913B).
66. GNO X.19.21 (= PG 46, 913C).
67. GNO X.20.7–8 (= PG 46, 913C). Cf. 14.10f. (= PG 46, 908C) for the parallel language used to describe his abandonment of urban life for solitude.
68. Basil, *De spiritu sancto* 29.73 and Letter 28.1–2.
69. This title did not become customary until the sixth century. See W. Telfer, "The Cultus of St. Gregory Thaumaturgus," *HTR* 29 (1936): 240. For the Cappadocians, Gregory Thaumaturgus was normally Gregory the Great.
70. GNO X.36.3–41.15 (= PG 46, 933B–940B).
71. GNO X.36.17 (= PG 46, 933C).
72. GNO X.40.6–7 (= PG 46, 937C).
73. *Ouk anagkē penias,* GNO X.38.10 (= PG 46, 936C).
74. GNO X.40.5–7 (= PG 46, 937C).
75. GNO X.40.25–41.1 (= PG 46, 940A). See also 36.22–37.5 (= 933D), where Nyssan compares Gregory Thaumaturgus to Samuel in his indifference to external qualities in the choice of a king.
76. See Thomas A. Kopeček, "The Social Class of the Cappadocian Fathers," *CH* (1973): 458. On tensions between bishops and local gentry see also Barnim Treucker, *Politische und sozialgeschichtliche Studien zu den Basilius: Briefen* (Bonn: Habelt, 1961), pp. 26–28. For a thorough discussion of the relevant ecclesiastical legislation see R. Gryson, "Les elections épiscopales en Orient au IVe siècle," *RHE* (1979): 301–345.
77. *CTh* 16.1.3. See the discussion below, Chapter 7.
78. See Letter 2.12 regarding his voyage to Arabia for this purpose, and Maraval, ed., *Lettres,* p. 119 n. 2.
79. The precise dating of *De vita Moysis* is still uncertain, though it is generally attributed to the twilight of Gregory's career. For internal evidence to this effect see the Prologue, section 2, in *Gregory of Nyssa: The Life of Moses,* trans. Abraham J. Malherbe and Everett Ferguson, Classics of Western Spirituality (New York: Paulist Press, 1978) (= GNO VII.1.2.12–14). For the Greek text see also *Grégoire de Nysse: La vie de Moïse,* ed. Jean Daniélou, SC 1 bis (Paris: Éditions du cerf, 1955). The English translation follows the subdivisions of Daniélou's edition.
80. For an outline of Gregory's life and growing involvement with the monastic communities of Asia Minor after 385 see Jean Daniélou, "Le mariage de Grégoire de Nysse et la chronologie de sa vie," *REA* 2 (1956): 71–78. There is, however, still debate about a number of dates and events in his life.
81. *Life of Moses* II, 280, p. 126; GNO VII.1.129.6–10. See also II, 278, p. 125.
82. *Life of Moses* II, 286, p. 127; GNO VII.131.11–14. See Letter 1 regarding Gregory's dispute with Bishop Helladius of Caesarea, mentioned above. Cf. Letter 17.28.

83. *Life of Moses* II, 10–17, pp. 57–59; GNO VII.36.7–38.20.

84. Ibid., II, 115–116, p. 81; GNO VII.68.23–69.3.

85. Ibid., II, 18–19, p. 59; GNO VII.38.21–39.5.

86. Ibid., II, 55, p. 67; GNO VII.49.1–2.

87. See S. Giet, ed. and trans., *Basile de Césarée, Homélies sur l'Hexaémérun,* SC 26 bis (Paris: Éditions du cerf, 1968), p. 91 n. 4.

88. *Life of Moses,* II, 89, p. 75; GNO VII.60.1–7.

89. The text is in Maraval, *Lettres,* pp. 214–232. On the dating and circumstances see Jean Daniélou, "L'évêque d'après une lettre de Grégoire de Nysse," *Euntes Docete* 20 (1967): 86–89, and Reinhart Staats, "Gregor von Nyssa und das Bischofsamt," *ZKG* 84 (1973): 157–159. Both authors date the letter around 390.

90. See Letter 17.2 and 3.

91. Letter 17.5. In 17.4 Gregory spoke not only of "dissidence" but also of "secession" from the church. There is difference of opinion as to the heresy in question here. Compare Daniélou, "L'éveque," and Staats, "Gregor von Nyssa."

92. Letter 17.10. For the following description see 17.10–15.

93. Letter 17.14. The example of Peter in this passage is only one of a lengthy list of biblical figures Gregory employed to illustrate his point.

94. Sozomen, *HE* 8.6. See also the discussion of this account in Staats, "Gregor von Nyssa," especially p. 157, and Maraval, *Lettres,* pp. 39–40.

95. Staats, "Gregor von Nyssa," points out that Gregory's negative assessment of Helladius of Caesarea in Letter 1 accords with these events. In addition to outlining the portrait of Gregory's ideal bishop, Maraval, "Grégoire de Nysse," pp. 392–393, has described Letter 17 as an indirect attack on the candidate who would be appointed by Helladius.

96. Letter 17.28.

97. Letter 17.6, 7.

98. Letter 17.8, 9.

99. Letter 17.20; Letter 17.21, alluding to 2 Timothy 2:21.

100. Letter 17.22–24; Letter 17.26. Maraval, *Lettres,* p. 230 n. 1, suggests that Gregory's concluding words about the incompetence of a worldly leader may well be aimed against Gerontius.

101. See Staats, "Gregor von Nyssa," pp. 169–170. Cf. Basil, Letter 217, regarding neophytes.

102. The concept of the harbor *(limein)* was widely used to express the meaning of monastic life. See Staats, "Gregor von Nyssa," pp. 164–168.

103. See the comments of Maraval, *Lettres,* pp. 38–39; for the text of Letter 1, pp. 82–105.

104. See *CTh* 16.1.3 for the decree of Theodosius. Canon 2 of Constantinople

explicitly forbids bishops to be involved in ordinations or any other ecclesiastical activities outside their dioceses.

105. See especially Letter 1.19 and 35.

106. According to Sozomen, *HE* 8.6, Gerontius was in fact ordained by Helladius, though he was eventually deposed by John Chrysostom.

107. Letter 19.12–13, and see the comments of Maraval, *Lettres,* pp. 28–29.

108. On the election of Peter see P. Devos, "Saint Pierre Ier, évêque de Sébastée, dans une lettre de Grégoire de Nazianze," *AB* 70 (1961): 359–360. For Nyssan's description of Peter's character and virtues, see *VSM* 12 and 14.

109. Letter 2.12–13 mentions a mission to Arabia; Letter 3 speaks of the same journey. On Gregory's largely failed intervention in ecclesiastical affairs mentioned in Letters 2 and 3 see Maraval, *Lettres,* pp. 33–38.

110. See Letter 7; also Letters 8.4–5 and 13.3. Letters 26 and 27 show his response to the request of a pagan rhetor. See Letters 2, 19, 21 for Gregory's discussion of monastic concerns. Letters 6.10, 18.5, and 21.2 refer to monastic communities in Nyssa itself.

111. GNO X.1.2, 15.9–10 (= PG 46.909 AB). Cf. *VSM* 14, 4–6.

112. On this shift in Gregory's theology see Anthony Meredith, *The Cappadocians* (New York: St. Vladimir's Seminary Press, 1995), pp. 59–62.

113. *Life of Moses* II, 319, p. 137 (= GNO X.1.2, 144.8–14).

114. On the treatment of the life of Moses in Jewish, Christian, and Islamic traditions see the collection of essays in *Moïse l'homme de l'alliance,* ed. H. Cazelles et al., Cahiers Sioniens (Paris: Desclée, 1955). Jean Daniélou's essay, "Moïse exemple et figure chez Grégoire de Nysse," pp. 267–282, focuses on Gregory's *De vita Moysis* and demonstrates his dependence on Philo.

115. Gregory discussed both baptism and the Eucharist in his *Great Catechism,* chapters 33–40. However, he said very little about the function of the priest with respect to the sacraments.

116. For Severus's comment see E. W. Brooks, ed. and trans., *The Sixth Book of the Select Letters of Severus of Antioch* 2 (London: Williams and Norgate, 1904), p. 393.

5. Gregory of Nazianzus

1. This has been emphasized by Neil McLynn, "A Self-Made Holy Man: The Case of Gregory Nazianzen," *JECS* 6/3 (1998): 463–483, and Susanna Elm, "A Programmatic Life: Gregory of Nazianzus' *Orations* 42 and 43 and the Constantinopolitan Elites," *Arethusa* 33 (2000): 411–427, especially pp. 414–415.

2. *De rebus suis,* lines 455–457, in Denis Molaise Meehan, trans., *Saint Greg-*

ory of Nazianzus: Three Poems (Washington, D.C.: Catholic University of America Press, 1986); cf. lines 262–267. Meehan, p. 20, dates this poem tentatively c. 371. For the Greek text see PG 37, 969–1017.

3. *De vita sua* 231–232, in *Gregor von Nazianz: De vita sua: Einleitung, Text, Übersetzung, Kommentar,* ed. Christoph Jungck (Heidelberg: Carl Winter Universitätsverlag, 1974); trans. Meehan, p. 83. The Greek text is also in PG 37, 1029–1166. For Gregory's description of these years in Athens see also Oration 43.14–24.

4. Oration 43.24, line 4. Cf. Letter 1.1. On the Cappadocians' use of the term *philosophy* to denote monastic life see A.-M. Malingrey, *"Philosophia": Étude d'un groupe de mots dans la littérature grecque, des Présocratiques au IVe siècle après J.-C.* (Paris: C. Klincksieck, 1961), pp. 237–260, and 220–22, nn. 19–22. For the scope of their usage of this term see also Jaroslav Pelikan, *Christianity and Culture: The Metamorphosis of Natural Theology in the Christian Encounter with Hellenism* (New Haven: Yale University Press, 1993), pp. 177–183. At this early stage of their careers (in the mid-350s) they certainly did not have in mind anything like the organized monastic communities that would eventually spread throughout Asia Minor.

5. Oration 43.25. Cf. *De rebus suis,* Meehan, lines 261–267. On his parents, see Letter 1.2, and *De rebus suis* 267–272. However, see McLynn, "A Self-Made Holy Man," pp. 467–468 and nn. 18–19, regarding Gregory's portrayal of the influence of Basil and his father.

6. Paul Gallay, *La vie de Grégoire de Nazianze* (Lyons: Vitte, 1943), p. 70, places his stay in Annesi around 360–361. More likely this retreat with Basil took place in 358–359 for reasons discussed by Philip Rousseau, *Basil of Caesarea* (Berkeley: University of California Press, 1994), pp. 65–68.

7. See Letters 4 and 5 in Paul Gallay, ed., *Saint Grégoire de Nazianze: Lettres,* vol. 1 (Paris: Belles lettres, 1964), which offer a satirical response to Basil's glowing description of his monastic retreat in Letter 14. For divergent interpretations of their expectations of monastic life see Stanislas Giet, *Sasimes: Une méprise de Saint Basile* (Paris: Gabalda, 1941), pp. 51–54, and Gallay, *Grégoire de Nazianze,* pp. 71–72.

8. Letter 6.3. Note that the two friends were not alone or completely isolated in their retreat, as has often been assumed. See Susanna Elm, *"Virgins of God": The Making of Asceticism in Late Antiquity* (Oxford: Clarendon, 1994), pp. 63–66, and Rousseau, *Basil of Caesarea,* pp. 68–70.

9. *De vita sua,* Meehan, lines 284–332. See also Oration 2.6, 7 in Jean Bernardi, ed., *Grégoire de Nazianze: Discours 1–3,* SC 247 (Paris: Éditions du cerf, 1978), pp. 94–98, and *De rebus suis,* Meehan, lines 261–306.

10. *De vita sua,* Meehan, lines 352–352, 354–355. See Gregory's description of Basil in Oration 43.62 for a different perspective.

11. *De vita sua,* Meehan, lines 357–363, and Oration 2.112. On the importance of this period of retreat in the formation of Gregory's ideas on orthodox leadership see Susanna Elm, "The Diagnostic Gaze: Gregory of Nazianzus' Theory of Orthodox Priesthood in his Orations 6 *De Pace* and 2 *Apologia de fuga sua,*" in *Orthodoxy, Christianity, History,* ed. Susanna Elm, Éric Rebillard, and Antonella Romano (Rome: École française de Rome, 2000), pp. 83–100, here 91.

12. See Hermann Dörries, "Erneuerung des kirchlichen Amts im vierten Jahrhundert: Die Schrift De sacerdotio des Johannes Chrysostomus und ihre Vorlage, die Oratio de fuga sua des Gregor von Nazianz," in Bernd Moeller and Gerhard Ruhbach, eds., *Bleibendes im Wandel der Kirchengeschichte* (Tübingen: Mohr, 1973), pp. 1–46.

13. On the Council of Rimini-Constantinople and its aftermath see H. C. Brennecke, *Studien zur Geschichte der Homöer: Der Osten bis zum Ende der homöischen Reichskirche,* Beiträge zur historischen Theologie 73 (Tübingen: Mohr, 1988), pp. 23–86.

14. Leaders of the dissident group, apparently monastics, received ordination by "foreign hands." Oration 6.11, lines 1 and 12. Gregory would later excuse his father for his "simplicity" and would reconcile the schismatic ascetics of Nazianzus with Gregory the Elder. See Neil McLynn, "Gregory the Peacemaker: A Study of Oration Six," *Kyoyo-ronso* 101 (1996): 183–216.

15. On Gregory the Elder's signing of the *homoian* creed as background to Nazianzen's Orations 2 and 6 see Elm, "The Diagnostic Gaze," pp. 88–90.

16. See especially Oration 4.31, lines 9–12, in Jean Bernardi, ed., *Grégoire de Nazianze: Discours 4–5,* SC 309 (Paris: Éditions du cerf, 1983). See also Oration 4.14, 32, and 49, and Oration 5.34.

17. Oration 2.87, line 1. Gregory alludes to Julian in this section. See Bernardi, *Discours 1–3,* p. 203 n. 1. Cf. Oration 2.85, where Gregory speaks of the mutual war between Christians. See also Bernardi, "Introduction," *Discours 4–5,* p. 63.

18. Oration 2.8, lines 3–7, and 2.111.

19. For lack of preparation see Oration 2.8, lines 3–7, and 2.47, lines 10–15. Regarding motives, see especially 2.8, lines 8–10, 2.41, and 2.46–49. On character and presumptuousness, see 2.46–47, 2.71, 2.95–99.

20. Oration 2.8, lines 11–12 and 17–22.

21. Oration 2.71, lines 9–12. See also 2.69, lines 8–11, where Gregory stresses the celestial conduct that should mark the priest's life.

22. Oration 2.16–22 and 28–34. Cf. Basil, RF 43: PG 31, 1029A.

23. Oration 2.26, line 1.

24. Oration 2.49.

25. Oration 2.72; and 2.91, lines 10–19.

26. Oration 2.92. Cf. Orations 20.2, 32.16–17, and 28.2–3, where the theologian rather than the priest is in view. For other uses of Moses as a model leader see Orations 7.2, 11.2, 18.14, 21.3, 43.72.

27. Oration 2.92, line 9.

28. See Oration 2.97–99.

29. Oration 2.114. On refusal of church office as a motif for late antique bishops see Rita Lizzi, *Il potere epsicopale nell'oriente romano: Rappresentazione ideologica e realità politica (IV–V sec. d.C.)* (Rome: Edizioni dell'Ateneo, 1987), pp. 33–55, for references to its classical political roots, pp. 36–37, and especially J. Béranger, "Le réfus du pouvoir: Recherches sur l'aspect idéologique du principat," in *Principatus: Études de notions et d'histoire politiques dans l'Antiquité gréco-romaine,* ed. F. Paschoud and P. Ducrey (Geneva, 1973), pp. 165–190.

30. Letter 8.

31. Letter 19. For Nazianzen's interpretation of the disagreement and its eventual resolution see Oration 43.28–33; 43.28, lines 8–11, for reference to the Nazarites.

32. In Letter 40 Gregory expresses anger that his friend is seeking higher ecclesiastical office.

33. Letter 41.4 and 8. This letter is written by Gregory in the name of his father, Gregory the Elder.

34. Letter 47.2.

35. Indeed *praxis* is sometimes described by Gregory as a prerequisite for *theoria*. See Orations 20.12, line 7, and 40.37, PG 35, 1080, and PG 36, 412C, respectively. These passages are cited and the theme discussed in T. Špidlik, "La *theoria* et la *praxis* chez Grégoire de Nazianze," *SP* 14 (= TU 117) (Berlin: Akademie-Verlag, 1976), pp. 358–364. On Gregory's notion of a "middle way," see also *De vita sua* 284–332, cited above at n. 9.

36. Garth Fowden, "The Pagan Holy Man in Late Antique Society," *Journal of Hellenic Studies* 102 (1982): 50–51, gives several examples.

37. See Peter Brown, "The Philosopher and Society in Late Antiquity," Protocol Series of the Colloquies 34 (Berkeley: Center for Hermeneutical Studies, 1980), pp. 1–17. Brown's essay is followed by several responses from which I have borrowed the phrase "contemplative worldliness."

38. See Brian Daley, "Building a New City: The Cappadocian Fathers and the Rhetoric of Philanthropy," *JECS* (1999): especially 437–440. For Nazianzen's particular emphasis on *ptōchotrophia* see Oration 14, discussed by Daley, pp. 455–458. See also Jean Bernardi, *La prédication des pères cappadociens: Le prédicateur et son auditoire* (Paris: Presses universitaires de France, 1968), pp. 400–402. For Gregory's commendation of Basil's efforts on behalf of the masses see Oration 43.34–36 and 64.

39. Letter 49.1–2; but see *De vita sua,* Meehan, lines 440–449, for a different perspective.

40. For example, Letter 58.1. Following Basil's death, Nazianzen dedicated several epitaphs to his friend. See *Epitaphia* 119.2, 4, 5, 7, 9, 10, in Hermann Beckby, ed., *Anthologia Graeca,* Books VII–VIII (Munich, 1957), pp. 448–453; PG 38, 72A–73B.

41. Marie-Ange Calvet-Sebasti, "Introduction," in *Discours 6–12,* SC 405 (Paris: Éditions du cerf, 1995), pp. 99–103. On the circumstances and dating of these four Orations see pp. 84–99.

42. Oration 10.1, lines 9–15.

43. For continued complaints about friendship see especially Orations 9.5, 10.2, 11.3. For Gregory's claims to have been reconciled to his charge and to Basil personally see Orations 9.3 and 10.3. On the relationship between Basil and Gregory see Carolinne White, *Christian Friendship in the Fourth Century* (Cambridge: Cambridge University Press, 1992), pp. 61–84.

44. See Orations 9.2; 9.5, lines 13–25; 11.2; 12.2.

45. See Jean Bernardi, *Saint Grégoire de Nazianze* (Paris: Éditions du cerf, 1995), pp. 150–151.

46. *De vita sua,* Meehan, lines 553–556.

47. For Gregory's account see *De se ipso et de episcopis,* 71–135, in *Über die Bishöfe (Carmen 2.1.12): Einleitung, Text, Übersetzung, Kommentar,* ed. Beno Meier (Paderborn: Schöningh, 1989); also PG 37, 1166–1227; English trans. in Meehan, *Three Poems.* See also *De vita sua,* Meehan, 563–606, and Oration 42.2–5. Writing in the mid-fifth century, Socrates, HE 5.3–6, gives a similar survey of the chaos in Constantinople around the time of Theodosius I's ascension.

48. McLynn, "A Self-Made Holy Man," pp. 474–477. For a more extensive treatment of this phase of his career see Gallay, *Grégoire de Nazianze,* pp. 132–211, and Bernardi, *Saint Grégoire,* pp. 175–192.

49. In *De vita sua,* Meehan, lines 609–664, Gregory recounts his opposition to Apollinarianism and Arianism in Constantinople; in lines 1146–1186 he lists various other heresies he confronted there. According to lines 665–735, Gregory's position was contested because he had been consecrated bishop of Sasima and the Council of Nicaea had prohibited episcopal transfers.

50. According to Gallay, *Grégoire de Nazianze,* p. 137, 1,297 of the 1,949 verses of *De vita sua* deal with events in Constantinople.

51. Justin Mossay, ed. and trans., *Grégoire de Nazianze: Discours 20–23,* SC 270 (Paris: Éditions du cerf, 1980). According to Mossay, p. 50, Oration 20 was probably delivered between February and late summer 380, but it is not clear whether it was given before or after Gregory's other theological ora-

tions (27–31). Mossay, p. 93, surmises that Oration 21, "In Honor of Athanasius," was composed in Constantinople for a feast of Athanasius in 379, 380, or 381.

52. Oration 20.1; Oration 21.9. See also Oration 42.18, and for similar complaints about priests, Oration 2.8, 46–47, 71, 95–99.

53. Oration 20.2. Cf. Oration 2.92, and Bernardi, *Saint Grégoire*, p. 209 n. 5. Oration 32.16, one of the earliest orations from Constantinople, contains a parallel appeal to Moses as a leader.

54. Oration 28.3, line 18, in Paul Gallay, ed. and trans., *Grégoire de Nazianze: Discours 27–31 (Discours Théologiques)*, SC 250 (Paris: Éditions du cerf, 1978). For an illuminating study of these theological orations see Frederick Norris, *Faith Gives Fullness to Reasoning: A Commentary on Gregory Nazianzen's "Theological Orations,"* Supplements to *Vigiliae Christianae* 13 (Leiden: Brill, 1991).

55. Oration 21.9.

56. See Oration 21.3–4 for the whole comparison. Mossay, *Discours 20–23*, p. 118 n. 1, notes that this type of *synkrisis* is typical of the second sophistic. Gregory uses it again in his panegyric of Basil. Compare Oration 43.70–76.

57. Oration 21.19, line 21, to 21.20, line 5.

58. Oration 21.37, line 2. Compare Gregory of Nyssa, Encomium, GNO X.1.2, 120.7–21. On Nazianzen's ideal of the bishop in Oration 21 see also Jean-Robert Pouchet, "Athanase d'Alexandrie, modèle de l'évêque, selon Grégoire de Nazianze, Discours 21," in *Vescovi et pastori pastori in epoca teodosiana* (Rome: Institution Patristicum "Augustinianum," 1997), vol. 2, pp. 347–357.

59. I.e., Sasima. See Oration 36.6, lines 17–28, in *Grégoire de Nazianze: Discours 32–37*, ed. Claudio Moreschini and trans. Paul Gallay, SC 318 (Paris: Éditions du cerf, 1984), pp. 254–256. On the development of this doctrine in patristic writings and canon law see Jean Gaudemet, *L'Église dans l'Empire romain (IVe–V Siècles)* (Paris: Sirey, 1958), pp. 357–358.

60. For Gregory's lengthy, highly derogatory description of Maximus and his consecration see *De vita sua*, Meehan, lines 736–1043.

61. See Gilbert Dagron, "Les moines et la ville: Le monachisme à Constantinople jusqu'au Concile de Chalcédoine (451)," *Travaux et Mémoires* 4 (1970): 261–272; on Gregory in particular, p. 262.

62. *De vita sua*, Meehan, lines 1745–1870.

63. See Jean Bernardi, "La composition et la publication du discours 42 de Grégoire de Nazianze," Studia Ephemeridis "Augustinianum" 27, *Mémorial Dom Jean Gribomont (1920–1986)* (Rome: Institutum Patristicum "Augustinianum," 1988), pp. 131–143. For the text of Oration 42 along with Oration 43 see Jean Bernardi, ed. and trans., *Grégoire de*

Nazianze, Discours 42–43, SC 384 (Paris: Éditions du cerf, 1992); also PG 36, 457–492; English trans. by Charles Gordon Browne and James Edward Swallow, NPNF, 2nd ser., vol. 7, pp. 385–395.

64. Two recent analyses of Oration 42 also connect its content and themes with these other three pieces from the same period: Elm, "A Programmatic Life," pp. 411–427, and Neil McLynn, "The Voice of Conscience: Gregory Nazianzen in Retirement," in *Vescovi e pastori* 2, pp. 299–308.

65. Oration 42.14; Oration 42.21, line 2. Bernardi, *Discours 42–43,* p. 94 n. 2, notes that Gregory uses a parallel phrase, *ho polemos . . . tōn episkopōn,* "the war of the bishops," to describe similar circumstances in Oration 43.58, line 3.

66. Oration 42.24, lines 15–16, 24–25; Browne and Swallow, pp. 393–394.

67. Oration 42.25, lines 13–14; Browne and Swallow, p. 394.

68. Bernardi, *La prédication,* p. 238. Bernardi suggests that the speech was delivered at the anniversary celebration of Basil's death, January 1, 382, though of course the date of Basil's death remains uncertain. Rousseau, *Basil of Caesarea,* p. 3 n. 2, suggests August or September 381 for its delivery. For the text and French trans. see SC 384; PG 36, 493–605; English trans. Browne and Swallow, pp. 395–422.

69. For parallels see Paul Jonathan Fedwick, *The Church and the Charisma of Leadership in Basil of Caesarea* (Toronto: PIMS, 1979), p. 55. See also the sensitive treatment of Frederick W. Norris, "Your Honor, My Reputation: St. Gregory of Nazianzus's Funeral Oration on St. Basil the Great," in *Greek Biography and Panegyric in Late Antiquity,* ed. Tomas Hägg and Philip Rousseau (Berkeley: University of California Press, 2000), pp. 140–159.

70. Oration 43.3–10. For a rhetorical analysis of Oration 43 see George A. Kennedy, *Greek Rhetoric under Christian Emperors* (Princeton: Princeton University Press, 1983), pp. 228–234. Kennedy categorizes the speech as an *epitaphios,* traditionally delivered some time after the death of the person being eulogized. On the difficulty of defining its precise genre see also Norris, "Your Honor, My Reputation," p. 143.

71. Oration 43.11, lines 2–7.

72. Oration 43.20, lines 12–15; Browne and Swallow, p. 402; on Basil's zeal for "philosophy," see 43.19, line 2.

73. Oration 43.26. Cf. Orations 2.8, 21.9, 42.18.

74. Oration 43.25, lines 25–28, and 43.27, lines 7–10, respectively; Browne and Swallow, pp. 404–405. See also Oration 32.11–12 on the importance of proper order in the church.

75. Oration 43.29, lines 14–16. His retreat was provoked by a disagreement with his episcopal predecessor, Bishop Eusebius. See 43.33 on his governance of the church from a lower position.

76. Oration 43.36.

77. Oration 43.37; Oration 43.38, lines 2–6. For the same idea in Nyssan's writings, namely that ordination need not compromise the philosophical (i.e., monastic) life, see *VSM* 14, 4–6, and his account of the ordination of Gregory Thaumaturgus, GNO X.1.2, 15.16f. (= PG 46, 909AB).

78. Oration 43.40, lines 10–11; Browne and Swallow, p. 409.

79. Oration 43.56, lines 21–22; 43.57, line 26; 43.58, especially lines 11–12; Browne and Swallow, pp. 413–414. On healing see Oration 43.54–55. The force of Basil's personal presence caused the disease of the emperor's son to abate, but the ruler's failure to trust Basil and his simultaneous consultation with the heterodox caused the boy to die. The prefect, however, was healed of his affliction through Basil's powerful mediation.

80. Oration 43.58, 59. For helpful comment on Gregory's deft handling of this and other difficult episodes see Norris, "Your Honor, My Reputation," especially pp. 152–154.

81. See especially Oration 43.66, 67.

82. Oration 43.60, line 26; 43.61, lines 13–16; Browne and Swallow, 415.

83. Oration 43.63.

84. *Hina mēte to philosophon akoinōnēton ē mēte to praktikon aphilosophon,* Oration 43.62, lines 28–39; Browne and Swallow, p. 416. Compare Gregory's similar praise of Athanasius in Oration 21.19–20.

85. See also Oration 43.23, lines 19–20. Elm, *"Virgins of God,"* pp. 209–210, notes that Gregory sometimes uses the term *migades* to describe such a mixture of contemplative and practical life as might characterize the lives of ascetic bishops. More often in this oration, however, Gregory reserves the terms *migas* or *migados bios* for communal as opposed to eremitic monasticism.

86. Oration 43.71, lines 22–23; Oration 43.75.

87. Oration 43.77; Oration 43.78, lines 9–10. Who were these *gnēsiōtatoi therapeutoi* whom Basil ordained? Bernardi, *Discours 42–43,* p. 298 n. 1, suspects they were monks who had been assisting Basil in his ecclesiastical duties. If so, this provides one of many examples of Basil's selection of monks for positions of ecclesiastical authority.

88. These are the goals suggested by Kennedy, *Greek Rhetoric,* p. 230.

89. See C. Moreschini, "Il platonismo cristiano di Gregorio Nazianzeno" and "Luce e purificazione nella dottrina di Gregorio Nazianzeno," *Augustinianum* (1973): 535–549; also Anthony Meredith, "Gregory of Nazianzus and Gregory of Nyssa on Basil," *SP* 32 (1997): 168–169, who argues for a stronger Platonic bent in Nazianzen. Both Moreschini and Anthony Meredith, *The Cappadocians* (New York: St. Vladimir's Seminary Press, 1995), pp. 42–49, demonstrate the predominance of light imagery in Nazianzen's references to God or the Trinity and therefore in his notions of

spiritual progress as well. See, for example, Oration 2.5. In Oration 43.65 Gregory speaks of Basil's purification by the Spirit and subsequent illumination so that "with God he examined the things of God."

90. See Oration 43.11 for Gregory's critique of the anti-intellectualism of many Christians.

91. Oration 43.60–66.

92. *De ipso et de episcopis,* Meehan, lines 181–182. This affirmation immediately follows a lengthy complaint about lower-class infiltration of the episcopate (lines 154–175). On this aspect of Gregory's episcopal ideals see Andrew Louth, "St. Gregory of Nazianzen on Bishops and the Episcopate," *Vescovi i pastori* 2, pp. 282–284.

93. *De ipso et de episcopis,* Meehan, line 775. For Gregory's harshest invectives against the character and preparation of bishops see lines 136–183 and 330–453. The account of Gregory's resignation, lines 136–175, makes it clear that his own experience with bishops in Constantinople lies behind many of his bitter reproaches. For a fuller analysis of this poem and the roughly contemporaneous *De vita sua,* see McLynn, "Voice of Conscience."

94. See *De se ipso et de episcopis,* Meehan, lines 503–574, for Gregory's remarks on this issue. For further discussion of ordination in Nazianzen's writings see André de Halleux, "Grégoire de Nazianze témoin du caractère sacerdotal'?" in *Memorial Jean Gribomont,* pp. 331–347.

95. *De se ipso et de episcopis,* Meehan, lines 576–609.

96. See *De vita sua,* Meehan, lines 1219–1224; see also lines 1433–1434.

97. See Letters 87.3, 95, 125, 130, 133.3–4, 136.3–4, 185.

98. Gregory's constant vacillation between ascetic withdrawal and active service to church and community has been analyzed by Raymond Van Dam, "Self-Representation in the Will of Gregory of Nazianzus," *JTS* n.s. 46 (1995): 118–148; here 137–142. See also Rosemary Radford Ruether, *Gregory of Nazianzus: Rhetor and Philosopher* (Oxford: Clarendon, 1969), pp. 32–33.

99. See the brief discussion of Jean Bernardi, "Saint Grégoire de Nazianze, observateur du milieu ecclésiastique et théoricien de la fonction sacerdotale," in A. Mandouze and J. Fouilheron, eds., *Migne et le renouveau des études patristiques,* Théologie historique 66 (Paris: Beauchesne, 1985), p. 356. On Gregory's neglect of the sacraments in his treatment of the priesthood see Rowan Greer, "Who Seeks for a Spring in the Mud? Reflections on the Ordained Ministry in the Fourth Century," in Richard John Neuhaus, ed., *Theological Education and Moral Formation* (Grand Rapids, Mich.: Eerdmans, 1992), pp. 22–55; here especially p. 40 n. 49.

100. For Gregory's estimation of Eulalios see Letters 182 and 183, and Gallay, *Grégoire de Nazianze,* pp. 227–228.

101. Jan Sajdak, "Die Scholiasten der Reden des Gregor von Nazianz," *BZ* 30 (1929): 269, and Michael Wittig, "Introduction," *Gregor von Nazianz: Briefe* (Stuttgart: Anton Hiersemann, 1981), p. 68. See also George T. Dennis, "Gregory of Nazianzus and the Byzantine Letter," in Thomas Halton and Joseph P. Williman, eds., *Diakonia: Studies in Honor of Robert T. Meyer* (Washington, D.C.: Catholic University of America Press, 1986), pp. 3–13.

102. Jacques Noret, "Grégoire de Nazianze, l'auteur le plus cité, après la Bible, dans la littérature ecclésiastique byzantine," in Justin Mossay, ed., *II. Symposium Nazianzenum* 2 (Paderborn: Schöningh, 1983), p. 265 n. 38, suggests that the possibility that sections of Nazianzen's orations were memorized would explain some of the many tacit borrowings from them. See also Francesco Trisoglio, "Mentalità ed atteggiamento degli scoliasti di fronte agli scritti di S. Gregorio di Nazianzo," ibid., p. 188 n. 5, and Kennedy, *Greek Rhetoric*, p. 238. On the fame and veneration of Nazianzen in the fifth and sixth centuries see Friedhelm Lefherz, *Studien zu Gregor von Nazianz: Mythologie, Überlieferung, Scholiasten* (Bonn: Rheinische Friedrich-Wilhelms-Universität, 1958), pp. 111–147.

103. Jean Bernardi, "Introduction," *Discours 1–3*, p. 39.

104. For his influence on Chrysostom see Chapter 6. Regarding Jerome, see Philip Rousseau, *Ascetics, Authority and the Church in the Age of Jerome and Cassian* (Oxford: Oxford University Press, 1978), p. 107. On Gregory the Great see R. A. Markus, *The World of Gregory the Great* (Cambridge: Cambridge University Press, 1997), pp. 17–33, and brief comments of Andrew Louth, "St. Gregory of Nazianzen on Bishops," *Vescovi e pastori* 2, pp. 284–285.

105. Kennedy, *Greek Rhetoric*, 237.

106. Oration 43.77. E. W. Brooks, ed., *The Sixth Book of the Select Letters of Severus of Antioch*, 2 (London: Williams and Norgate, 1904), p. 393. Though it is not completely clear whether this passage refers to Nyssan's or Nazianzen's funeral oration, considering the latter's particular influence on Severus and in the Syrian milieu, it seems likely that Nazianzen's speech is in view. Alongside the Bible no other texts interested the ancient schools of Syrian philology more than Gregory's orations. See André de Halleux, "La version syriaque des *Discours* de Grégoire de Nazianze," in Mossay, *II. Symposium Nazianzenum*, especially p. 75.

107. On written borrowings see Noret, "Grégoire, l'auteur le plus cité," pp. 262–264. On iconography see D. Stiernon, "Basilio il Grande: Vita, opere, culto, reliquie, iconografia," *Bibliotheca sanctorum* II, p. 937f., and Wilma Fitzgerald, "Notes on the Iconography of Saint Basil the Great," in Paul Jonathan Fedwick, ed., *Basil of Caesarea: Christian, Humanist, Ascetic, A Sixteen-hundredth Anniversary Symposium* (Toronto: Pontifical Institute of Mediaeval Studies, 1981), 2, pp. 533–564. K. Weitzmann, *Greek Mythol-*

ogy in Byzantine Art (Princeton: Princeton University Press, 1951), pp. 6–92, devotes considerable space to representations of Gregory's texts, which were among the most illustrated of the Byzantine era.

108. Susanna Elm has stressed the Greco-Roman rhetoric of political office as the background to Gregory's ideals of ecclesiastical leadership. See Elm, "Orthodoxy and the True Philosophical Life: Julian and Gregory of Nazianzus," *SP* 37 (2001): 69–85, especially pp. 75–76.

6. John Chrysostom

1. Palladius, *Dialogus de vita Iohannis Chrysostomi* 5.1–15, in Anne-Marie Malingrey and Philippe Leclercq, eds., *Palladios: Dialogue sur la vie de Jean Chrysostome,* SC 341 (Paris: Éditions du cerf, 1988).

2. Socrates, *HE* 6.3.1–8, Günther Christian Hansen and Manja Sirinian, *Sokrates Kirchengeschichte,* GCS n.F. 1(Berlin: Akademie Verlag, 1995), 313–314; trans. A. C. Zenos, *Church History from A.D. 305–439,* NPNF 2nd ser., 2 (Grand Rapids, Mich.: Erdmans, 1979), pp. 138–139. In a parallel passage Sozomen, *HE* 8.2, also omits mention of Meletius but includes Diodore, the *asketerion,* and Chrysostom's colleagues, Maximus and Theodore. The identity of the Evagrius in Socrates' account is uncertain. The Basil mentioned at the end is mistakenly identified as Basil of Caesarea by both Socrates and Sozomen. Among other things, the dating of this period (c. 368–372) makes such an association impossible, since the Cappadocian was serving as priest and then bishop in Caesarea at this time. This other Basil, Chrysostom's close friend, is very likely the future bishop of Raphanea in Syria and the addressee and rather reticent interlocutor of *De sacerdotio.*

3. *De sacerdotio* 1.2 in Anne-Marie Malingrey, ed. and trans., *Jean Chrysostome: Sur le sacerdoce,* SC 272 (Paris: Éditions du cerf, 1980).

4. David Hunter suggests that Diodore's school "may have provided the equivalent of seminary training" for aspiring clerics and that his relationship with Chrysostom may have been "more academic." See the introduction in David Hunter, *A Comparison between a King and a Monk / Against the Opponents of the Monastic Life: Two Treatises by John Chrysostom* (Lewiston, N.Y.: Edwin Mellen, 1988), p. 9.

5. Robert L. Wilken, *John Chrysostom and the Jews: Rhetoric and Reality in the Late Fourth Century* (Berkeley: University of California Press, 1983), pp. 6–7, suggests that John's change in career plans might well be understood in this light by contemporaries.

6. J. N. D. Kelly, *Golden Mouth: The Story of John Chrysostom—Ascetic, Preacher, Bishop* (Ithaca: Cornell University Press, 1995), pp. 18–20.

7. *Ad Theodorum lapsum* 1.4–5 in Jean Dumortier, ed., *Jean Chrysostome: A*

Théodore, SC 117 (Paris: Éditions du cerf, 1966). John warns Theodore that for him to marry would be adultery, since he has been attached to a "heavenly bridegroom." See 3.23–33.

8. *Ad Thedorum lapsum* 1.48–55.

9. The text and English translation of the fragmentary letter appear as Letter 55 in *The Works of the Emperor Julian,* 3, trans. Wilmer Cave Wright, LCL (London, 1923), pp. 186–191. Julian attributes Diodore's ill health to the punishment of the gods rather than a sign of his ascetic or philosophic life. The passage is discussed by A. J. Festugière, *Antioche païenne et chrétienne: Libanius, Chrysostome et les moines de Syrie* (Paris: Éditions de Boccard, 1959), pp. 182–183.

10. *Laus Diodori episcopi,* PG 52.761–766. John twice refers to Diodore in this speech as his "father" as well as his "teacher."

11. Ibid., PG 52.761; 52.763–4.

12. See Basil, Letters 135 and 160; also his description of Diodore in Letter 244.3. Concerning their relationship and mutual influence see Robert Pouchet, "Les rapports de Basile avec Diodore," *Bullétin de littérature ecclésiastique* 87 (1986): 243–272.

13. Palladius, *Dial.* 5.16–21.

14. See, for example, *De compunctione* 1.6, PG 47.403, where he speaks of leaving the city for "the huts of the monks" and performing tasks allotted by someone in a supervisory role. See Kelly, *Golden Mouth,* pp. 28–35, for a reasonable approximation of John's routine during this period.

15. *Comparatio regis et monachi,* PG 47.387–392; and *Adversus oppugnatores vitae monasticae,* PG 47.319–386. Both treatises are available in English in Hunter, *Two Treatises,* pp. 69–76 and 77–176, respectively.

16. For example, Hunter, *Two Treatises,* pp. 37–39. See Kelly, *Golden Mouth,* p. 21, for a different argument.

17. On the significant pagan population see J. H. W. G. Liebeschuetz, *Antioch: City and Imperial Administration in the Later Roman Empire* (Oxford: Clarendon, 1972). For the substantial Jewish population see Wilken, *Chrysostom and the Jews,* pp. 34–65.

18. *Adv. oppug.* 2.5: Hunter, p. 107. The ascetic ideal as the standard for true leadership is a major theme of the brief *Comparatio.* See especially *Comparatio* 2: Hunter, pp. 70–72.

19. See *Comparatio* 3, and *Adv. oppug.* 3.11, 19. On this dominant motif for monastic life in Syrian sources see Peter Brown, *The Body and Society: Men, Women, and Sexual Renunciation in Early Christianity* (New York: Columbia University Press, 1988), pp. 323–338.

20. See especially *Adv. oppug.* 2.4–5, where Chrysostom treats an assortment of classic Hellenic values and compares monks favorably with specific pagan

philosophers. Hunter, *Two Treatises,* p. 31, notes that Chrysostom's positive evaluation of pagan philosophers in this section of the work is unique
in his writings and is related to his particular apologetic purpose here.

21. *Adv. oppug.* 3.11: Hunter, p. 150.
22. Much of *Adv. oppug.,* Book 3, "To the Christian Parent," presents argu-
    ments supporting this practice.
23. *Adv. oppug.* 3.14: Hunter, pp. 156–157.
24. *Adv. oppug.* 3.18: Hunter, p. 168. See also 2.7–8.
25. *Adv. oppug.* 1.8.
26. On Chrysostom's understanding of the role of monks in these areas see M.
    Jean-Marie Leroux, "Monachisme et communauté chrétienne d'après saint
    Jean Chrysostome," in *Théologie de la vie monastique: Études sur la tradition
    patristique,* Théologie 49 (Paris: Aubier, 1961), pp. 143–190.
27. For suggestions about dating see Festugière, *Antioche païenne et chrétienne,*
    pp. 14–15 n. 2, and Kelly, *Golden Mouth,* pp. 42–43. For the text of *De
    compunctione* see PG 47.393–432.
28. *De compunctione* 1.6, PG 47.403. Presumably the rest mentioned here is in-
    tended for contemplation.
29. *De compunctione* 2.2, PG 47.412–413.
30. *De compunctione* 2.3, PG 47.414.
31. *De incomprehensibili Dei natura* 6.3, PG 48.752; passage translated in Blake
    Leyerle, *Theatrical Shows and Ascetic Lives: John Chyrsostom's Attack on
    Spiritual Marriage* (Berkeley: University of California Press, 2001), p. 197.
    See Leyerle, pp. 196–202, for a fuller discussion of Chrysostom's praise for
    and criticisms of ascetics, especially in his homilies.
32. On the dating and alleged circumstances see the introduction in Anne-Ma-
    rie Malingrey, ed. and trans., *Jean Chrysostome: Sur le sacerdoce,* SC 272
    (Paris: Éditions du cerf, 1980), especially pp. 10–13, 19–22.
33. *De sacerdotio* 1.3.
34. See Malingrey, ed., *Sur le sacerdoce,* pp. 19–21; also Kelly, *Golden Mouth,*
    pp. 27–28, who presents and responds to the major counterarguments.
35. See A.-M. Malingrey, "Le clergé d'Antioche vu par S. Jean Chrysostome," in
    *Mélanges offerts à Jean Dauvillier, professeur à l'Université des sciences
    sociales de Toulouse,* (Toulouse: Centre d'histoire juridique méridionale,
    1979), pp. 507–515.
36. Like Nazianzen in Oration 2, Chrysostom wrote *De sacerdotio* ostensibly as
    an apology for his flight. It was written long after the event, however, and
    it is much less autobiographical than Gregory's oration. For a direct com-
    parison of the treatises see Hermann Dörries, "Erneuerung des kirchlichen
    Amts im vierten Jahrhundert: Die Schrift De sacerdotio des Johannes
    Chrysostomus und ihre Vorlage, die Oratio de fuga sua des Gregor von

Nazianz," in Bernd Moeller and Gerhard Ruhbach, eds., *Bleibendes im Wandel der Kirchengeschichte* (Tübingen: Mohr, 1973). For a comparison with both Ambrose's *De officiis* and Nazianzen's Oration 2 see Rowan Greer, "Who Seeks for a Spring in the Mud? Reflections on the Ordained Ministry in the Fourth Century," in Richard John Neuhaus, ed., *Theological Education and Moral Formation* (Grand Rapids, Mich.: Eerdmans, 1992), pp. 38–54.

37. *De sacerdotio* 3.10, lines 22–25.

38. *De sacerdotio* 3.11, lines 59–62 and 82–91; for the comparison with civil rulers, 3.11, lines 8–23 and 66–71.

39. *De sacerdotio* 3.9.

40. Homily 3 on Acts in *The Homilies of St. John Chrysostom on the Acts of the Apostles*, trans. J. Walker et al., NPNF, 1st ser., vol. 11 (Grand Rapids, Mich.: Eerdmans, 1980), p. 23. In the same homily he echoes Nazianzen's lamentation over the honors awarded bishops.

41. On John's use of *hierosunē* see Malingrey's comments in *Sur le sacerdoce*, pp. 72–73 n. 1, and 143 n. 1. See also Anne-Marie Malingrey, "Le ministère épiscopal dans l'oeuvre de Jean Chrysostome," in Charles Kannengiesser, ed., *Jean Chrysostome et Augustin*, Théologie historique 35 (Paris: Éditions Beauchesne, 1975), pp. 87–88. On p. 76 she cites the passage in John's *In epist. I ad Tim. 3, hom.* XI (PG 62, 553) where he suggests that the only real difference between the offices of priest and bishop is that the latter has the power to ordain.

42. *De sacerdotio* 3.1 and 2.4, respectively.

43. *De sacerdotio* 6.2, lines 4–5.

44. *De sacerdotio* 3.4, lines 1–8. For references to the clergy as the counterpart of the Old Testament priesthood in other patristic writers—specifically Ambrose, Paulinus, Jerome, and Nazianzen—see Greer, "Reflections on the Ordained Ministry," p. 39 n. 46.

45. *De sacerdotio* 3.4–6.

46. John describes many pastoral and administrative tasks in *De sacerotio* 3.12–14 while devoting almost all of Books 4 and 5 to the prophetic duties of the priest as a preacher and teacher of the Word of God.

47. *De sacerdotio* 2.1, lines 57–65.

48. *De sacerdotio* 3.10, lines 108–126, 195–200. These themes are developed more fully in 6.6–8.

49. *De sacerdotio* 4.8, line 47, to 4.9, line 11.

50. See especially *De sacerdotio* 6.2–6.6 on this theme. The argument bears close resemblance to that of the sermon *De renunciatione saeculi*, PG 31, 648BC, originating from the Cappadocian monastic milieu.

51. *De sacerdotio* 3.11, lines 24–38; 6.3–4; and 6.6–8.

52. *In Mattaeum homiliae* 72.4 (PG 58, 672); cited in Kelly, *Golden Mouth*, p. 85.

53. *In Matt. hom.* 68.4 and 69.4 (PG 58.645 and 654), and *De inani gloria* 78, in Anne-Marie Malingrey, *Jean Chyrsostome: Sur la vaine gloire et l'éducation des enfants,* SC 188 (Paris: Éditions du cerf, 1972), p. 180, lines 931–932. The purpose of these father-son visits was to help boys struggling to rein in their sexual passions. Unlike his recommendation in *Against the Opponents,* however, John expresses esteem for the monastic vocation while advising parents to raise their children on their own rather than send them to monasteries. *De inani gloria* 18–19.

54. *De sacerdotio* 3.11, lines 46–47.

55. *De sacerdotio* 2.4, lines 57–59.

56. See especially *De sacerdotio* 2.3–4, 4.6, and 6.4. That these traits derive from the ascetic rather than the clerical tradition has been emphasized in a paper by George Demacopoulos, "Spiritual Direction in the Early Byzantine Church: Ammonas, Athanasius and Chrysostom," Byzantine Studies Conference, November 2001.

57. *De sacerdotio* 3.5, lines 25–27; *De sacerdotio* 6.2. On the "angelic life" as a metaphor for monks see also Leroux, "Monachisme et communauté chrétienne," pp. 176–179.

58. *De sacerdotio* 6.8, lines 9–15; ibid., 6.4, lines 69–71.

59. *Sermo cum presbyter,* lines 159–199, especially lines 166–172, in Malingrey, ed., *Sur le sacerdoce,* pp. 367–419. Malingrey describes the sermon as "the necessary complement" to Chrysostom's dialogue on the priesthood. On Bishop Flavian see also Theodoret, *HE* 4.11 and 25, and 5.23.

60. *Sermo cum presbyter,* lines 220–222. Abraham is mentioned only in passing. The Moses *synkrisis* emphasizes the patriarch's rejection of worldly honors and pleasures.

61. *Sermo cum presbyter,* lines 235–248, 253–268.

62. See Ivo auf der Maur, *Mönchtum und Glaubensverkündigung in den Schriften des Hl. Johannes Chrysostomus,* Paradosis 14, (Freiburg, 1959), pp. 124–141, for John's use of monks in missions.

63. See Jean-Marie Leroux, "Jean Chrysostome et le monachisme," in Kannengiesser, *Jean Chrysostome et Augustin,* especially pp. 139–144, and Leroux, "Monachisme et communauté chrétienne," pp. 182–190.

64. Sozomen, *HE* 8.6; Socrates, *HE* 6.11. On John's consecration of monks for various church offices see Leroux, "Jean Chrysostome et le monachisme," pp. 141–142, and the more extensive treatment in auf der Maur, *Mönchtum und Glaubensverkündigung,* pp. 118–124.

65. On Palladius's life and association with John see the editors' introduction in Malingrey and Leclercq, *Palladios,* pp. 10–18, 25–33. See also Robert T.

Meyer, trans., *Palladius: Dialogue on the Life of St. John Chrysostom,* ACW 45 (New York: Newman Press, 1985), pp. 3–4.

66. Most notably by Gilbert Dagron, "Les moines et la ville: Le monachisme à Constantinople jusqu'au Concile de Chalcédoine (451)," *Travaux et Mémoires* 4 (1970): especially pp. 262–265.

67. On Issac as the leader of Constantinopolitan monasticism see the mid-fifth-century reflections of Callinicus, *Vita Hypatii* 1.6 and 11.1–4, in G. J. M. Bartelink, ed., *Callinicus: Vie d'Hypatios,* SC 177 (Paris: Éditions du cerf, 1971), pp. 74 and 110, respectively. For a very different perspective on this Isaac see Palladius, *Dial.* 6.

68. Dagron, "Les moines et la ville," p. 246.

69. Sozomen, *HE* 8.9.4–5: Joseph Bidez, ed., rev. Günther Christian Hansen, *Sozomenus Kirchengeschichte,* GCS n.F. 4 (Berlin: Akademie Verlag, 1995), p. 362; trans. Chester D. Hartranft, *The Ecclesiastical History of Sozomen,* NPNF 2nd ser. (Grand Rapids, Mich.: Eerdmans, 1989), p. 405. Sozomen attributes John's seeming disdain for monks and society in general to the rigors of his ascetic life, which had permanently injured his stomach and head.

70. See in particular Dagron, "Les moines et la ville," p. 258 n. 148.

71. *Homiliae de statuis ad populum Antiochenum* 17.5 (PG 49, 174). Leyerle, *Theatrical Shows and Ascetic Lives,* p. 199, mentions this episode in the context of Chrysostom's ambivalence about monks.

72. On Olympias and her involvement with Chrysostom see Palladius, *Dial.* 16 and 17, and "Vie d'Olympias" in Anne-Marie Malingrey, ed., *John Chrysostome: Lettres à Olympias,* 2nd ed., SC 13 bis (Paris: Éditions du cerf, 1968), pp. 393–449; English translation and notes in Elizabeth A. Clark, *Jerome Chrysostom, and Friends: Essays and Translations* (New York: Edwin Mellen Press, 1979), pp. 107–144.

73. Toward the beginning of the *Dialogue,* Palladius alludes to a calumnious letter about John; this may have been a literary invention to justify Palladius's writing the *Dialogue* so shortly after John's death. See Meyer's comments, *Dialogue,* pp. 4–5. On date and place of composition see Malingrey and Leclercq, *Palladios,* pp. 19–31.

74. *Dial.* 17.206–208: Meyer, p. 115.

75. *Dial.* 20.5–6: Meyer, p. 131.

76. For comparisons with Moses see *Dial.* 9.38, 18.225, 19.133. See the comments on Palladius in Claudia Rapp, "Comparison, Paradigm and the Case of Moses in Panegyric and Hagiography," in Mary Whitby, ed., *The Propaganda of Power: The Role of Panegyric in Late Antiquity* (Leiden: Brill, 1998), p. 291.

77. For what follows see *Dial.* 5.15–33.

78. *Dial.* 12 and 18. See *Dial.* 20 for his final days.

79. *Dial.* 19.16–27 and 19.118–153.
80. *Dial.* 6.16–17: Meyer, p. 41.
81. On John's support of the monastic party in the controversy with Theophilus see especially *Dial.* 7–8; on his exemplary life, see 18.47–57.
82. *Dial.* 8.226–231.
83. *Dial.* 11.120–156.
84. *Dial.* 10.72 and 87–88: Meyer, pp. 67–68. Palladius attributes no miracles to John himself, although this was characteristic of hagiography from this period onward.
85. *Dial.* 17.30–63. Compare GNaz, Oration 43.54, and Socrates, *HE* 6.19.
86. See *Dial.* 5.100–166 for Palladius's discussion of John's reforms, and 5.158–161 for the alleged results. Regarding the calumnies such reforms provoked, see especially *Dial.* 6.1–7.
87. *Dial.* 20.523–528: Meyer, p. 146.
88. *Dial.* 17.115–119. Notice here Palladius's pun on the name Theophilus, literally "lover of God." Other Egyptian monk-bishops are mentioned in chapters 7 and 8. See also *Historia lausiaca* 46.
89. See especially *Dial.* 20.31–106.
90. See *Vita Hypatii* 11.8 and 9, SC 177.
91. On Hypatius's forced ordination see *Vita Hypatii* 13.2. For an example of his independence see chapter 32. On Hypatius and the place of his *Vita* in Constantinopolitan monastic developments see Dagron, "Les moines et la ville," especially pp. 233–236 and 244–246.
92. *Vita Hypatii* 11.1–4.

7. From Nuisances to Episcopal Ideals

1. Jean Gaudemet, *La formation du droit séculier et du droit de l'église aux IVe et Ve siècles,* 2nd ed. (Paris: Sirey, 1979), p. 3. This overview was an attempt to fill in the gap.
2. John F. Matthews, *Laying Down the Law: A Study of the Theodosian Code* (New Haven: Yale University Press, 2000), provides an indispensable introduction to the way in which the text was conceived, edited, and published. See also Jill Harries, *Law and Empire in Late Antiquity* (Cambridge: Cambridge University Press, 1999), and Jill Harries and Ian Wood, eds., *The Theodosian Code* (Ithaca: Cornell University Press, 1993). On the intersection of civil and ecclesiastical legislation see J. Gaudemet, P. Siniscalco, and G. L. Falchi, *Legislazione imperiale e religione nel IV secolo* (Rome: Istituto Patristico Augustinianum, 2000), and Lucio De Giovanni, *Il libro XVI del Codice Teodosiano,* Associazione di studi tardoantichi (Naples: M. D'Auria, 1985).
3. Leo Ueding, "Die Kanones von Chalkedon in ihrer Bedeutung für

Mönchtum und Klerus," in *Das Konzil von Chalkedon,* ed. Alois Grillmeier and Heinrich Bacht, vol. 2 (Würzburg: Echter, 1953), p. 660.

4. Matthews, *Laying Down the Law,* pp. 118–120, points out the contrast with the *Codex Justinianus,* in which the subjects of religious belief and practices and the privileges of the church come first, suggesting that the authority of God stands before that of emperors.

5. *CTh* 12.1.63. Clyde Pharr, ed. and trans., *The Theodosian Code and Novels and the Sirmondian Constitutions* (Princeton: Princeton University Press, 1952). All quotations are from Pharr. For a collection of most of the religious laws in imperial legislation from 312 to 476 see Périclès-Pierre Joannou, *La législation impériale et la christianisation de l'Empire Romain (311–476)* (Rome: Pontificium institutum orientalium studiorum, 1972). Laws on monasticism are summarized by Charles Frazee, "Late Roman and Byzantine Legislation on the Monastic Life from the Fourth to the Eighth Centuries," *CH* 51 (1982): 263–279. For more extensive discussion of monastic legislation see Giorgio Barone Adesi, *Monachesimo ortodosso d'oriente e diritto romano nel tardo antico* (Milan: Giuffrè, 1990), pp. 118–142.

6. *CTh* 13.3.7.

7. *CTh* 9.45.3.

8. On the function of *curiales* and decline of the curial order during this period see Jones, *Later Roman Empire,* 1, pp. 737–757. For a reevaluation of the concept of the "decline of the *curiales,*" see Claudia Rapp, "Bishops in Late Antiquity," in J. Haldon, ed., *Elites Old and New in the Byzantine and Early Islamic Near East,* Studies in Late Antiquity and Early Islam 6 (Princeton: Darwin Press, 2003), pp. 144–173. For the situation in Cappadocia see Thomas A. Kopeček, "Curial Displacements and Flight in Later Fourth-Century Cappadocia," *Historia* 23 (1974): 319–342.

9. *NVal.* 35.1.3; Pharr, p. 546. A. H. M. Jones, *The Later Roman Empire, A.D. 284–602* (Oxford: Clarendon, 1964; repr. 1986), 1, p. 746, notes that this is the only law that explicitly forebade *curiales* to enter monasteries. They were generally permitted entry, provided they demonstrated the genuineness of their commitment by relinquishing their estates.

10. Jerome, *Chronicle,* twelfth year of Valens, in Malcolm Drew Donalson, *A Translation of Jerome's Chronicon with Historical Commentary* (Lewiston, N.Y.: Mellen, 1996), p. 55. On deportation of Egyptian monks to the mines of Pontus and Aremenia see Cassian, *Collationes* 7, and Socrates, *HE* 4.24.

11. Cassian, *Collationes* 8. Compare Jerome, Letter 22.34.

12. See Jones, *Later Roman Empire,* 2, pp. 932–933, and Jean Gaudemet, *L'Église dans l'Empire Romain (IVe–Ve siècles)* (Paris: Sirey, 1958), p. 198.

13. *CTh* 16.3.1. On the background to this decree and associated legislation see Gaudemet, *L'Église dans l'Empire Romain,* p. 199. See also G. L. Falchi,

"La diffusione della legislazione imperiale ecclesiastica nei secoli IV e V," in Gaudemet, Siniscalo, and Falchi, *Legislazione imperiale e religione,* p. 169.

14. Regarding the temple see Libanius, Oration 30.44f.; for its probable identification with Edessa see A. F. Norman, trans., *Libanius: Selected Works,* 2, LCL (Cambridge, Mass.: Harvard University Press, 1977), p. 141, note b. For a discussion of the various incidents of temple destruction see Garth Fowden, "Bishops and Temples in the Eastern Roman Empire A.D. 320–435," *JTS* n.s. 29/1 (1978): 53–78, especially pp. 62–71.

15. Libanius, Or. 30.8–9: Norman, p. 109. On the oft-quoted invectives of the pagans Libanius and Eunapius against monks see the discussion "Ascetic Politics" in H. A. Drake, *Constantine and the Bishops: The Politics of Intolerance* (Baltimore: Johns Hopkins University Press, 2000), pp. 409–418.

16. Libanius, Or. 30.46–47.

17. Ambrose, Letter 41.27. On the role of praetorian prefects in promulgating and enforcing antipagan legislation in the late fourth century see Fowden, "Bishops and Temples," pp. 54–56. For links between ascetics and the court of Theodosius I see John Matthews, *Western Aristocracies and Imperial Court A.D. 364–425* (Oxford: Clarendon, 1975), pp. 127–145, who discusses Cynegius in particular; on the appointment of Tatianus, who had also held court office under Valens, pp. 113–114.

18. *CTh* 16.3.2; see Pharr, p. 449 n. 2, and especially De Giovanni, *Il libro XVI del Codice Teodosiano,* p. 70.

19. *CJ* 1.3.22, in *Corpus Iuris Civilis,* 2: *Codex Iustinianus,* ed. Paul Krueger (Berlin: Weidmannsche Verlagsbuchhandlung, 1954), p. 16. On conflicts between monks and bishops in Constantinople see Gilbert Dagron, "Les moines et la ville: Le monachisme à Constantinople jusqu'au Concile de Chalcédoine (451)," *Travaux et mémoires* 4 (1970): pp. 261–275.

20. Chalcedon, canon 23, in *Acta conciliorum oecumenicorum (ACO)* 2.1, ed. Eduard Schwartz (Berlin: de Gruyter, 1933), p. 162 [358].

21. *CJ* 1.3.29: Krueger, p. 22. This law exemplifies the reception and incorporation of canonical legislation, in this case the canons of Chalcedon, in successive imperial legislation. See Falchi, "La diffusione della legislazione ecclesiastica," pp. 169–170 n. 93.

22. *CTh* 9.40.16; cf. *CTh* 11.30.57 and 16.2.32.

23. Karl Leo Noetlichs, "Materialen zum Bischofsbild aus den spätantiken Rechtsquellen," *JAC* 16 (1973): 38, notes that emperors were very reserved with regard to monks but considered them subject to bishops. On the great respect and extensive powers accorded bishops in the Code see David Hunt, "Christianising the Roman Empire: The Evidence of the Code," in Harries and Wood, eds., *Theodosian Code,* pp. 150–156.

24. *CTh* 5.3.1. According to B. Granić, "L'acte de fondation d'un monastère dans les provinces grecques du Bas-Empire au Ve et au VIe siècle," *Mélanges Charles Diehl*, 1 (Paris: Librairie Ernest Leroux, 1930), p. 102, this constitution of 434 was the first law to demonstrate clearly that the state viewed monasteries as an institution of the church with corporative rights.

25. *CTh* 16.5.7 and 9. See Barone Adesi, *Monachesimo e diritto romano*, pp. 126–128.

26. *CTh* 9.40.16.

27. *CTh* 16.2.32. The date of this law, 26 July 398, disagrees with the prefecture of Caesarius, to whom the decree is addressed. Pharr, p. 446 n. 99. On the interconnection of this decree with *CTh* 11.30.57 and 9.40.16 see Matthews, *Laying Down the Law*, p. 210.

28. See Frazee, "Late Roman and Byzantine Legislation," p. 266.

29. *CTh* 16.1.3. Cf. Sozomen, *HE* 7.9, where the list is accurately cited. On this legislation see Jean Gaudemet, "Politique ecclésiastique et législation religieuse après l'édit de Théodose I de 380," in *Atti dell'Accademia romanistica constantiniana, VI Convegno internazionale* (Perugia: Università di Perugia, Facoltà di giurisprudenza, 1986), pp. 1–22, especially 13–16, and more recently, idem, "La politique religieuse impériale au IVe siècle (envers les païens, les juifs, les hérétiques, les donatistes)," in Gaudemet, Siniscalo, and Falchi, *Legislazione imperiale e religione*, pp. 7–66.

30. The first three of these were monk-bishops discussed in earlier chapters. Pelagius of Laodicea on his wedding night agreed together with his wife to lead a life of continence. He was later said to have been raised to the episcopate because of his many virtues (Theodoret, *HE* 4.13). Timothy of Alexandria, brother and successor of Peter, was a monastic biographer. Optimus of Antioch was a devotee of Olympias in Constantinople, a member of the Cappadocian circle, and an admirer of Basil. Otreius of Melitene was a close friend of Gregory of Nyssa, a correspondent of Basil, and raised the monk Euthymius, whose Life was recounted by Cyril of Scythopolis. Regarding the other four bishops on Theodosius's list, Helladius of Caesarea had been a member of the curial class and Nectarius of Constantinople, a senator and neophyte. We know nothing of the relation of Terennius of Scythia and Marmarius of Martianopolis to the monastic movement.

31. Willibald M. Plöchl, *Geschichte des Kirchenrechts*, 1 (Vienna: Verlag Herold, 1960), p. 196, points out that the oldest legal measures that have come down to us regarding monks issue from popes rather than councils, especially Siricius (384–398), Innocent I (402–417), and Celestine I (423–432). For fuller discussion of this legal material, unfortunately limited to the West, see Paul Remy Oliger, *Les évêques réguliers: Recherche sur leur*

condition juridique depuis les origines du monachisme jusqu'à la fin du moyen âge (Paris, 1958).

32. Laodicea, canon 24. Together with clergy, those belonging to this order are warned against entering taverns. In canon 30 ascetics are listed alongside clergy as those prohibited from bathing with women.

33. According to Granić, "L'acte de fondation d'un monastère," p. 102, this is due to the fact that before Chalcedon monasteries were neither before the church nor before the state *de iure* recognized institutions. Ueding, "Die Kanones von Chalkedon," p. 579, points to the foundation of monasteries as an especially important indicator of relations between monasticism and the church hierarchy prior to Chalcedon.

34. Canon 14: Hefele-Leclercq 2/1, p. 129. Canon 80 in *Codex ecclesiae africanae* See Gaudemet, *L'Église dans l'Empire Romain*, p. 205 n. 7.

35. The authenticity and dating of these canons has been debated. Ueding, "Die Kanones von Chalkedon," pp. 590–591, suggests they may not date from before 451. However, Arthur Vööbus argues that these canons originate from western Syrian Christianity in the early fifth century. For an analysis and edition of these canons see Vööbus, "The So-Called Canons of Maruta," *Syriac and Arabic Documents*, Papers of the Estonian Theological Society in Exile 11 (Stockholm: Etse, 1960), pp. 115–149.

36. *Mar. can.* 25.1: Vööbus, p. 119.

37. *Mar. can.* 56–58: Vööbus, pp. 145–147.

38. Dagron, "Les moines et la ville," pp. 261–275, and idem, *Naissance d'une capitale: Constantinople et ses institutions de 330 à 451* (Paris: Presses universitaires de France, 1974), pp. 509–517. Dagron surveys several decades of turbulence. On the role of monks in the crises immediately preceding Chalcedon, from 448 to 451, see Heinrich Bacht, "Die Rolle des orientalischen Mönchtums in den kirchenpolitischen Auseinandersetzungen um Chalkedon (431–519)," in *Das Konzil von Chalkedon*, 2, pp. 193–243.

39. Chalcedon, canons 2–4, 6–8, 16, 18, 23, 24.

40. *ACO* 2.1, 159 [355]. For detailed discussion of the significance of the canons for both monks and clergy see Ueding, "Die Kanones von Chalkedon."

41. On the Eutychean affair as background to canon 4 see Ueding, "Die Kanones von Chalkedon," pp. 602–606, and Bacht, "Die Rolle des orientalischen Mönchtums," p. 197f. On the centrality of canon 4 and its implications see Barone Adesi, *Monachesimo e diritto romano*, pp. 323–333.

42. Canon 18: *ACO* 2.1, p. 161 [357].

43. Canon 23: *ACO* 2.1, p. 162 [358]. Ueding, "Die Kanones von Chalkedon," p. 610, also points out the parallel between canon 23 of Chalcedon and *CJ* I.3.22.2.

44. Canon 24: *ACO* 2.1, p. 162 [358].

45. Canon 16: *ACO* 2.1, p. 161 [357]; canon 2: *ACO* 2.1, p. 158 [354].

46. Canons 7 and 18, respectively: *ACO* 2.1, p. 159 [355] and p. 161 [357].

47. Canon 3: *ACO* 2.1, pp. 158–159 [354–355].

48. Canon 6: *ACO* 2.1, 159 [355]. Literally, *Mēdena de apolelumenōs cheirotoneisthai.*

49. Mansi 6, pp. 751–754. For other examples see Mansi 4, p. 1101, and 6, pp. 617, 677, 796, 861, 865. Similarly, Bacht, "Die Rolle des orientalischen Mönchtums," pp. 302–303, refers to monastic documents attesting that from the beginning of the fifth century it was increasingly common for leading monks of a monastery to be ordained.

50. Plöchl, *Geschichte des Kirchenrechts,* 1, pp. 195–197, points out in critique of Ueding that the movement would never have experienced such amazing growth if it had obtained its legal basis only through Chalcedon.

51. In 401 at the sixth Synod of Carthage bishops were already being warned not to ordain a monk from the monastery of another diocese. See canon 10: Hefele-Leclercq 2/1, p. 129. On later legislation and restrictions see also Ueding, "Die Kanones von Chalkedon," pp. 575–576, 592 n. 104.

52. Dagron, "Les moines et la ville," p. 267. Dagron is referring to a particular incident concerning Nestorius, but the description fits many scenarios of conflict presented in the article.

53. See the concluding comments of Dagron, "Les moines et la ville," p. 272.

54. *Nov.* 131.1 in *Corpus Juris Civilis,* 3: *Novellae,* ed. R. Schoell and W. Kroll (Berlin: Weidmannsche Verlagsbuchhandlung, 1954), pp. 654–655. See Matthews, *Laying Down the Law,* pp. 120 and 290, regarding the ideological shift in the treatment of religion.

55. For a full treatment of this subject see Noetlichs, "Materialen zum Bischofsbild."

56. On Justinianic legislation on monasticism, particularly its incorporation of Chalcedonian material, see Ueding, "Die Kanones von Chalkedon," pp. 662–670, and Frazee, "Late Roman and Byzantine Legislation," pp. 272–276. Barone Adesi, *Moncahesimo e diritto romano,* discusses some of the decrees in the *Codex,* which, he points out, lacks any specific title concerning monasticism (p. 141), but he does not mention the *novellae,* where most of the direct treatment of monasticism is found.

57. *Nov.* 5, preface, 14–19: Schoell and Kroll, p. 28. Cf. *Nov.* 133, preface: Schoell and Kroll, pp. 666–667, for a similarly high appraisal of monastic life. *Novella* 133, entitled *Quomodo oportet monachos vivere,* treats various aspects of monastic life and organization.

58. *Nov.* 5, preface, 25–29: Schoell and Kroll, p. 28. *Novella* 6 (Schoell and Kroll, pp. 35–47) is devoted to regulations for bishops and clergy. The rest

of *Novella* 5 is divided into nine chapters concerning the proper ordering of monastic life, treating such themes as the importance of the novitiate, the superiority of cenobitic life, the abandonment of religious life, the disposition of the monk's property, requirements for monks who take clerical orders, and the choice of the *higoumen,* or abbot. Both this *novella* and the monastic rulings of *Novella* 123 (issued in 546), a long, eclectic edict on bishops, clerics and monks, are discussed by Frazee, "Late Roman and Byzantine Legislation," pp. 272–273 and 274–276, respectively.

59. *Nov.* 5.8. Cf. *Nov.* 123.15.
60. *Nov.* 79; *Nov.* 123.44.
61. The subordination of monasteries to episcopal authority, which Ueding refers to as the "Grundgesetz" of Chalcedonian monastic legislation, is particularly clear in *CJ* 1.3.39: Krueger, p. 25.
62. *Nov.* 79.1. Cf. *Nov.* 123.21, 22, 27, regarding legal processes against clergy, bishops, and monks. This legislation essentially corresponds to canons 9 and 21 of Chalcedon, although the Chalcedonian canons do not explicitly include monks.
63. *Nov.* 67.1.
64. Regarding mixed houses see *CJ* 1.3.43 and *Nov.* 133.3. On the bishop's responsibility to maintain discipline see *CJ* 1.3.39, *CJ* 1.3.41.8, and *Nov.* 123.36. On choosing an abbot see *CJ* 1.3.46.3–4 (530), and *Nov.* 5.9 (535).
65. See the index to Noetlichs, "Materialen zum Bischofsbild," pp. 52–59, a thematic and chronological listing of imperial legislation concerning the bishop. The category of episcopal functions receives by far the most attention.
66. Similar prohibitions occur more than once in both the *Codex* and the *Novellae: CJ* 1.3.41.2–4, *CJ* 1.3.44.pr–3, *CJ* 1.3.47; *Nov.* 6.1.3–4, *Nov.* 123.1.pr, *Nov.* 123.29.10, and *Nov.* 137.2. It was possible, however, for a bishop to have been married previously. Also, this legislation was not retroactive; it did not apply to bishops elected prior to the establishment of this law.
67. Antioch, canon 24; and Apostolic canon 40. See Peter L'Huillier, "Episcopal Celibacy in the Orthodox Tradition," *SVQR* 35/2–3 (1991): 280.
68. While Justinian was reticent on possible financial concerns connected with the decrees requiring episcopal celibacy, Jones, *Later Roman Empire,* 2, p. 929, notes that Pope Pelagius I (556–561) interpreted the intention of the recent Justinianic legislation "more crudely." He required a bond indicating that a married candidate would not alienate to his family any church lands or other property he acquired after his consecration. See Pelagius I, *Ep.* 33.
69. *CJ* 1.3.41.2–4: Krueger, p. 26; *CJ* 1.3.47: Krueger, p. 34.

70. See Jean Gaudemet, "Le symbolisme du mariage entre l'évêque et son église et ses conséquences juridiques," *Kanon, der Bischof und seine Eparchie* 7 (1985): 110–123. Peter l'Huillier, "Episcopal Celibacy," p. 280, points to the phrase "a widowed church" *(chēreuousa ekklēsia)* in canon 25 of Chalcedon to describe a local church bereft of its bishop.

71. *Nov.* 6.1.7 (535). *Nov.* 123 1.2.7 (546) required only three months.

72. *Nov.* 123.1.1 (546) and 137.2 (565). On earlier imperial legislation regarding access of *curiales* to church office see Jones, *Later Roman Empire,* 1, p. 746, and especially 2, pp. 923–927.

73. The canons of the Council of Trullo are edited in Mansi 11 and 12, and in Périclès-Pierre Joannou, *Fonti* 9, *Discipline generale antique* (Rome: Pontificia Commissione per la Redazione del Codice di Diritto Canonico orientale, 1962), 1/1, pp. 101–241. For an introduction to this legislation see V. Laurent, "L'oeuvre canonique du Concile en Trullo (691–692), source primaire du droit de l'église orientale," *REB* 23 (1965): 7–41. On the relation of imperial and ecclesiastical law in Byzantium see Hans-Georg Beck, *Nomos, Kanon und Staatsraison in Byzanz,* Philosophisch-historische Klasse Sitzungsberichte 384 (Vienna: Verlag der österreichischen Akademie der Wissenschaften, 1981), pp. 9–20.

74. Trullo, canon 12.

75. Trullo, canon 48. Frazee, "Late Roman and Byzantine Legislation," pp. 276–277, discusses the Trullan legislation on monasticism, but he does not mention canons 12 or 48.

76. On law and practice relating to bishops, celibacy, and the growing role of monks in the East in subsequent centuries, see L'Huillier, "Episcopal Celibacy," pp. 284–296.

8. Normalizing the Model

1. For observations on monasticism in Egypt and the Holy Land see Jerome, Letter 108.14, and for Melania's visit to Nitria and the Cells, Elizabeth A. Clark, trans., *The Life of Melania the Younger* (New York: E. Mellen Press, 1984), chap. 39, pp. 53–54.

2. Epiphanius of Salamis, *Expositio fidei* 21, PG 42, 824B.

3. See Egeria's visits to Bathnae, Edessa, and Carrhae in George E. Gingras, trans., *Egeria: Diary of a Pilgrimage,* ACW 38 (New York: Newman Press, 1970), chaps. 19 and 20.

4. For missionary monks in Syria see Sozomen, *HE* 6.34. On the ordination of Peter see *VSM* 14.1–6; on the *gnēsiōtatoi therapeutoi* whom Basil ordained, GNaz, Oration 43.78. On Sacerdos, GNaz, Letter 211, and Gregory's Letters 99, 168–170, 209.

5. PG 31, 648BC. On the provenance and dating of this sermon see W. K. L. Clarke, trans., *Ascetic Works of Saint Basil* (London: S.P.C.K., 1925), pp. 9–10. On the same theme from a monk-priest in Egypt see Isidore of Pelusium, Letter 284, PG 78, 714BC.

6. Athanasius, *Epistola ad Dracontium* 7, PG 50, 532A, and *Ep. fest.* 40 in L.-Th. Lefort, ed., *Lettres festales et pastorales en Copte* (Louvain: CSCO, 1965), pp. 22–23; R. G. Coquin, "Les Lettres festales d'Athanase (CPG 2102), un nouveau complément: Le manuscrit IFAQ copte 25," *Orientalia Louvainensia Periodica* 15 (1984): 144–146. For an English translation of this fragmentary text see David Brakke, *Athanasius and the Politics of Asceticsm* (Oxford: Clarendon, 1995), pp. 332–334.

7. On Athanasius's linkage of the roles of monk and bishop see Brakke, *Athanasius and Asceticism,* pp. 80–141; on his political and ecclesiastical motives for appointing monks to the episcopate see especially pp. 99–110. See Susanna Elm, *"Virgins of God": The Making of Asceticism in Late Antiquity* (Oxford: Clarendon, 1994), pp. 331–372, for another perspective on Athanasius's recruitment and employment of monks.

8. Evagrius, *HE* 1.preface and 5.24 in *The Ecclesiastical History of Evagrius Scholasticus,* trans. Michael Whitby, Translated Texts for Historians 33 (Liverpool: Liverpool University Press, 2000), pp. 4 and 285. Evagrius completed his ecclesiastical history in 593/594. On Evagrius's methods and style see Pauline Allen, *Evagrius Scholasticus the Church Historian* (Louvain: Spicilegium Sacrum Lovanienses, 1981), pp. 44–52.

9. On their perspectives and approaches see Glenn F. Chesnut, *The First Christian Histories: Eusebius, Socrates, Sozomen, Theodoret and Evagrius,* 2nd ed. (Macon, Ga.: Mercer University Press, 1986); Mario Mazza, "Sulla teoria della storiografia cristiana: osservazioni sui proemi degli storici ecclesiastici," *La storiografia ecclesiastica nella tarda antichità* (Messina: Centro di studi umanistici, 1980); R. A. Markus, "Church History and Early Church Historians," in Derek Baker, ed., *The Materials, Sources and Methods of Ecclesiastical History,* Studies in Church History 11 (Cambridge: Cambridge University Press, 1975), pp. 1–17; Glanville Downey, "The Perspective of the Early Christian Historians," *Greek, Roman, and Byzantine Studies* 6 (1965): 57–70, though also note Markus's criticism of Downey, "Church History," p. 4 and n. 15.

10. In particular see Pauline Allen, "The Use of Heretics and Heresies in the Greek Church Historians: Studies in Socrates and Theodoret," in Graeme Clark, ed., *Reading the Past in Late Antiquity* (Rushcutters Bay: Australian National University Press, 1990), pp. 265–268.

11. Arnaldo Momigliano, "Popular Religious Beliefs and the Late Roman Historians," in G. J. Cuming and Derek Baker, eds., *Popular Belief and Practice,*

Studies in Church History 8 (Cambridge: Cambridge University Press, 1972), pp. 15–16.

12. See Arnaldo Momigliano, "Pagan and Christian Historiography in the Fourth Century A.D.," in idem, ed., *The Conflict between Paganism and Christianity in the Fourth Century* (Oxford: Clarendon, 1963), especially pp. 92–93. See also Chesnut, *First Christian Histories,* pp. 205–206, 253–255.

13. Chesnut, *First Christian Histories,* pp. 240–241. For changes in the writing of history see Momigliano, "Popular Religious Beliefs," especially p. 11.

14. This is particularly evident in the preface to Sozomen's work, where he addresses the emperor directly.

15. Markus, "Church History," p. 9.

16. For the text of Socrates' Church History see Günther Christian Hansen, ed., *Sokrates Kirchengeschichte* GCS n.F. 1 (Berlin: Akademie Verlag, 1995); also PG 67, 29–841. For Sozomen see J. Bidez, ed., *Sozomenus Kirchengeschichte,* GCS (Berlin: Akademie Verlag, 1960); also PG 67, 843–1629. For Theodoret see L. Parmentier, ed., GCS 44 (Berlin: Akademie Verlag, 1954), recently rev. G. C. Hansen, GCS n.F. 5 (Berlin: Akademie Verlag, 1998); also PG 82, 881–1280. English quotations of Socrates and Sozomen are from translations by A. C. Zenos and Chester D. Hartranft, respectively, in NPNF, 2nd ser., vol. 2 (Grand Rapids, Mich.: Eerdmans, 1957). Quotations of Theodoret are from Blomfield Jackson's translation, NPNF, 2nd ser., vol. 3 (Grand Rapids, Mich.: Eerdmans, 1983).

17. Sozomen, *HE* 1.1; Socrates, *HE* 4.23f.

18. Socrates, *HE* 7.22.4–5.

19. Sozomen, *HE* 4.10.

20. Socrates, *HE* 4.26 and 4.24.

21. Sozomen, 3.14–16. See Guy Sabbah, ed., *Sozomène: Histoire ecclésiastique,* Books III–IV, SC 418 (Paris: Éditions du cerf, 1996), pp. 9–43.

22. Sozomen, *HE* 6.27. See also 6.34.

23. For example, Sozomen *HE* 4.2–3, 20, 27. Compare his treatment of monasticism in Egypt, Palestine, and Syria in 3.14–16. On the church historians' distinctive treatment of Constantinopolitan monasticism see Gilbert Dagron, "Les moines et la ville: Le monachisme à Constantinople jusqu'au Concile de Chalcédoine (451)," *Travaux et mémoires* 4 (1970): especially 238–239.

24. Theodoret, *HE* 1.6, 2.30, 3.24, and 4.25 and 27. Theodoret's *Philotheus,* more commonly referred to as the *Historia religiosa,* was a group biography of famous Syrian ascetics composed approximately five years prior to his ecclesiastical history. On the dating of his Church History see the arguments for a *terminus ante quem* of 449 in G. F. Chesnut, "The Date of Composition of Theodoret's Church History," *VC* 35 (1981): 245–252.

25. Allen, "Use of Heretics and Heresies," p. 272f., illustrates this underlying Antiochene focus. See also Chesnut, *First Christian Histories*, pp. 210–212.

26. Theodoret, *HE* 4.27.5: Jackson, p. 128. For other examples of monks in the Arian struggle see 4.28–29.

27. Theodoret, *HE* 4.20 and 5.4.

28. For examples see Theodoret, *HR* 2.15, 26.27, 21.15–18, 3.11, and discussion below, Chapter 9.

29. Sozomen, *HE* 6.34 and 3.14, respectively.

30. On Eulogius and Protogenes see Theodoret, *HE* 4.18. Both monks were later consecrated bishops. For the Egyptians see Theodoret, *HE* 4.21; Socrates, *HE* 4.24; Sozomen, *HE* 6.20. In all these accounts the two famous Macarii numbered among Egyptian monks who were banished.

31. For example, see Socrates, *HE* 7.8, for the mission of Marutha of Mesopotamia and Abdas of Persia.

32. See the descriptions of the destruction of the Serapeum: Socrates, *HE* 7.15; Socrates, *HE* 5.16; Theodoret, *HE* 5.22. For the destruction of other pagan shrines and the involvement of bishops and monks in these acts see Socrates, *HE* 3.2; Sozomen *HE* 5.7, 5.15, 5.10; and Theodoret *HE* 5.21. For further discussion of many of these texts and the broader context see Garth Fowden, "Bishops and Temples in the Eastern Roman Empire A.D. 320–435," *JTS* (1978): 53–78.

33. Sozomen, *HE* 3.17.

34. Socrates *HE* 4.24. The incident was also mentioned by Sozomen, *HE* 6.30.

35. Socrates, *HE* 7.35.

36. Socrates, *HE* 7.37.

37. Socrates, *HE* 4.36; Theodoret, *HE* 4.23. In Sozomen's rendition of this affair, *HE* 6.38, Moses refused ordination at the hands of the Arian bishop.

38. Socrates, *HE* 7.17, 39, and 46. On Socrates' sympathetic treatment of Novatianism see Allen, "Use of Heretics and Heresies," pp. 266–271.

39. Sozomen, *HE* 3.14.

40. Sozomen, *HE* 7.28. Acacius is mentioned in Theodoret's Church History as well (*HE* 5.5) and appears frequently in his *Historia religiosa*.

41. Sozomen, *HE* 6.31.

42. Sozomen, *HE* 6.32.

43. On Vitus and Protogenes see Sozomen, *HE* 6.33. For Ephrem's descriptions of these and other ascetic bishops of Syria see above, Chapter 1. On Barses and Eulogius see Sozomen, *HE* 6.34. Regarding the ordination of Barses and Eulogius, compare Theodoret, *HE* 5.4.

44. Sozomen, *HE* 6.34.

45. Theodoret, *HE* 4.13.2–3: Jackson, p. 115. Cf. Socrates, *HE* 3.25 and 5.8, and Sozomen, *HE* 6.12, 7.9.

46. Theodoret, *HE* 2.30, 4.16, 4.23, 4.17–18. On Eulogius and Protogenes compare Sozomen, *HE* 6.33, 34.
47. Theodoret, *HE* 5.4.
48. For Theodoret's self-description see Ep. 113, NPNF, 2nd ser., vol. 3, p. 294. See also the section "Der Mönch-Bischof Theodoret von Cyrrhus," Stephan Schiwietz, *Das Morgenländische Mönchtum,* 3: *Das Mönchtum in Syrien und Mesopotamien und das Asketentum in Persien* (Mödling bei Wien: Missionsdruckerei St. Gabriel, 1938), pp. 238–241.
49. Chesnut, *First Christian Histories,* p. 240 n. 62.
50. Sozomen, *HE* 6.21.
51. Theodoret, *HE* 2.30.15. For other confrontations with emperors see the accounts involving Eusebius of Samosata (2.32), Ambrose (4.7), Aphraates (4.26), and Vetranio (4.35).
52. Chesnut, *First Christian Histories,* pp. 240–241. See also Peter Brown, "The Rise and Function of the Holy Man in Late Antiquity," in *Society and the Holy in Late Antiquity* (Berkeley: University of California Press, 1982), pp. 136–141.
53. Both historians included accounts of Maris of Chalcedon vs. Julian (Socrates, *HE* 3.12; Sozomen, *HE* 5.4) and of Basil of Caesarea vs. Valens and Modestus (Socrates, *HE* 4.26; Sozomen, *HE* 6.16). The other confrontations all appear in Sozomen's history: Athanasius of Alexandria vs. Constantius (3.20), Liberius of Rome vs. Constantius (6.16), Vetranio vs. Valens (6.21), Amphilochius of Iconium vs. Theodosius (7.6; the protagonist here is an "old priest," but in Theodoret's account, *HE* 5.16, he is identified as Amphilochius), Flavian of Antioch vs. Theodosius (7.23), Ambrose vs. Theodosius (7.25), and Chrysostom vs. Arcadius (8.4). The other two confrontations involved the whole church of Edessa, with special reference to a woman, vs. Valens and the prefect Modestus (6.18), and a monk named Issac vs. Valens (6.40).
54. For example, Theodoret recounts at considerable length the trials and exiles of Athanasius of Alexandria. Other notable examples occur in *HE* 1.21; 2.7, 27, 31–32; and 4.13–21, 25, 30.
55. For discussion and references see Allen, "Use of Heretics and Heresies," pp. 273–282.
56. See especially Theodoret, *HE* 2.24, 4.25, 4.11, and 5.23, although 4.25.5–6 also exalts his piety and virtue and connects him with the famous Syrian ascetic Aphrahat.
57. Socrates, *HE* 6.13. Socrates also viewed Flavian in a negative light for continuing the schism of Antioch. See Socrates, *HE* 5.9.10 and 15; cf. Sozomen, *HE* 7.11.
58. For criticism of Theophilus of Alexandria see Socrates, *HE* 6.7, 9, 10, and 17.

59. On Eusebius, see Socrates, *HE* 2.21 and 3.7; on the Origenism of the others, *HE* 4.25–27. On Socrates' Origenism see also Chesnut, *First Christian Histories,* pp. 177–181.

60. See especially Socrates, *HE* 7.2, 3, 11, 41; Sozomen, *HE* 7.12 and 15, and 8.3. The historians' praise of tolerant emperors was even more pronounced. See Chesnut, *First Christian Histories,* p. 239.

61. On Proclus, Socrates, *HE* 7.41; On Atticus, *HE* 6.20, 7.2, 7.21, 7.25. On Atticus see also Dagron, "Les moines et la ville," p. 265.

62. Socrates, *HE* 1.11.

63. Sozomen, *HE* 6.16. See also 6.15. Socrates, *HE* 4.26, emphasizes Origen's influence on Basil and Gregory Nazianzen.

64. Theodoret, *HE* 4.19.

65. GNaz, Oration 43.54.

66. The accounts occur in Socrates, *HE* 4.26; Sozomen, *HE* 6.16; Theodoret, *HE* 4.19. In Socrates' narrative Basil is brought from Caesarea to Antioch to be questioned by the prefect.

67. Socrates suggests the former while Sozomen and Theodoret suggest the latter behavior.

68. Sozomen, *HE* 6.16. His comment regarding the boy's improvement at Basil's arrival agrees with Nazianzen's account.

69. Theodoret, *HE* 4.19.15–16: Jackson, p. 120.

70. Henry Chadwick, "The Role of the Christian Bishop in Ancient Society," Protocol Series of the Colloquies 35 (Berkeley: Center for Hermeneutical Studies, 1980), p. 14.

71. Peter Brown, response to Chadwick, "Role of the Christian Bishop," in ibid., pp. 15–16, and idem, *Power and Persuasion in Late Antiquity: Towards a Christian Empire* (Madison: University of Wisconsin Press, 1992), p. 5.

72. Ramsey MacMullen, response to Chadwick, "Role of the Christian Bishop," in ibid., p. 29.

73. Peter Brown, "Rise and Function of the Holy Man," *JRS* 61 (1971): 95f. In this original version of the article, Brown contrasts the role of the holy man in the East with the situation in the West, where the hierarchical church stood unchallenged. However, in a footnote in his updated version of this article, Brown also mentions parenthetically the continuity between expectations of the Christian bishop and the later holy man. See "Rise and Function," in *Society and the Holy,* p. 127 n. 119.

74. Brown, *Power and Persuasion,* pp. 71–117.

9. The Broadening Appeal

1. Benedicta Ward, trans., *The Sayings of the Desert Fathers: The Alphabetical Collection* (Kalamazoo, Mich.: Cistercian Publications, 1975), p. 33.

2. Palladius, *Historia Lausiaca (HL)* 38, in Cuthbert Butler, ed., *The Lausiac History of Palladius,* Texts and Studies 6, vol. 2 (Cambridge: Cambridge University Press, 1898), p. 116, lines 15–16, says that Basil ordained Evagrius of Pontus lector, and after Basil's death none other than Gregory Nazianzen ordained him deacon. Both Socrates (*HE* 4.23) and Sozomen (*HE* 6.30) attest to the latter ordination by Gregory. For an English translation of the Syriac texts see Joseph Philip Amar, "The Syriac *Vita* Tradition of Ephrem the Syrian," Ph.D. diss., Catholic University of America, 1988, pp. 280–281. For Amar's comparison of the Syriac tradition with the pseudo-Amphilochian account of this incident see pp. 24–25.

3. For examples of monk-bishops see the accounts of Apphy and Netras. See also Graham Gould, *The Desert Fathers on Monastic Community* (Oxford: Clarendon, 1993), pp. 147 and 174, on the harmony between episcopal and monastic vocations in these sayings. On the milieu in which the *Apophthegmata* developed, reasons for its compilation, and the extent of its influence, see Derwas J. Chitty, *The Desert a City* (Crestwood, N.Y.: St. Vladimir's Seminary Press, 1966), pp. 67–77. On the stages of compilation and proposed dating see Jean Claude Guy, *Apophtegmes des pères: Collection systématique, chapitres I–IX,* SC 387 (Paris: Éditions du cerf, 1993), pp. 23–35, 79–84.

4. Regarding this approach see Claudia Rapp, "Storytelling as Spiritual Communication in Early Greek Hagiography: The Use of *Diegesis,*" *JECS* 6/3 (1998): 431–462.

5. See T. Kauser, "L'Hagiographie: Un 'genre' chrétien ou antique tardif?," *AB* 111 (1993): 135–188, and Claudia Rapp, "'For Next to God, You Are My Salvation': Reflections on the Rise of the Holy Man in Late Antiquity," in John Howard-Johnston and Paul Anthony Hayward, eds., *The Cult of the Saints in Late Antiquity and the Middle Ages: Essays on the Contribution of Peter Brown* (New York: Oxford University Press, 1999), pp. 63–81.

6. On this function see Garth Fowden, "Religious Communities," in G. W. Bowersock, Peter Brown, and Oleg Grabar, eds., *Late Antiquity: A Guide to the Postclassical World* (Cambridge, Mass.: The Belknap Press of Harvard University Press, 1999), pp. 92–96.

7. Patricia Cox Miller, "Strategies of Representation in Collective Biography: Constructing the Subject as Holy," in Thomas Hägg and Philip Rousseau, eds., *Greek Biography and Panegyric in Late Antiquity* (Berkeley: University of California Press, 2000), p. 232.

8. On these qualities of hagiographical literature see Averil Cameron, *Christianity and the Rhetoric of Empire: The Development of Christian Discourse* (Berkeley: University of California Press, 1991), pp. 141–154. Also idem, "Ascetic Closure," in Vincent L. Wimbush and Richard Valantasis, eds., *Asceticism* (Oxford: Oxford University Press, 1997), pp. 147–161.

9. *Presbuteriou ēxiōmenos.* See, for example, Elpidius, who later became a chorbishop. *Historia Lausiaca* 48, lines 14–16, in Butler, ed., *Lausiac History* 2. For very similar phrases see descriptions of Macarius of Egypt (*HL* 17, p. 43, lines 2–3); Rufinus of Aquileia (*HL* 46, p. 136, line 2); Sisinnius (*HL* 49, p. 144, line 1); and Dorotheus (*HL* 58, p. 151, lines 18–19).

10. See Philip Rousseau, *Ascetics, Authority, and the Church in the Age of Jerome and Cassian* (Oxford: Oxford University Press, 1978), pp. 16–17.

11. Palladius, *Dialogue,* 17.

12. Palladius, *HL* 11 and 46 (Butler, p. 134, line 18). The incident is also related by Socrates, *HE* 4.23 and Sozomen, *HE* 6.30.

13. Jacob Muyser, "Contribution à l'étude des listes épiscopales de l'Église copte," *Bulletin de la Société d'archéologie copte* 10 (1944): 134.

14. For the Syriac text of *Life of Rabbula* see J. J. Overbeck, ed., *S. Ephraemi Syri, Rabulae episcopi Edesseni, Balaeit aliorumque opera selecta* (Oxford: Clarendon, 1865), pp. 159–209; German translation in G. Bickell, *Ausgewählte Schriften der syrischen Kirchenvater Aphraates, Rabulas und Isaak von Ninive,* Bibliothek der Kirchenväter (Kempten, 1874), pp. 155–211. On Rabbula see Georg Günter Blum, *Rabbula von Edessa: Der Christ, der Bischof, der Theologe,* CSCO 300, Subsidia 34 (Louvain: CSCO, 1969); also P. Peeters, "La vie de Rabboula, évêque d'Édesse (+7 août 436)," *RSR* 18 (1928): 170–204. On the connection of the vita with anti-Nestorianism, the Council of Ephesus, and its aftermath, see Han J. W. Drijvers, "Rabbula, Bishop of Edessa: Spiritual Authority and Secular Power," in Jan Willem Drijvers and John W. Watt, eds., *Portraits of Spiritual Authority: Religious Power in Early Christianity, Byzantium and the Christian Orient* (Leiden: Brill, 1999), 139–154, especially pp. 148–152. Drijvers, p. 138, notes that the *vita Rabbulae* is technically not a Life but a panegyric.

15. Arthur Vööbus, ed., *Syriac and Arabic Documents Regarding Legislation Relative to Syrian Asceticism,* Papers of the Estonian Theological Society in Exile 11 (Stockholm: Etse, 1960), pp. 24–50 and 78–86.

16. Bickell, pp. 168–170. On the background of these ascetics see Pierre Canivet, *Le monachisme syrien selon Théodoret de Cyr,* Théologie historique 42 (Paris: Éditions Beauchesne, 1977), pp. 185–186 and 248–252.

17. Bickell, pp. 168–174. On Rabbula as an *alter Christus* see Drijvers, "Rabbula, Bishop of Edessa," pp. 144–145, 151.

18. Bickell, p. 177.

19. Bickell, pp. 187, 190. See also Blum, *Rabbula von Edessa,* pp. 83–86.

20. See Han J. W. Drijvers, "The Man of God of Edessa, Bishop Rabbula, and the Urban Poor: Church and Society in the Fifth Century," *JECS* 4 (1996): 235–248, and Susan Ashbrook Harvey, "The Holy and the Poor: Models from Early Syriac Christianity," in E. Albu Hanawalt and C. Lindberg, eds.,

Through the Eye of a Needle: Judeo-Christian Roots of Social Welfare (Kirksville, Mo.: Thomas Jefferson University Press, 1994), pp. 43–66.

21. Bickell, p. 172.
22. Rabbula's biographer claims in one passage that he undertook no new building projects because he believed that the church's wealth should be used to support the poor and needy. Bickell, p. 194. For different perspectives on this passage compare Harvey, "The Holy and the Poor," p. 48, and Drijvers, "The Man of God," pp. 242–243.
23. See Bickell, pp. 204–207, on the hospitals.
24. Bickell, p. 181.
25. Bickell, p. 175. See also Blum, *Rabbula von Edessa,* pp. 30–32.
26. Bickell, p. 206.
27. Bickell, pp. 180–182, 185–186, 187–188, 191–192. See Drijvers, "Rabbula, Bishop of Edessa," p. 145, who assumes these are physical punishments.
28. References to Rabbula's fearsome character or the people's fear of him abound. See, for example, Bickell, pp. 183, 188, 192, 193. The epithet "Tyrant of Edessa" was ascribed to Rabbula by Ibas, whom he exiled in 433. See Drijvers, "Rabbula, Bishop of Edessa," pp. 146, 148–152.
29. See Garth Fowden "Bishops and Temples in the Eastern Roman Empire A.D. 320–435," *JTS* (1978): 53–78; Timothy E. Gregory, *Vox Populi: Popular Opinion and Violence in the Religious Controversies of the Fifth Century A.D.* (Columbus: Ohio State University Press, 1979); N. McLynn, "Christian Controversy and Violence in the Fourth Century," *Kodai* 3 (1992): 15–44; Ramsey MacMullen, *Christianity and Paganism in the Fourth to Eighth Centuries* (New Haven: Yale University Press, 1997), pp. 11–31; and Michael Gaddis, "There Is No Crime for Those Who Have Christ': Religious Violence in the Christian Roman Empire," Ph.D. diss., Princeton University, 1999.
30. Averil Cameron, "Ascetic Closure and the End of Antiquity," in Wimbush and Valantasis, *Asceticism,* p. 149; also idem, "On Defining the Holy Man," in Howard-Johnston and Hayward, *The Cult of the Saints,* p. 42, and idem, *Rhetoric of Empire,* chap. 6.
31. This is among the motives proposed by Canivet, *Le monachisme syrien,* p. 41. For the text see Pierre Canivet and Alice Leroy-Molinghen, *Theodoret de Cyr: Histoire des moines de Syrie,* SC 234 and 257 (Paris: Éditions du cerf, 1977, 1979); English trans., R. M. Price, *Theodoret of Cyrrhus: A History of the Monks of Syria* (Kalamazoo, Mich.: Cistercian Publications, 1985).
32. See, for example, *HR* 10.6, 26.10, and 27.3.
33. For examples of such services see *HR* 2.15–17, 21.15–18, 3.11, and 26.27.
34. *HR* 14.5, lines 5–6. Here Theodoret is referring to the example of the

monk-priest Maësymas. For other examples of monks ordained as priests see *HR* 3.11, 4.10, 13.4, 15.4, 19.2.

35. *HR* 1.4, 6, and 11, respectively. In connection with the first and last of these feats he is compared with Moses. The historical Jacob of Nisibis was the first metropolitan bishop of the city and died in 337/338. He was one of several bishops served by Ephrem the Syrian and is hymned in Ephrem's *Carmen Nisibenum* 14.

36. *HR* 1.7, lines 4–13.

37. *HR* 2.9, line 15.

38. *HR* 5.8 (Aphthonius of Zeugma); *HR* 10.9, lines 4–5 (Helladius of Cilicia).

39. *HR* 17.1; 17.11, line 3.

40. On the possible context of *HR* 31's composition see Canivet and Leroy-Molinghen, *Theodoret de Cyr,* pp. 53–55, and Canivet, *Le monachisme syrien,* pp. 91–94. Price, *Monks of Syria,* p. 206 n. 1 casts doubt on Canivet's arguments for precise dating of the treatise.

41. *HR* 31.10, lines 30–33. Theodoret's exegesis of this passage closely follows that of Theodore of Mopsuestia. Canivet, *Le monachisme syrien,* pp. 67–68, compares the two interpretations.

42. Canivet, *Le monachisme syrien,* p. 229. In his Letter 81, written during his period of exile, Theodoret says that he was ordained bishop against his will. For references to the burden of episcopal office and his continued longing for the peace and solitude of monastic life see Canivet, p. 28 n. 102. For his sense of duty to his episcopal charge see especially Letter 113.

43. Henri Grégoire and M.-A. Kugener, eds., *Marc le Diacre: Vie de Porphyre évêque de Gaza* (Paris, 1930), ciii–cix. An English translation by Claudia Rapp of most of the *Life* is in Thomas Head, ed., *Medieval Hagiography: An Anthology* (New York: Garland, 2000), pp. 53–74.

44. On Gaza see C. A. M. Glucker, *The City of Gaza in the Roman and Byzantine Periods,* BAR International Series 325 (Oxford: B.A.R., 1987). On the context of Porphyry's struggle with paganism see Raymond Van Dam, "From Paganism to Christianity in Late Antique Gaza," *Viator* 16 (1985): 1–20. See *Life of Porphyry,* 41 for the emperor's initial response to Porphyry, and 45–46 for the bishop's request.

45. *Life of Porphyry,* 63–79, 82, 92.

46. *Life of Porphyry,* 4.

47. *Life of Porphyry,* 16. On his priesthood see chap. 10, especially lines 12–13, which seems to be drawn from Theodoret's *Historia religiosa.*

48. *Life of Porphyry,* 66–69 and 77–79.

49. For this theme in Socrates, see Chapter 8, n. 60. For a much fuller analysis of factors underlying Porphyry's acts against paganism see Van Dam, "From Paganism to Christianity."

50. See John Binns, "Introduction," in *Lives of the Monks of Palestine by Cyril of Scypotholis*, trans. R. M. Price (Kalamazoo: Cistercian Publications, 1991), pp. xi and xl. The Greek text is edited by Eduard Schwartz, *Kyrillos von Skythopolis*, TU 49:2 (Leipzig, 1939). Price, whose translation I cite here, has synchronized his line numbering with Schwartz's edition.

51. For a comparative treatment of Cyril's sources see Bernard Flusin, *Miracle et histoire dans l'oeuvre de Cyrille de Scythopolis* (Paris: Études augustiniennes,1983), pp. 41–86. See also the section entitled "Cyril's Library" in John Binns, *Ascetics and Ambassadors of Christ: The Monasteries of Palestine, 314–631* (Oxford: Clarendon, 1994), pp. 57–66, which offers several corrections and additions to Flusin. On Theodoret's influence see pp. 63–64.

52. Successors of the martyrs, monks bear "the impression of apostolic virtue." Cyril, *Lives*, 8.3. See 7.15–8.10 for Cyril's chain of apostles, martyrs, and monks culminating with the monk Euthymius. The monk Sabas is called a "new Moses" in 117.5. On Cyril's apologetic purpose see Cynthia Jean Stallman-Pacitti, *Cyril of Scythopolis: A Study in Hagiography as Apology* (Brookline, Mass.: Hellenic College Press, 1991).

53. Binns, "Introduction," p. xliii.

54. On the cosmopolitan nature of Palestinian monastic life see Binns, *Ascetics and Ambassadors*, pp. 77–147.

55. Cyril, *Lives*, 102.19–21. See also 100.14–16.

56. *Ton tēs archēs kindunon uforōmenos.* Cyril, *Lives*, 242.5. For Theodosius see 237.1.

57. Cyril, *Lives*, 10.5–14.2.

58. On Martyrius and Elias see Cyril, *Lives*, 51.4–51.15. On Stephen, Gaianus, and Cosmas, see 33.30–31, 53.3–4, and 55.21–22, respectively.

59. Cyril, *Lives*, 25.4–9.

60. Cyril, *Lives*, 35.11–25 and 52.1–9 (Anastasius); 51.6–9 (Martyrius and Elias); 26.4–5 and 55.23–24 (Cosmas). All of these bishops were monks.

61. See *Lives* 103.8–105.2 for the circumstances of Sabas's ordination. For his appointment as archimandrite see 114.23–115.26. Cyril mentions several monks ordained to the episcopate: Sergius and Paul (112.23–27); George (126.20–127.3); Marcianus, Antony, and John (127.4–14).

62. For the full account of John the Hesychast see Cyril, *Lives*, 201.4–222.16, here 202.24–25; for Abraamius, 243.20f.; for Theognius, 241.12–13.

63. The adverb *akousiōs* is most often inserted in the account to signal their reservations. See the cases of Euthymius (*Lives*, 13.15), John the Hesychast (202.23), and Theognius (242.25–26). Obviously Theognius overcame his initial fear of wielding authority (242.5).

64. Cyril, *Lives,* 247.4–5, regarding Abraamius.

65. On the nature and use of miracles see Flusin, *Miracle et histoire,* especially chap. 3, and Binns, *Ascetics and Ambassadors,* pp. 218–246.

66. For examples of the humility and respect with which archbishops approached holy men see Cyril, *Lives,* 54.17–55.12 (Anastasius), 103.6–105.1 (Martyrius and Sallustius), and 244.31–32 (bishops who delighted in conversation with Theognius). In addition, monks manifested power in cases where bishops were powerless. For examples see *Lives,* 167.25–169.20 and 170.1–171.5. For the authority of monks before imperial powers see the following incidents: *Lives,* 47.5–49.23 (Euthymius and Empress Eudocia), 141.5–144.30 (Sabas before Anastasius), and 174.24–178.19 (Sabas before Justinian).

67. For examples and discussion of these factors underlying the popularity of monks in the Christian East see Heinrich Bacht, "Die Rolle des orientalischen Mönchtems in den kirchenpolitischen Auseinandersetzungen um Chalkedon (431–519)," in *Das Konzil von Chalkedon,* ed. Alois Grillmeier and Heinrich Bacht (Würzburg: Echter, 1953), 2, pp. 310–313.

68. Cyril, *Lives,* 121.14–122.17 and 246.8–247.5.

69. Cyril's accounts of the foundation of Castellium (*Life of Sabas,* 27), the Cenobium of the Cave (37), the Cenobium of the Tower (38), and the Cenobium of Zannus (42) say nothing of episcopal consultation or consent. Similarly Abba Theodosius founded a cenobium and appointed his successor as superior without any mention of a bishop. *Life of Theodosius,* 3 and 5. Both Euthymius and Sabas also appointed superiors without any indication of episcopal approval. See *Life of Euthymius,* 37, in *Lives,* 55.13–19, and *Life of Sabas,* 27 (112.20–23), 36 (124.2–4), 38 (128.17–21), and 76 (182.20–21). At the same time, there are examples of appointments where knowledge or consent of the bishop is expressly indicated. For references and discussion see Leo Ueding, "Die Kanones von Chalkedon in ihrer Bedeutung für Mönchtum und Klerus," in *Das Konzil von Chalkedon,* 2, pp. 672–673.

70. For Sabas's diplomatic missions to Emperors Anastasius and Justinian see *Lives,* 141.25–147.9 and 173.12–178.19, respectively. On his role as a patron and diplomat see Binns, *Ascetics and Ambassadors,* pp. 170–182.

71. See especially Cyril, *Lives,* 41.4–45.4, 47.21–49.13, 66.18–67.20 on Euthymius; and 103.12–17, 141.24–144.28, 198.7–200.16 regarding Sabas. For a discussion of the role of Palestinian monks in the doctrinal struggles of the day see Binns, *Ascetics and Ambassadors,* pp. 183–217; also Chitty, *The Desert a City,* pp. 101–122.

72. See Cyril, *Lives,* 238.25, though in the case of Theodosius no specific op-

ponents are named. For other examples see 221.18–22 (John the Hesychast vs. followers of Orgien and Theodore of Mopsuestia) and 229.7–230.30 (Cyriacus vs. Nonnus and Leontius of Byzantium).

73. Susan Ashbrook Harvey, *Asceticism and Society in Crisis: John of Ephesus and The Lives of the Eastern Saints* (Berkeley: University of California Press, 1990), p. 139.

74. On the distinction between Miaphysites and Monophysites see "Monophysites," in Bowersock, Brown, and Grabar, *Late Antiquity*, p. 586. Nonetheless, until very recently most of the secondary literature has used the term Monophysite for all non-Chalcedonians.

75. John Rufus, *Plérophories*, ed. F. Nau, Patrologia Orientalis 8 (Paris: Firmin-Didot, 1912).

76. The notion of Juvenal as an almost a literal embodiment of the deceased Nestorius is graphically represented in *Plerophoriae* 40: Nau, p. 91.

77. For an overview of theological developments leading up to Chalcedon, the roles of monks and bishops in the proceedings, and the rise of the anti-Chalcedonian party see Binns, *Ascetics and Ambassadors*, pp. 1–17; for a much fuller treatment, Grillmeier and Bacht, eds., *Das Konzil von Chalkedon*. On the aftermath see W. H. C. Frend, *The Rise of the Monophysite Movement: Chapters in the History of the Church in the Fifth and Sixth Centuries* (Cambridge: Cambridge University Press, 1972), and Patrick T. R. Gray, *The Defense of Chalcedon in the East (451–553)* (Leiden: Brill, 1979).

78. See *Plerophoriae* 46 and 47, respectively, for these two accounts: Nau, pp. 98–99. The "Encyclical" was an anti-Chalcedonian document issued by the usurper Basilicus in order to rally support for himself in the east. See Gray, *Defense of Chalcedon*, pp. 25–26. Faced with protest from Constantinople and Rome, Basilicus quickly changed his mind and issued an anti-Encyclical; but almost all the eastern bishops subscribed to the original Encyclical.

79. *Plerophoriae* 16: Nau, pp. 32–33.

80. *Plerophoriae* 22: Nau, p. 47. On the Encyclical see n. 78 above.

81. Binns, *Ascetics and Ambassadors*, pp. 6–11, discusses the Henoticon in a subsection of his introduction aptly entitled "The Forgetting of Chalcedon."

82. *Plerophoriae* 22; Nau, p. 52. For the whole incident see chaps. 47–54.

83. John Rufus, *Vita Petri Iberi*, 24, ed. and [German] trans. R. Raabe, *Petrus der Iberer* (Leipzig: J. C. Hinrichs'sche Buchhandlung, 1895). There are two extant biographies of Peter, the Syrian translation of the original Greek composed by John Rufus, edited by Raabe, and a later Georgian version. Modified by redactors after the Georgians were reconciled to Chalcedon, this later vita studiously avoids any mention of Peter's connection with non-Chalcedonians. See David Marshall Lang, "Peter the Iberian and

his Biographers," *JEH* 2/2 (1951): 159–168; for an abridged English version of the Syriac text see idem, *Lives and Legends of the Georgian Saints,* 2nd ed., rev. (London: Mowbrays, 1976), pp. 57–80.

84. *Vita Petri Iberi,* 51.

85. *Vita Petri Iberi,* 53–54. Regarding Theodosius see also *Plerophoriae* 56: Nau, pp. 111–113.

86. Peter, already in hiding in Egypt in 457 with many other non-Chalcedonian bishops, was one of the two bishops to ordain Timothy Aelurus, known as the Weasel because he was inordinately thin. *Vita Petri Iberi,* 65–66.

87. *Vita Petri Iberi,* 106; for his consequent journey to Beirut and influence on students there, 107. The circle of law students included John Rufus himself and later Severus of Antioch.

88. *Vita Petri Iberi,* 124.

89. On this phase of non-Chalceodonian organization see W. H. C. Frend, "Severus of Antioch and the Monophysite Hierarchy," *OCA* 195 (1972): 261–275.

90. John of Ephesus, *Lives of the Eastern Saints* 49, ed. and trans., E. W. Brooks, PO 18 (Paris: Firmin-Didot, 1924), p. 514.

91. John of Ephesus, *Lives* 49, pp. 522 and 519, respectively. The number 170,000 is surely exaggerated.

92. John of Ephesus, *Lives* 24, p. 521.

93. Severus of Antioch, *Sixth Book of the Select Letters of Severus of Antioch,* 5.14, ed. and trans. E. W. Brooks (London: Williams and Norgate, 1904), II, pp. 345–350.

94. John of Ephesus, *Lives* 25, p. 529.

95. Ibid., p. 534. For John of Ephesus's account of the refugee community in Constantinople and the protective role of Theodora see also *Lives* 47, pp. 676–684.

96. For one of the best examples of the spiritual leadership of a nonordained monk see the biography of Thomas the Armenian, John of Ephesus, *Lives* 21, PO 17, pp. 283–298.

97. John of Ephesus, *Lives* 25, pp. 526–527.

98. On Severus see the chapter on the five patriarchs in John of Ephesus, *Lives* 48, pp. 684–688. The two *Lives* of Severus were originally written in Greek but have survived only in Syriac translation. See *Vita Severi* (Zacharias Rhetor), "*Vie de Sévère, Patriarche d'Antioche 512–518* par Zacharie le scholastique," ed. and trans. M.-A. Kugener, PO 2 (Paris: Firmin-Didot, 1907), pp. 7–115, and *Vita Severi* (John of Beith-Aphthonia), "*Vie de Sévère* par Jean de Beith-Aphthonia," ed. and trans. M.-A. Kugener, PO 2, pp. 204–264. The former was the work of a lawyer and friend of Severus; the latter

was written by John, hegumen of the monastery of Beith-Aphthonia in Syria. For an overview of Severus's career see Frend, *Rise of the Monophysite Movement,* pp. 201–220, and idem, "Severus and the Monophysite Hierarchy," pp. 261–275. For the representation of Severus in the *Life of Sabas* see Cyril, *Lives,* 148.20–152.15 and 154.24–155.11.

99. Severus, *Sixth Book of Select Letters* 2, 5.11, p. 328.

100. See Zacharias Rhetor, *Vita Severi:* Kugener, PO 2, p. 78. Peter's monastic vocation is also prominent in John of Beith-Aphthonia's discussion of his influence, *Vita Severi:* Kugener, PO 2, pp. 218–223.

101. John of Ephesus, *Lives,* p. 685. For Severus's involvment in administering the churches during this period see also Frend, "Severus and the Monophysite Hierarchy," pp. 268–275.

102. See Frend, *Rise of the Monophysite Movement,* pp. 208–211.

103. Zacharias Rhetor, *Vita Severi:* Kugener, PO 2, p. 13; John of Beith-Aphthonia, *Vita Severi:* Kugener, PO 2, pp. 215–218.

104. For example, Severus of Antioch, *Sixth Book of Select Letters,* I.1, pp. 9–10; I.2, pp. 13–15; II.3, pp. 220–221; V.1, p. 276.

105. Harvey, *Asceticism and Society,* pp. 135–145.

106. Carl Laga, ed., *Eustratii Presbyteri Vita Eutychii Patriarchae Constantinopolitani,* Corpus Christianorum, Series Graeca 25 (Turnhout: Brepols, 1992); also PG 86.2.2273–2389. (I cite line numbers from Laga.) There is no modern translation of this work, but Averil Cameron has indicated in several footnotes that an English translation and commentary are in process.

107. On the importance of this work for the Fifth Ecumenical Council, for which it is the major literary source, see Averil Cameron, "Eustratius' *Life* of the Patriarch Eutychius and the Fifth Ecumenical Council," in J. Chrysostomides, ed., *Kathēgētria: Essays Presented to Joan Hussey for her 80th Birthday* (Camberley: Porphyrogenitus, 1988), pp. 225–247. See also Paul Van den Ven, "L'Accession de Jean le Scholastique au siège patriarcal de Constantinople en 565," *Byzantion* 35 (1965): 320–352.

108. For references to Eutychius's career outside Eustratius's Life, see the ecclesiastical history of Evagrius Scholasticus, *HE* 4.38, 5.16 and 18, and the non-Chalcedonian history of John of Ephesus, *HE* 2.36, 51; 3.15, 17f.; 2.40, 52; and 3.19. The former is relatively neutral, but the latter has nothing positive to say about Eutychius. Another version of Eutychius's career is offered in Paul the Silentiary's encomium of the patriarch in classicizing Greek hexameters, recited on the occasion of the rededication of St. Sophia in 562. See Mary Whitby, "Eutychius, Patriarch of Constantinople: An Epic Holy Man," in Michael Whitby et al., eds., *Homo Viator: Classical Essays for John Bramble* (Bristol: Classical Press, 1987), pp. 297–308.

109. *Vita Eutychii,* 322–513. On Eutychius's family see 162–197; for his education, 198–321.

110. *Vita Eutychii,* 613–638. Cf. Evagrius, *HE* 4.38, for a very similar rendering of this episode.

111. Aphthartodocetism was the theory proposed by Julian of Halicarnassus that Christ's body was always incorruptible *(aphthartos)* and impassible. For Eutychius's opposition to this doctrine and consequent arrest, deposition, banishment, and condemnation, see *Vita Eutychii,* 912–1145. On this affair see also Van den Ven, "L'Accession de Jean le Scholastique," especially pp. 324–328, and Cameron, "Eustratius' *Life,*" pp. 233–246.

112. For events leading up to Eutychius's return see *Vita Eutychii,* 1780–1952. For the comparison of his return from exile with that of Athanasius, see 2049–2070.

113. For an overview of the Council and its failures see Herrin, *Formation of Christendom,* pp. 119–127.

114. *Vita Eutychii,* 2449–2454. This passage is cited and Eustratius's approach to authority discussed in Averil Cameron, "Models of the Past in the Late Sixth Century: The Life of Patriarch Eutychius," in Graeme Clarke, ed., *Reading the Past in Late Antiquity* (Rushcutters Bay: Australian National University Press, 1990), pp. 205–223; here p. 216.

115. *Vita Eutychii,* 2740–2759. Compare GNaz, Oration 43.81. Eustratius cites the entire chapter verbatim except for the replacement of Gregory's *ekeinou* (referring to Basil) with *tou neou Basileiou,* i.e., Eutychius. The citation of "the great Basil" in the prologue (20–23) is from *De fide.* Cameron, "Eustratius' *Life,*" p. 227, comments that "Eustratius was well read in the Cappadocians, of whom Basil was his hero." Laga's index of sources (pp. 102–104) makes this abundantly clear. Eustratius's author of choice was Gregory Nazianzen, and Laga lists no fewer than thirteen citations of Oration 43, the panegyric of Basil.

116. Three of the four explicit references to Athanasius are based on Nazianen's Oration 21. See lines 2051–2063, 2298–2311, 2311–2319, where Eutychius is dubbed "the new Athanasius." In his index, 102, Laga lists twelve citations of this oration in Eustratius's Life.

117. *Vita Eutychii,* 317–320; 445–450. Though there is no specific quotation, the wording as well as the ideas recall Nazianzen's description of Basil, who "embraced the desert with Elijah and John" (Oration 43.29, lines 9–10).

118. For his entry into the monastery in Amasea see *Vita Eutychii,* 451–459; for his position as catholicos, 499f.

119. *Vita Eutychii,* 578–595; also 658–687.

120. For Eustratius's exposition of this scheme at the moment of Eutychius's patriarchal ascent see *Vita Eutychii,* 708–751. In his index of names in the

Vita Eutychii, Laga, p. 94, lists eight references to Moses, who appears second only to Basil.

121. *Vita Eutychii,* 2432–2445. The specific citation is in 2437–2438.

122. Only 134 of 2,831 lines—i.e., less than 5 percent of the *Life,* is devoted to the Council: *Vita Eutychii,* 777–911. In contrast, 577 lines (*Vita Eutychii,* 1202–1779) recount Eutychius's miracles during his monastic exile in Amasea. This does not include the later account of miracles on his reinstitution as patriarch (2294–2419).

123. See *Vita Eutychii,* 533–751, for the miraculous events leading up to Eutychius's presence in Constantinople. The phrase "obscure monk" is from Cameron, "Models of the Past," p. 210.

124. *Vita Eutychii,* 184–192.

125. For Eustratius's apologetic intent see especially *Vita Eutychii,* 1902f. On his careful crafting of the *Life* in light of Eutychius's involvement in theological controversies see Van den Ven, "L'Accession de Jean le Scholastique," and Cameron, "Eustratius' *Life.*"

126. On Eustratius's style see Averil Cameron, *Christianity and the Rhetoric of Empire: The Development of Christian Discourse* (Berkeley: University of California Press, 1991), pp. 204–209; also Anna Wilson, "Biblical Imagery in Eustratios's Life," pp. 303–309.

127. See Hippolyte Delehaye, *Les passions des martyrs et les genres littéraires* (Brussels: Société des Bollandistes, 1966), especially pp. 136 and 312.

128. Hippolyte Delehaye, *L'Ancienne hagiographie: Les sources—Les premiers modèles—La formation des genres,* Conférences prononcées au Collège de France en 1935 par Hippolyte Delehaye, Subsidia Hagiographica no. 73 (Brussels: Société des Bollandistes, 1991), p. 21.

129. For discussion of the role of texts in conferring identities see Teresa M. Shaw, "*Askesis* and the Appearance of Holiness," *JECS* 6/3 (1998): 485–499; M. Douglas, *How Institutions Think* (London: Routledge, 1986), pp. 100–102.

Epilogue

1. For example, Peter L'Huillier, "Episcopal Celibacy in the Orthodox Tradition," *SVQR* 35/2–3 (1991), though he does at least mention the earlier background; Peter Charanis, "The Monk as an Element in Byzantine Society," *DOP* 25 (1971): 84; J.-L. Van Dieten, *Geschichte der Patriarchen von Sergios I. bis Johannes VII: (610–715)* (Amsterdam, 1972), pp. 161f.; J. F. Haldon, *Byzantium in the Seventh Century* (Cambridge: Cambridge University Press, 1990), p. 296; and especially Louis Bréhier, *Le monde byzantin,* 2: *Les institutions de l'empire byzantin* (Paris: Éditions Albin Michel, 1949),

pp. 511–512. Surprisingly, many excellent discussions of posticonoclast monasticism do not even mention its connection to the recruitment of bishops.

2. Bréhier, *Le monde byzantin*, 2, p. 483. For a laudatory perspective on the entry of monks into high ecclesiastical positions in the aftermath of Iconoclasm see R. P. J. Pargoire, *L'Église byzantine de 527 à 847* (Paris: Librairie Victor LeCoffre, 1923), pp. 300–303.

3. This oversimplified scenario is particularly evident in older treatments of Iconoclasm like Pargoire, *L'Église byzantine*, pp. 300–310; see also P. van den Ven, "La patristique et l'hagiographie au Concile de Nicée de 787," *Byzantion* 25–27/1 (1955–57): 331–332. For an opposing view of monks in the context of First Iconoclasm and its aftermath see M. F. Auzépy, "La place des moines à Nicée II (787)," *Byzantion* 58 (1988): 5–21. See also the more balanced treatment of Joan Hussey, *The Orthodox Church in the Byzantine Empire* (Oxford: Clarendon, 1986), pp. 38–44, 65–68.

4. On tension between bishops and holy men in the period leading up to Iconoclasm see Peter Brown, "A Dark Age Crisis: Aspects of the Iconoclastic Controversy," in *Society and the Holy in Late Antiquity* (Berkeley: University of California Press, 1982), especially pp. 280–281, 294–301.

5. For a survey of relevant seventh-century developments see Haldon, *Byzantium in the Seventh Century*, chap. 3. On the status and functions of bishops in this context see also Gilbert Dagron, "Le Christianisme dans la ville byzantine," *DOP* 31 (1977): 19–23; and especially Friedhelm Winkelmann, "Kirche und Gesellschaft in Byzanz vom Ende des 6. bis zum Beginn des 8. Jahrunderts," *KLIO* 59 (1977): 477–489, reprinted in idem, *Studien zu Konstantin dem Grossen und zur byzantinischen Kirchengeschichte: Ausgewählte Aufsätze* (Birmingham: Center for Byzantine, Ottoman and Modern Greek Studies, 1993).

6. Peter Hatlie, "Spiritual Authority and Monasticism in Constantinople during the Dark Ages (650–800)," in Jan Willem Drijvers and John W. Watt, eds., *Portraits of Spiritual Authority: Religious Power in Early Christianity, Byzantium and the Christian Orient* (Leiden: Brill, 1999), p. 215. Hatlie's essay is a welcome addition to the few studies on monks or spiritual authority during this period.

7. The epithet *episkotos,* a play on the word *episkopos* (bishop), is used three times in this vita. See Marie-France Auzépy, ed. and trans., *La vie d'Étienne le Jeune par Étienne le Diacre,* Birmingham Byzantine and Ottoman Monographs 3 (Aldershot: Variorum, 1997), 127.11, 127.16, 142.6.

8. See especially Theodore's Letter 9 to his brother Joseph, Archbishop of Thessalonica, PG 99, 1140. See also Letters 267, 269, 281 in *Theodori*

Studitae Epistulae, Corpus fontium historiae Byzantinae 31/2, ed. Georgios Fatouros (New York: DeGruyter, 1992), pp. 394–395, 397–399, 421–422.

9. Although the rhetorical *topoi,* idealized portraits, and didactic intent of saints' Lives complicate their use for the historian, Byzantine hagiographical texts have proven invaluable as sources on social and religious attitudes and ideals. See E. Patlagean, "Ancienne hagiographie byzantine et histoire sociale," *Annales ESC* 23 (1968): 104–124, and idem, "Sainteté et pouvoir," in Sergei Hackel, ed., *The Byzantine Saint* (London: Fellowship of St. Alban and St. Sergius, 1981); also F. Halkin, "L'Hagiographie byzantine au service de l'histoire," *Proceedings of the 13th International Congress of Byzantine Studies* (New York: Oxford University Press, 1967), pp. 345–354.
   On the background to Iconoclasm see E. Kitzinger, "The Cult of Icons before Iconoclasm," *DOP* 8 (1954): 83–150; Peter Brown, "Dark Age Crisis"; J. F. Haldon, "Some Remarks on the Background to the Iconoclast Controversies," *Byzantinoslavica* 38 (1977): 161–184; and for a response to Brown and a discussion of theological issues, P. Henry, "What Was the Iconoclast Controversy About?" *CH* 45 (1976): 16–31. See, too, the essays collected in A. Bryer and J. Herrin, eds., *Iconoclasm* (Birmingham: Center for Byzantine Studies, 1977). For a survey of events see Hussey, *Orthodox Church,* pp. 30–68.

10. Milton V. Anastos, "The Ethical Theory of Images Formulated by the Iconoclasts in 754 and 815," *DOP* 8 (1954): 153–160, has underscored the importance for iconoclasts of the Lives of saints.

11. For a full list and discussion of the patristic citations (including Greek texts) that make up the florilegium see Anastos, "Ethical Theory of Images." For the text cited from Basil in the iconoclastic floriglegium of 754, see Mansi 13, 300AB.

12. Ihor Ševčenko, "Hagiography of the Iconoclast Period," in idem, *Ideology, Letters and Culture in the Byzantine World* (London: Variorum, 1982), V.1–42; originally published in Bryer and Herrin, eds., *Iconoclasm,* pp. 113–129. A similar point about the relative paucity of hagiographical texts from the period of Iconoclasm itself has been made by Alice-Mary Talbot, ed., *Byzantine Defenders of Images: Eight Saints' Lives in English Translation* (Washington, D.C.: Dumbarton Oaks, 1998), pp. xvi–xvii.

13. The *Life of George of Amastris* (hereafter *VGA*) is edited with a Russian translation in V. G. Vasil'evskij, *Trudy* 2 (St. Petersburg, 1915), pp. 1–71. (I cite section numbers followed by page and line numbers.) See http://www.byzantine.nd.edu/Amastris.pdf. for an English translation.

14. That Ignatius had once been an iconoclast, most likely an iconoclast met-

ropolitan, is especially evident in the epilogue to his vita of Patriarch Nikephoros, written after 842. See Carl DeBoor, ed., *Bibliotheca hagiographicae graecae* (= BHG) no. 1335, 215.13–217.36, and Elizabeth A. Fisher's English translation in Talbot, ed., *Byzantine Defenders of Images*, pp. 41–142; 138–142 for the epilogue. Extensive evidence of Ignatius's iconoclast phase and authorship of *VGA* is presented by Ševčenko, "Hagiography," especially pp. 13–17. Another reason for the editor's oversight with regard to the iconoclastic nature of the text, he suggests, is that George of Amastris himself was an iconodule.

15. See Stephanos Efthymiadis, "On the Hagiographical Work of Ignatius the Deacon," *JÖB* 41 (1991): 73–83, who confirms Ševčenko's arguments about the dating and noniconodule character of *VGA*. See also Warren Treadgold, *The Byzantine Revival* (Stanford: Stanford University Press, 1988), pp. 375–376, 457 n. 496.

16. See Marie-France Auzépy, "L'Analyse littéraire et l'historien: L'exemple des vies de saints iconoclastes," *Byzantinoslavica* 53 (1992): 57–67. The eucharistic theology of *VGA* has been analyzed by Stefanos Alexopoulos, "The Life of George of Amastris as a Source of Liturgical Information: 'Private' Liturgy and Eucharistic Doctrine," paper presented at the Byzantine Studies Conference, University of Notre Dame, 2001. See also Ševčenko, "Hagiography," for points of comparison.

17. *VGA* 2, 3.16–17.

18. For his rejection of academic pursuits see *VGA* 8, 14.7–11. Compare GNaz, Oration 43.10, lines 20–31. For his renunciations, *VGA* 8–11, pp. 13–19; for the reference to the biblical saints, p. 17. This is the first of four comparisons of George with Moses. For the other three analogies see *VGA* 11 (19.21), 26 (40.9–11), and 38 (58.10).

19. *VGA* 14, 25.4–5. For his ascetic rigor and study of Scripture at Bonyssa see *VGA* 12–13, 21–25.

20. *VGA* 15, 25.7–10.

21. *VGA* 16, 27.3–5. Auzépy, "L'Analyse littéraire," p. 62, cites this passage alone to demonstrate that the social and collective notion of holiness in the *Life of George* is contradictory to the ascetic ideal, ignoring the ensuing response of the monk to the envoys' appeal.

22. *VGA* 17, 28.3–5.

23. *VGA* 23, 36.5–8.

24. *VGA* 35, 55–56.

25. The monastic chroniclers of the period emphasize Nicephorus's hypocrisy and cupidity and recount his antimonastic acts. See *The Chronicle of Theophanes Confessor*, trans. Cyril Mango and Roger Scott (Oxford: Claren-

don, 1997). See also, however, the more balanced treatment of Nicephorus's reign in Treadgold, *Byzantine Revival,* pp. 127–195.

26. For these specific miracles see *VGA* 25, 36, 31–32, and 41, respectively.

27. Ševčenko, "Hagiography," p. 14. See also his appendix, pp. 24–27, where he lists several borrowings from Nazianzen's oration on Basil. Borrowings from Gregory's Oration 43 in *VGA* were analyzed in 1895 by the Russian scholar P. Nikitin, "O nekotorych grečeskych tekstach žitij svjatych," *Zapiski Imp. Akademii Nauk po istor.-filol. otdeleniju,* 8th ser., I, 1 (1895), pp. 27–51. He listed some thirty-five parallel passages, though I have found additional reminiscences.

28. *VGA* 8, 14.7–11. Cf. GNaz, Oration 43.10, lines 29–31.

29. For the direct borrowings compare *VGA* 10, 18.16–19.1 with GNaz, Oration 43.29, and *VGA* 11, 19.13 with Oration 43.12, line 8. For comparisons with biblical and classical heroes see *VGA* 27, 41.14–42.4; cf. Oration 43.3, lines 17–19.

30. Compare *VGA* 30, 46–47, and GNaz, Oration 43.33.

31. See BHG 1335 147.18–149.2; Talbot, ed., *Byzantine Defenders of Images,* pp. 50–52.

32. Anthony I Cassimatas (821–837) and John VII the Grammarian (837–843). See S. Gero, "Byzantine Iconoclasm and Monachomachy," *JEH* 28 (1977): 241–248; also Haldon, "Iconoclast Controversies," p. 161f. Both articles provide evidence to counter the popular notion that "iconomachy in action is monachomachy."

33. See Wolfgang Lackner, "Die Gestalt des Heiligen in der byzantinischen Hagiographie des 9. und 10. Jahrhunderts," in *The 17th International Byzantine Congress: Major Papers* (New Rochelle, N.Y.: Caratzas, 1986), p. 522. In the same volume Lennart Rydén, "New Forms of Hagiography: Heroes and Saints," pp. 537–551, counts at least seventy Lives written in the ninth and tenth centuries.

34. Lackner, "Die Gestalt des Heiligen," pp. 526–527.

35. Methodius (843–847), Ignatius (847–858), Antonios Kauleas (893–901), and Euthymius (907–912) had monastic backgrounds. Nicephorus (806–815) lived a life of ascetic withdrawal and became a monk on his rise to the patriarchal dignity. Only Tarasius (786–815) had been a layman and administrator in the imperial service.

36. François Halkin, ed., *Hagiologie byzantine,* BHG 2452, Subsidia hagiographica 71 (Brussels: Société des Bollandistes, 1986), p. 174. In addition to this shorter biography of Theophylact, written in the late ninth or early tenth century, a fuller Life, published by Albert Vogt (BHG 2451), was composed c. 870.

37. See Halkin, ed., *Hagiologie byzantine,* BHG 2452, p. 176 for a graphic illustration of his loving care for the lame.

38. For the Lives of Peter of Argos and Nicephorus of Miletus see BHG 1504 and BHG 1338, respectively. Along with Theophylact of Nicomedia they are included and briefly described in Lackner's list of new, more active bishops that characterized this period of hagiography. They also appear in the discussion of "monastic founders" in Rosemary Morris, *Monks and Laymen in Byzantium, 843–1118* (Cambridge: Cambridge University Press, 1995), especially pp. 76–79.

39. Claudia Rapp, "Byzantine Hagiographers as Antiquarians, Seventh to Tenth Centuries," in *Bosphorus: Essays in Honor of Cyril Mango,* ed. Stephanos Efthymiadis et al., Byzantinische Forschungen 21 (Amerstdam: Adolf M. Hakkert, 1995), pp. 31–44. Hagiographic *metaphraseis* did not end with the work of Symeon, for saints' Lives were recast for the consumption of late Byzantine readers as well. See A.-M. Talbot, "Old Wine in New Bottles: The Rewriting of Saints' Lives in the Palaeologan Period," in *The Twilight of Byzantium: Aspects of Cultural and Religious History in the Late Byzantine Empire,* ed. S. Ćurčić and D. Mouriki (Princeton: Princeton University Press, 1991), pp. 15–26.

40. See PG 105, 488–574. On Nicetas and his works see H. G. Beck, *Kirche und theologische Literatur im Byzantinischen Reich* (Munich, 1959), pp. 548–549, and A. Solignac, *Dictionnaire de Spiritualité* 11 (Paris: Beauchesne, 1982), pp. 221–224.

41. James John Rizzo, ed. and trans., *The Encomium of Gregory Nazianzen by Nicetas the Paphlagonian,* Subsidia Hagiographica 58 (Brussels: Société des Bollandistes, 1976). On Nicetas's choice and use of sources see pp. 7–18.

42. The letter is from Arethas, the irascible archbishop of Caesarea, a bibliophile famed for his copying of manuscripts. See L. G. Westerink, ed., *Arethae Scripta Minora* I (Leipzig, 1968), pp. 267–270.

43. See especially *Encomium of Gregory Nazianzen* 1.27–31.

44. *Encomium of Gregory Nazianzen* 8.61–62: Rizzo, p. 93. See also 5.35–45 and 8.27–32 on Gregory's preparation with Basil in the desert.

45. This comparison is the subject of chap. 20, filling 209 lines in Rizzo's edition.

46. *Encomium of Gregory Nazianzen,* 20.60–75: Rizzo, p. 112.

47. For an overview of Byzantine missionary activity in the ninth and tenth centuries see Gilbert Dagron, "Missions, chrétienté et orthodoxie," in Gilbert Dagron et al., eds., *Évêques, moines et empereurs (610–1054)* (Paris: Desclée, 1993), pp. 216–240, especially 216–226 for the Slavic lands.

48. On the impact of the Byzantine ascetic tradition and specific Slavic monks and monasteries in the ecclesiastical and cultural life of eastern Europe see

Dimitri Obolensky, *The Byzantine Commonwealth: Eastern Europe, 500–1453* (Crestwood, N.Y.: St. Vladimir's Seminary Press, 1971), pp. 377–404.

49. Best on Sava in English is Dimitri Obolensky, "Sava of Serbia," in *Six Byzantine Portraits* (Oxford: Clarendon, 1988), pp. 115–172; see p. 121 for the comparison with Alexander the Great. In the vast bibliography of Serbian scholarship on the saint, most valuable is the collection of essays titled *Sava Nemanjić—Sveti Sava: Istorija i predanje* (Sava Nemanjić—Saint Sava: History and Tradition), ed. V. Djurić (Belgrade: Serbian Academy of Sciences and Arts, 1979).

   For the history of medieval Serbia, and particularly on Sava's own political role, see John V. Fine, Jr., *The Late Medieval Balkans: A Critical Survey from the Late Twelfth Century to the Ottoman Conquest* (Ann Arbor: University of Michigan Press, 1987), chaps. 1–3. On the church in medieval Serbia see Đjoko Slijepcević, *Istorija srpske pravoslavne crkve* (History of the Serbian Orthodox Church), 1 (Munich, 1962), especially pp. 56–141.

50. The controversy that arose with the sanctioning of a self-governing Serbian church is discussed briefly by Obolensky, "Sava of Serbia," pp. 157–161, and more fully in my unpublished paper, "The Attainment of Serbian Autocephaly: Its Significance in Byzantine History and Orthodox Canon Law," presented at the Byzantine Studies Conference, Princeton, 1993.

51. Domentijan, *Život svetoga Simeuna i svetoga Save,* ed. Dj. Daničić (Belgrade, 1865), and Teodosije Hilandarac, *Život svetoga Save,* ed. Dj. Daničić (Belgrade, 1860; repr. 1973). There are also modern Serbian translations of these Old Slavonic texts: Domentijan, *Životi svetoga Save i svetoga Simeona,* trans. Lazar Mirković (Belgrade: Srpska Književna Zadruga, 1938); Teodosije Hilandarac, *Žitije svetog Save,* trans. Lazar Mirković (Belgrade: Srpska Književna Zadruga, 1984). Ensuing references cite these two Serbian translations. For a comparison of the two accounts see Dimitrije Bogdanović's preface to Mirković's translation of Teodosije, especially pp. xxx–xxxii. On distinctive features of the medieval Serbian hagiographic genre, including some discussion of these Lives of Sava see H. Birnbaum, "Byzantine Tradition Transformed: The Old Serbian *Vita,*" in H. Birnbaum and S. Vyronis, eds., *Aspects of the Balkans: Continuity and Change* (The Hague: Mouton, 1972), pp. 243–280.

52. Teodosije, p. 3.

53. Teodosije, p. 95.

54. In Bulgaria and Serbia in the twelfth to fifteenth centuries schools were primarily monastic, focusing on the education of monks and the study of religious texts. See Fine, *Late Medieval Balkans,* pp. 118, 436, 445–446.

55. The next example in Serbia was the youngest son of Stefan Nemanjić. He

served as archbishop of Serbia from 1263 to 1270. Fine, *Late Medieval Balkans,* pp. 135–136.

56. Starting with Stefan Nemanja it became the practice or duty of Serbian rulers to found at least one major monastery for the salvation of their souls. On these magnificent royal monasteries (known as *zadužbine,* literally "obligations") see Obolensky, *Byzantine Commonwealth,* pp. 388–389. On the importance of imperial patronage and the foundation of monasteries in the portrayals of orthodox rulers in post-iconoclastic Byzantium see Morris, *Monks and Laymen,* p. 19. For examples of these expensive building and decorating projects see Domentijan, pp. 59–62, 67, 83–84, 102–103; Teodosije, pp. 43, 51, 66–67, 97, 135.

57. Domentijan, pp. 123, 126; Teodosije, pp. 129–130, 133, 135. The monks were from Studenica and Žiča monasteries. Both Lives also speak of Sava traveling through the land visiting monasteries, supervising, and instructing monks; for example, Teodosije, pp. 146, 166–167.

58. Domentijan, pp. 135–136; Teodosije, pp. 145–146.

59. Domentijan, p. 177; Teodosije, p. 172.

60. On Sava's continued ascetic rigors in Serbia see especially Teodosije, p. 95.

61. Teodosije, p. 27; for a similar distribution of wealth, p. 61. Cf. Domentijan, p. 40. On Byzantine monks as lovers of the poor *(philotheoi)* and the special role of monasticism in society see Demetrios Constantelos, *Byzantine Philanthropy and Social Welfare,* 2nd (rev.) ed. (New Rochelle, N.Y.: Aristide D. Caratzas, 1991), pp. 75–88.

62. Teodosije, p. 90. Domentijan's version, pp. 90–92, speaks more broadly of Nemanja as a model of faith and good works.

63. See Dimitrije Bogdanović's comment in Teodosije, *Žitije Svetog Save,* p. 272, referring to Teodosije, p. 167. See also pp. 68–69. Sava's posthumous miracles included the healing of multitudes of the sick, blind, deaf, and lame.

64. Teodosije, p. 100.

65. Domentijan, pp. 139–146; Teodosije, pp. 147–153. The anti-Latin bias appears only in Teodosije's fourteenth-century *Life.* Writing toward the middle of the thirteenth century, Domentijan expressed no hostility toward Rome. A number of Serbian bishoprics at this time were still in the hands of Latin prelates.

66. Domentijan, pp. 146–149; Teodosije, pp. 154–158.

67. Cited in Ivan Dujčev, "Les rapports hagiographiques entre Byzance et les Slaves," *Proceedings of the XIIIth International Congress,* p. 365.

68. See Robert Browning, "Serbian Literature," *Oxford Dictionary of Byzantium,* 3, pp. 1874–1875, for comments on Byzantine sources of medieval Serbian vitae. Of some value on sources of these Lives are Alois Schmaus, "Die

literarhistorische Problematik von Domentijans Sava-Vita," in *Slawistische Studien zum V. Internationalen Slawistenkongress in Sofia 1963*, Opera Slavica 4, ed. Maximilian Braun and Erwin Koschmieder (Göttingen: Vandenhoeck and Ruprecht, 1963), pp. 121–142, and Cornelia Müller-Landau, *Studien zum Stil der Sava-Vita Teodosijes* (Munich: Verlag Otto Sagner, 1972). There has been virtually no discussion of patristic influences.

69. This is particularly evident in the opening pages of both Lives. See Domentijan, pp. 27–28, and Teodosije, pp. 3–4.

70. Obolensky, *Byzantine Commonwealth,* pp. 381–382. Other influential models for Slavic monasticism were the *Historia monachorum,* the *Historia Lausiaca,* and the *Pratum spirituale* of John Moschus for sustaining the anchoritic life; also the monastery of Studios in Constantinople, founded by St. Theodore the Studite in the ninth century and largely based on earlier Basilian cenobitic organization.

71. For example, Teodosije, pp. 101 and 144. Cf. GNaz, Oration 43, 29.10 and 74.1–3.

72. Teodosije, p. 128. Cf. GNaz, Oration 43.27, lines 7–10. The parallel is almost exact.

73. For example, Domentijan, p. 194. Sava's *Nomocanon,* known as the *Kormčaja Knjiga* (Book of the Pilot) to Slavs, also served as the basic constitution of the Bulgarian and Russian churches. See Obolensky, "Sava of Serbia," pp. 154–155, on Sava's role in its compilation; on its broader influence, idem, *Byzantine Commonwealth,* pp. 407–408, 410–413.

74. Teodosije, pp. 101 and 176.

75. Domentijan, pp. 192–200.

76. See Domentijan, pp. 193–194 and 195–196, respectively. See also Teodosije, p. 158.

77. Domentijan, p. 192. The title *bogovidac* occurs more than thirty times in this *synkrisis.* Even after this formal Moses-*synkrisis* the comparison with Moses as a *bogovidac* is repeated in the description of the journey to Trnovo to recover Sava's relics. See Domentijan, p. 208.

78. Dagron, *Évêques, moines et empereurs,* p. 247, cites the *Life of Leontios* (BHG 985) as an example.

79. See Dagron, *Évêques, moines et empereurs,* pp. 245–250.

80. J. Hausherr and G. Horn, eds. and trans., *Un grand mystique byzantin: Vie de Syméon le Nouveau Théologien (949–1022) par Nicétas Stéthatos,* Orientalia Christiana XII/45 (Rome: Pontificium Institutum Orientalium Studiorum, 1928).

81. In many instances conventional *topoi* of Byzantine saints' Lives reflected the actual state of affairs. See Morris, *Monks and Laymen,* pp. 75–80, who

refers to the *Life of Symeon* as a case in point. On Symeon's life see also H. J. M. Turner, *Symeon the New Theologian and Spiritual Fatherhood,* Byzantina Neerlandica 11 (Leiden: Brill, 1990), especially pp. 16–36.

82. *Life of Symeon the New Theologian,* 72: Hausherr and Horn, p. 98. Symeon wrote a Life of his mentor, composed hymns in his honor, and had his image painted on icons for veneration.

83. *Life of Symeon the New Theologian,* 103: Hausherr and Horn, p. 142.

84. For what follows see especially Turner, *Symeon and Spiritual Fatherhood;* Morris, *Monks and Laymen,* pp. 90–102; Dagron, *Évêques, moines et empereurs,* pp. 323–326, and Jean Darrouzès, "Introduction," in *Syméon le Nouveau Théologien: Traités théologiques et éthiques,* trans. Darrouzès, SC 122 (Paris: Éditions du cerf, 1966), 1, especially pp. 13–37. On Symeon's theology see also Archbishop Basil Krivocheine, *In the Light of Christ: St. Symeon the New Theologian (949–1022),* trans. Anthony P. Gythiel (Crestwood, N.Y.: St. Vladimir's Seminary Press, 1986).

85. For Symeon's description of his first vision see Discourse XXII, 89–105, in *Symeon the New Theologian: The Discourses,* trans. C. J. de Catanzaro (New York: Paulist Press, 1980), pp. 245–246. See also *Life of Symeon the New Theologian,* 30–31: Hausherr and Horn, pp. 40–42.

86. *Life of Symeon the New Theologian,* 71: Hausherr and Horn, p. 96.

87. For Symeon's fullest exposition of this doctrine see *Traité éthique* (= *Eth*) V. The vision of God is also prominent in *Discourses* 28, 32, and 33, and is a continual theme of Symeon's *Hymns.*

88. *Eth* V, 523–538; Darrouzès 2, pp. 116–118.

89. *Eth* VI, 434–435; Darrouzès 2, pp. 151–152.

90. Turner, *Symeon and Spiritual Fatherhood,* p. 56, citing Symeon's Epistle 1, or *Letter on Confession,* published in Karl Holl, *Enthusiasmus und Busssgewalt beim griechischen Mönchtum: Eine Studie zu Symeon dem Neuen Theologen* (Leipzig, 1898; repr. 1969), pp. 110–127. For an illuminating discussion of Symeon's *Letter on Confession,* see Alexander Golitzin, "Hierarchy versus Anarchy? Dionysius Areopagita, Symeon the New Theologian, and Nicetas Stethatos," in Bradley Nassif, ed., *New Perspectives on Historical Theology* (Grand Rapids, Mich.: Eerdmans, 1996), pp. 250–276.

91. See Morris, *Monks and Laymen,* p, 94; also pp. 100–101, for some specific relationships between monks and rulers or aristocratic circles including the circle around Symeon.

92. *Life of Symeon the New Theologian,* 29–30; Hausherr and Horn, pp. 40–42. See also Discourse IV.8–21: de Catanzaro, p. 70, where Symeon instructed laymen and monks always to communicate with tears, a practice he himself observed throughout his life. See Dagron's comments on this passage,

Évêques, moines et empereurs, p. 322. Regarding ordination and sacraments in Symeon's thought see also Darrouzès, "Introduction," pp. 25–29.

93. *Eth* XV, 68–73. This particular progression is strongly reminiscent of Nazianzen's use of the example of Moses in Orations 2, 20, and 28. See also XV, 169–187. See Turner, *Symeon and Spiritual Fatherhood,* pp. 46–49, on Symeon's extensive use of the writings of Nazianzen, the Father he quotes or refers to more than any other.

94. Symeon's strongest opposition came from the official court theologian of his day, Archbishop Stephen of Nicomedia. The conflict between them is presented by Nicetas, *Life of Symeon the New Theologian,* especially 74–99; Hausherr and Horn, pp. 100–138. See also Hausherr's introduction, pp. li–lvi, and Turner, *Symeon and Spiritual Fatherhood,* pp. 11 and 33f. For Symeon's likeness to and distinction from neo-Messalian and other "enthusiastic" sects of his day that were officially denounced see Dagron, *Évêques, moines et empereurs,* pp. 327–328.

95. For an insightful discussion of what has often been regarded as a "paradoxical relationship" between Nicetas, Symeon, and Dionysius, see Golitzin, "Hierarchy versus Anarchy?"

96. Nicétas Stéthatos, *On the Hierarchy,* 36.6, in J. Darrouzès, ed., *Nicétas Stéthatos, Opuscules et lettres,* SC 81 (Paris: Éditions du cerf, 1961), p. 338. For the larger argument see 34–38: Darrouzès, pp. 334–342.

97. Nicétas Stéthatos, *On the Hierarchy,* 42–54: Darrouzès, pp. 342–344.

98. Regarding the roles and influence of Symeon and two other eleventh-century saints outside the monastic milieu see Rosemary Morris, "The Political Saint of the Eleventh Century," in Hackel, ed., *Byzantine Saint,* pp. 43–50. See Charanis, "The Monk as an Element in Byzantine Society," especially p. 85 and n. 161, for examples of emperors who befriended or sought counsel from monks.

99. Cited (with the Greek text) by Darrouzès, *Traités théologiques et éthiques,* 1, p. 34, and Dagron, *Évêques, moines et empereurs,* p. 326. Written between 1075 and 1078, Cecaumenus's *Strategicon* is an important text for the political and cultural history of Byzantium and the Balkans.

100. Dagron, *Évêques, moines et empereurs,* p. 320.

101. For the changing situation of monasticism during this period see the final chapter of Morris, *Monks and laymen,* pp. 267–295. On social, cultural, and ecclesiastical developments that prompted changes in perspective on holy men and monks see Paul Magdalino, "The Byzantine Holy Man in the Twelfth Century," in Hackel, ed., *Byzantine Saint,* pp. 51–66. In the same volume Ruth Macrides, "Saints and Sainthood in the Early Palaiologan Period," pp. 67–87, shows that negative attitudes toward the holy man were passed on to the thirteenth century as well.

102. Morris, "The Political Saint of the Eleventh Century," p. 50, associates this politicization with the new popularity of cenobitic monasticism as over against the individual holy man or wandering monk.

103. Magdalino, "Byzantine Holy Man," p. 65.

104. There is a vast bibliography on Palamas and the hesychast controversy. See especially John Meyendorff, *Byzantine Hesychasm* (London: Variorum, 1974), and idem, *Introduction à l'étude de Grégoire Palamas* (Paris, 1959). See also Hussey, *Orthodox Church*, pp. 259–60, regarding the unfortunate use of the label "hesychast" for this controversy.

105. On the significance of this passage of the Tome (PG 150, 1225–1236) see John Meyendorff, *The Byzantine Legacy in the Orthodox Church* (Crestwood, N.Y.: St. Vladimir's Seminary Press, 1982), pp. 212–213.

106. On monastic patriarchs of Constantinople from 705–1204 see Bréhier, *Le monde byzantin*, 2, pp. 483–484. On fourteenth-century monk-bishops who served as patriarchs see Hussey, *Orthodox Church*, p. 289.

107. See Meyendorff, "St. Basil, the Church, and Charismatic Leadership," in *Byzantine Legacy*, pp. 197–215.

108. Ibid., p. 213.

Frequently Cited Works

Bacht, Heinrich. "Die Rolle des orientalischen Mönchtums in den kirchen-politischen Auseinandersetzungen um Chalkedon (431–519)," in *Das Konzil von Chalkedon,* ed. Alois Grillmeier and Heinrich Bacht, vol. 2, pp. 193–314. Würzburg: Echter, 1953.

Bernardi, Jean. *La prédication des pères cappadociens: Le prédicateur et son auditoire.* Paris: Presses universitaires de France, 1968.

Brakke, David. *Athanasius and the Politics of Asceticism.* Oxford: Clarendon, 1995.

Bréhier, Louis. *Le monde byzantin, 2: Les institutions de l'empire byzantin.* Paris: Éditions Albin Michel, 1949.

Brown, Peter. *Power and Persuasion in Late Antiquity: Towards a Christian Empire.* Madison: University of Wisconsin Press, 1992.

———. "The Rise and Function of the Holy Man in Late Antiquity," in *Society and the Holy in Late Antiquity.* Berkeley: University of California Press, 1982, pp. 103–152. (Revised from *JRS* 61 (1971): 80–101.)

Chadwick, Henry. "The Role of the Christian Bishop in Ancient Society." Protocol Series of the Colloquies 35. Berkeley: Center for Hermeneutical Studies, 1980.

Chesnut, G. F. *The First Christian Histories: Eusebius, Socrates, Sozomen, Theodoret and Evagrius.* Macon, Ga.: Mercer University Press, 1986.

Chitty, Derwas J., *The Desert a City.* Crestwood, N.Y.: St. Vladimir's Seminary Press, 1966.

Clarke, Graeme, ed. *Reading the Past in Late Antiquity.* Ruschcutters Bay: Australian National University Press, 1990.

Dagron, Gilbert. "Les moines et la ville: Le monachisme à Constantinople jusqu'au Concile de Chalcédoine (451)." *Travaux et Mémoires* 4 (1970): 229–276.

Dagron, Gilbert, et al., eds., *Évêques, moines et empereurs (610–1054).* Histoire du christianisme 4. Paris: Desclée, 1993.

Daley, Brian, S. J. "Building a New City: The Cappadocian Fathers and the Rhetoric of Philanthropy." *JECS* 7/3 (1999): 431–461.

Drake, H. A. *Constantine and the Bishops: The Politics of Intolerance*. Baltimore: Johns Hopkins University Press, 2000.

Elm, Susanna. *"Virgins of God": The Making of Asceticism in Late Antiquity*. Oxford: Clarendon, 1994.

Fedwick, Paul Jonathan. *The Church and the Charisma of Leadership in Basil of Caesarea* Toronto: Pontifical Institute of Mediaeval Studies, 1979.

———, ed. *Basil of Caesarea: Christian, Humanist, Ascetic, a Sixteen-hundredth Anniversary Symposium*. 2 vols. Toronto: Pontifical Institute of Mediaeval Studies, 1981.

Gaudemet, Jean. *L'Église dans l'Empire Romain (IVe–Ve siècles)*. Histoire du droit et des institutions de l'église en Occident 3. Paris: Sirey, 1958.

Goehring, James. *Ascetics, Society and the Desert: Studies in Egyptian Monasticism*. Harrisburg, Pa.: Trinity International Press, 1999.

Gribomont, Jean. *Saint Basile, Évangile et Église: Mélanges*. 2 vols. Bégrolles-en-Mauges: Abbaye de Bellefontaine, 1984.

Jones, A. H. M. *Cities of the Eastern Roman Provinces*, 2nd ed. Oxford: Clarendon, 1971.

———. *The Later Roman Empire, A.D. 284–602*. 2 vols. Oxford: Clarendon, 1964; reprint, 1986.

Kelly, J. N. D. *Golden Mouth: The Story of John Chrysostom—Ascetic, Preacher, Bishop*. Ithaca: Cornell University Press, 1995.

Koschorke, Klaus. *Spuren der alten Liebe: Studien zum Kirchenbegriff des Basilius von Caesarea*. Paradosis 32. Freiburg: Universitätsverlag Freiburg Schweiz, 1991.

Lizzi, Rita. *Il potere episcopale nell'oriente romano: Rappresentazione ideologica e realtà politica (IV–V sec. d.C.)*. Rome: Edizioni dell'Ateneo, 1987.

Pouchet, Robert. *Basile le Grand et son univers d'amis d'après sa correspondance*. Studia Ephememeridis Augustinianum 36. Rome: Institutum Patristicum "Augustinianum," 1992.

Rapp, Claudia. "Comparison, Paradigm and the Case of Moses in Panegyric and Hagiography," in Mary Whitby, ed., *The Propaganda of Power: The Role of Panegyric in Late Antiquity*. Leiden: Brill, 1998.

———. "The Elite Status of Bishops in Late Antiquity in the Ecclesiastical, Spiritual and Social Context," *Arethusa* 33 (2000): 379–399.

Rousseau, Philip. *Basil of Caesarea*. Berkeley: University of California Press, 1994.

———. "The Spiritual Authority of the 'Monk-Bishop': Eastern Elements in Some Western Hagiography of the Fourth and Fifth Centuries." *JTS* n.s. 23 (1971): 380–419.

Sterk, Andrea. "On Basil, Moses, and the Model Bishop: The Cappadocian Legacy of Leadership." *CH* 67 (1998): 227–253.

Ueding, Leo. "Die Kanones von Chalkedon in ihrer Bedeutung für Mönchtum und Klerus," in *Das Konzil von Chalkedon,* ed. Alois Grillmeier and Heinrich Bacht, vol. 2. Würzburg: Echter, 1953.

Vescovi e pastori in epoca teodosiana, XXV Incontro di studiosi dell'antichità cristiana. Studia Ephemeridis Augustinianum 58. 2 vols. Rome: Institutum Patristicum "Augustinianum," 1997.

Wimbush, Vincent L., and Richard Valantasis, eds., *Asceticism.* Oxford: Oxford University Press, 1997.

Index